Crochet Mega-Bundle 23 In 1:

244 Projects And 23 Books On Crocheting From Beginner To Advanced Level

Table of content

First Steps In Crocheting 20

Book 1

Crochet Introduction 22

20 Home Crochet Ideas Any Beginner Crocheter Should Start With 22

Introduction 23

Chapter 1 – Kitchen and Bath 26

Chapter 2 – Cushions and Poufs 31

Chapter 3 – Baskets, Bowls, and Containers 33

Chapter 4 – Blankets 38

Chapter 5 – Toys 42

Conclusion 45

Book 2

Professional Crochet Stitch Guide: 48

Learn The Most Popular Modern Crochet Stitches: Chinese Puzzle Stitch, Cable Stitch, Crocodile Stitch, Picot Stitch, Waffle Stitch, Popcorn Stitch, Shell Stitch, Seed Stitch! 48

Introduction 49

Chapter 1 – Tutorial for Crocodile Stitch, Picot Stitch and Waffle Stitch 51

Stitch 01: Crocodile Stitch 51

Stitch 02: Picot Stitch 52

Stitch 03: Waffle Stitch 57

Chapter 2 – Learn Chinese Puzzle Stitch and Cable Stitch 61

Stitch 04: Chinese Puzzle Stitch 61

Stitch 05: Cable Stitch 71

Chapter 3 – Learn how to make Popcorn Stitch, Seed Stitch and Shell Stitch 75

Stitch 06: Popcorn Stitch 75

Stitch 07: Shell Stitch 80

Stitch 08: Seed Stitch 82

Chapter 4 – Tips to hold the yarn and hook while crocheting? 86

Chapter 5 – Work on Some Basic Stitches 88

Chain Stitch 88

Slip Stitch 88

Single Crochet 89

Double Crochet 90

Half Double Crochet 91

Tips to Make an FPdc 92

Conclusion 94

Book 3

Filet Crochet In One Day 96

Learn The Most Elegant Crochet Techniques In No Time! 96

Introduction 97

Chapter 1 – What Is Filet Crochet? 99

Chapter 2 – The Technique 105

Conclusion 112

Book 4

African Flower Crochet 115

Learn to Crochet Basic African Flower Hexagon And Use It In Wonderful Crochet Projects... 115

Introduction 116

Chapter 1 – Creating The African Flower Hexagon Stitch 118

Chapter 2 – African Flower Hexagon Projects 129

All About that Flower Baby Blanket 129

An African Hexagon Pin Cushion 130

Conclusion 133

Book 5

One Day Afghan Crochet 136

10 Pretty Afghan Crochet Patterns You Can Master in One Day! 136

Introduction 137

Chapter 1 – Cozy Afghan Blankets 138

Project 01: Rainbow Afghan Blanket 138

Project 02: Afghan Throw 140

Chapter 2 – Afghan Booties and Flip Flops 142

Project 03: Afghan Flip Flops Women 142

Chapter 3 – Beautiful Afghan Jewelry 145

Project 04: The Tunisian cuff bracelet 145

Project 05: Afghan crochet Necklace and earrings 147

Project 6: Necklace: The necklace is made roughly around 20-22 inches. 148

Project 7: Earing: The earing is made roughly an inch or more for both in the pair. 148

Chapter 4 – Beautiful Afghan Scarves 150

Project 08: Tunisian crochet scarf 150

Project 09: Infinity scarf 153

Project 10: Isle Cowl 154

Conclusion 157

Book 6

Crochet Projects For Home 158

Crochet Projects In One Hour 160

15 Adorable Ideas For Everyone Who Loves Crocheting But Has No Time! 160

Introduction 161

Chapter 1 – The Projects 163

Winter Sunset Crochet Headband 163

The Mandala Vase Holder.. 164

Mandala Wall Art... 165

The Springtime Skinny Scarf 166

Fast and Easy Crochet Cuff.. 167

Waste Basket Camo Cover.. 168

A Fairy Trinket Bag 170

The Catch All Crochet Bowl 172

The Mandala Pendant.. 173

Fruity Coasters 175

The Coin Catcher... 176

Grass Is Always Greener Scarf... 177

Fast and Easy Dish Scrubby 179

Mother's Favorite Washcloth 180

Chunky Crochet Beanie... 181

Conclusion... 183

Book 7

Crochet Keychains 185

15 Must Have Crochet Keychains To Rock This Fashion Season 185

Introduction 186

Chapter 1 – The Keychains 188

Simple Strawberry... 188

Sam the Squid.. 189

Easy Elegant Cross.. 190

Tony the Teddy Bear... 191

Tiny Foot Sock... 192

Luck of the Irish Charm 193

The Serious Strawberry 194

Tiny Heart Trinket 196

Speedy the Snail 197

Flower Power 198

Baloo the Blue Whale 199

Henrietta the Hen 201

Brown Mouse Keychain 202

Starburst Trinket 203

Harry the Hedgehog 204

Conclusion 206

Book 8

Crochet: 208

18 Beautiful One-Night Crochet Projects To Try Right Now! 208

Introduction 209

Chapter 1 – Christmas Around the House 210

Pretty Party Napkin Ring 210

Winter Chill Scarf 211

Snow Trinket Snowflakes 212

Winter Cranberry Phone Sock 213

Chapter 2 – Last Minute Stocking Stuffers 216

Mini Doll Beanie 216

Tiny Teddy 217

Smiling Snakes 220

Sammy the Stocking Mouse 222

Chapter 3 – Warm Crochet 224

One Night Neck Warmer 224

Winter Wind Beanie 225

For the Little One Mittens 226

Sassy Headband 228

Chapter 4 – Winter Wonderland Crochet 230

Skater Ornament 230

Fast and Easy Lap Throw 231

Texting Gloves 233

Men's Smooth and Silky Scarf 234

Chapter 5 – The Best of the Rest 236

Mantle Stockings 236

Ho Ho Holidays 237

Conclusion 241

Book 9

Crochet Book Covers 243

15 Wonderful Crochet Patterns To Cover Your Books 243

Introduction 244

Chapter 1 – The Basics 246

Zig Zag Zipper 246

Owl's Eyes Cover 247

Blue And Gold Besties 249

Chapter 2 – Cute As a Button 251

Green Striped Goodness 252

Meadow Madness 254

Chapter 3 – Just What You Wanted 256

Handy Handle 256

The Lady of Lace 257

Crazy Days 259

Chapter 4 – Books and Books 261

Multi-Goodness Goddess 261

Pleased as a Plum 262

Green Machine 263

Chapter 5 – The Best of the Rest 264

The Pretty Pastel 265

Rainbow Valley Beauty Book 266

The Scholar Cover 268

Chapter 6 – Making It Your Own 270

Conclusion 272

Book 10

Crochet Mandala: 275

12 Most Gorgeous Patterns With Easy Instructions 275

Introduction 276

Chapter 1 – 12 Most Gorgeous Patterns With Easy Instructions 277

Pattern 01: Blooming Mandala 277

Pattern 02: Flower Madala 281

Pattern 03: Mandala Beanie 282

Pattern 04: Crochet Doily 286

Pattern 05: Spring Rug 289

Pattern 06: Colorful Mini Mandala 291

Pattern 07: Flower Mandala 292

Pattern 08: Black Mandala 294

Pattern 09: Mandala Blanket 295

Pattern 10: Mandala Pouch 298

Pattern 11: Mandala Bag for Market 302

Pattern 12: Mandala Shoulder Bag 304

Conclusion 308

Book 11

Crochet Pillow: 310

10 Brilliant Crochet Pillow Cases To Make Your Home Super Cozy 310

Introduction 311

Design no. 1 Checkerboard Pillow crochet Pattern 314

Design no. 2 Circular pillow at top 317

Design no. 3 Second round pillow 320

Design no. 4 Square Yellow Pillow 322

Design no. 5 324

Design no. 6 Diagonal pillow 326

Design no. 7 329

Design no. 8 Simple Round pillow 332

Design no. 9 Ribbon laced crochet cushion 335

Design no. 10 339

Conclusion 341

Book 12

Crochet Dishcloth 343

15 Colorful And Pretty Crochet Dishcloth Patterns To Brighten Your Kitchen 343

Introduction 344

Chapter 1 – Getting Started 346

Chapter 2 – Your First Dishcloths 348

Easy Peasy Dishcloth 348

White as Snow Dishcloth 349

All About Those Waves Dishcloth 351

The Black and White Classics Dishcloth 352

Chapter 3 – Bringing In Your Style 354

Be My Valentine Dishcloths 354

The Spring Mix Dishcloth 356

The Happy Rainbow Dishcloth 358

Fun and Flirty Dishcloths 359

Chapter 4 – The Jazzy Section 361

Triple Crochet Border Dishcloth 361

Summer Patriot Dishcloths 362

Muted Moss Dishcloths 364

Chapter 5 – Variation Patterns 366

The Self Striper Dishcloths 367

The Triple Crochet Self Striper Dishcloth (Photo Above) 368

Storm Cloud Dishcloth 369

The Open Work Storm Cloud Dishcloth (Photo Above) 370

Conclusion 372

Book 13

Crochet Ovals 375

6 Afghan Patterns To Use For Cozy Crochet Rugs 375

Introduction 376

The Patterns 377

Basic but Beautiful Rug 377

Rainbow Rug 379

Perfect for Fall Rug 381

Rags to Riches Rug 383

Seasonal Sensation Rug 385

The Hodge Podge Edition 388

Conclusion 391

Book 14

Crochet Dream Catchers: 394

10 Mystic Dream Catchers To Protect Your Sleep 394

Introduction 395

The Dream Catchers 397

Mystic Mountain Dreamcatcher 397

King of the Sea Dreamcatcher 399

Perfect for Fall Dreamcatcher 401

Spring Center Dreamcatcher 403

Pretty in Pink Dreamcatcher 406

Delicate Lace Dreamcatcher 408

Catching the Wind Dreamcatcher 411

Mini Beaded Dreamcatcher 413

Triple Crown Dreamcatcher 415

Crochet Feathers 417

Conclusion 419

Book 15

Seasonal Crocheting 420

Winter Crochet: 422

Wonderful Crochet Projects To Warm You And Your Loved Ones 422

Introduction 423

The Projects 425

Pretty Kitty Cuffs 425

That's A Wrap Scarf And Beanie Set 428

Around the World Eternity Scarf 430

Magical Mermaid Cozy Blanket 431

Snowball Fight Christmas Gloves 433

The Diva Wrap 434

Fireside Warmth Cardigan 437

Holiday Happiness Winter Cardigan 439

Conclusion 443

Book 16

Crochet Mittens: 446

6 Crochet Mittens Patterns For The Whole Family 446

Introduction 447

Chapter 1 – Mittens for Male Members 448

Chapter 02: Crochet Mitten for Adult Girls 452

Chapter 03: Crochet Mitten for Baby Girl 455

Chapter 04: Crochet Mitten for Baby Boy 458

Chapter 05: Crochet Mitten with Flaps 461

Chapter 06: Fingerless Crochet Mitten 465

Conclusion 467

Book17

Crochet Neck Warmer 469

15 Beautiful Neck Warmers To Keep You Nice And Cozy 469

Introduction 470

Chapter 1 – Beautiful Holiday Warmers 472

Snowflake Slate Neck Warmer 472

Rose Garden Warmer 473

Hippy Holiday Neck Warmer 475

Chapter 2 – Elegant Wraps 477

Flower Power Neck Warmer 477

Camo Colored Neck Warmer..479

Royally Wise Neck Warmer...480

Chapter 3 – Upscale Neck Warmers...482

Buttoned Burgundy Wrap..482

Catherine's Favorite Neck Warmer..484

Highland Hooded Cowl..486

Chapter 4 – Wraps All Around...488

Spectacular Striped Neck Warmer...488

Filled Up Neck Warmer...490

Buttoned Back Around Neck Warmer..491

Chapter 5 – All the Best of all the Rest...493

Two Toned Warmer...493

Lovely Lady's Scalloped Neck Warmer...495

Wavy Wonder Neck Warmer...496

Conclusion...499

Book 18

Crochet Angel..502

15 Wonderful Crochet Angel Patterns To Prepare Your Home For Christmas Miracle.............502

Introduction...503

Chapter 1 – Angels From On High...504

The Angel Choir..504

Highlight Angel..506

Glorious Day Angel...509

Chapter 2 – Small Packages..511

Elegant Wraps...511

Mini Little Singer..512

Chubby Little Cherub..514

Chapter 3 – Spreading Christmas Cheer 518

Greetings from the Lamp Post 518

Christmas Carols Angels 520

Candy Corny Angel 522

Chapter 4 – Unique Little Cherubs 524

Mini Wing Angel's Sing 524

Photo made by: Picture Institute- Bristol Margate Nida London 524

Golden Glory Angel 526

Twist and Turned Angel 528

Chapter 5 – Small and Sweet 530

Open Work Joy 530

Little Miss Silent Night 532

The Wings of Christmas Past 534

Conclusion 537

Book 19

Christmas Crochet 539

15 Beautiful Christmas Crochet Patterns To Give Your Home A Christmas Look 539

Introduction 540

Chapter 1 – Simplicity Crochet 542

Simple Little Snowflake 542

Mini Helpers 544

Noel, the Mini Angel 546

Chapter 2 – Christmas Everywhere 549

Christmas Bulb Cover 549

Christmas Tree Coasters 551

Christmas Skate Ornaments 552

Chapter 3 – That Little Touch 554

Elegant Napkin Holders 554

Christmas Pine Throw 555

Perfect Ornaments for Every Tree 556

Chapter 4 – Christmas Cheer 559

Starry Night Christmas Garland 559

Christmas Stocking Mini Decoration 561

The Littlest Angel 563

Chapter 5 – The Best of Christmas Decorations 565

Basket Bundle 565

Your Favorite Christmas Wreath 567

He Sees You Christmas Bulb 569

Conclusion 570

Book 20

Crochet Bikini For Everyone 573

5 Masterpiece Crochet Bikinis To Rock On The Beach 573

Introduction 574

Chapter 1 – The Bikini Patterns 576

Ruby Red Bikini Set 576

Mesmerizing Pearl Top 579

Flirty Ruffle Bottoms 581

High Wasted Bikini Set 583

The Wonder Top + Ruffle Bottoms 587

Conclusion 591

Book 21

Crochet Bag DIY: 594

10 Pretty and Trendy Crochet Bag Patterns 594

Introduction 595

Chapter 1 – Beach Crochet Bags.. 596

Pattern 01: Cutest Beach Bag 596

Pattern 02: Triple Pattern Beach Bag 599

Chapter 2 – Summer Crochet Bags 602

Pattern 03: Sling Pattern for Summer.. 602

Pattern 04: Flower Crochet Bag 605

Chapter 3 – Crochet Clutch Bags 611

Pattern 05: Cash and Card Case 611

Pattern 06: Bright Clutch... 613

Chapter 4 – Flowery Crochet Patterns.. 616

Pattern 07: Flower Crochet Bag 616

Pattern 08: Roses Tote.. 619

Chapter 5 – Crochet Pouch Bags... 621

Pattern 09: Crochet Pouch... 621

Pattern 10: Draw String Crochet Bag... 625

Conclusion... 628

Book 22

Crochet Jewelry.. 630

20 Crochet Bracelets, Earrings, and Rings You Can Make Yourself! 630

Introduction 631

Chapter 1 – Crochet Earrings 633

Red as a Ruby Dangle Earrings.. 633

Key Lime Earring Set.. 635

All the Gum Drops Earrings... 636

Bleeding Heart Earrings 637

Hoops and Swoops Earrings... 639

Mottled Magic Earrings 640

Star of the Show Earring Set 641

Chapter 2 – Crochet Bracelets 643

Sea Bracelet 643

It's All in the Braid 645

The Cage of Glory Bracelet 646

It's Hip to be a Square 647

The Simple Solution 648

Sunny Day Bracelet 650

Fall Fantasy Bracelet 651

Chapter 3 – Crochet Rings 653

The Simple Things Ring 653

The Fairy Garden Ring 654

Barely There White Ring 656

The Oversized Statement Ring 658

The Plum Summer Ring 659

Oh So Tiny Ring 661

Conclusion 663

Book 23

Fall Crochet Patterns 665

20 Cozy Fall Crochet Projects For You And Your Home 665

Introduction 666

Chapter 1 – The Projects 667

Pumpkin Patch 667

Fall Wraps 669

Carrie the Cranberry 670

The Fall Bangle 671

Not Your Mother's Scarf 672

Fall Bash Beanie 673

The Fall Collection Washcloths 674

Maroon Madness 675

Around the Globe Cowl 676

Super Stripes Autumn Throw 678

Every Season Throw 679

Fall Harvest Coasters 680

Droopy Back Beanie 682

Fall's Fun Fur Scarf 683

Pumpkin Spice Scarf 684

Tabletop Owl 685

Bright and Bold Pumpkin Scarf 687

Basic Fall Nights Pillow 688

Fall Toaster Coasters 689

Fireside Warmth 690

Conclusion 692

First Steps In Crocheting

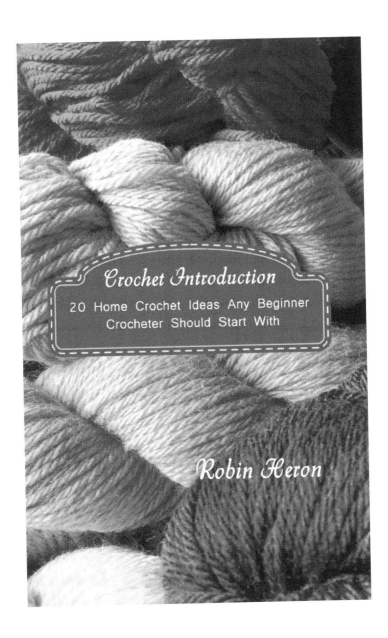

Crochet Introduction

20 Home Crochet Ideas Any Beginner Crocheter Should Start With

Robin Heron

Crochet Introduction
20 Home Crochet Ideas Any Beginner Crocheter
Should Start With

Introduction

Sometimes it happens. Maybe all of your plans got cancelled, or your house is just cleaner than you expected. Maybe you somehow managed to get a nice, quiet weekend to yourself, or you're recuperating and need to take it easy for a few days. However you got to this point, you've decided you want to spend a soothing weekend with your yarn stash, making things for your home.

Of course, part of what we like about crochet is the satisfaction of getting things done, isn't it? We're busy people. We don't want to have to come back to a project weeks later and hope we remember where we were in this project. We want to be able to hold up our work and the end of the week and say, "I was productive! I made this!"

That's where this book comes in. While the projects will be soothing and enjoyable for people at all levels of crochet practice, all you need to know are the basic crochet stitches and where you want to put your projects when you're done with them.

Resources

You aren't alone in your efforts. As someone new to the craft, it can feel like you're floating in a sea of string, with no guidance. There are scads of people out there who want to help guide you, whether it's in the form of tutorials, patterns, or just images of projects they made for you to sigh over.

Yarn Manufacturers' Websites

I have had fantastic luck finding patterns, tutorials, and guidance on yarn manufacturers' websites. Yarnspirations (http://www.yarnspirations.com/) is a personal favorite. Yarnspirations is the online home of several yarn manufacturers, to include Bernat, Caron, and Paton's. They offer patterns at a variety of skill levels, and they have kits that they will ship to you that include printed patterns and all the yarn you will need to complete that project. My very first completed crochet project was a blanket that came from Yarnspirations, which my daughter promptly fell in love with and cannot sleep without.

Lion Brand Yarns offers similar services, although only for Lion Brand yarns. They also offer tutorials. If you're sitting there looking at a pattern, suddenly suffer a brain cramp and forget how to make a single crochet (look, it happens, no judging), you can pick up your phone and look it up. *No one will ever know. I promise.*

Other Websites

Check out The Crochet Crowd (www.thecrochetcrowd.com) for some fun, exciting patterns. They also have some fantastic tutorials, videos, community features, and other benefits. It's a very encouraging place to be new to crochet while still having a lot to offer people who've been doing this for a while.

Ravelry (www.ravelry.com) is a little harder to use, and it's easy to get intimidated by some of the incredible projects some of the users have made. It's worth joining, though. You can find plenty of free patterns, connect with other crafters, and keep track of your projects. You can also link up with folks coordinating charity drives as outlets for your endeavors.

Pinterest (www.pinterest.com) can be addictive. You can find thousands of beautiful projects, and you can get links to tons of free patterns. Beware, though – some links may not work. It's also possible to spend more time hoarding patterns on Pinterest than actually crocheting. The site is still useful, though, and it makes a great place to store links you find on other websites.

Craftsy (www.craftsy.com) offers classes and sells yarn. The classes are helpful and the yarns they sell are a bargain, considering their quality. The patterns and classes are not free. I've found them incredibly helpful, though.

Social Media

Facebook has a group specifically for Yarnspirations members. It's an incredibly supportive place. Some of the projects I've seen have been intimidating, but they've also been inspiring. There is also a group just for free crochet patterns, at varying skill levels.

Chapter 1 – Kitchen and Bath

Your kitchen and bath are two of the most important areas of your home. Crochet projects for these areas can be deeply rewarding, and they're practical as well. They make fantastic gifts, and they can be a great way for beginners to practice techniques and stitches.

There are a few caveats, of course. Projects for both rooms call for yarns made from natural fibers. If you're making a dishcloth, a washcloth, or a bathmat, use cotton yarn.

You can get away with wool if you're making a potholder or a trivet, but wool tends to be on the pricey side for use in a washcloth and it has the added downside of making the user smell like a wet sheep if used for washing up. Cotton is best, because of its heat resistance.

A dishcloth or washcloth – they work out to being the same thing for our purposes – is the easiest project to start out with. It doesn't have to be fancy. A simple washcloth can be done in single crochet:

- Chain as many stitches as you need to get the width you want, 9" is about average

- Add 1 chain for your turning chain, turn.

- Single crochet across the row. Chain 1, turn.

- Repeat until you've reached a height of 9".

- Create a border in SC.

- Fasten off and weave in your ends.

See? It's easy. If you want to try something that's a little more involved, try this:

- Chain 35
- Row 1: Chain 1, skip 1, single crochet (sc) in each stitch across.
- Row 2: Chain three, turn. Make a double crochet (dc) in the first stitch. Skip two stitches, and then make three dcs in the next stitch. Repeat until the end.
- Repeat rows 1 and 2 until you've gotten to 9" height.
- Create your border in SC.
- Fasten off and weave in your ends.

If you have a blanket pattern that's giving you trouble, and it's one with a repeating pattern, you can use it to make a washcloth. This can help you to work out whatever part of the blanket pattern might be causing your difficulty. Personally, I tend to have trouble keeping my edges straight. Shrinking the scale down helps me to see where I'm messing up and helps me to correct my problems.

Are you looking for something a bit more challenging than that? Do you like granny squares? (This is a trick question. Everyone likes granny squares.) Most of the types of squares we would use to make an afghan would make fantastic washcloths. Go ahead and take your favorite afghan square, work it up in your favorite cotton yarn, and you'll have a fantastic washcloth or dishcloth you can smile at every time you suds up.

A bathmat is a little bit trickier, only because it's larger and you have to work faster to get your project done in a weekend. When you want to get a large project done quickly, a good rule of thumb is "go big or go home." In an ideal world, you would have some bulky or super bulky cottons on hand and be able to work these up in a jiffy. Bernat has a pattern for a bath mat up on Yarnspirations (http://www.yarnspirations.com/patterns/bubble-bathmat.html?id=200811) made in a cotton/nylon blend (72%/s8%) that is still presumably absorbent, so you probably don't have to be a natural-fiber purist for this project.

So use a good, big yarn, bulky or heavier. A large hook will be helpful too. Your crochet teacher probably told you to use a larger hook if you were having trouble making your stitches too tight, right? Using a big hook will help make larger stitches, which will help your project move right along. Don't overdo it – using an L hook on lace weight yarn gets silly. But if you want to make a simple bath mat in double crochet with an N hook instead of a K, that shouldn't be a problem.

Projects for the kitchen can be similar to those for the bathroom. The same patterns you used to make washcloths can be used to make dishcloths, or potholders, or trivets for your counters and tables. I do have one caveat here that did not apply in your bathroom. It is more important to use natural fibers in the kitchen due to the risk of fire.

When natural fibers catch fire, they burn. When synthetic fibers catch fire, they melt. This is especially risky if the item is going to be used near your skin, such as a potholder.

Other quick weekend projects for the kitchen include tea and cup cozies.

These cute and fun accessories can make quick gifts, or they can help to class up promo or novelty mugs that have been hanging around your cabinet forever. They're also portable, so you can bring them to your favorite coffee shop and use them in place of the disposable cup sheaths that protect your hands from the super-hot coffee inside.

Placemats and coasters are other options. You have a lot of fun options for these, especially if your skills extend to color work and to some fun animal shapes. Even if they don't, imagine the elegance and satisfaction of setting your table with handmade placemats in lovely jewel tones! Think about setting out some lovely coasters that look like delicate granny squares that you yourself made!

Crochet offers endless possibilities for your kitchen and bath. You'll get immense satisfaction from using something you made with your own hands every day.

Chapter 2 – Cushions and Poufs

Cushions and poufs are a fun way to update the look of your home, and to make it more comfortable as well. A pouf, which tends to be a larger object, might be a bit of a stretch for a weekend project. Someone who crochets quickly might be able to pull it off, so don't discount the idea completely. You know your skill level and your hook speed best.

Cushions, on the other hand, could be completely doable. All you'd need is stuffing (or a pillow form, depending on the pattern or project), yarn, and a pattern. As I mentioned in the Kitchen and Bath chapter, the general rule of thumb is "go big or go home." If you use a big yarn, and a big hook, your project will speed right along.

At its easiest, a pillow is very simple to make:

- Take a pillow form. You can get these at most craft stores. They don't cost a lot of money. If you're new to all of this, you might prefer to start with a rectangular or square pillow.

- Chain enough stitches in your chosen yarn to go a little beyond the edges of your pillow.

- Make two equally sized pieces, a little bit taller than your pillow.

- Stitch the pieces together, around your pillow form.

- Enjoy your new cushion.

If you're working with a round pillow form, the theory is basically the same. All you would really do differently is start with a magic ring at the center and work your way out, making two sides and stitching them together just as you did for the rectangular cushion.

If you want to add some colors, go right ahead! It's easy to change colors at the end of a row. You can match cushions to a favorite afghan. You can also make cushions based on your favorite granny squares, although you might want to carefully consider which ones you choose lest the pillow form show through more than you want.

You can get more elaborate if you like, and you're feeling up to it. If you want to be able to change the pillow form, you can find a pattern for an envelope-style pillow case with ties or a button closure. You can add little arms and legs, and a face, and make a huggable pillow for a small child. (Ravelry has several examples of projects just like this. More advanced crocheters can add texture, or words.

If novelty pillows are your cup of tea, the Yarnspirations website has some very clever ideas and even offers kits to help build them. They include a rabbit floor pillow, which makes a fantastic segue into the subject of poufs.

A pouf is a much larger project, sized more like a hassock or beanbag chair cover. Some crocheters might be able to work one of them up in a weekend, although I'd suggest not trying to work so quickly if you're newer to the craft.

If you want to try to get a pouf done over the weekend, remember that bigger is better. Use a super bulky yarn, or bigger. Use a big hook. And again, if you want to get it done over the weekend, don't overcomplicate it. Poufs can be a fun way to add a splash of color to a casual living space, and they can be a great way to cover an old beanbag that's seen better days.

Chapter 3 – Baskets, Bowls, and Containers

One of the things about human beings is that we tend to accumulate stuff. If we didn't, there wouldn't be much for archaeologists to study. As the number of things we have increases, we need places to put those things, ways to transport them, and ways to contain them when we aren't using them.

Sure, we're supposed to be downsizing and turning to minimalism and all that. You still have crochet hooks, right? You still have yarn, and stitch markers, and... right. Most people have basic household necessities that they'd like to keep contained in one place, if for no other reason than the need to know where it is.

I keep my keys in a hammered copper bowl that I made myself. It's not huge, but it's a single place to keep my keys. If I need my house keys, or the keys to my spouse's car, or the keys to my parents' house, I always know where to find them. I can tell my daughter to go get them if my hands are full, because they're always in the same place. Baskets and other containers can be some of the most useful items you can create. They can be some of the most beautiful, too.

I have yet to find a basket pattern that isn't worked in rounds, even when the basket itself is rectangular. The basic pattern is generally pretty simple. If you're looking to get the job done in a weekend, I'd recommend going with a larger yarn, and not trying to get too fancy. A lined basket might not be in your best interest, but something made with a nice bulky yarn and a large-sized hook should be nice.

The type of yarn you use doesn't seem to be all that important. Yarnspirations has a series of nesting baskets intended for beginners that is made with worsted weight yarn in cotton here (http://www.yarnspirations.com/patterns/lily-sugar-n-cream-crochet-nesting-baskets.html?id=201506) that would be just adorable as a gift or set up on a shelf. No one has to know you filled it up with crochet supplies.

Rescued Paw Designs, a blog that has a fantastic newsletter and offers a ton of free patterns, has a fairly simple basket pattern that looks elegant and quite lovely. You can find it here: http://rescuedpawdesigns.com/2015/06/08/chunky-crochet-basket-pattern/ .

The great thing about baskets – as well as bowls, bags, totes, and other containers – is that you aren't limited to regular yarns. Darn Good Yarn, a company that offers a yarn-of-the-month subscription service, recently sent out a skein of ribbon made from recycled sari fabric as their yarn of the month. Their recommended project for this skein was a crochet bowl: https://www.darngoodyarn.com/products/classic-fiber-bowl (please note that this was previously a free pattern, but now costs $0.99.)

I've seen baskets made with t-shirt yarn, baskets made with plastic tubing (!), and baskets made with shredded plastic bags. I've seen baskets crocheted from twine and rope, too. If you happen to have any of these things lying around the house, and the right size crochet hook, you could make baskets from any of these products. If you're still a beginner, though, I'd recommend sticking with yarn.

Another option for your home is the tote or bag. These are similar to baskets, but they offer a little more flexibility in that they don't need the rigidity of a basket and they can be made to close. Again, if you're looking to finish a project in a weekend, I would recommend finding a project with a bulky yarn and a large hook.

This bear-faced pencil case from Yarnspirations is an adorable example of a beginner-friendly project that you should be able to whip together in a weekend without a problem. It would be a great way to contain your child or grandchild's school supplies, and it would make an incredible gift for a school-bound young or young-at-heart person. http://www.yarnspirations.com/patterns/grin-and-bear-it-case.html?id=198835

This pattern, on All Free Crochet (https://www.allfreecrochet.com/Totes/Easy-Crochet-Tote), is a pretty basic pattern that that should be pretty easy for people to get through in a weekend.

This pattern, from Lion Brand Yarns, makes a stylish market tote that is intended for beginners and looks good on your arm. Find it here: http://www.lionbrand.com/patterns/pattern-market-tote-bag.html.

With more and more jurisdictions banning plastic shopping bags, it's worth your while to consider making some reusable bags to bring with you as you go about your business every week. It's certainly better for the environment, and if you find crochet as soothing as I do it's better for your mind and soul.

Maybe you're looking for a project that's on a smaller or more personal scale. While I'm not sure that purses and handbags qualify as projects "for the home," they're found in the same section on most websites and are therefore worth a mention here. Since they're smaller than the kind of bag you might take to the beach or the grocery store, they're easier to finish in a weekend. They can be fun and easy, too.

The easiest purses to get through in one weekend would be envelope-style clutches. An example of an envelope clutch can be found for free from Lion Brand Yarns, here: http://www.lionbrand.com/patterns/crochet-pattern-envelope-bag-1.html. When you've learned the basic concept, of course, you can customize it by adding appliqué or stripes.

Totes and baskets are some of the most useful and versatile objects you can make for your home. With the right yarn, they can be some of the most beautiful as well.

Chapter 4 – Blankets

I'll be perfectly honest here. I learned to crochet specifically because I wanted to make blankets. Throws, afghans, bedspreads – I wanted to make them all. I still do. When I buy yarn, I buy it in quantities to make blankets. This may have something to do with why I'm running out of storage space…

Making a blanket can be a time-consuming proposition. You may be looking at this section and thinking, *There is no possible way that I can make a blanket in a weekend. Not even a long weekend.* I'm here to tell you that it IS possible, but only if you stay positive, don't get too sidetracked, and plan your work with the end goal in mind.

That gorgeous blanket with thirty different squares or more, each one having five different colors and a three-dimensional design on each? That's not a realistic goal for one weekend. It sounds like a fun long-term project and I'd love to see your finished project, though.

A blanket you make in one piece? Now that we can probably manage, especially if we use a bulky yarn and a large hook. Big stitches are a great time saver, too.

The first crochet project I ever made was a blanket. I made a ton of mistakes. I see them every day. It was the Hibernate Blanket from Yarnspirations (http://www.yarnspirations.com/patterns/hibernate-blanket.html?id=200172) and my daughter fell in love with it, flaws and all. The whole blanket is done in one stitch, single crochet. The yarn is Bernat Blanket, which is a super bulky yarn. It works up incredibly fast, it's fun to make, and it has a fluffy and warm texture that makes a person feel comfortable every time they touch it.

My daughter carries it around the house with her all the time, and she has ever since I finished it.

So there is something deeply satisfying and intensely soothing about making a blanket, even a simple one that you can finish in a weekend. I highly recommend this yarn to make blankets quickly.

Maybe the thought of sitting on the couch and making the same stitch over and over again doesn't exactly appeal to you. It's a good way to learn the stitch, if you're a raw beginner, but some people just like the look of granny squares. I know I just said that you shouldn't try to finish a blanket made of granny squares in one weekend, but what if you tried to make a giant granny square?

This free pattern, also from Yarnspirations (http://www.yarnspirations.com/patterns/classic-granny-square-throw.html?id=200388), is essentially just that. You start from the middle and work your way out, until your throw is done. It's made with a smaller yarn and a smaller hook, but it works up quickly and looks very elegant once completed.

This pretty blanket from Lion Brand looks like it should be fussy and complicated, but it's actually very simple. It's even called Beginner's Delight, and it does look like a delight to make, doesn't it? The pattern is free: http://www.lionbrand.com/patterns/beginners-delight-afghan-l70176.html.

The Crochet Crowd offers a free blanket pattern and tutorial here (http://thecrochetcrowd.com/crochet-toy-box-baby-blanket-tutorial/) for a colorful baby blanket that is made in this way. It would probably work just as well if you were to add extra rounds with more skeins of the same wool. They say the baby blanket can be made in about three hours, give or take, so it definitely fits in to our one-weekend time limit.

Maybe you're feeling rebellions with regards to rectangles. I can respect that. Check out this hexagonal blanket from MyPoppet, an Australian blogger (http://www.notey.com/@mypoppet_unofficial/external/15057316/let%E2%80%99s-try-self-striping-yarn-cakes-2-bonus-crochet-patterns.html?utm_content=buffere36a7&utm_medium=social&utm_source=pinterest.com&utm_campaign=buffer). This one took her a full weekend to produce, which fits our timeframe, and it makes a simply stunning baby blanket.

Here is another rectangular afghan, a free pattern I found through Pinterest. It's got a clever name that tells me it's right up our alley: Fast And Easy Weekend Afghan (https://babytoboomer.com/2014/02/18/free-pattern-fast-and-easy-crochet-throw/2/?utm_content=buffer7d14d&utm_medium=social&utm_source=pinterest.com&utm_campaign=buffer). I love how they used a smaller yarn and a giant crochet hook. It gives the finished product an interesting texture that really catches the eye.

Blankets and afghans are a wonderful way to perk up almost any room. They are soothing to make, and they comfort the people who use them for years to come. My mother still has a crocheted afghan that was given to her when I was born. The neighbor who made it is no longer with us, but we remember her and her kindness through her gentle and comforting gift. Now it keeps my daughter and my nephews warm whenever they go to visit, extending the neighbor's legacy far beyond her own lifespan.

I love blankets. I can't get enough of them. I can all but guarantee that once you've seen the bright smile on a recipient's face when you've made your first blanket or afghan, you'll be just as hooked on them as I am.

Chapter 5 – Toys

This is a book about projects you can make in a weekend, that are for your home. If you are someone who interacts with children on anything like a regular basis, you probably have toys. They might indeed be everywhere. I have friends who are child-free who keep a supply of toys in their home, simply because so many of their friends have children that visit.

Aren't handmade toys better than store bought? For one thing, they don't have batteries. For another, they're not loud. While it can be fun to buy loud toys for the children of those friends of our spouses whom we never did like, there's always the threat of retaliation. Nice, homemade toys that don't suddenly turn on in the middle of the night like something out of a horror movie are best in my book!

An added benefit of handmade toys is the personal touch they bring. If your child, or your young at heart person, has a fondness for penguins and her favorite color is purple, your options are kind of limited at the store. There aren't a lot of purple penguins out there. At home, you can make as many purple penguins as you want, in as many shapes as you want, and chances are they will all be different.

There are a few different types of toy you can make for your child. One popular trend is amigurumi. Amigurumi are traditionally small crocheted stuffed things, animals or food items. There is no technical restriction on the size of the finished item, but as the craft has become more popular in the West it has become associated with very small toys.

Remember how I told you that "go big or go home was the rule of thumb for weekend crochet projects? When it comes to toys, the opposite is true. A small amigurumi project, if it isn't too elaborate, might well take you less time than a big caterpillar. Amigurumi are very popular right now, and there are a number of books and websites that will be happy to share their wisdom with you.

Some are still available for free, though. One relatively simple example of a free pattern can be found here: https://www.ravelry.com/patterns/library/vegetables-amigurumi-food. If you have a budding chef or foodie, or a toddler with a fixation on gardening, they might enjoy these cheery little food items.

Another simple toy that most kids will love is the ball. A pattern to get you started can be found here: http://www.lovethispic.com/image/38346/diy-crochet-ball. The pattern consists entirely of photos, so you would need to know how to increase and decrease on your own.

The above ball is essentially a hackey-sack, but once you've mastered the basics you can expand it and make it larger as you see fit. My nephew, eighteen months old, loves these. His mother loves them too, because they're less likely to break things than the hard plastic balls she's able to find in the store.

And here's another fun one. Yarnspirations has given us a pattern for a simply adorable chicken, right here: http://www.yarnspirations.com/patterns/free-range-chicken.html?id=191506. I'm a little bit in love with this big guy, possibly because I have all of the yarn to make it sitting right here in my office. The colors are bright and cheerful, toy looks eminently squishable, and everything about it screams love. Maybe the child in your life is into farming. Maybe they just have a thing for chickens. Either way, this is a simply adorable project that any kid would be proud to have.

There are plenty of toys that require more involved work than the ones I've presented here. I've seen elephants made out of granny squares that were so elaborate that they might have been made from the finest china. They were breathtaking. I don't know anyone who could make them in a weekend!

The important thing to remember, when crocheting toys, is that these will be in the hands of children. I'm not sure how old the children in your life are, but kids can be kind of destructive. They don't necessarily understand how hard you worked to make this beautiful product you gave to them, and they have a limited amount of control over themselves and their environment. If they see a pulled thread, they will keep pulling that thread just to see what happens. They're kids, it's what they do, and it's something we as adults have to compensate for rather than trying to stifle it in the children.

That's why we need to make sure that all of our ends are securely fastened. We need to use safety eyes on our toys, or better yet sew eyes out of scrap yarn. We use smaller hooks than the yarn calls for so the stuffing doesn't poke through, and the kids don't eat it and choke or get sick. We make an extra effort to make sure these projects won't unravel, so the yarn doesn't wind up around a baby's neck.

It might sound like I'm trying to discourage you from crocheting projects for your children, or giving them as gifts. On the contrary, my daughter's been receiving crocheted gifts since she was too tiny to roll over and we've never had a problem. All I'm saying is that it's best to double check, and not to get too upset if something gets torn or broken.

It's crochet. We can probably fix it.

Conclusion

Your home is your haven, your castle. It's the most personal space you have. It's where most of the important events in your life, and your family's life, take place. You build your relationships there. You nurture your hopes and dreams there. You raise your children there. You grow old there.

There's no better way to personalize space that is so intimately yours than with everyday objects you make yourself. An expensive mattress covered in high-end sheets is very comfortable, but you can't wrap yourself in them and remember the weekend you spent making them with a smile on your face. A fancy couch looks great in your living room, but the cushions you crocheted bring it an added touch that marks it as yours.

It can be intimidating to think about making objects for the home. They sound big and scary. They sound like the kind of thing that should take weeks or months, the labor of love your grandmother told you about. Those projects are out there, and they can be a lot of fun to work on too.

But it's okay to get your feet wet. Go ahead and treat yourself to the satisfaction of seeing a project through from beginning to end in a single weekend. You'll end up with a lovely finished product, and you'll build up the confidence to tackle those bigger projects a little further down the road.

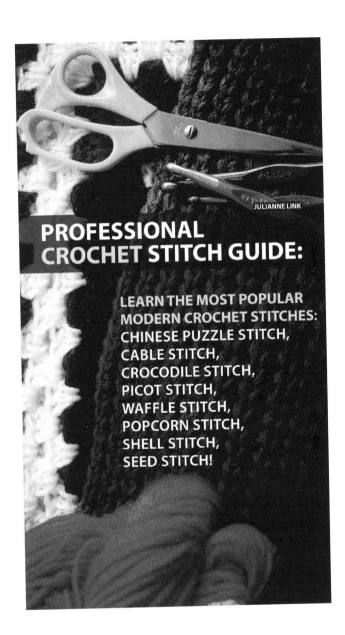

JULIANNE LINK

PROFESSIONAL
CROCHET STITCH GUIDE:

LEARN THE MOST POPULAR
MODERN CROCHET STITCHES:
CHINESE PUZZLE STITCH,
CABLE STITCH,
CROCODILE STITCH,
PICOT STITCH,
WAFFLE STITCH,
POPCORN STITCH,
SHELL STITCH,
SEED STITCH!

Professional Crochet Stitch Guide:

Learn The Most Popular Modern Crochet Stitches: Chinese Puzzle Stitch, Cable Stitch, Crocodile Stitch, Picot Stitch, Waffle Stitch, Popcorn Stitch, Shell Stitch, Seed Stitch!

Introduction

Crocheting is a fantastic art, and you can design lots of patterns with crochet after learning its simple and modern stitches. Your practice will help you to design all simple to complicated patterns. Initially, it can be problematic to learn the stitches and techniques of crochet, but with the passage of time and practice, you can be a master in this art. The followings are some tips that can make the crocheting easy for beginners and finally, you will be able to do it while watching TV, in the car and cooking food.

Keep your Fingers and Hands Relaxed

The non-stop crocheting of 45 minutes is enough to make you tired; therefore, you should break your routine and give some time to your hand for relaxation. The stress relieving gloves will help you to get rid of pain, and you will be able to start a new session. The continuous routine can make you bore; hence, you should break the stretch of your hands and fingers to avoid cramping.

Sit in a Relaxed Posture

As you start to crochet, you have to sit in a comfortable position because an uncomfortable posture can be the reason of a backache and tiredness. There is no need to keep your head down for a longer period because this posture is not good for your backbone and shoulder. Start your work in moderation and watch for the posture while you are sitting to crochet.

Check the Tension of Yarn

The position of the yarn in your hands and tension in it matters a lot because you need to pull each loop and hold the other end tightly in your left hand. The tight and loose yarn matters a lot in your left and right hand. You should work consistently to make each row. The stitches should be super tight, and it will be based on your control on yarn. The right number of stitches will help you to design a perfect pattern.

Slowly Work on Your Patterns

The haste always makes waste; therefore, you should start slowly, but consistently to win the race. There is no need to start various projects at a time because it will ruin all your efforts. You should focus on one pattern at a time before starting another.

Fake Sticks are Good to Practice

To become a master, you need a lot of practice because you may mess up patterns in the end. If you miss even a single loop, it will make a massive hole in your pattern. You may feel aching in your hands while holding loops for a long time, but you can fake the practice to reduce tiredness. You can add a border at the start to cover up the pattern and then start working on it. Initially, the use of chunky yarn can make your work easy because it can hide lots of mistakes. You may mess up the pattern in your first attempt, but don't be disheartened because you will improve it in the next attempt.

Selection of Yarn to Crochet

The thickness of the yarn can be based on the kind of pattern, such as if you are making a blanket or thick knit cloth, then you have to use finest yarn. The chunky yarn is used to make shawls and blankets. You should check the colors, price, and quality of yarn by its pattern.

The yarn is the most important factor of crocheting because the selection of yarn can make a clear difference in the end results of the design. The yarn can be made of wool, acrylic, and cotton, but you have to consider the thickness and weight of the thread. The natural yarn may be based on cashmere, cotton, angora, silk, mohair or wool. Using the blend of natural and synthetic yarns will be good. Consider the thickness of your yarn and check the number of strands that are twisted together to make the yarn.

Selection of Crocheting Hook

A crochet hook is the most important tool with a slender handle and hook at one or both ends. You need to pull the yarn through the loops to create the crochet stitches. The crochet hooks are made of steel, plastic, Tunisian, aluminum and bamboo. The size of the crochet hook may base on the material and brand. The sizes may vary from the 0.6 mm thick hooks to 3 mm thickness. If you are going to work on larger and large patterns, such as blankets and shawls, then it will be good to use heavy hooks. The lightweight hooks are good for smaller patterns.

Chapter 1 – Tutorial for Crocodile Stitch, Picot Stitch and Waffle Stitch

Crocodile stitch is really beautiful and this stitch can turn the shapes of your projects. By adding these stitches to your project, you can give a look of art piece to your work. There will be different layers to give a unique flare to your project. You can use these stitches in different things from simple scarves to bags. Learn this stitch:

Stitch 01: Crocodile Stitch

If you want to start your crocodile stitch project, start with one slip knot, similar to all other projects, and chain 5 (make five chains) and make one chain extra. Usually, your project will determine the actual number of crochet chains. Before starting crocodile stitch, you should remember that this stitch will not work on the upper (top) layer, but work well on posts and the base of the project. If you are learning it for the first time, you should have patience and practice them slowly:

Chain multiples of five + one.

Flip and, start working into back loops, double crochet in the second chain from a crochet hook. Chain 1, *skip two chains, two double crochet into following stitch*. Replicate from * to* crosswise row.

Flip, single crochet at the base of chain. Working all the way on the back of initial post (only first one instead of both posts), five double crochet around the similar post. Now, your stitches will heap on the top of one another (each other). See in the image.

Revolve your crochet work to move back up to the opposite side and to conclude scale - working all the way around the similar singular post, front post stitch from the bottommost of your stitch up toward the top (upper part) and now work in five double crochet. The one scale is successfully completed.

Single crochet into the upper/top of the 2nd post (it will be after the only one that you have been working) to carefully hold everything to its place and continue working crosswise the row.

After completing your scales rows, you have to set up a new foundation row formerly you start your subsequent scales set: chain one at the finishing point of this scale row and flip, single crochet into the foundation of the chain. Single crochet into the center of this scale and two double crochet in the top chain between scales. Carry one crosswise row.

Once you finish and reach till the end of this row, chain 1, flip and work crosswise and make scales.

Stitch 02: Picot Stitch

This stitch is used to make edging and you can add it on the finished garment. There are numerous patterns that use combination of stitches. You can make beautiful afghan or square patterns. It will be simple to practice this stitch with the help of given tutorial:

Small PICOT Stitch:

You have to start working along the boundary of finished items. (You can make one length of the picot boundary/edge to add to your ready to wear items. You can start with one chain or one strip of sc (single crochet) or dc (double crochet)

Work Single crochet (SC) in initial stitch.

Now, Chain 3, SC (single crochet) in the subsequent stitch.

Work single crochet (SC) in the subsequent three stitches. Now, Chain 3, SC in the subsequent stitch. (The Picot is formed).

Replicate the 4th step crosswise the row.

Medium PICOT Stitch:

Replicate the instruction of small picot, but you have to chain five as an alternative of chain three.

If you want to make flared edge with picot (similar to the image), you have to work the sequence of SC (single crochet) and chain five and then single crochet again in the similar stitch.

It will help you to slightly flare out the pattern and it may become useful for the base of your tank tops, sleeves, hats and skirts.

Bauble Ended PICOT Stitch:

You have to follow all the instructions of small picot, but you have to make chain seven as a replacement of chain three.

Now Slip stitch (sl st) in the sixth stitch from your crochet hook.

Sl st in the final stitch of the crochet chain. SC in the subsequent three stitches.

Replicate 1,2&3 steps crosswise the row.

Picot Stitch

The picot is a little round-shaped crochet stitch that can give a decorative edge to your work. The picots are used to fill an empty space in a web design. These are particularly made with thread, but you can try them with your yarn:

You need to create three chain stitches from the particular point in the row where you want to add a picot stitch.

Insert the hook in the 3rd chain to create the chain stitch for the preceding step.

Yarn through and design the yarn over the stitch and over the loop on the hook. You will get one complete picot stitch.

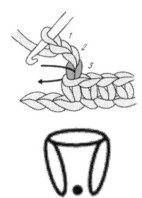

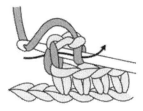

Stitch 03: Waffle Stitch
You will work on this stitch with 5.5 mm crochet hook and 4 ply worsted yarn. You will also need tapestry needle.

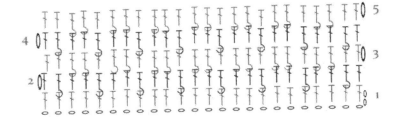

Abbreviations
DC - Double Crochet
HDC - Half Double Crochet
CH - Chain
SL ST - Slip Stitch
FPDC - Front Post Double Crochet

Instructions for Stitches:

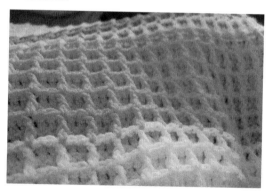

Version for Right Hand - FPDC – Start by wrapping the YO your crochet hook, now insert the crochet hook toward the right side of your post, among the stitches, all the way around the rear and by the conflicting side among the crochet stitches toward the left side of your post. Now, wrap the YO, draw it through, finish the dc (double) crochet.

Version for Left Hand - FPDC - YO on your crochet hook, now insert the crochet hook toward the leftward of this post, among the stitches, nearby the back and by the conflicting side among the stitches toward the right area of this post. Now YO, draw it through, conclude the dc (double crochet).

Important Note: You have to work on this stitch pattern with different crochet hooks and yarn.

Now Multiple: 03

Directions:

Chain 26

Row 1: Omit two chains, work 1 DOUBLE CROCHET in every chain crosswise. (24 DOUBLE CROCHET total) flip.

Row 2: Work a chain, this will not count as a stitch, Work a double crochet in the initial stitch, *FRONT-POST-DOUBLE CROCHET around the subsequent stitch. Work a DOUBLE CROCHET in every of the subsequent two stitches. Continue crosswise from *; the last two stitches will be an FRONT-POST-DOUBLE CROCHET and a DOUBLE CROCHET, flip.

Row 3: Work a chain, this is the step up, this will not count as a stitch, Work a double crochet in the first stitch, work a DOUBLE CROCHET in the subsequent stitch, work an FRONT-POST-DOUBLE CROCHET around every of the subsequent 2 stitches. *Work a DOUBLE CROCHET in the subsequent stitch, work an FRONT-POST-DOUBLE CROCHET around the subsequent 2 stitches. Continue crosswise from *; the last two stitches will be a DOUBLE CROCHET in every stitch, flip.

Row 4: Work a chain, this is the step up, this will not count as a stitch, Work a double crochet in the initial stitch, *Work an FRONT-POST-DOUBLE CROCHET in the subsequent stitch. Work a DOUBLE CROCHET in every of the subsequent two stitches, Continue crosswise from *, the last two stitches will be an FRONT-POST-DOUBLE CROCHET and DOUBLE CROCHET in every stitch, flip.

Row 5: Work a chain, this is the step up, this will not count as a stitch, Work a double crochet in the initial stitch, *Work an FRONT-POST-DOUBLE CROCHET in every of the subsequent two stitches. Work a DOUBLE CROCHET in the subsequent stitch, Continue crosswise from *, the last two stitches will be a DOUBLE CROCHET in every stitch, flip.

Replicate Rows 2,3,4 and5.

Chapter 2 – Learn Chinese Puzzle Stitch and Cable Stitch

There are some beautiful stitches that will help you to make your own crochet patterns. You should try these stitches.

Stitch 04: Chinese Puzzle Stitch

5.5 mm crochet hook

Multiple of Stitch: CH (chain) one multiple of seven stitches and add one additional four stitches for the initial chain.

Final Dimensions: 8x8 inches block

Abbreviations:

ch – chain

R – row

RS – right side

st – stitch

sts – stitches

dc – double crochet

dc5tog – double crochet 5 together

FPdc2tog – front post double crochet 2 together

FPdc5tog – front post double crochet 5 together

decrease – is used to refer to any of the dc5tog, FPdc2tog or FPdc5tog sts

Learn Special Stitches:

dc5tog: (double-crochet-five-stitches-together) – For this stitch, you have to make five stitches – * YO (yarn over) the crochet hook, inset your crochet hook into subsequent stitch; YO the hook and draw up one loop; YO the crochet hook and draw the crochet hook through two loops on the crochet hook* reiterate from *to* four more times; YO the crochet hook and pull through six loops on your crochet hook.

FPdc2tog (front-post-double-crochet-2-together) – For this stitch, you have to make two stitches – * YO the crochet hook, inset the crochet hook from front-to-back, to front, around this post of subsequent double crochet, YO the crochet hook and draw up one loop, YO the crochet hook and pull through two loops on your crochet hook * replicate from *to* one time again; YO the crochet hook and drag through all three residual loops on your crochet hook

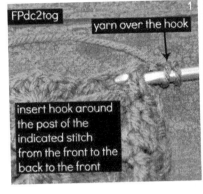

FPdc2tog

yarn over the hook

insert hook around the post of the indicated stitch from the front to the back to the front

yarn over the hook

yarn over the hook and pull through 2 loops

two loops left on the hook

yarn over the hook and insert the hook around the post of the next st, from front to back to front

yarn over hook

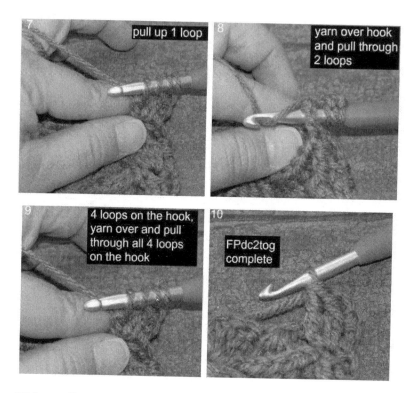

FPdc5tog (front-post-double-crochet-5-together): For this stitch, you have to make more than five stitches – * YO your crochet hook, and insert the crochet hook from the front-to-back, to facade, around the following double crochet, YO the crochet hook and draw up one loop, YO the crochet hook and drag through two of the loops on crochet hook * replicate from *to* four more times; YO the crochet hook and pull through all six residual loops on crochet

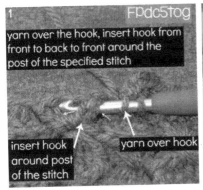

1 FPdc5Tog

yarn over the hook, insert hook from front to back to front around the post of the specified stitch

insert hook around post of the stitch

yarn over hook

2 yarn over

3 pull up 1 loop

4 yarn over and pull through two loops

after you have pulled through 2 loops you have 2 loops left on the hook; now you repeat the process for the next 4 posts

5 4 3 2 1

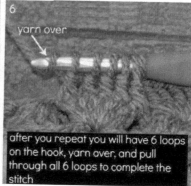

6

yarn over

after you repeat you will have 6 loops on the hook, yarn over, and pull through all 6 loops to complete the stitch

Chain 25

Row 1 (RS): 2 double crochet in the 4th ch from the hook (Note: the skipped three chains count as one double crochet st), double crochet5tog, ch 1, * skip the subsequent ch, five double crochet in the subsequent chain, double crochet5tog, ch 1 *. Replicate from * to * to the last two chains; skip the subsequent ch, three double crochet in the last chain.

Row 2: chain 3 (Note: the chain three taken as one double crochet stitch), flip; Front-post-double crochet2tog, work five double crochet in the subsequent ch, * skip the subsequent reduction, work Front-post-double crochet5tog, chain 1, work five double crochet in the subsequent ch *. Replicate from * to * crossways to the last four stitches. Skip the subsequent decrease; Front-post-double crochet2tog then work one double crochet in the last double crochet of the row

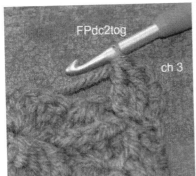

FPdc2tog

ch 3

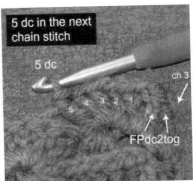

5 dc in the next chain stitch

5 dc

5 4 3 2 1

ch 3

FPdc2tog

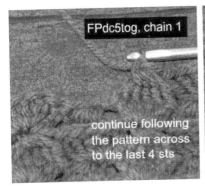

FPdc5tog, chain 1

continue following the pattern across to the last 4 sts

across to the last 4 sts

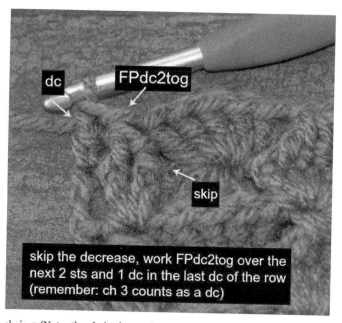

dc FPdc2tog

skip

skip the decrease, work FPdc2tog over the next 2 sts and 1 dc in the last dc of the row (remember: ch 3 counts as a dc)

Row 3: chain 3 (Note: the chain three taken as one double crochet stitch), flip; 2 double crochet in the subsequent decrease, work Front-post-double crochet5tog, ch 1, * work five double crochet in the subsequent ch, skip the subsequent decrease, work Front-post-double crochet5tog, ch 1 *. Replicate from * to * crossways to the last two stitches. Work 2 double crochet in the subsequent decrease and one double crochet in the last double crochet.

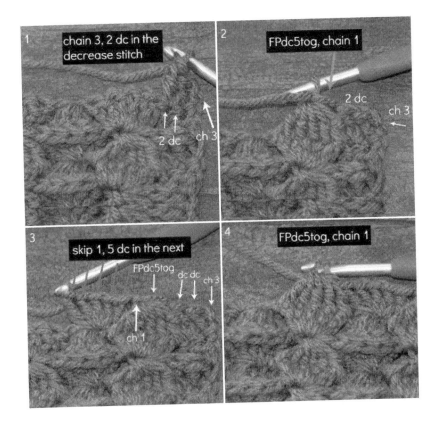

1. chain 3, 2 dc in the decrease stitch

2 dc   ch 3

2. FPdc5tog, chain 1

2 dc   ch 3

3. skip 1, 5 dc in the next

FPdc5tog   dc dc   ch 3
ch 1

4. FPdc5tog, chain 1

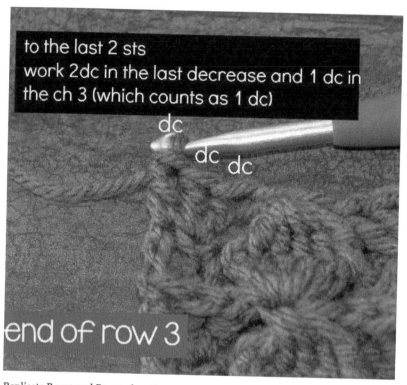

to the last 2 sts
work 2dc in the last decrease and 1 dc in the ch 3 (which counts as 1 dc)

dc
dc dc

end of row 3

Replicate Row 2 and Row 3: four times

Replicate Row 2 1 more time

There is no need to finish it off and proceed to the border.

Border

Row 1: chain 2, flip, 1 half-double-crochet in the following st, 1 single crochet in every of the following 5 stitches, skip the ch1, 1 half-double-crochet in the following st, 1 single crochet in every of the following 5 stitches, skip the ch st, 1 half-double-crochet in the following st, 1 single crochet in every of the following 5 stitches, 1 half-double-crochet in the last st, (19)ch 1 flip to complete the work along the side corner

R2: half-double-crochet 19 times equally along the side corner, chain 1, flip to finish the work along the initial chain row

R3: single crochet 19 times equally along the bottom corner, chain 1, flip to finish the work along the side corner

R4: half-double-crochet 19 times equally along the side corner, chain 1, flip to finish the work along the 1st row of the border

You are now back to the initial corner, two single crochet in every chain stitch (corner), flip one FPdc in every st crossway, two single crochet in every ch st (corner), flip to complete the work along the side corner

one FPdc in every st crossway, two single crochet in every chain stitch (corner), flip to finish the work along the initial chain row

one FPdc in every st crossway, two single crochet in every chain stitch (corner), flip to finish the work along the final corner

one FPdc in every st crossway, finish off with an invisible join and weave in ends.

Stitch 05: Cable Stitch
This stitch looks similar to one twisted rope and you can use it in decoration projects. It is good to make borders of hats, sweaters and scarves. Follow these directions to make cable stitches:

If you want to make one crocheted cable, you should have four stitches on your crochet hook. For this purpose, you have to chain in multiples of four and add three. For instance, four cables can be 16 stitches + 3 will be equal to 19. Hence, the 19 chain stitches will be there. Now, single crochet (SC) in the second stitch from the crochet hook and in every stitch of this chain.

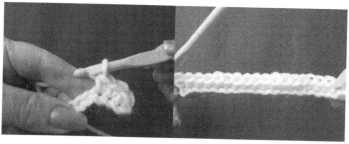

Now chain three and flip.

Avoid the subsequent stitch, dc (double crochet) in every of the subsequent three stitches.

Now, insert the crochet hook, from front-to-back, into the initial stitch avoided.

Pull up one loop, sloppily (loosely), bring this loop toward top of your final double crochet (dc) worked, and complete this double crochet with one yarn over (YO), and over the loops.

Replicate 3,4&5 steps crossways the row. Finish this row with one double crochet in the final stitch.

Chain (ch) 1 and flip, sc (single crochet) in every stitch crossways the row.

Replicate the steps by starting from 2nd step.

In the photo, you can see the three cable stitch rows and these are completed.

Chapter 3 – Learn how to make Popcorn Stitch, Seed Stitch and Shell Stitch

There are three modern stitches that prove helpful to increase the beauty and versatility of your designs:

Stitch 06: Popcorn Stitch

You can easily make popcorn stitch by following all the directions properly. You have to make clusters with double crochet in similar stitch. You can follow the given tutorial to make your work easy:

1. Make one foundation chain that you can easily divide by 3. SC in the second stitch from the crochet hook and in every crochet stitch of this chain.

2. Ch (chain) 1 and flip, SC in the subsequent 2 stitches. * In the subsequent stitch, make 5 DC, keeping the final loop of every stitch on the crochet hook.

3. Sl St (slip stitch) into complete six loops on your crochet hook.

4. SC in the subsequent 3 stitches.

5. Replicate 2,3,and4 crosswise the row, start at * in the 2nd step.

6. Chain (CH) 1 and flip, SC in every stitch crosswise the row. (In your popcorn stitch, SC in the middle stitch.)

(SC (SC) in the middle stitch of back area of your popcorn stitch.)

Replicate the series of steps, such as 2,3,4and5, to make desired number of rows to complete this project.

(Two complete rows of popcorn stitch.)

(Three complete rows of popcorn stitch.)

2nd Tutorial for Popcorn Stitch

The popcorn crochet looks really nice because the round and compact oval stitches will give a unique look to your fabric. It may take a bit more time or efforts, but it will be fun to work in the front and back of the fabric. You need to work 5 double-crochet popcorn stitches that may pop to the front design:

Start 5 double crochet stitches in the similar stitch and drop the loop from your hook.

Pop in your hook from front to back under the upper two loops of the initial dual crochet of the group.

Grasp the plummeted loop with your hook and drag it through your stitch.

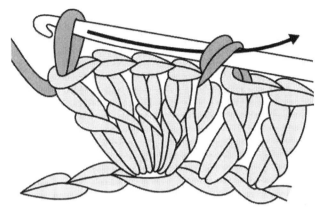

You can notice complete front-popping popcorn.

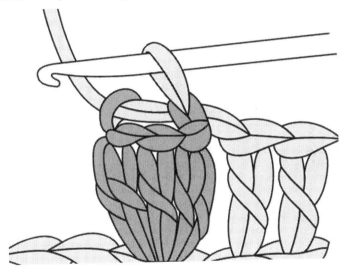

Now it is time to work on the back of the pattern:

Work the 5 dc stitches in the similar stitch. Drop the ring from your hook and pop in your hook from back to front under the upper 2 loops of the initial dc of the group. Grasp the dropped circle with your hook and pull it over the stitch.

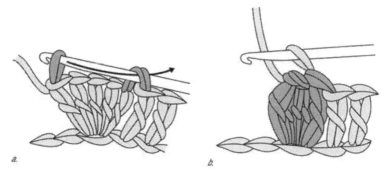

You can see complete back-popping popcorn.

Stitch 07: Shell Stitch

Shell stitch is really beautiful because you can use this stitch in any pattern as per your wish. You can use it to make border or create a variety of patterns, such as beanie, scarf, shrug, etc. See the given tutorial:

This stitch is really simple, just follow the pattern and you are done.

Initiate with one chain.

Now double crochet (dc) in the third stitch from your crochet hook.

You will make four more dc (double crochet) stitches in the similar stitch.

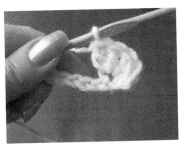

Omit the subsequent three stitches, and make five double crochet in the subsequent stitch.

Replicate 4th step crosswise the row.

Now, at the finishing point of this row, flip and sl st (slip stitch) in the initial three stitches, now chain 2, form four double crochet (dc) in the similar stitch. Replicate 4th crosswise the row. Replicate 6th step for every next row of your shell stitch.

Stitch 08: Seed Stitch

There are only seven steps that will help you to learn this stitch. This stitch will be easy to work with the alternate working of double and single crochet. This stitch looks like a close stitch and you can accomplish it successfully with the help of given tutorial:

1. Initiate with one chain. Flip, SC (single crochet) in the second stitch from your crochet hook.

2. DC (double crochet) in the subsequent stitch.

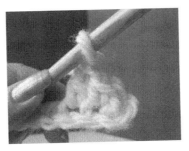

3. SC in the subsequent stitch.

4. Replicated 2nd and 3rd steps crosswise the row.

5. Now you have one complete row of this seed stitch. You can replicate rounds to make this row longer.

6. At the finishing point of this row, flip. If you are ending in one DC, then you have to SC in the initial stitch. To end in one single crochet, Sl St (slip stitch) in your initial stitch, then chain 2, (it will replace the initial double crochet), SC (single crochet) in the subsequent stitch.

7. You can continue crosswise this row, interchanging it by creating one single crochet (SC) in the DC (double crochet) of the earlier row, and vice-versa. See the photo.

You can replicate this tutorial to make your own patterns with the help of these stitches.

Chapter 4 – Tips to hold the yarn and hook while crocheting?

- There are a number of projects that you can follow because every project is based on the basic crochet stitches from a single stitch to double crochet. In the first step, you need to learn how to hold the yarn and hook:

- There is no critical rule or a specific way to hold the hook and yarn. You can select any way you are comfortable with. For some people, pencil grip is excellent and they hold the hook in the right hand just like a pencil.

- It is necessary to maintain the slight tension in yarn for easy stitching and it will be good to wrap the around your fingers of the other hand opposite to the one you are holding the hook. You can try a way in which you are comfortable to work.

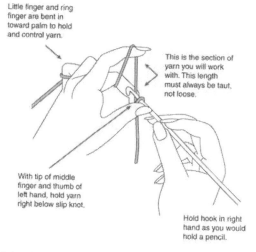

Little finger and ring finger are bent in toward palm to hold and control yarn.

This is the section of yarn you will work with. This length must always be taut, not loose.

With tip of middle finger and thumb of left hand, hold yarn right below slip knot.

Hold hook in right hand as you would hold a pencil.

- In the left hand, you will handle the crochet work and tension of the yarn. The middle finger of the left hand, you can control the yarn, and the index finger and thumb will hold your crochet work.

- In short, there is no strict rule to follow to hold and control the yarn and hook. You can choose any way that helps you to design any pattern comfortably. Some people like pencil grip and they hold it in the right hand just like a pencil.

- Some people prefer knife grip and they also carry the hook just like a knife in the right hand as they hold it while cutting the vegetables.

86

- For some people. It is more comfortable to control the yarn with the index finger and hold the crochet work with their thumb and middle finger. You can try any way that can make you comfortable while working.

Chapter 5 – Work on Some Basic Stitches

There is a range of visual effects that you can achieve with the use of right pattern. The crochet looks really cool with the combination of right stitches. You need to tackle the pattern with the use of basic stitches, such as chain stitch, single crochet, and double crochet. Start your practice with basic stitches and then move to advanced stitches. Following are some basic stitches for your help:

Chain Stitch

Every crochet project starts with a chain stitch, and it is important for you to learn this pattern. You can try it with the help of the given below steps:

- In the first step, you will tie a slip loop and glide it over the hook as the first knot.

- Now wrap the yarn around the hook from flipside to frontage and create another loop of yarn on the hook.

- Depict that loop via an already available knot on your hook and complete the chain stitch. Continue this process and design a desired pattern.

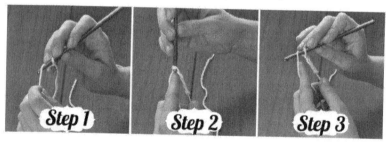

Slip Stitch

If you want something different, then try the pattern of slip stitch. Following are some simple steps for this:

- Make a loop with yarn by wrapping it around your first two fingers.

- The hook should be inserted into the first loop of the yard and try to reach for one loop from behind.

- Hook will help you to grab the yarn at the back of the loop and pull it all the way through.

- Pull to make your slip knot tight and the following picture will help you to tie this knot. You will get one loop and dual pieces of yarn. Carefully cut the free end and another will be known as working end. This will be used to crochet.

Single Crochet

Single crochet is really simple and the following steps will make your work easy:

- Insert your hook into the 2nd chain from hook and pass the yarn under both loops to make a V-shaped chain at the top of the stitch.

- Yarn over and draw a new loop via existing stitch and now you will get two loops on your hook.

- It is time to yarn over once again.

- Draw the loop back and on the hook and continue this process.

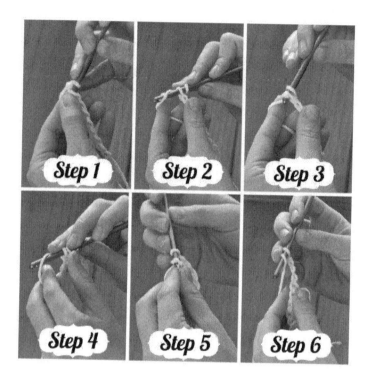

Double Crochet

This crochet is three times taller than a single crochet stitch. You can complete it at a faster rate and to do it, you have to create a double loop at the first stage.

- Yarn over and put on the hook into 2nd stitch.

- Yarn over once again and then draw the yarn with the help of a loop.

- You should have three loops on the hook and yarn over to draw the first two loops on your hook.

- Now your hook will have two loops and you can draw two more loops over your hook. Continue the DC after previous SC row.

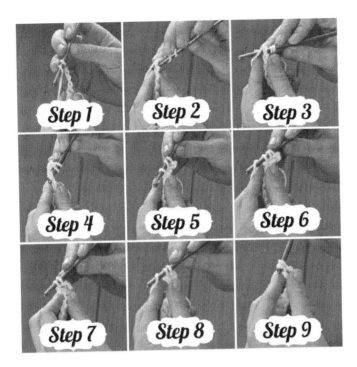

Half Double Crochet

It is a unique design with some glimpses of single crochet and double crochet on the basis of its height.

- It can be completed through particular steps used on the double crochet.

- Just yarn over, insert your hook in the stitch that you are working on and draw the loop back via existing stitch.

- Your hook should have three loops and to complete the stitch, you need to yarn over and draw a new knot back through all existing knots on the hook.

- The following image will give you a better idea of half double crochet:

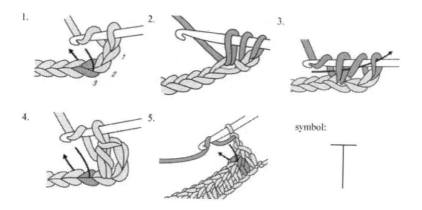

Tips to Make an FPdc

It is a specialized version of double crochet via front post. The actual process is same, but the only thing is the insertion of loops on the hook.

- Start by yarning over and then run the hook from right to the left direction or in the vertical position of the stitches.

- Yarn over once again and then pull it back after the post. It will help you to create a third loop on the hook.

- Now it is time to follow the similar process just like you follow while designing double crochet design.

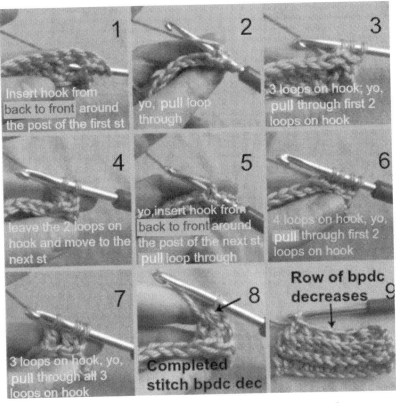

1. Insert hook from back to front around the post of the first st

2. yo, pull loop through

3. 3 loops on hook; yo, pull through first 2 loops on hook

4. leave the 2 loops on hook and move to the next st

5. yo, insert hook from back to front around the post of the next st, pull loop through

6. 4 loops on hook, yo, pull through first 2 loops on hook

7. 3 loops on hook, yo, pull through all 3 loops on hook

8. Completed stitch bpdc dec

9. Row of bpdc decreases

If you want to learn crochet, then in initial level, it will be good to try these patterns. These will help you to become a master in your work.

Conclusion

There are different types of stitches in Crochet, but in the beginning, you can focus on small stitches like a chain. You will make an oval symbol by pulling this loop through another loop to make an interlocking oval. The single crochet is known as a squat cross that is slightly smaller in the length than double crochet. The symbol of double crochet contains a bar in the middle of its post. Remaining symbols are arranged in the line with the same reasoning. The symbol of the short stitch will be short as well, but the puffs out stitches may have similar symbols.

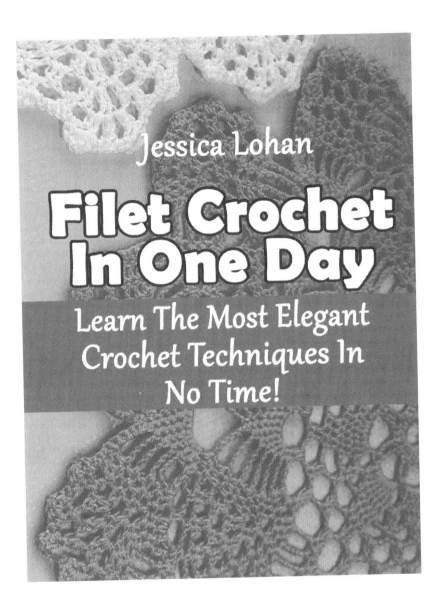

Jessica Lohan

Filet Crochet In One Day

Learn The Most Elegant Crochet Techniques In No Time!

Filet Crochet In One Day
Learn The Most Elegant Crochet Techniques In No Time!

Introduction

You look through the different crochet patterns you find on the internet, and each one looks amazing. You think of the ways you could make your own projects look like that, or how you would use those patterns but add a little of this here and a little of that there.

As you work through the different crochet patterns, you can't help but think of the ways you like to embellish and do your own thing. You love doing new and exciting techniques, and you love showing off your crochet skills. But, there are times when your skills tend to feel a little repetitive, and you want to do something new.

Crochet is a simple hobby, and it doesn't matter how long you have been doing it – though you can use different kinds of stitches as you work on your projects, you always end up feeling like you are doing the same things as you work back and forth across the rows. Now, you want to get creative, you want to show off something new, and you want to get started now.

But what are you going to do? All the other projects you've been working on are feeling like you've done them a million times already.

If you are ready to try a new technique with your crochet, you have come to the right place. This book is going to show you how to do filet crochet – a crochet method that is going to blow your mind.

It doesn't matter how long you have been crocheting, and it doesn't matter if you are a beginner or if you know how to do every stitch in the book. This is a new kind of crochet that is going to blow your mind, and give you the chance to be creative in ways you have never before thought possible in the world of crochet.

Filet crochet is like a counted cross stitch crochet hybrid, and it's going to give you the chance to write messages, show off images, and create a new kind of pattern that your friends and family have never seen before. When you learn how to filet crochet, you give yourself the chance to step out from the other patterns, and do something that is fresh and exciting.

When you look at the projects as a seasoned crochet artist, they don't look possible. But trust me, in no time at all you will be hooked on this new method, and you're going to fall in love with the results time and time again. Grab your hook and your favorite yarn, it's time to dive into a whole new method of crochet that's going to blow open the doors to creativity.

There's a new kind of crochet in town, and it's just waiting for you to dive in and express yourself. So what are you waiting for? You know you're excited.

Let's get started.

Chapter 1 – What Is Filet Crochet?

As you know, the world of crochet entails so many different kinds of work, it's almost impossible to list them all. From the beautiful and intricate doily patterns to the thick and chunky scarves and sweaters – and everything in between. You can make a world of projects from just a single stitch, or you can practice and expand your skills until you know how to create dozens if not hundreds of crochet stitches.

Yet it seems that the more you advance in crochet, the more opportunities there are to advance. You can go bigger, better, more intricate, less intricate, even inside out in some cases, making crochet one of the most versatile hobbies on the planet.

If you have been crocheting for very long, odds are you have heard of a different kind of crochet technique that has been around for ages, but has yet to gain the same popularity of other methods. Perhaps it is the challenge and patience that is involved with this kind of technique, perhaps it's the imagination and skill that is required to follow through with the patterns.

Whatever the reason, filet crochet is one branch of the hobby that manages to stay on the fringes.

Until now.

With this book, you are going to learn everything you need to know about this style of crochet, and how you can take the designs you have in your mind, and put them down into a hobby that is sure to wow your friends and family.

But, you may wonder – what exactly is filet crochet?

Photo made by: noricum

In a way, filet crochet is like a hybrid between counted cross stitch and crochet. You are going to create flat projects that you can turn into either pillows, scarves, blankets, or just leave as they are, and you are going to use a mix of double crochet and single crochet to create elaborate patterns within the squares you have created.

Traditionally, filet crochet is created using thread weight yarn and really small crochet hooks – whether those be sizes G or E or even the much smaller hooks. Depending on the intricacy of the project, the weight of the yarn and the crochet hook vary.

As a filet crochet beginner, it is important to note that you are going to use a different kind of crochet pattern in most of your projects – the graph. Crochet graphs are different from other patterns in that they aren't written out line by line or space by space as traditional patterns are.

They are drawn more like the graph you would use for a counted cross stitch process, and you work through them row by row in much the same way. When it comes to the use of a graph with your filet crochet, it is important that you pay attention to where you are on the project, and that you are careful to mark off your progress as you move along.

One of the biggest challenges you are going to face is whether you are marking off the right part of the project or not, and this is something that can be accomplished by simply paying careful attention to where you are when you mark off on the pattern.

As with all other forms of crochet, if you make a mistake at any time, all you need to do is pull out the work you have done and start fresh. While this is a more intricate form of crochet then others you have done in the past, it is still done using the traditional crochet stitches – just in a less traditional manner.

Photo made by: noricum

Although the standard for filet crochet is using thread weight yarn and a small crochet hook, you are free to use any weight yarn you like, as well as any size crochet hook you like.

Among those who have used this form of crochet there are artists who are now using it to create accessories such as scarves and blankets. While this certainly is an admirable feat in and of itself, you know that you wouldn't want to make such things using the thread weight yarn.

As with other forms of crochet, you are going to have a good amount of freedom that allows you to create the kinds of projects you wish to create, though you are using the same pattern as everyone else. Just make sure you are paying attention to where you are on the project, and where you are on the pattern you are using. One of the biggest benefits that comes from using the graph when you are creating a crochet project is that you get to check what you have against the graph as you move along.

This is going to give you greater control over what happens when you make a mistake, as well as give you a better idea of what you need to do to make the finished project look like the pattern. Although there is a specific technique you need to follow with filet crochet, bear in mind that you are going to also have the freedom to through in some of your own preferences.

As long as you are following the pattern as it is written, you are going to end up with the end result that you see on the graph – whatever that image may be.

Filet crochet is a great way to create patterns with messages – common messages include "Home Sweet Home", "I love you," "Bless This House," and others like it.

Photo made by: leeives

How does filet crochet work?

To anyone who is familiar with the hobby, they may be confused when they see a filet crochet project. After all, when you are working with a pattern that runs back and forth and back and forth, how are you going to know when to add in the filler stitches that create the look of the piece?

The answer is simple: Filet crochet is created using a combination of the single crochet stitch and the double crochet stitch. Some artists choose to add in the triple crochet stitch for some of the wider parts of the piece, although this isn't nearly as common as sticking to the other two stitches.

When you are creating your own crochet patterns, you have the freedom to decide which is going to work best for you, and what you want to do for the end result of your pattern. If there is a place in which you want to add a triple crochet, feel free to do so in order to get the pattern to lie flat.

The key to working with filet crochet is to take your time as you work through all your pieces, ensuring that you get the end result you want with the pattern.

Chapter 2 – The Technique

Now that you have an understanding of what filet crochet is, it's time to put the method to the test. Although many people choose to use smaller hooks and thinner, threadlike yarn to create these patterns, you are free to use any size hook and yarn that you wish.

I find that it is easier to learn with the bigger hooks and thicker yarn, as you are better able to see what you are doing with the stitches. Practice with the bigger hook and thicker yarn in the beginning if you would like, then when you feel like you are better able to handle the smaller hook and smaller stitches, you can change what you are doing to accommodate those.

As I have said, there are many different ways you can enjoy this kind of crochet, you just have to find the method that you enjoy best. Most people use these lace patterns to create decorations for their home, so they tend to leave them in more of a lacelike way. However, there are more and more crochet artists who are using thicker yarn and bigger hooks to create actual crochet pieces to place around their home or even wear, so you can do what you want with it really.

I recommend for the beginning of this project that you find the yarn you like using the best and your favorite crochet hook, to ensure that you are completely comfortable and ready to start the new hobby. There are few things more irritating than when you are trying to start a new hobby, but you simply do not like the tools that they are recommending you use.

If this is the first time you are crocheting at all, I still recommend that you start with a larger hook and some thicker yarn. It is going to be easier for you to see what you are doing, and you're going to be more comfortable holding the thicker hook in your hands for a long period of time.

Of course, if you wish to start with the traditional manner, you can also use the thread weight yarn with the smaller hooks, just keep in mind that this is going to require you to pay closer attention both to what the pattern is telling you to do, and what you have in front of you.

Thinner yarn also tends to knot up easier than the thicker yarn, so you may spend more time fixing the mistakes that you make with this size, too. Choose which you would like to do to begin, gather all the supplies you will need, and you are ready to start your filet crochet.

Make sure when you move on to using a pattern that you also have a pen and a pencil handy so you can mark off the places you have done on the pattern – this is going to make it much easier for you to see where you are on the piece as you move along with the project.

Now let's begin.

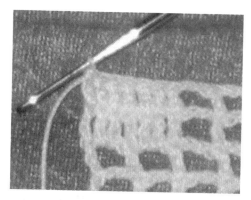

Photo made by: noricum

When you filet crochet, each of the open squares you make is going to be a total of 4 stitches wide. If you are making a larger project, keep this in mind so you can properly gauge how big you need to make the project as a whole.

I recommend when you are planning a bigger project using this technique, that you begin with a small swatch to give you an idea of what the tension is going to look like. Make sure you stay consistent with your tension throughout the piece as well, as there are going to be a lot of open spaces that could cause bigger gaps.

When you begin your filet crochet, you are going to begin with making the mesh area. You create the entire mesh area first, then you are going to go back over it and fill in the blanks, so to speak.

With this in mind, this means you are going to create the overall size of the project at first, then you are going to go back over the piece and add the décor. This is going to put you in greater control of the final look of the piece.

For this starter project, we are going to crochet a smaller swatch until you get the hang of the movement. When you have that down, you will be ready to move onto the bigger pieces.

Start by chaining 26 stitches.

Begin by double crocheting in the 8th chain from the hook. Chain 2, then skip the next 2 chains, then double crochet in the next chain. Chain 2, then skip the next 2 chains, then double crochet in the next chain. Chain 2, then skip the next 2 chains, then double crochet in the next chain. Chain 2, then skip the next 2 chains, then double crochet in the next chain. Chain 2, then skip the next 2 chains, then double crochet in the next chain. Chain 2, then skip the next 2 chains, then double crochet in the next chain.

You should now be across the row with 7 squares in your swatch.

For the next row you are going to begin with chaining 5, and you are going to skip the first double crochet stitch on the row and the chain 2 gap. Double crochet in the next double crochet, then chain 2. Double crochet in the next double crochet, then chain 2. Double crochet in the next double crochet, then chain 2. Double crochet in the next double crochet, then chain 2. Double crochet in the next double crochet, then chain 2.

When you are at the end of the row, double crochet in the third chain of the previous row's turning chain.

For the next row you are going to begin with chaining 5, and you are going to skip the first double crochet stitch on the row and the chain 2 gap. Double crochet in the next double crochet, then chain 2. Double crochet in the next double crochet, then chain 2. Double crochet in the next double crochet, then chain 2. Double crochet in the next double crochet, then chain 2. Double crochet in the next double crochet, then chain 2.

When you are at the end of the row, double crochet in the third chain of the previous row's turning chain.

For the next row you are going to begin with chaining 5, and you are going to skip the first double crochet stitch on the row and the chain 2 gap. Double crochet in the next double crochet, then chain 2. Double crochet in the next double crochet, then chain 2. Double crochet in the next double crochet, then chain 2. Double crochet in the next double crochet, then chain 2.

When you are at the end of the row, double crochet in the third chain of the previous row's turning chain.

For the next row you are going to begin with chaining 5, and you are going to skip the first double crochet stitch on the row and the chain 2 gap. Double crochet in the next double crochet, then chain 2. Double crochet in the next double crochet, then chain 2. Double crochet in the next double crochet, then chain 2. Double crochet in the next double crochet, then chain 2. Double crochet in the next double crochet, then chain 2.

When you are at the end of the row, double crochet in the third chain of the previous row's turning chain.

For the next row you are going to begin with chaining 5, and you are going to skip the first double crochet stitch on the row and the chain 2 gap. Double crochet in the next double crochet, then chain 2. Double crochet in the next double crochet, then chain 2. Double crochet in the next double crochet, then chain 2. Double crochet in the next double crochet, then chain 2. Double crochet in the next double crochet, then chain 2.

When you are at the end of the row, double crochet in the third chain of the previous row's turning chain.

For the next row you are going to begin with chaining 5, and you are going to skip the first double crochet stitch on the row and the chain 2 gap. Double crochet in the next double crochet, then chain 2. Double crochet in the next double crochet, then chain 2. Double crochet in the next double crochet, then chain 2. Double crochet in the next double crochet, then chain 2. Double crochet in the next double crochet, then chain 2.

When you are at the end of the row, double crochet in the third chain of the previous row's turning chain.

For the next row you are going to begin with chaining 5, and you are going to skip the first double crochet stitch on the row and the chain 2 gap. Double crochet in the next double crochet, then chain 2. Double crochet in the next double crochet, then chain 2. Double crochet in the next double crochet, then chain 2. Double crochet in the next double crochet, then chain 2. Double crochet in the next double crochet, then chain 2.

When you are at the end of the row, double crochet in the third chain of the previous row's turning chain.

For the next row you are going to begin with chaining 5, and you are going to skip the first double crochet stitch on the row and the chain 2 gap. Double crochet in the next double crochet, then chain 2. Double crochet in the next double crochet, then chain 2. Double crochet in the next double crochet, then chain 2. Double crochet in the next double crochet, then chain 2. Double crochet in the next double crochet, then chain 2.

When you are at the end of the row, double crochet in the third chain of the previous row's turning chain.

You should now have a perfect square grid to work with. There should be 7 squares running across, as well as 7 squares running vertically. If you need to add another row or remove on, adjust accordingly.

Now it's time to fill in the blanks!

To create a pattern like you see below, you are going to work with the same grid as before, only you are going to fill in the blanks as you go.

Once again, set the foundation chain for your work.

Start by chaining 26 stitches.

Begin by double crocheting in the 8th chain from the hook. Chain 2, then skip the next 2 chains, then double crochet in the next chain. Chain 2, then skip the next 2 chains, then double crochet in the next chain. Chain 2, then skip the next 2 chains, then double crochet in the next chain. Chain 2, then skip the next 2 chains, then double crochet in the next chain. Chain 2, then skip the next 2 chains, then double crochet in the next chain. Chain 2, then skip the next 2 chains, then double crochet in the next chain.

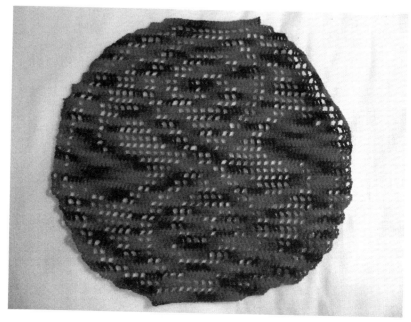

You should now be across the row with 7 squares in your swatch.

Now, to create a block pattern you are going to work on filling in the blanks.

Chain 2, and double crochet in the first 4 stitches, filling that block. Chain 2 and skip the next 2 stitches, then double crochet in the next double crochet chain. Double crochet in the next 3 stitches, then chain 2 and skip the next 2 stitches, then double crochet in the next double crochet chain. Double crochet in the next 3 stitches, then chain 2 and skip the next 2 stitches, then double crochet in the next double crochet chain. Double crochet in the next 3 stitches, then chain 2 and skip the next 2 stitches, then double crochet in the next double crochet chain.

Continue with this until you are at the end of the row. chain 2 and turn.

To create an alternating pattern do the opposite as you did in the last row.

Chain 5 and skip the first double crochet and the chain 2 space, then double crochet in the next 4 stitches. Chain 2 and skip the next 2 stitches, then double crochet in the next double crochet chain. Double crochet in the next 3 stitches, then chain 2 and skip the next 2 stitches, then double crochet in the next double crochet chain. Double crochet in the next 3 stitches, then chain 2 and skip the next 2 stitches, then double crochet in the

110

next double crochet chain. Double crochet in the next 3 stitches, then chain 2 and skip the next 2 stitches, then double crochet in the next double crochet chain.

Continue with this until you are at the end of the row. chain 2 and turn.

To create an alternating pattern do the opposite as you did in the last row.

Chain 5 and skip the first double crochet and the chain 2 space, then double crochet in the next 4 stitches. Chain 2 and skip the next 2 stitches, then double crochet in the next double crochet chain. Double crochet in the next 3 stitches, then chain 2 and skip the next 2 stitches, then double crochet in the next double crochet chain. Double crochet in the next 3 stitches, then chain 2 and skip the next 2 stitches, then double crochet in the next double crochet chain. Double crochet in the next 3 stitches, then chain 2 and skip the next 2 stitches, then double crochet in the next double crochet chain.

Continue with this until you are at the end of the row. chain 2 and turn.

To create an alternating pattern do the opposite as you did in the last row.

Chain 5 and skip the first double crochet and the chain 2 space, then double crochet in the next 4 stitches. Chain 2 and skip the next 2 stitches, then double crochet in the next double crochet chain. Double crochet in the next 3 stitches, then chain 2 and skip the next 2 stitches, then double crochet in the next double crochet chain. Double crochet in the next 3 stitches, then chain 2 and skip the next 2 stitches, then double crochet in the next double crochet chain. Double crochet in the next 3 stitches, then chain 2 and skip the next 2 stitches, then double crochet in the next double crochet chain.

Continue with this until you are at the end of the row. chain 2 and turn.

To create an alternating pattern do the opposite as you did in the last row.

Chain 5 and skip the first double crochet and the chain 2 space, then double crochet in the next 4 stitches. Chain 2 and skip the next 2 stitches, then double crochet in the next double crochet chain. Double crochet in the next 3 stitches, then chain 2 and skip the next 2 stitches, then double crochet in the next double crochet chain. Double crochet in the next 3 stitches, then chain 2 and skip the next 2 stitches, then double crochet in the next double crochet chain. Double crochet in the next 3 stitches, then chain 2 and skip the next 2 stitches, then double crochet in the next double crochet chain.

Of course you can see as you do this that you are moving in a checkered shape, and that's all you really need to know how to do with the filet crochet. With this method, you can follow any graph pattern you can dream of.

Conclusion

There you have it, everything you need to know when it comes to the world of filet crochet, and the simple steps you need to take to make the hobby a reality in your own crafting. I hope this book was able to not only give you the inspiration you need to create your own projects, but that you take what you have learned here and apply them to other pieces you are working on.

When it comes to the world of filet crochet, you have so many choices of things you can make and do. You can create the images on the patterns as you see them, or you can bring in all new kinds of shapes and colors, throwing in your own creativity with each of the pieces.

There really is no way you can do it wrong if you are getting the end results you wish to be getting, and when you attach the pieces to pillows, scarves, or anything else that you want, you are giving new life to a hobby that can get boring with repetition if you aren't careful.

I hope this new method of crochet opens to the door for you in a whole new way, and that you take what you have learned here and find new patterns to work on. There really is no end to the ways you can bring filet crochet into the projects that you are already working on, and when you get good at it, you are going to be able to do even more.

Don't let yourself get overwhelmed, and don't feel intimidated with the different patterns you see. Each of these methods is done with the same filet, and each one is going to give you the results that you see in the patterns. Just make sure you pay attention to where you are, and that you mark off on the pattern where you wish to be.

It takes practice, just as you did with the other kinds of crochet you have done, but if you are willing to put in the time and effort to do the practice, you're going to end up with a new skill you can use any time that you want. I hope you bring this new kind of crochet into your crafting rotation, and that you are able to create all kinds of wonderful projects with it.

Take your creativity and apply it to what you are already doing, and learn from the methods that I outlined in this book. Filet crochet may not be as common as other methods, but the more you create using it, the more it's going to be around.

Now get out there and find the projects you wish to create, then settle in with a crochet method that will show off your crochet skills like a true champion. You are going to fall in love with each and every one of these patterns, and be able to express yourself like never before.

Get ready to blow some minds with a creativity that few people have seen.

Happy crocheting!

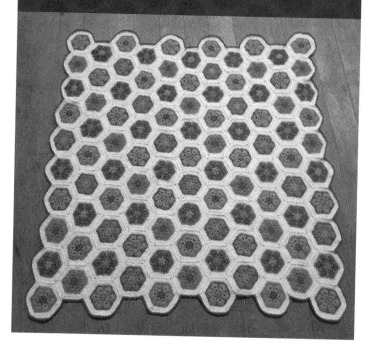

African
Crochet Flower
Learn To Crochet Basic African
Flower Hexagon And Use It
In Wonderful Crochet Projects

African Flower Crochet

Learn to Crochet Basic African Flower Hexagon
And Use It In Wonderful Crochet Projects

Introduction

You browse Pinterest, looking for new inspiration. You want to make something that is new and exciting, and you are tired of the same old stitches. But, you are also short on time, and you don't want to have to spend hours trying to learn a new stitch.

You want something that's easy to make, something you can do in a single afternoon, and something that gives you the results you want. You want to learn a stitch like the African Hexagon stitch.

But when you look at the photos of the stitch, it feels overwhelming. You want to make something that looks like that, but it seems impossible. How do you get the shape of a flower in the center of the stitch, but yet you have a hexagon around the border?

It looks difficult, and like something that's going to take a lot of time for you to learn how to do.

I would love to be able to make the hexagon stitch, but it looks so difficult.

I want to make the African Hexagon stitch, but with all the different shapes and colors, I don't know if I can.

I want to make the hexagon stitch, but how am I supposed to make the edges a hexagon and a flower in the center?

If you haven't ever made this stitch before, you are sure to feel confused. But, I am here to clear this up for you. Using an easy, step by step method that anyone can understand, I am going to show you how to make the African flower stitch in mere hours.

Sit down and grab your crochet hook, your favorite yarn, and brew a cup of coffee – you are about to learn how to make the African flower you have wanted. It's so much easier than you think it is, and with the right set of directions, anyone can learn how to do it.

116

Let me show you a stitch that is going to open the door to a whole new world of crochet. It might look hard now, but the projects you can make are incredible, and you will be so very glad you did.

Chapter 1 – Creating The African Flower Hexagon Stitch

With all the different stitches you can make with crochet, it can be hard to find something new. The African Hexagon flower stitch, you can get a fresh, new look without having to stress about the stitch.

Though this is considered a single unit, much like a granny square, you are going to create it using a combination of single and double crochet. Don't worry, for as intimidating as it looks, you'll find that it's both fast and incredibly easy to make if you have the right set of directions.

Before we get into those directions, however, you need to gather all your supplies. None of these flowers take much yarn, and you can easily use your scraps to assemble them. However, if you want to use fresh yarn to make them, use a skein in each color you choose.

You will need a size G crochet hook, and for many of the projects you use these flowers to create, you will also need a yarn needle to sew them together. A yarn needle is not necessary for making the flowers themselves, however, so don't worry about that at this point.

Keep your stitches even throughout, and change colors as you like. As I said, these are a great way to use up scraps, but you can do it however you want.

Once you have all your supplies, you are ready to get started.

Let's start your flower.

To begin, chain 5. Make a slip stitch into the first stitch, forming a ring.

Next, chain 3. You are going to count this chain 3 as your first double crochet stitch. Work 1 double crochet stitch into the center of this ring you have just created. Chain 1, then work 2 more double crochet stitches into the center of the ring.

As I said, the first chain 3 you have made counts as your first double crochet, so at this point you should now have a set of 4 double crochet stitches separated by a chain space.

Chain 1, and double crochet in the center of the ring 2 times, chain 1 again, then double crochet in the center of the ring 2 more times. Chain 1, and double crochet in the center of the ring 2 times, chain 1 again, then double crochet in the center of the ring 2 more times. Chain 1, and double crochet in the center of the ring 2 times, chain 1 again, then double crochet in the center of the ring 2 more times.

Continue to work with this same sequence until you have a total of 6 groups in the center of the ring. These will be groups of 2 double crochet, chain space, followed by 2 double crochet.

By this time you should be back to the beginning, with your final stitch next to your chain 3 that you made at first. Join with a slip stitch to the top stitch in this chain 3, closing your loop and forming a complete disc.

Tie off this color, and join with a new color of your choice.

Now it's time to add the next row to the center of the flower.

To join the next color to the flower, insert the hook into the chain space, and grab the yarn. Pull it through, then push the hook through the chain space once more. Bring the yarn up and around the hook, then grab the yarn and pull it through.

You have made a single crochet stitch.

Chain 3.

Next, you are going to make 1 double crochet stitch into this same space you just pulled the yarn through.

Chain 1. Now, work 2 more double crochet stitches in the same space as you made your first double crochet stitch. The space is going to be stretched to accommodate the amount of stitches are putting into it, but don't worry about that, it will be fixed as you move along the row.

Chain 1, and work 2 double crochet into the next space.

Make 2 double crochet stitches into the next space, then chain 1, then make 2 double crochet into the next chain space. Make 2 double crochet stitches into the next space, then chain 1, then make 2 double crochet into the next chain space.

Make 2 double crochet stitches into the next space, then chain 1, then make 2 double crochet into the next chain space. Make 2 double crochet stitches into the next space, then chain 1, then make 2 double crochet into the next chain space.

Make 2 double crochet stitches into the next space, then chain 1, then make 2 double crochet into the next chain space. Make 2 double crochet stitches into the next space, then chain 1, then make 2 double crochet into the next chain space.

Make 2 double crochet stitches into the next space, then chain 1, then make 2 double crochet into the next chain space. Make 2 double crochet stitches into the next space, then chain 1, then make 2 double crochet into the next chain space.

It's important that you keep track of where you are on the pattern, but this is easy to do when you are watching your stitches as you work.

Join with a slip stitch when you get back to the beginning. By now you should have 6 groups of 2 double crochet, chain space, 2 double crochet, 2 double crochet, chain space, 2 double crochet.

Now you have finished the end of the second row, and you can see the center shape of your flower formed.

Now add the petals to the center of your flower.

Begin the next row the same as you have the previous rows, with a chain 3. This is the first double crochet on the row, and will be counted with the rest of the double crochets as you work.

As this is the petal of the flower, you are going to work enough double crochet stitches in the space to form a rounded edge. To do this, work 6 more double crochet stitches in the same stitch as you have made your chain 3 space.

Count to make sure you have the right number of double crochet stitches. You are going to have a total of 7 double crochet stitches in a single chain space, as the first chain 3 you made counts as the first double crochet stitch on the row.

Next, bring the yarn up and over the hook, then make another double crochet in the next chain space.

Work 6 more double crochet stitches in the same stitch as you have made your chain 3 space.

Count to make sure you have the right number of double crochet stitches. You are going to have a total of 7 double crochet stitches in a single chain space.

Next, bring the yarn up and over the hook, then make another double crochet in the next chain space.

Work 6 more double crochet stitches in the same stitch as you have made your chain 3 space.

Count to make sure you have the right number of double crochet stitches. You are going to have a total of 7 double crochet stitches in a single chain space.

Next, bring the yarn up and over the hook, then make another double crochet in the next chain space.

Work 6 more double crochet stitches in the same stitch as you have made your chain 3 space.

Count to make sure you have the right number of double crochet stitches. You are going to have a total of 7 double crochet stitches in a single chain space.

Next, bring the yarn up and over the hook, then make another double crochet in the next chain space.

Work 6 more double crochet stitches in the same stitch as you have made your chain 3 space.

Count to make sure you have the right number of double crochet stitches. You are going to have a total of 7 double crochet stitches in a single chain space.

Next, bring the yarn up and over the hook, then make another double crochet in the next chain space.

Work 6 more double crochet stitches in the same stitch as you have made your chain 3 space.

Count to make sure you have the right number of double crochet stitches. You are going to have a total of 7 double crochet stitches in a single chain space.

Next, bring the yarn up and over the hook, then make another double crochet in the next chain space.

With each rounded edge you make, you can see the shape of the flower coming together. Continue until you have reached the beginning of the flower.

Now it's time to shape the hexagon out of the flower shape.

Join the yarn with a slip stitch, finishing the row.

Cut this color, then join the next color to the flower. Remember to push the hook through the space, then bring the yarn up and over the side of the hook. Yarn pull the yarn through the space, then finish forming your single crochet stitch, attaching the yarn to the flower.

This is going to count as the first single crochet stitch on the loop. Next, follow the edge of the flower as you work 6 more single crochet stitches along the side of the petal.

Counting the first stitch you made, you now have a total of 7 single crochet stitches on the flower.

In the next stitch, you will form a double crochet. make sure the yarn reaches down to the space in the row below, you can see in the photo where this ought to be. This is going to be a very tall stitch, but it forms the shape of the flower.

Once this double crochet stitch is completed, form 7 more single crochet stitches in the next 7 stitches on the flower.

In the next stitch, you will form a double crochet. make sure the yarn reaches down to the space in the row below, you can see in the photo where this ought to be. This is going to be a very tall stitch, but it forms the shape of the flower.

Once this double crochet stitch is completed, form 7 more single crochet stitches in the next 7 stitches on the flower.

In the next stitch, you will form a double crochet. make sure the yarn reaches down to the space in the row below, you can see in the photo where this ought to be. This is going to be a very tall stitch, but it forms the shape of the flower.

Once this double crochet stitch is completed, form 7 more single crochet stitches in the next 7 stitches on the flower.

In the next stitch, you will form a double crochet. make sure the yarn reaches down to the space in the row below, you can see in the photo where this ought to be. This is going to be a very tall stitch, but it forms the shape of the flower.

Once this double crochet stitch is completed, form 7 more single crochet stitches in the next 7 stitches on the flower.

In the next stitch, you will form a double crochet. make sure the yarn reaches down to the space in the row below, you can see in the photo where this ought to be. This is going to be a very tall stitch, but it forms the shape of the flower.

Once this double crochet stitch is completed, form 7 more single crochet stitches in the next 7 stitches on the flower.

In the next stitch, you will form a double crochet. make sure the yarn reaches down to the space in the row below, you can see in the photo where this ought to be. This is going to be a very tall stitch, but it forms the shape of the flower.

Once this double crochet stitch is completed, form 7 more single crochet stitches in the next 7 stitches on the flower.

You should now be back to the beginning of your flower. Remember to join with a slip stitch at the end of the row, sealing the ring of the flower.

The Final Two Rows

Cut the yarn, then join with a new color. Remember to push the hook through the yarn space, then yarn over from the other side. Grab the yarn with your hook, then draw it through the chain space. Form the rest of the single crochet stitch.

You are going to chain 3 with this new color, and count it as the first double crochet stitch on the row.

Double crochet into the next stich on the row, then double crochet into the stitch after that. Double crochet into the next stich on the row, then double crochet into the stitch after that. Continue to work your way up the side of the flower, making only 1 stitch in each of the stitches along the way.

You should now be at the center of the first petal on the flower. This is when you are going to form the angle of the hexagon. To do this, double crochet in this stitch, chain 1, then double crochet into this same stitch once more. Double crochet in the next stitch, double crochet in the next stitch, and double crochet into the next stitch. You are going to continue with this set of double crochet, one in each stitch until you reach the center of the next petal.

Now, chain 1, then double crochet into this same stitch once more. Double crochet in the next stitch, double crochet in the next stitch, and double crochet into the next stitch. You are going to continue with this set of double crochet, one in each stitch until you reach the center of the next petal.

Next, chain 1, then double crochet into this same stitch once more. Double crochet in the next stitch, double crochet in the next stitch, and double crochet into the next stitch. You are going to continue with this set of double crochet, one in each stitch until you reach the center of the next petal.

Again, chain 1, then double crochet into this same stitch once more. Double crochet in the next stitch, double crochet in the next stitch, and double crochet into the next stitch. You are going to continue with this set of double crochet, one in each stitch until you reach the center of the next petal.

Again, chain 1, then double crochet into this same stitch once more. Double crochet in the next stitch, double crochet in the next stitch, and double crochet into the next stitch. You are going to continue with this set of double crochet, one in each stitch until you reach the center of the next petal.

One more time, chain 1, then double crochet into this same stitch once more. Double crochet in the next stitch, double crochet in the next stitch, and double crochet into the next stitch. You are going to continue with this set of double crochet, one in each stitch until you reach the center of the next petal.

Join with a slip stitch, then cut the yarn. You are going to work 1 more row in a new color.

Cut the yarn, then join with a new color. Remember to push the hook through the yarn space, then yarn over from the other side. Grab the yarn with your hook, then draw it through the chain space. Form the rest of the single crochet stitch.

You are going to chain 3 with this new color, and count it as the first double crochet stitch on the row.

Double crochet into the next stich on the row, then double crochet into the stitch after that. Double crochet into the next stich on the row, then double crochet into the stitch after that. Continue to work your way up the side of the flower, making only 1 stitch in each of the stitches along the way.

You should now be at the center of the first petal on the flower. This is when you are going to form the angle of the hexagon. To do this, double crochet in this stitch, chain 1, then double crochet into this same stitch once more. Double crochet in the next stitch, double crochet in the next stitch, and double crochet into the next stitch. You are going to continue with this set of double crochet, one in each stitch until you reach the center of the next petal.

Now, chain 1, then double crochet into this same stitch once more. Double crochet in the next stitch, double crochet in the next stitch, and double crochet into the next stitch. You are going to continue with this set of double crochet, one in each stitch until you reach the center of the next petal.

Next, chain 1, then double crochet into this same stitch once more. Double crochet in the next stitch, double crochet in the next stitch, and double crochet into the next stitch. You are going to continue with this set of double crochet, one in each stitch until you reach the center of the next petal.

Again, chain 1, then double crochet into this same stitch once more. Double crochet in the next stitch, double crochet in the next stitch, and double crochet into the next stitch. You are going to continue with this set of double crochet, one in each stitch until you reach the center of the next petal.

Again, chain 1, then double crochet into this same stitch once more. Double crochet in the next stitch, double crochet in the next stitch, and double crochet into the next stitch. You are going to continue with this set of double crochet, one in each stitch until you reach the center of the next petal.

One more time, chain 1, then double crochet into this same stitch once more. Double crochet in the next stitch, double crochet in the next stitch, and double crochet into the next stitch. You are going to continue with this set of double crochet, one in each stitch until you reach the center of the next petal.

Join with a slip stitch.

Tie off, and that's it! You have completed your first African Hexagon Stitch.

You can clearly see all the different rows and the longer stitches in the photo, as well as how I finished the hexagon. Remember to take your time with this, and count as you go.

This is a very straight forward pattern, and when you follow each of the steps you are going to see the shape come together right before your very eyes. Remember that practice makes perfect, and the more you practice these hexagons, the easier they will be to complete.

Tie off each one as you finish it, then set it aside. When you have enough, you can make virtually any project you can think of!

Chapter 2 – African Flower Hexagon Projects

All About that Flower Baby Blanket

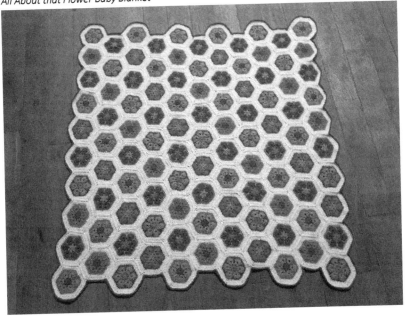

Photo made by: pandatomic

Use scrap yarn or 1 skein of yarn for each of the colors you wish to have in your project. Use a size G crochet hook, and a yarn needle.

For this blanket, you can make as many hexagons as you like. To make it the same size I did, you will need a total of 106. I did row by row of 10, 9, 10.

You are going to start this project by making each of the hexagon stitches as I outlined in the last chapter. Remember to keep your stitches even so each of the flowers turn out close to the same size.

As you can see by the photo, I used white as the primary color, with red and blue as the secondary and third colors. You can follow the same color scheme as I used, or you can choose your own. If you use scrap yarn, you are going to end up with an entirely hodge podge blanket.

Remember to keep the stitches even so all the flowers end up close to the same size, and as you complete each one check it against the others you have made to ensure that it's the right size. Tie off each one as you finish it, then set it aside until you have completed all the flowers.

The first strip has 10 flowers in it, then the next strip has 9 flower in it. The next strip has 10 flowers in it, then the next strip has 9 flower in it. Follow this pattern until you run out of the flowers, then tie off.

Now, you are going to finish the blanket with a border. Join the color of your choice to the side of the blanket with a slip stitch, then work a single crochet row around the entire blanket. You can add another row if you like, or tie it off as it is now.

That's it! Your African baby blanket is done and ready for that special little one in your life.

An African Hexagon Pin Cushion

Photo made by: Charyl

Use scrap yarn or 1 skein of yarn for each of the colors you wish to have in your project. Use a size G crochet hook, and a yarn needle.

You will also need stuffing for the center of the piece.

This is a little project, and you can likely make it in just a single afternoon if you try. Decide which color scheme you want, or use the scrap yarn you have in your basket to put together a pin cushion of scraps. Either way, you are going to end up with an adorable project you can use for all your other crafting needs.

If you would rather not use your scrap yarn, you can purchase each of the colors you need for your own particular scheme.

Once you have chosen the color scheme that works for you, you are ready to form the flowers. Follow the same sequence that I outlined in chapter 1. Take your time, and make both the flowers as close to the same size as you can. Of course, following the same pattern you are going to end up with flowers that are close to the same size anyway, but if you make the stitches the same tension, you will get an even better fit.

Make one, then repeat for the other end of the pin cushion.

Once you have both of your flowers created and set aside, you are going to make the center strip.

Start by measuring around the outside of both your flowers, and chain a length that is equal to this measurement. Single crochet across the row. Chain 1, turn, and single crochet back to the other side. chain 1, turn, and single crochet back to the beginning.

Chain 1, turn, and single crochet to the other side.

You can make this strip as thin or as thick as you like. When you are happy with how thick it is, tie it off.

Take your yarn needle now, and fit the strip to one of the flowers as you sew it together. Sew all the way around the flower, using one part of the flower against the edge of the strip as you work.

Work your way around the entire border, and you will finish with a cup shape.

Next, sew the opposite flower to the top of the piece, only this time, leave one of the ends open, so you can stuff the pin cushion with your stuffing.

Stuff the center of the flower firmly, making sure all ends are tucked in. Stuff as firmly as you like, the firmer the better, in my opinion! When you are happy with the size of the flower, tie it off.

Snip off the loose ends, and your pin cushion is ready for action!

Conclusion

There you have it, everything you need to know to make your own African flower stitch, and what you need to know to put it into as many projects as you like. I hope this book gave you the inspiration you need to make the African Hexagon, and to put it into the projects you have been wanting to make.

With the two projects provided in this book, you are going to realize just how easy it is to bring this stitch into your day to day crochet. Think of it as a spin on the granny square, and a way you can show off your skills in a whole new way.

You don't have to be an expert at crochet, and with practice, you are going to see that it's just as easy as single and double. All you need to do is keep track of where you are on the hexagon and the flower, and where you need to put the chain spaces.

It's going to take some deliberate effort for a while, but witch practice, it's all going to come as second nature, and you'll be able to form the flowers without giving it a second thought.

Have fun and express yourself with all the different colors you can use, and make the flowers as large as you want with a few extra rows on the border. There's no end to the ways you can make your own African Hexagon flowers, and when you let your creativity flow, you can make them even more elaborate.

The African Hexagon stitch may look hard, but you will quickly see that you can make it no matter what your skill level happens to be, and the projects you can make are going to impress anyone and everyone who sees them.

Now get out there and show the world what you can do.

Happy crocheting.

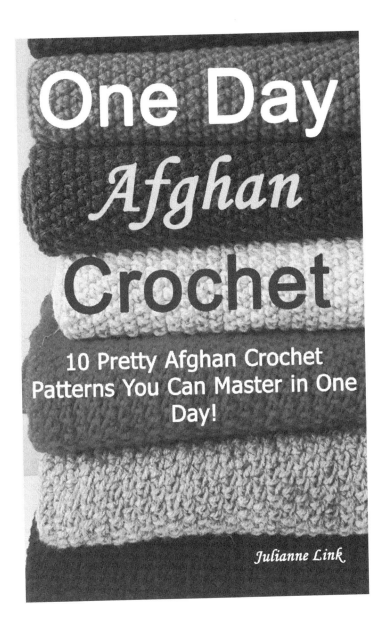

One Day *Afghan* Crochet

10 Pretty Afghan Crochet Patterns You Can Master in One Day!

Julianne Link

One Day Afghan Crochet
10 Pretty Afghan Crochet Patterns You Can Master in One Day!

Introduction

Crochet is a beautiful and unique form of domestic art. In countries in the east, domestic skills and arts like these are very popular and are very values. As difficult as it looks, it is worth learning due to its uniqueness and value as well as beauty. Crochet items have become really popular in the recent past. All these age old fashions that are ever green and golden classics are making thrilling comebacks and crochet is one of those trends. This will never get old. A crochet throw blanket on your couch or accent chair or a crochet article of clothing will always something to value in the winter months.

As beautiful and colorful as crochet is, its items that are pleasing to the eyes are often very heavy and unpleasing on the pocket. Crochet can be expensive. Well with this book that will not be the case anymore. We will show you how to make beautifully ethnic as well as unusual items of clothing and décor in no time. With the simple and easy to follow steps, you will be able to complete these projects in a single day. Being able to make your own items from crochet has myriad benefits. Not only are you able to add your sense of personal touch but they are also ridiculously customizable. You can go for whatever colors and patterns that you like and make things that match perfectly with your personality and with the vibe and décor of your house. How exciting is that? So without further delay, lets grab those crochet hooks and get crocheting.

Chapter 1 – Cozy Afghan Blankets

Anybody who is new to the amazing and colorful world of arts and crafts would most certainly be intimidated by something that sounds as complicated as crochet stich. While it sounds like a daunting task it is definitely not difficult at all to do. With the easy and simple guidelines, we have discussed in this book you will be able to master it in no time at all.

We will take you through afghan crochet stich patterns of all kinds but first let us look at how to make blankets. Blankets are a beautiful accessory to be added anywhere in your house. It can liven up your boring bed spread or awaken the plain couch in your living room when used as a throw. The touch stich of personal sense that you will get by making your own is just an added bonus. So let us learn a few different kinds of afghan crochet stich patterns for blankets.

Project 01: Rainbow Afghan Blanket

This is a beautiful and colorful blanket that you can use as a throw or curl up into while you read your favorite book.

Materials Required

1. Crochet Needle/Hook – These come in different sizes. The best to start with when you are a beginner is the I-9 hook. Here we will be using a K hook.

2. Yarn (color of your chain choice) – Get solid, bright colored yarn when you are a beginner since multi colored chain stiches will be difficult to distinguish when you are at beginner level. Get worsted weight yarn made out of wool fiber or acrylic fiber.

3. A pair of scissors – Make sure it is a nice and sharp one.

Methods

1. First thing to decide is what do you want the width of your blanket to be. Measure it out and plan accordingly. Planning ahead is very important in crochet stiches especially if you are a beginner to avoid any time waste and effort. Here we will use 122 chain stiches to make medium sized blanket.

2. Once the width is decided, make a classic crochet stich chain stich or chain stich of the desired length. In our example we will uses 121.

3. Now for row 1, using the color of your choice, make a single crochet stich in to the second crochet hook from the initial chain stich and then keep working a single crochet stich in every single chain until the end. When you are making 120 stiches this will have created your foundation row.

4. Now for row 2, keep using the same color as you were using before for the chain stich, chain stich 1 and then and then make a turn. Now make 1 single crochet stich into the next stich, and 1 and then make a turn chain into the next stich. Do this in repetition and finish with a single crochet stich in the last chain stich of the row. You have now created your first row of the chain stiches. These are referred to as bubble or popcorn stiches.

5. Now for row 3, keep using the same color as you were using before for the chain stich, chain stich 3 and then make a turn. Into the next chain stich work

one single crochet stich. (Remember that this single crochet stich is worked into the top of what was a turn chain in the previous row.) Into the next chain stich, make and then make a turn chain stich. (Remember, this and then make a turn chain stich is made into the top of what was a single crochet stich in the previous row.) Now single crochet stich in next chain stich, and then make a turn the chain stich in next chain stich* across. This way you will make and then make a turn chain stich into the last single chain stich of the last row and then a double crochet stich into chain stich was the and then make a turning chain stich in the previous row.

6. For row number 4, repeat the exact same procedure as the previous row 3. Each row starts with a chain stich 3 and ends with a double crochet stich. Between these two, you simply be working with a repeat of single crochet stiches and turn chain stiches. Isn't that easy?

7. Here we have used different color for each chain in a row. The color chain changes of yarn will happen in row 5 and after that in row 7 after which every other row will be a different color. And the resulting pattern is shown as an image below.

Project 02: Afghan Throw

This is ideal for use over your bed or even to decorate a colorful couch. The pattern is very ethnic and afghan and not difficult to do at all. Just the simple steps below.

Material Required

1. Crochet Needle/Hook – These come in different sizes. Here we will be using a H-8 hook.

2. Yarn (color of your chain choice) – Get solid, bright colored yarn when you are a beginner since multi colored chain stiches will be difficult to distinguish when you are at beginner level. Get worsted weight yarn made out of wool fiber or acrylic fiber. Here we will be using three colors, green, white and pink. You can go for any of your choice.

3. A pair of scissors – Make sure it is a nice and sharp one.

Method

1. For row 1, make a chain stich of 143 classic crochet stiches, double crochet stich in 4th chain stich from the hook, and in next chain, chain stich 2, * now skipping 2 chain stich, double crochet in every one of the coming 5 chain chains, stich 2, repeat from and across to the last 5 chain stiches, now skipping 2 chain stiches, double crochet in each stich of last 3 chain stiches and then make a turn.

2. For row 2, chain stich 3, Shell stich in next chain stich 2 space, now skipping 2 make double crochet stich, back post double crochet stich around next double crochet stich, Shell in next chain stich 2 space, repeat from last row across to the last 3 double crochet, skipping 2 double crochet, double crochet in last double crochet and then make a turn.

3. For row 3: Chain stich 3, double crochet in next 2 double crochet, chain stich 2, *skipping 2 double crochet, double crochet in next 2 double crochet, Front post double crochet around next back post double crochet, double crochet in next 2 double crochet, chain stich 2, repeat from * across to the last 5 double crochet, skipping 2 double crochet, double crochet in last 3 double crochet and then make a turn.

4. For row 4: Chain stich 3, Shell in next chain stich 2 space, *skipping 2 double crochet, back post double crochet around next Front post double crochet, Shell stitch in next chain stich 2 space, repeat from * across to the last 3 double crochet, skipping 2 double crochet, double crochet in last double crochet, bind off and then make a turn.

5. For row 5: Join pink in first chain stich, chain stich 2 and then keep going with the 3rd row.

6. For row 6, repeat all the process of row 2.

7. For row 7: repeat all the process of row 3.

8. For row 8: Repeat the process of row 2, bind off and then make a turn.

Chapter 2 – Afghan Booties and Flip Flops

Afghan style f crochet is one of the most beautiful ones. You will never see an afghan crochet article that is not beautiful. It makes everything look so much more ethnic. It adds color to your home.

Another great use of afghan crochet is using it to add color not only to your home and living but also to your wardrobe. A very popular application of afghan crochet is to utilize those beautiful stiches to make flip flops and booties for your young ones as well as for yourself. A lot of people use it for making shawls sweaters and throws but here will discuss the innovative way in which you can make beautiful and colorful flip flops and booties.

Project 03: Afghan Flip Flops Women

These can be the sweetest little accessory to glamorize your feet and at the same time staying comfortable. So let us get started.

Material Required

1. Crochet Needle/Hook – These come in different sizes. Here we will be using a 6mm hook.

1. Yarn (color of your chain choice) – Get solid, bright colored yarn and get worsted weight yarn made out of wool fiber or acrylic fiber. You can go for any of your choice.

2. A pair of scissors

Method

1. Chain 9 stiches. Make 3 single crochet in 2nd chain from the crochet hook, single crochet in next 3 chains, half double crochet in next chain, double crochet in next 2 chains, 7 double crochet in last chain. Now start work across the opposite side and follow this: Double crochet in next 2 chains, half double crochet in next chain, single crochet in next 3 chains. This makes 22 stiches. Remember to stich the marker and shift it up with every single round.

2. 2 single crochet in the next 3 stiches. Single crochet in next 7 stiches. 2 single crochet in next 5 stiches. Single crochet in next 7 stiches. This makes 30 stiches.

3. Single crochet in next stich, 2 single crochet in next stitch. Do this thrice. Single crochet in next 7 stiches. *Single crochet in next stich, 2 single crochet in next stitch and do this 5 times then single crochet in next 7 stiches. This makes 38 stiches. Now just bind off.

4. Count the slip stich, count 7 toward your right side. Here attach another second color of your choosing. Chain 1. Single crochet in same stich. Single crochet 2. Chain 7. Skip 8 stiches, single crochet in next stich. Single crochet 2. Chain 14. Attach with a slip stich with the very first stich of the round

5. Chain 1. Single crochet in same stich. Single crochet. Now attach with slip stich. Bind off.

6. For the strap, begin with a long tail end of 8 inches and this will be a separate piece.

7. Chain 3. Single crochet into 2nd chain from hook. Single crochet 1. Then turn.

8. Chain 1. Single crochet into same stich. Single crochet 1. Now turn.

9. Single crochet in same stich. Tilt 90 degrees. Make 5 single crochet across the side. Single crochet 2 in last stich. Single crochet in the other corner. Bind off after leaving a tail to tie.

143

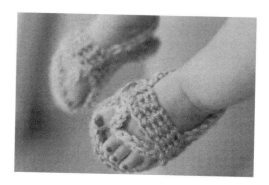

The project can also be altered to make adult flip flops or booties, a great idea is to try making the pattern using a flip flop soul as a base and make the shoes wearable outdoors Make them for adults or babies, it will all be easy now.

Chapter 3 – Beautiful Afghan Jewelry

If you are a crocheting fan and a knitting fan, then the afghan crochet is the way to go. Also referred to as "Tunisian" crochet sometimes, afghan crochet is a merger between knitting and crocheting, and the products of these techniques speak for themselves. Whatever you create with the afghan crochet, would have the distinct "knit look" while having been made with a crocheting needle and technique. With this, most people are familiar with the

Afghan blankets, which is a popular manifestation of this crocheting technique. However, much like any other, the technique can be used to make a lot more than just blankets and throws for your living room. The afghan crochet has its own particular stitches and techniques that can be used to make simple crocheted jewelry. For a beginner, this is easy and can be increased in the difficulty level one by one, as each afghan crochet begins with a simple chain stitch, and picks up from there. As always, the crocheting requires a yarn of thread in the choice of your material, and the crocheting hook. However, the afghan crocheting hook is a bit different from the usual one. They are longer than the regular crochet hooks, and have the proper shape on their tip needed to hold the many loops that constitute an afghan crochet. In this guide, we will discuss some easy DIY afghan crochet ideas for fun and stylish jewelry that you can make in an evening and pair with you lovely outfit for a special day.

Project 04: The Tunisian cuff bracelet

Cuff bracelets are an edgy yet elegant jewelry item, and are fairly easy to make with crochet. The Tunisian cuff bracelet is made using afghan crochet technique and gives the unique knitted look. Let's look at a simple technique to make a two colored cuff bracelet.

Materials required

1. Afghan crochet hook, preferably size F.

2. Two colors of yarn thread

3. Scissors, glue etc.

Method

1. Begin with making a slip knot by passing your yarn on the crochet needle. Use the yarn thread to make a loop, and allow the needle to pass through this loop. Around the hook of the needle, wrap the yarn and pull it through the loop. This will give you a basic slipknot which will serve as a starting point for the chain stitch.

2. Start a simple chain stitch from your slip knot using the first color yarn. This is made simply by wrapping the yarn again on the hook and pulling it through the loop as you did with the slip knot. Do 10 of the chain stitch, more if you want a thicker one, or less stitches if you want a thinner bracelet. This is now the foundation row.

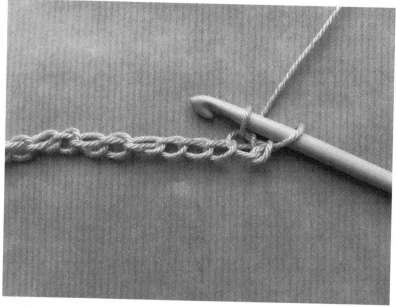

3. With the same color yarn, do the yarn over to make a loop in the second chain stitch and all the following chain stitch loops on the hook.

4. Now use the second color yarn, and use it to yarn over and draw a loop on the first loop that is on your hook. Use the next two loops on the hook to yarn over them a draw another loop. Keep the similar technique for all the next loops until only one is left on your hook. This is your second vertical bar.

5. Continue with the second color yarn, and under the second vertical bar, insert the hook to yarn over and draw a loop. Do the same with inserting hook under the next vertical bar and yarning over to make loops for all the next loops on the hook.

6. Use the first color yarn again to draw a loop by another yarn over the first loop on the hook. Again, use the next two loops on the hook to yarn over them a draw another loop and do it for all the next loops until one loop is left on the hook.

146

7. Continue with the first color yarn, and under the second vertical bar, insert the hook to yarn over and draw a loop. Do the same with inserting hook under the next vertical bar and yarning over to make loops for all the next loops on the hook.

8. Repeat steps 4 to 7 t increase the length of your cuff bracelet, or keep it at this by finishing off with doing a border of single crochet on around the length of both long sides. On the short side, finish the border 2 single crochets on each stitch in the corner and fasten off.

9. End with making button holes on the edge of one short side, while stitching button on the opposite short side. Your bracelet cuff should look similar to this:

Project 05: Afghan crochet Necklace and earrings

A fairly simple pattern that goes for a long loopy necklace and then for its matching pair of earrings to make a complete set.

Materials

1. Nylon thread yarn of the color of your choice

2. Tapestry needles

3. Afghan hook, crochet hook (size of your choice)

4. Fish hook steel earrings of approximately 1 inch.

Method

Project 6: Necklace: The necklace is made roughly around 20-22 inches.

Row 1. Leave about a space of 10-11 inches' empty on your crochet hook and using the afghan hook, chain stitch 75. Insert the crochet hook on the second stitch, pull a loop through by doing a yarn over, and then insert hook in the next chain stitch, and pull a loop through by doing a yarn over. Finish the first row by doing a work loops off hook. Do this by doing a yarn over by pulling a single loop on the hook. Use the next two loops on the hook to yarn over them a draw another loop. Keep the similar technique for all the next loops until only one is left on your hook.

Row 2. Slipknot the first vertical bar, insert the hook from front to back with the yarn in back. Do a yarn over by pulling a single loop on the hook. Use the next two loops on the hook to yarn over them a draw another loop. Keep the similar technique for all the next loops until only one is left on your hook.

Row 3-5. For these three rows, repeat the technique for row 2.

Button: Use the crochet hook to make a 5 long chain stitch and then from the hook, use the second chain stitch to make 10 single crochet stitches. Fasten off here. Finish the button by making weaving its end through the single crochets for the button hole. Roll the rows of the necklace to a close by sewing the edges of the rows on an angle that causes them to spiral the necklace. Make a 1-inch loop for the other end of the necklace and sew it off, making a button hole.

Project 7: Earing: The earing is made roughly an inch or more for both in the pair.

Row 1. Leave about a space of 8 inches' empty on your crochet hook and using the afghan hook, chain stitch 7. Insert the crochet hook on the second stitch, pull a loop through by doing a yarn over, and then insert hook in all the next chain stitches across, and pull a loop through by doing a yarn over. Finish the first row by doing a work loops off hook. Do this by doing a yarn over by pulling a single loop on the hook. Use the next two loops on the hook to yarn over them a draw another loop. Keep the similar technique for all the next loops until only one is left on your hook.

Row 2 & 3. Do a slip knot from the first vertical bar and insert the hook from front to back with the yarn in back. Do a yarn over by pulling a single loop on the hook. Use the next two loops on the hook to yarn over them a draw another loop. Keep the similar technique for all the next loops until only one is left on your hook. Fasten off after leaving a 12-inch end.

Finish off by threading the ends of the earrings through the fishhooks and do two slip stitches to reinforce them in place with the hooks. Sew the edges at an angle similar to the necklace to give the earrings the same spiral, by sewing the first stitch on the bottom with the second stitch on the top. Your necklace and earrings set will look something like this:

Chapter 4 – Beautiful Afghan Scarves

Afghan scarves are incredibly popular among scar lovers because of their knitted look and use for both warm and cold seasons. Although they require a lot more work than a few simple jewelry items, the techniques of afghan crochet are more or less the same and with slight modifications, can be done by a beginner or an intermediate crocheted. Here we discuss a few patterns to make DIY afghan scarves and make your outfit ensemble a little more edgy and personal.

Project 08: Tunisian crochet scarf

The words afghan crochet and Tunisian crochet often interchange and mean the same thing. A simple overlay of this stitch pattern in the form of a scarf is a great way to go. Opt for a neutral toned warm color to make an equally warm feeling scarf.

Materials

1. A large yarn or about 6-7 skeins of a single colored thread.

2. A 6 mm long afghan crochet hook.

3. Scissors.

Method

Row 1

1. Begin with a slip knot and a foundation row of approximately 42 chain stitches.

2. Start the preparation row by inserting hook into the 2nd chain stitch at the back, yarn over to pull a loop over the hook and continue it on for all the loops across.

3. Use the next two loops on the hook to yarn over them a draw another loop. Keep the similar technique for all the next loops until only one is left on your hook.

4. To make the first forward row, insert hook through the first space as shown in figure right between the vertical strands from right to left and yarn over to pull a loop through, which you leave on the hook. Continue this for all the vertical strands till the very end of the entire row. Leave the last loop. Now insert the hook into the chain stitch and pull a loop onto the hook for all 42 stitches in the chain.

5. Chain a single stitch here, and yarn over to pull a loop through the next two chain stitches, continuing till the end, where you leave one loop on the hook.

Row 2

1. Insert the hook in space next to the first in the figure in between the vertical strands from right to left and yarn over to pull a loop through, which you leave on the hook. Continue this for all the vertical strands till the very end of the entire row and this time include the last loop. Now insert the hook into the chain stitch and pull a loop onto the hook for all 42 stitches in the chain.

2. Chain a single stitch here, and yarn over to pull a loop through the next two chain stitches, continuing till the end, where you leave one loop on the hook.

For rows 3 onwards

Repeat these steps for another 4 rows until the material begins to become of around 70 inches in size and then end with a yarn over to pull a loop through the next two chain stitches, continuing till the end, where you leave one loop on the hook.

Finish off by using the space marked 1 in the first forward row as shown in the figure to pull up a loop and yarn it over to pull further two more loops. Repeat the step by putting hook through the next space and repeat for all the spaces between the vertical strands till the end of row. End with one loop still remaining on the hook. Here, cut the remaining yarn to pull through the remaining loop. Ensuring that the side is facing towards you, make a single crochet along the bind off edge at every stitch. Again, cut the remaining yarn to pull through the remaining loop. For the cast on edge, repeat this pattern. For all the ends, weave in properly and block as you desire for your scarf.

Material

1. Afghan long hook.

2. Large yarn needle

3. Full yarn of the color and material of your choice

Method

Row 1. To make the first forward row, insert hook through the first space right between the vertical strands from right to left and yarn over to pull a loop through, which you leave on the hook. Chain stitch 17 and use the second loop on the hook to work into pulling up a loop from each stitch in the chain to make 17 loops on the hook. Use the next two loops on the hook to yarn over them a draw another loop. Keep the similar technique for all the next loops until only one is left on your hook.

Row 2. Leave the first stitch and make the second forward row by this time making the hook insert under the back horizontal bar from right to left and yarn over to pull a loop through, which you leave on the hook. Chain stitch 17 and use the second loop on the hook to work into pulling up a loop from each stitch in the chain to make 17 loops on the hook. Use the next two loops on the hook to yarn over them a draw another loop. Keep the similar technique for all the next loops until only one is left on your hook.

Row 3 to onwards. Continue with the steps for Row 2 onwards till the yarn is left enough to stitch up the ends of the scarf. To give the look of the infinity scarf, twist the scarf and stitch the ends together by any seam stitch such as the mattress for a nice and almost invisible seam. You can also opt for keeping the sides straight for the scarf to lack the twisty look, and then sew its ends together. The scarf should come out too look like this:

Infinity scarf is a lot more popular these days, and while both scarves essentially differ in simply sewing together the ends, more or less, it gives you a great room to choose the one you like. You can use a lighter and less warm material yarn to make an open scarf for slightly warmer seasons, whereas an infinity scarf made from warm wool or alpaca that completely covers your neck is a great option for winters. Be sure to know if you are allergic to any of these materials before using them.

Project 10: Isle Cowl

Crochet Hook: 5.5 mm or I/9

Weight of Yarn: (4) Aran and Worsted Weight and Medium Weight (16 to 20 stitches to four inches)

Crochet Gauge: 14 single crochet = 4(ten cm); 16 rounds is equal to four (ten cm) in sc (single crochet) and Isle Chart

Keep an eye on your gauge.

Final Size: 9.5 inches x 22 inches

Material:

- 1 balls of Wheat A
- 1 ball of Sea B
- 1 ball of Grey C
- 1 ball of Seafoam D

Notes: You will work this cowl in rounds and every round worked with RS (right side) face.

The stitches will work in the back loops, unless you work in both loops.

Pick your yarn from old to turn yarns and avoid holes. You can carry colors that are not in use slackly along WS (wrong side) of your work. On subsequent round, you have to work on carried yarn of proceeding round to hide everything.

While changing colors, you will work in the last step of the final stitch of former color with a new color.

COWL Directions:

With A, chain 80 [100], slip st in first chain to form a ring, being careful not to twist chain.

Round 1 (Right Side): Chain 1 (don't consider it as a stitch here and all over), working in both loops, single crochet in similar stitch as join and every chain around, slip stitch in first single crochet to join, 80(100) single crochet.

Round 2: Chain 1, working in the back loops merely and start with 2nd round of Isle Chart, work 20-stitches replicate of Chart in single crochet around.

Working in the back loops merely, work Isle Chart in single crochet until Round 32 is completed, and work in Rounds 1 to 5 again. Tie off.

FINISHING

Now, weave all ends

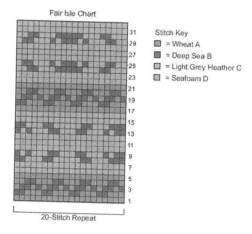

Fair Isle Chart

Stitch Key
- □ = Wheat A
- ■ = Deep Sea B
- □ = Light Grey Heather C
- □ = Seafoam D

20-Stitch Repeat

Conclusion

For anybody, there is no satisfaction greater than the ability to fashion your own articles of clothing and decor. First of all, the customization that it comes with it is absolutely unmatched. You can alter everything from colors to patterns and designs. about it to cater to your own liking. And as far as making your own stuff goes from crochet goes, it is a phenomenal experience. You can take advantage of this beautiful and fun hobby by practicing the easy beginner friendly projects that you learned from this book. Not only is crocheting fun but it is a great way to pass some time without getting bored. The activities like this that are craft and art related have a very calming effect on your mind. Just put music, get that kettle going and get your grandma on! Hey, we all need that at some point.

These projects are one day and they assure the level of ease assures that you learn afghan style crochet in just one day. How great is that? Make stuff for yourself or impress friends and family, you are a pro!

Most tutorials of the items discussed in the chapters above will make for amazing gifts. Make beautiful ethnic throw blankets to match with your living room décor or even to jazz up your plain bedroom. The world is your oyster! Follow the simple, beginner friendly tutorials and you will see is not as difficult as it is made out to be. So without further delay, let us make something colorfully cultural.

Crochet Projects For Home

One Hour Crochet Projects

15 Adorable Ideas For Everyone Who Loves Crocheting But Has No Time!

Alisa Hatchenson

Crochet Projects In One Hour

15 Adorable Ideas For Everyone Who Loves
Crocheting But Has No Time!

Cover photo made by: dsoltesz

snarledskein

hellomomo

Introduction

You spend your day running around like a busy bee, trying to get everything done, and make sure everyone in your family is fed, healthy, and happy. By the end of the night, you are so tired you don't want to start a big project, although you do find crochet to be incredibly relaxing.

But you don't want to start something now that you know is going to take you months to complete. And you don't want to get into something that is going to require as much effort out of you as the daily duties that crop up. You want something that you can do quickly and easily, and something that will give you an actual project when you are done.

If this sounds like you, then you have come to the right place. This book is full of many different crochet patterns, and each one can be completed in an hour or less. There's no need to worry or stress that you are going to have to commit to a big project, because these projects are going to give you the results that you want in a matter of minutes.

Think of it as the best of both worlds, and you are going to get the projects you want every time you sit down to crochet. Last minute gifts? Only have a few minutes to sit down and you want to spend it doing something with your hands?

Want to make something quickly while you relax?

If you answered 'yes' to any of those questions, then you are going to be thrilled with the items you find in this book. There's no end to the ways you can make them your own, and in no time at all, you're going to have settled into a new kind of routine.

Make the patterns as they are, or throw in your own creativity with size, texture, and color, and you are going to have the solution to every five minute project you have ever wanted to make.

You live a busy life, but you deserve a few minutes to yourself. Grab your favorite yarn and your collection of crochet hooks and put your feet up.

Let's get started.

Winter Sunset Crochet Headband

Photo made by: peregrine blue

You will need 1 skein of yarn in multi-color and a size J crochet hook

Chain a length that is 5 inches long.

Single crochet across the row. Chain 1, turn, and single crochet back to the beginning, in the front loop only. Chain 1, turn, and single crochet back to the other side of the row, again in the front loop only. Chain 1, turn, and single crochet across the row in the front loop only. Chain 1, turn, and single crochet back to the beginning in the front loop only.

Chain 1, turn, and single crochet across the row, in the front loop only. Chain 1, turn, and single crochet back to the beginning, in the front loop only. Chain 1, turn, and single crochet back to the other side of the row, again in the front loop only. Chain 1, turn, and single crochet across the row in the front loop only. Chain 1, turn, and single crochet back to the beginning in the front loop only.

Chain 1, turn, and single crochet across the row, in the front loop only. Chain 1, turn, and single crochet back to the beginning, in the front loop only. Chain 1, turn, and single crochet back to the other side of the row, again in the front loop only. Chain 1, turn, and

163

single crochet across the row in the front loop only. Chain 1, turn, and single crochet back to the beginning in the front loop only.

Measure as you go, and keep an eye on your tension. When the piece can reach comfortably around your head, tie off.

Take your yarn needle now, and sew up the open end of the headband. Use a whip stitch and make sure all is secure, then tie off.

That's it! your headband is done!

The Mandala Vase Holder

Photo made by: <u>peregrineblue</u>

You will need 1 skein of yarn in multi-color and a size J crochet hook

Chain 4 and join with a slip stitch to form a ring. Single crochet in the center of this ring 10 times, and join with a slip stitch.

Chain 1, turn, and single crochet around the row, joining with a slip stitch. Chain 1, turn, and single crochet back around to the other side, and join with a slip stitch. Chain 1, turn, and single crochet back to the beginning, joining with a slip stitch. Chain 1, turn, and single crochet back to the other side, joining with a slip stitch.

Chain 1, turn, and single crochet around the row, joining with a slip stitch. Chain 1, turn, and single crochet back around to the other side, and join with a slip stitch. Chain 1, turn, and single crochet back to the beginning, joining with a slip stitch. Chain 1, turn, and single crochet back to the other side, joining with a slip stitch.

Continue until you are happy with the size of your vase base, then tie off, and you are done!

Mandala Wall Art

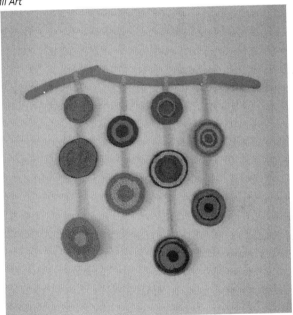

Photo made by: peregrineblue

You will need scrap yarn or 1 skein of yarn in multi-color and a size G crochet hook

You are going to make a total of 10 mandalas, choosing the colors you prefer. Make each one the size you wish for it to be, and tie off and set aside each one as it is completed.

Chain 4 and join with a slip stitch to form a ring. Single crochet in the center of this ring 10 times, and join with a slip stitch.

Chain 1, turn, and single crochet around the row, joining with a slip stitch. Chain 1, turn, and single crochet back around to the other side, and join with a slip stitch. Chain 1, turn, and single crochet back to the beginning, joining with a slip stitch. Chain 1, turn, and single crochet back to the other side, joining with a slip stitch.

Chain 1, turn, and single crochet around the row, joining with a slip stitch. Chain 1, turn, and single crochet back around to the other side, and join with a slip stitch. Chain 1, turn, and single crochet back to the beginning, joining with a slip stitch. Chain 1, turn, and single crochet back to the other side, joining with a slip stitch.

Tie off each one and set aside when you are happy with the size.

Once you have created all the mandalas, you are going to chain 3 or 4 different lengths of chain, and single crochet across the row for a total of 3 rows each. Secure them to your wall mount, and sew each of the mandalas onto the chains.

The Springtime Skinny Scarf

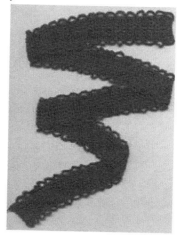

Photo made by: elainegreycats

You will need 1 skein of yarn in the color of your choice and a size J crochet hook

Chain a length that is 4 inches long.

Single crochet across the row. Chain 1, turn, and single crochet back to the beginning. Chain 1, turn, and single crochet across the row. Chain 1, turn, and single crochet back to the beginning. Chain 1, turn, and single crochet across the row. Chain 1, turn, and single crochet back to the beginning.

Single crochet across the row. Chain 1, turn, and single crochet back to the beginning. Chain 1, turn, and single crochet across the row. Chain 1, turn, and single crochet back to the beginning. Chain 1, turn, and single crochet across the row. Chain 1, turn, and single crochet back to the beginning.

Single crochet across the row. Chain 1, turn, and single crochet back to the beginning. Chain 1, turn, and single crochet across the row. Chain 1, turn, and single crochet back to the beginning. Chain 1, turn, and single crochet across the row. Chain 1, turn, and single crochet back to the beginning.

Continue for as long as you want your scarf to be. When you are happy with the length, chain 5, and skip the next 2 stitches, and join with a slip stitch in the next stitch. Chain 5, skip the next 2 stitches, and join with a slip stitch into the next stitch. Chain 5, and skip the next 2 stitches, and join with a slip stitch into the next stitch.

Repeat this around the entire border, and you are done!

Fast and Easy Crochet Cuff

You will need 1 skein of yarn in the color of your choice and a size G crochet hook

Measure around your wrist, and chain a length that is equal to this measurement. This can either be loose enough to slip over your hand, or snug fitting with a clasp.

Single crochet across the row. Chain 5, turn, and skip the first 2 stitches, then work a slip stitch into the next stitch. Chain 5, skip the next 2 stitches, and work a slip stitch into the next stitch. Continue across the row.

Chain 5, and join with a slip stitch in the center of the chain space. Chain 5, and join with a slip stitch in the center of the chain space. Chain 5, and join with a slip stitch in the center of the chain space. Continue across the row.

Chain 1, turn. Single crochet across the row. Chain 1, turn. Single crochet across the row.

Tie off, and assemble according to your preference.

That's it! Your cuff is ready to rock and roll!

Waste Basket Camo Cover

You will need 1 skein of yarn in the color of your choice and a size J crochet hook

Chain 4 and join with a slip stitch to form a ring. Single crochet in the center of this ring 10 times, and join with a slip stitch.

Chain 1, turn, and single crochet around the row, joining with a slip stitch. Chain 1, turn, and single crochet back around to the other side, and join with a slip stitch. Chain 1, turn, and single crochet back to the beginning, joining with a slip stitch. Chain 1, turn, and single crochet back to the other side, joining with a slip stitch.

Chain 1, turn, and single crochet around the row, joining with a slip stitch. Chain 1, turn, and single crochet back around to the other side, and join with a slip stitch. Chain 1, turn, and single crochet back to the beginning, joining with a slip stitch. Chain 1, turn, and single crochet back to the other side, joining with a slip stitch.

When you are happy with the size of the base, you are going to begin with the decrease row.

Chain 1, and single crochet in the first 4 stitches, then skip the next stitch. Single crochet in the next 4 stitches, and skip the next stitch. Single crochet in the next 4 stitches, and skip the next stitch. Repeat this around.

Work 1 more decrease row.

Now, continue to work your way up the side of the cover, until you are happy with the overall size of the piece.

Chain 1, turn, and single crochet around the row, joining with a slip stitch. Chain 1, turn, and single crochet back around to the other side, and join with a slip stitch. Chain 1, turn, and single crochet back to the beginning, joining with a slip stitch. Chain 1, turn, and single crochet back to the other side, joining with a slip stitch.

Chain 1, turn, and single crochet around the row, joining with a slip stitch. Chain 1, turn, and single crochet back around to the other side, and join with a slip stitch. Chain 1, turn, and single crochet back to the beginning, joining with a slip stitch. Chain 1, turn, and single crochet back to the other side, joining with a slip stitch.

Once the cover is the right height, tie off.

Chain a length that will reach around the entire cover, then use your yarn needle to carefully feed this through the top of the basket. Tie off, and you are done!

A Fairy Trinket Bag

Photo made by: dsoltesz

You will need 1 skein of yarn in the color of your choice and a size G crochet hook

Chain 4 and join with a slip stitch to form a ring. Single crochet in the center of this ring 10 times, and join with a slip stitch.

Chain 1, turn, and single crochet around the row, joining with a slip stitch. Chain 1, turn, and single crochet back around to the other side, and join with a slip stitch. Chain 1, turn, and single crochet back to the beginning, joining with a slip stitch. Chain 1, turn, and single crochet back to the other side, joining with a slip stitch.

Chain 1, turn, and single crochet around the row, joining with a slip stitch. Chain 1, turn, and single crochet back around to the other side, and join with a slip stitch. Chain 1, turn,

170

and single crochet back to the beginning, joining with a slip stitch. Chain 1, turn, and single crochet back to the other side, joining with a slip stitch.

When you are happy with the size of the base of your pouch, you are going to begin with the decrease row.

Chain 1, and single crochet in the first 4 stitches, then skip the next stitch. Single crochet in the next 4 stitches, and skip the next stitch. Single crochet in the next 4 stitches, and skip the next stitch. Repeat this around.

Work 1 more decrease row.

Now, continue to work your way up the side of the pouch, until you are happy with the overall size of the piece.

Chain 1, turn, and single crochet around the row, joining with a slip stitch. Chain 1, turn, and single crochet back around to the other side, and join with a slip stitch. Chain 1, turn, and single crochet back to the beginning, joining with a slip stitch. Chain 1, turn, and single crochet back to the other side, joining with a slip stitch.

When you have the right size, tie off.

Take a length of yarn and feed it through the top portion of the pouch. Pull this tight to form the drawstring on the piece. You can add beads and lengths of yarn to the bottom of a more decorative effect. Tie off, and you are done!

Photo made by: <u>dainee</u>

You will need 1 skein of yarn in the color of your choice and a size J crochet hook

Chain 4 and join with a slip stitch to form a ring. Single crochet in the center of this ring 10 times, and join with a slip stitch.

Chain 1, turn, and single crochet around the row, joining with a slip stitch. Chain 1, turn, and single crochet back around to the other side, and join with a slip stitch. Chain 1, turn, and single crochet back to the beginning, joining with a slip stitch. Chain 1, turn, and single crochet back to the other side, joining with a slip stitch.

Chain 1, turn, and single crochet around the row, joining with a slip stitch. Chain 1, turn, and single crochet back around to the other side, and join with a slip stitch. Chain 1, turn, and single crochet back to the beginning, joining with a slip stitch. Chain 1, turn, and single crochet back to the other side, joining with a slip stitch.

When you are happy with the size of the base of the bowl, you are going to begin with the decrease row.

Chain 1, and single crochet in the first 4 stitches, then skip the next stitch. Single crochet in the next 4 stitches, and skip the next stitch. Single crochet in the next 4 stitches, and skip the next stitch. Repeat this around.

One decrease row is fine, as you want this to fan out rather than move straight up the side of the bowl.

Now, continue to work your way up the side of the bowl, until you are happy with the overall size of the piece.

Chain 1, turn, and single crochet around the row, joining with a slip stitch. Chain 1, turn, and single crochet back around to the other side, and join with a slip stitch. Chain 1, turn, and single crochet back to the beginning, joining with a slip stitch. Chain 1, turn, and single crochet back to the other side, joining with a slip stitch.

Change colors according to your preference, and when you are done, tie it off!

The Mandala Pendant

Photo made by: snarledskein

You will need 1 skein of yarn in the color of your choice and a size G crochet hook

173

Chain 4 and join with a slip stitch to form a ring. Single crochet in the center of this ring 10 times, and join with a slip stitch.

Chain 1, turn, and single crochet around the row, joining with a slip stitch. Chain 1, turn, and single crochet back around to the other side, and join with a slip stitch. Chain 1, turn, and single crochet back to the beginning, joining with a slip stitch. Chain 1, turn, and single crochet back to the other side, joining with a slip stitch.

Chain 1, turn, and single crochet around the row, joining with a slip stitch. Chain 1, turn, and single crochet back around to the other side, and join with a slip stitch. Chain 1, turn, and single crochet back to the beginning, joining with a slip stitch. Chain 1, turn, and single crochet back to the other side, joining with a slip stitch.

When you are happy with the size of the pendant, tie off.

Take your crochet hook and chain a length for the chain, and work 1 single crochet row across this piece. Tie off, and feed through the mandala pendant.

Secure the ends of the chain in place, and you are done!

Fruity Coasters

Photo made by: <u>hellomomo</u>

You will need 1 skein of yarn in the color of your choice and a size G crochet hook

Use the colors of your choice, or follow the colors listed above.

Chain 4 and join with a slip stitch to form a ring. Single crochet in the center of this ring 10 times, and join with a slip stitch.

Chain 1, turn, and single crochet around the row, joining with a slip stitch. Chain 1, turn, and single crochet back around to the other side, and join with a slip stitch. Chain 1, turn, and single crochet back to the beginning, joining with a slip stitch. Chain 1, turn, and single crochet back to the other side, joining with a slip stitch.

Chain 1, turn, and single crochet around the row, joining with a slip stitch. Chain 1, turn, and single crochet back around to the other side, and join with a slip stitch. Chain 1, turn, and single crochet back to the beginning, joining with a slip stitch. Chain 1, turn, and single crochet back to the other side, joining with a slip stitch.

When you are happy with the size of the coaster, tie off and set aside. Repeat for the other coasters, making each one the same size as the first coaster.

When you have finished, use green and chain a length of 10 stitches per piece. Sew this in place as you see in the photo, and your coasters are done!

The Coin Catcher

Photo made by: moonrat

You will need 1 skein of yarn in the color of your choice and a size G crochet hook

Chain 4 and join with a slip stitch to form a ring. Single crochet in the center of this ring 10 times, and join with a slip stitch.

Chain 1, turn, and single crochet around the row, joining with a slip stitch. Chain 1, turn, and single crochet back around to the other side, and join with a slip stitch. Chain 1, turn, and single crochet back to the beginning, joining with a slip stitch. Chain 1, turn, and single crochet back to the other side, joining with a slip stitch.

When you are happy with the size of the bottom of the bowl, you are going to begin with the decrease row.

Chain 1, and single crochet in the first 4 stitches, then skip the next stitch. Single crochet in the next 4 stitches, and skip the next stitch. Single crochet in the next 4 stitches, and skip the next stitch. Repeat this around.

Again, 1 decrease row is fine for a bowl, as you don't want it to go straight up, but rather fan out as you work.

Now, continue to work your way up the side of the bowl, until you are happy with the overall size of the piece.

Chain 1, turn, and single crochet around the row, joining with a slip stitch. Chain 1, turn, and single crochet back around to the other side, and join with a slip stitch. Chain 1, turn, and single crochet back to the beginning, joining with a slip stitch. Chain 1, turn, and single crochet back to the other side, joining with a slip stitch.

Tie off, and you are done!

Grass Is Always Greener Scarf

Photo made by: eldriva

You will need 1 skein of yarn in the green and a size J crochet hook

Chain a length that is 5 feet long.

Single crochet across the row. Chain 1, turn, and single crochet back to the beginning, in the front loop only. Chain 1, turn, and single crochet back to the other side of the row,

177

again in the front loop only. Chain 1, turn, and single crochet across the row in the front loop only. Chain 1, turn, and single crochet back to the beginning in the front loop only.

Chain 1, turn, and single crochet across the row, in the front loop only. Chain 1, turn, and single crochet back to the beginning, in the front loop only. Chain 1, turn, and single crochet back to the other side of the row, again in the front loop only. Chain 1, turn, and single crochet across the row in the front loop only. Chain 1, turn, and single crochet back to the beginning in the front loop only.

Chain 1, turn, and single crochet across the row, in the front loop only. Chain 1, turn, and single crochet back to the beginning, in the front loop only. Chain 1, turn, and single crochet back to the other side of the row, again in the front loop only. Chain 1, turn, and single crochet across the row in the front loop only. Chain 1, turn, and single crochet back to the beginning in the front loop only.

Tie off.

Cut a fistful of yarn that is the same length (about 5 inches long.) Using your yarn needle or crochet hook, feed these lengths through the ends of the scarf, creating the fringe as you see in the photo. Continue until the fringe is as thick as you like, then take your scissors and cut it all down to the same length.

That's it! Your scarf is done!

Fast and Easy Dish Scrubby

Photo made by: <u>dainec</u>

You will need 1 skein of cotton yarn in the color of your choice and a size G crochet hook

Chain 4 and join with a slip stitch to form a ring. Single crochet in the center of this ring 10 times, and join with a slip stitch.

Chain 1, turn, and single crochet around the row, joining with a slip stitch. Chain 1, turn, and single crochet back around to the other side, and join with a slip stitch. Chain 1, turn, and single crochet back to the beginning, joining with a slip stitch. Chain 1, turn, and single crochet back to the other side, joining with a slip stitch.

Chain 1, turn, and single crochet around the row, joining with a slip stitch. Chain 1, turn, and single crochet back around to the other side, and join with a slip stitch. Chain 1, turn, and single crochet back to the beginning, joining with a slip stitch. Chain 1, turn, and single crochet back to the other side, joining with a slip stitch.

Continue until you are happy with the size of the scrubby – when it fits comfortably in your hand you are ready to tie off.

Tie off, and you are done!

Mother's Favorite Washcloth

Photo made by: <u>smittenkittenoriginals</u>

You will need 1 skein of cotton yarn in the color of your choice and a size J crochet hook

Chain a length that is 6 inches long.

Single crochet across the row. Chain 1, turn, and single crochet back to the beginning. Chain 1, turn, and single crochet across the row. Chain 1, turn, and single crochet back to the beginning. Chain 1, turn, and single crochet across the row. Chain 1, turn, and single crochet back to the beginning.

Single crochet across the row. Chain 1, turn, and single crochet back to the beginning. Chain 1, turn, and single crochet across the row. Chain 1, turn, and single crochet back to the beginning. Chain 1, turn, and single crochet across the row. Chain 1, turn, and single crochet back to the beginning.

Single crochet across the row. Chain 1, turn, and single crochet back to the beginning. Chain 1, turn, and single crochet across the row. Chain 1, turn, and single crochet back to the beginning. Chain 1, turn, and single crochet across the row. Chain 1, turn, and single crochet back to the beginning.

When you have a square, tie off. You can create a single crochet border around the piece, or you can leave it as it is. Either way, your new washcloth is ready for anything!

Chunky Crochet Beanie

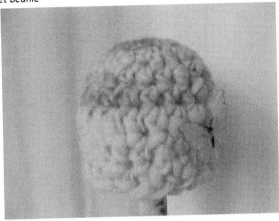

Photo made by: ilashdesigns

You will need 1 skein of chunky yarn in the color of your choice and a size J crochet hook

Chain 4 and join with a slip stitch to form a ring. Single crochet in the center of this ring 10 times, and join with a slip stitch.

Chain 1, turn, and single crochet around the row, joining with a slip stitch. Chain 1, turn, and single crochet back around to the other side, and join with a slip stitch. Chain 1, turn, and single crochet back to the beginning, joining with a slip stitch. Chain 1, turn, and single crochet back to the other side, joining with a slip stitch.

Chain 1, turn, and single crochet around the row, joining with a slip stitch. Chain 1, turn, and single crochet back around to the other side, and join with a slip stitch. Chain 1, turn, and single crochet back to the beginning, joining with a slip stitch. Chain 1, turn, and single crochet back to the other side, joining with a slip stitch.

When the hat can cover the top of your head, you are ready to decrease.

Chain 1, and single crochet in the first 4 stitches, then skip the next stitch. Single crochet in the next 4 stitches, and skip the next stitch. Single crochet in the next 4 stitches, and skip the next stitch. Repeat this around.

Work 1 more decrease row.

Now, continue to work your way around the hat, until you are happy with how it fits.

Chain 1, turn, and single crochet around the row, joining with a slip stitch. Chain 1, turn, and single crochet back around to the other side, and join with a slip stitch. Chain 1, turn, and single crochet back to the beginning, joining with a slip stitch. Chain 1, turn, and single crochet back to the other side, joining with a slip stitch.

Try it on as you go, and crochet it to fit your head. When you are happy with the size, tie off and you are done!

Conclusion

There you have it, a variety of adorable crochet projects you can make in just one hour. I know you love to crochet, but crochet can also take an incredibly long time to do, especially if you don't have a lot of time. I hope this book was able to give you the inspiration you need to create a variety of your own crochet projects, and that you create each and every one to be just what you want it to be.

You know you love to sit back and relax, and this book is going to give you the projects you need to make something in just a short amount of time. Let creativity flow, and have fun while you relax.

Happy crocheting!

Crochet Keychains

15 Must Have Crochet Keychains To Rock This Fashion Season

Crochet Keychains

15 Must Have Crochet Keychains To Rock This Fashion Season

Introduction

The world of fashion is a tricky one. You want to do what you want to do, but you don't want to be a copycat or follow what everyone else is doing. You want to show off your own style, and you want to flaunt the things you like the way you like them.

When it comes to fashion, the best way to show off what you like is through accessories. Whether it be a hat or a scarf or a little keychain, you know the best way to show off your style is through the simple things.

But these accessories are easy to find, and before you know it, everyone else has them, too. You become just another one of the crowd with whatever it was you picked, and you begin to feel as though you are blending in more than anything. There is no difference between what you are doing and what anyone else has, and you are simply following.

You aren't a follower. You are a leader, and you want to make a different statement. You want to show the world that you know how to flaunt your fashion style without any problems. You want to be able to get the accessories you want and you want to make a statement.

But how are you going to do this when you only have a limited selection?

You have come to the right place. Here, you are going to discover a variety of keychains that you can crochet in just a matter of minutes, giving you instant access to any accessory you want without having to do what everyone else is doing.

The keychains in this book are easy to make, so you can make them for any occasion, for anybody. Last minute gifts are no longer an issue with these keychains, and if you want to suddenly spice up your accessory list you have the instant access to do that.

Allow this book to change the way you view your accessories, and dive into a world that is fun, creative, and shows off your artistic side. There's no need to stress, no need to blend, and no need to do a thing that anyone else is doing. With these accessories, fashion is always in season.

All you need is your favorite yarn and a crochet hook, and you are going to get everything you have ever wanted from your accessories.

If you are ready, settle in.

It's time to begin.

Chapter 1 – The Keychains

Simple Strawberry

Photo made by: indiebandswithamission

You will need scrap yarn or 1 skein of yarn per color you wish to use, and a size E crochet hook.

Wrap the yarn around your index finger twice. **Insert the hook inside these loops, then grab the yarn and pull it through. Bring the yarn up and over, then pull this through the loop on the hook.

Insert the hook through the loop, then pull the yarn up. Bring the yarn up and over once again and pull it through the 2 loops on the hook. This is the first single crochet on the ring. Repeat from ** a total of 10 times, then pull the yarn through the opposite end to close the ring.

Work in the round and single crochet in each of the stitches. Continue to work in the round until you have completed 10 rows, then begin your invisible decrease.

To do an invisible decrease, you are going to insert the hook in the front post of both the next 2 stitches, then single crochet in the next stitch. Front post the next 2 stitches, then single crochet in the next stitch. Repeat around.

Continue with a steady decrease until you have a place that is just small enough to get stuffing inside. Tie off.

To assemble:

Cut a round piece of felt for the top of the strawberry, and either sew or glue this into place.

Stuff the piece, then sew the end closed around it. Add any details you wish to add with your yarn needle, and snip off the loose threads.

Feed the keychain loop through the top of the piece, then reinforce it with yarn. Snip off all the loose threads, and make sure all is secure. That's it!

Sam the Squid

Photo made by: jamieanne

You will need scrap yarn or 1 skein of yarn per color you wish to use, and a size E crochet hook.

Wrap the yarn around your index finger twice. **Insert the hook inside these loops, then grab the yarn and pull it through. Bring the yarn up and over, then pull this through the loop on the hook.

Insert the hook through the loop, then pull the yarn up. Bring the yarn up and over once again and pull it through the 2 loops on the hook. This is the first single crochet on the ring. Repeat from ** a total of 10 times, then pull the yarn through the opposite end to close the ring.

Work in the round and single crochet in each of the stitches. Continue to work in the round until you have completed 16 rows, then begin your invisible decrease.

189

To do an invisible decrease, you are going to insert the hook in the front post of both the next 2 stitches, then single crochet in the next stitch. Front post the next 2 stitches, then single crochet in the next stitch. Repeat around.

Continue with a steady decrease until you have a place that is just small enough to get stuffing inside. Tie off and set aside.

To assemble:

Cut lengths of yarn for the tentacles and secure them in place. You can also chain lengths of yarn for the thicker tentacles. Make sure they are securely in place on the bottom of the piece.

Stuff the piece, then sew the end closed around it. Add any details you wish to add with your yarn needle, and snip off the loose threads.

Feed the keychain loop through the top of the piece, then reinforce it with yarn. Snip off all the loose threads, and make sure all is secure. That's it!

Easy Elegant Cross

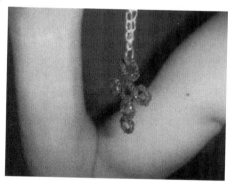

Photo made by: moiracrochetsplarn

Use a stiff yarn or even plastic yarn for this piece. Use a size E crochet hook.

Chain 5 and join with a slip stitch to form a stiff ring. Single crochet in the center of this ring 10 times, and join with a slip stitch. Tie off and repeat 5 more times.

Use your yarn needle to assemble the shape into the shape of a cross, as you see here. Insert the keychain through the top of the cross, and make sure all is secure.

That's it!

Tony the Teddy Bear

Photo made by: toadstool_ring

You will need scrap yarn or 1 skein of yarn per color you wish to use, and a size E crochet hook.

Wrap the yarn around your index finger twice. **Insert the hook inside these loops, then grab the yarn and pull it through. Bring the yarn up and over, then pull this through the loop on the hook.

Insert the hook through the loop, then pull the yarn up. Bring the yarn up and over once again and pull it through the 2 loops on the hook. This is the first single crochet on the ring. Repeat from ** a total of 10 times, then pull the yarn through the opposite end to close the ring.

Work in the round and single crochet in each of the stitches. Continue to work in the round until you have completed 10 rows, then begin your invisible decrease.

To do an invisible decrease, you are going to insert the hook in the front post of both the next 2 stitches, then single crochet in the next stitch. Front post the next 2 stitches, then single crochet in the next stitch. Repeat around.

Continue with a steady decrease until you have a place that is just small enough to get stuffing inside. Tie off and set aside.

Repeat for the body, only work up to 20 rows before decreasing.

To assemble:

Create the arms and legs of the bear by making a magic ring, then crocheting long, narrow tubes. Repeat a total of 4 times for the arms and legs, then sew these in place on the body.

Sew the head to the base of the body as well.

Stuff the piece, then sew the end closed around it. Add any details you wish to add with your yarn needle, and snip off the loose threads.

Feed the keychain loop through the top of the piece, then reinforce it with yarn. Snip off all the loose threads, and make sure all is secure. That's it!

Tiny Foot Sock

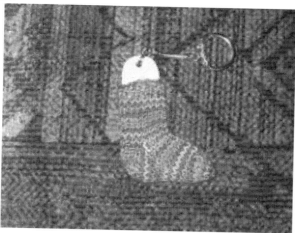

You will need scrap yarn or 1 skein of yarn per color you wish to use, and a size E crochet hook.

Chain 5 and single crochet across the row. Chain 1, turn, and single crochet back to the beginning. Chain 1, turn, and single crochet back to the other side. Chain 1, turn, and single crochet back to the beginning.

Continue with this for a strip that measures 1 inch long.

For the next row, chain 1, turn, and single crochet across the row, but continue on past the end of the row for 3 more stitches. Chain 1, turn, and single crochet back. Follow your new row for a total of ½ inch. Tie off.

Repeat for the other side of the sock, then use your yarn needle to sew both pieces together.

To assemble:

Using a thick piece of cardboard or a thin piece of wood, place a small hole near the top, then run glue down the sides. Slip the sock over this piece to glue it in place.

Feed the keychain loop through the top of the piece, then reinforce it with yarn. Snip off all the loose threads, and make sure all is secure. That's it!

Luck of the Irish Charm

193

You will need scrap yarn or 1 skein of yarn per color you wish to use, and a size E crochet hook.

Chain 4 and single crochet across the row. Chain 1, turn, and single crochet in the first stitch 2 times, single crochet across the row, then single crochet in the last stitch 2 times. Chain 1, turn, and single crochet in the first stitch 2 times, single crochet across the row, then single crochet in the last stitch 2 times. Chain 1, turn, and single crochet in the first stitch 2 times, single crochet across the row, then single crochet in the last stitch 2 times. Tie off.

Repeat 3 more times for the other portion of the leaves.

Place each section of the leaf together in the clover pattern, then sew them in place with your yarn needle. Snip off the loose threads.

To assemble:

Feed the keychain loop through the top of the piece, then reinforce it with yarn. Snip off all the loose threads, and make sure all is secure. That's it!

The Serious Strawberry

You will need scrap yarn or 1 skein of yarn per color you wish to use, and a size E crochet hook.

Wrap the yarn around your index finger twice. **Insert the hook inside these loops, then grab the yarn and pull it through. Bring the yarn up and over, then pull this through the loop on the hook.

Insert the hook through the loop, then pull the yarn up. Bring the yarn up and over once again and pull it through the 2 loops on the hook. This is the first single crochet on the ring. Repeat from ** a total of 10 times, then pull the yarn through the opposite end to close the ring.

Work in the round and single crochet in each of the stitches. Continue to work in the round until you have completed 10 rows, then begin your invisible decrease.

To do an invisible decrease, you are going to insert the hook in the front post of both the next 2 stitches, then single crochet in the next stitch. Front post the next 2 stitches, then single crochet in the next stitch. Repeat around.

Continue with a steady decrease until you have a place that is just small enough to get stuffing inside. Set aside.

Work in the round once more to crochet the top of the piece. Use green and create a disk that will reach over the top of the strawberry.

Sew this in place after stuffing.

To assemble:

Stuff the piece, then sew the end closed around it. Add any details you wish to add with your yarn needle, and snip off the loose threads.

Feed the keychain loop through the top of the piece, then reinforce it with yarn. Snip off all the loose threads, and make sure all is secure. That's it!

Tiny Heart Trinket

Photo made by: eraphernalia_vintage

You will need scrap yarn or 1 skein of yarn per color you wish to use, and a size E crochet hook.

Chain 8 and join with a slip stitch to form a ring. Single crochet in the center of this ring 10 times, and join with a sip stitch. Chain 1, turn, and single crochet around to the other side. chain 1, turn, and single crochet back to the beginning. Chain 1, turn, and single crochet back to the other side.

Take your yarn needle now and insert it through the front of the heart. Wrap the yarn up and around the top of the heart, then insert it once more through the center. Pull firmly to bring in the side of the heart, forming the heart shape.

Tie off securely, and you are ready to assemble.

To assemble:

Feed the keychain loop through the top of the piece, then reinforce it with yarn. Snip off all the loose threads, and make sure all is secure. That's it!

Speedy the Snail

Photo made by: <u>dumbledad</u>

You will need scrap yarn or 1 skein of yarn per color you wish to use, and a size E crochet hook.

Wrap the yarn around your index finger twice. **Insert the hook inside these loops, then grab the yarn and pull it through. Bring the yarn up and over, then pull this through the loop on the hook.

Insert the hook through the loop, then pull the yarn up. Bring the yarn up and over once again and pull it through the 2 loops on the hook. This is the first single crochet on the ring. Repeat from ** a total of 10 times, then pull the yarn through the opposite end to close the ring.

Work in the round and single crochet in each of the stitches. Continue to work in the round until you have completed 8 rows, then begin your invisible decrease.

To do an invisible decrease, you are going to insert the hook in the front post of both the next 2 stitches, then single crochet in the next stitch. Front post the next 2 stitches, then single crochet in the next stitch. Repeat around.

Continue with a steady decrease until you have a place that is just small enough to get stuffing inside. Tie off and set aside. This is the shell.

Repeat for the body, only work up to 5 rows, then continue without increasing for a total of 22 rows. Decrease quickly for the end of the tail.

To assemble:

Sew the shell to the body after you have finished stuffing both pieces.

Stuff the piece, then sew the end closed around it. Add any details you wish to add with your yarn needle, and snip off the loose threads.

Feed the keychain loop through the top of the piece, then reinforce it with yarn. Snip off all the loose threads, and make sure all is secure. That's it!

Flower Power

Photo made by: <u>sammy4586</u>

You will need scrap yarn or 1 skein of yarn per color you wish to use, and a size E crochet hook.

Chain 8 and join with a slip stitch to form a ring. Single crochet in the center of this ring 10 times, and join with a sip stitch. Chain 1, turn, and single crochet around to the other side. chain 1, turn, and single crochet back to the beginning. Chain 1, turn, and single crochet back to the other side.

198

For the next row, you are going to chain 8 and skip the first 3, then you are going to join with a slip stitch in the next stitch. Chain 8 and skip the next 3, then join with a slip stitch in the next stitch. Repeat this around.

Join with a slip stitch when you get back to the beginning, then chain 1 and turn.

Single crochet around the row.

For the next row, you are going to chain 1, and single crochet in the first stitch, then double crochet in the next 2 stitches. Single crochet in the next stitch, then double crochet in the next 2 stitches. Repeat this around.

Join with a slip stitch when you get back to the beginning, tie off, and assemble.

To assemble:

Feed the keychain loop through the top of the piece, then reinforce it with yarn. Snip off all the loose threads, and make sure all is secure. That's it!

Baloo the Blue Whale

Photo made by: <u>toadstool_ring</u>

You will need scrap yarn or 1 skein of yarn per color you wish to use, and a size E crochet hook.

Wrap the yarn around your index finger twice. **Insert the hook inside these loops, then grab the yarn and pull it through. Bring the yarn up and over, then pull this through the loop on the hook.

Insert the hook through the loop, then pull the yarn up. Bring the yarn up and over once again and pull it through the 2 loops on the hook. This is the first single crochet on the ring. Repeat from ** a total of 10 times, then pull the yarn through the opposite end to close the ring.

Work in the round and single crochet in each of the stitches. Continue to work in the round until you have completed 10 rows, then begin your invisible decrease.

To do an invisible decrease, you are going to insert the hook in the front post of both the next 2 stitches, then single crochet in the next stitch. Front post the next 2 stitches, then single crochet in the next stitch. Repeat around.

Continue with a steady decrease until you have a place that is just small enough to get stuffing inside. Set aside.

After you have finished stuffing the piece, you are going to join the hook once more with a slip stitch and finish the tail. The tail is worked as 2 disks, and is created to lie flat.

To assemble:

Stuff the piece, then sew the end closed around it. Add any details you wish to add with your yarn needle, and snip off the loose threads.

Feed the keychain loop through the top of the piece, then reinforce it with yarn. Snip off all the loose threads, and make sure all is secure. That's it!

Photo made by: amigurumiku

You will need scrap yarn or 1 skein of yarn per color you wish to use, and a size E crochet hook.

Wrap the yarn around your index finger twice. **Insert the hook inside these loops, then grab the yarn and pull it through. Bring the yarn up and over, then pull this through the loop on the hook.

Insert the hook through the loop, then pull the yarn up. Bring the yarn up and over once again and pull it through the 2 loops on the hook. This is the first single crochet on the ring. Repeat from ** a total of 10 times, then pull the yarn through the opposite end to close the ring.

Work in the round and single crochet in each of the stitches. Continue to work in the round until you have completed 10 rows, then begin your invisible decrease.

To do an invisible decrease, you are going to insert the hook in the front post of both the next 2 stitches, then single crochet in the next stitch. Front post the next 2 stitches, then single crochet in the next stitch. Repeat around.

Continue with a steady decrease until you have a place that is just small enough to get stuffing inside. Tie off and set aside.

Repeat for the body, only work up to 15 rows before decreasing.

To assemble:

Sew the head to the body after you have finished stuffing both pieces.

Stuff the piece, then sew the end closed around it. Add any details you wish to add with your yarn needle, and snip off the loose threads.

Feed the keychain loop through the top of the piece, then reinforce it with yarn. Snip off all the loose threads, and make sure all is secure. That's it!

Brown Mouse Keychain

You will need scrap yarn or 1 skein of yarn per color you wish to use, and a size E crochet hook.

Wrap the yarn around your index finger twice. **Insert the hook inside these loops, then grab the yarn and pull it through. Bring the yarn up and over, then pull this through the loop on the hook.

Insert the hook through the loop, then pull the yarn up. Bring the yarn up and over once again and pull it through the 2 loops on the hook. This is the first single crochet on the ring. Repeat from ** a total of 10 times, then pull the yarn through the opposite end to close the ring.

Work in the round and single crochet in each of the stitches. Continue to work in the round until you have completed 10 rows, then begin your invisible decrease.

To do an invisible decrease, you are going to insert the hook in the front post of both the next 2 stitches, then single crochet in the next stitch. Front post the next 2 stitches, then single crochet in the next stitch. Repeat around.

Continue with a steady decrease until you have a place that is just small enough to get stuffing inside. Set aside.

To assemble:

For his ears you are going to create 2 disks that are 4 rows across. Tie them off and sew them in place, then chain a length for his tail. You can make this length as long as you please.

Stuff the piece, then sew the end closed around it. Add any details you wish to add with your yarn needle, and snip off the loose threads.

Feed the keychain loop through the top of the piece, then reinforce it with yarn. Snip off all the loose threads, and make sure all is secure. That's it!

Starburst Trinket

Photo made by: <u>moiracrochetsplarn</u>

You will need scrap yarn or 1 skein of yarn per color you wish to use, and a size E crochet hook.

Chain 8 and join with a slip stitch to form a ring. Single crochet in the center of this ring 10 times, and join with a sip stitch. Chain 1, turn, and single crochet around to the other side. chain 1, turn, and single crochet back to the beginning. Chain 1, turn, and single crochet back to the other side.

For the next row, you are going to chain 8 and skip the first 3, then you are going to join with a slip stitch in the next stitch. Chain 8 and skip the next 3, then join with a slip stitch in the next stitch. Repeat this around.

Join with a slip stitch when you get back to the beginning, then chain 1 and turn.

Single crochet around the row.

For the next row, you are going to chain 1, and single crochet in the first stitch, then double crochet in the next stitch 3 times. Single crochet in the next stitch, then double crochet in the next stitch 3 times. Repeat this around.

Join with a slip stitch when you get back to the beginning, tie off, and assemble.

To assemble:

Feed the keychain loop through the top of the piece, then reinforce it with yarn. Snip off all the loose threads, and make sure all is secure. That's it!

Harry the Hedgehog

Photo made by: /toadstool_ring

You will need scrap yarn or 1 skein of yarn per color you wish to use, and a size E crochet hook.

Wrap the yarn around your index finger twice. **Insert the hook inside these loops, then grab the yarn and pull it through. Bring the yarn up and over, then pull this through the loop on the hook.

Insert the hook through the loop, then pull the yarn up. Bring the yarn up and over once again and pull it through the 2 loops on the hook. This is the first single crochet on the ring. Repeat from ** a total of 10 times, then pull the yarn through the opposite end to close the ring.

Work in the round and single crochet in each of the stitches. Continue to work in the round until you have completed 10 rows, then begin your invisible decrease.

To do an invisible decrease, you are going to insert the hook in the front post of both the next 2 stitches, then single crochet in the next stitch. Front post the next 2 stitches, then single crochet in the next stitch. Repeat around.

Continue with a steady decrease until you are where the nose will be. Once you have reached this point you are going to work 4 rows without decreasing. Stuff the body through the nose, then sew it closed.

To assemble:

Stuff the piece, then sew the end closed around it. Add any details you wish to add with your yarn needle, and snip off the loose threads.

Take your yarn needle and fun fir yarn next, and feed the fun fir through the back of the hedgehog. Continue until the back is covered in the yarn, as you can see in the photo.

Feed the keychain loop through the top of the piece, then reinforce it with yarn. Snip off all the loose threads, and make sure all is secure. That's it!

Conclusion

There you have it, everything you need to create a variety of keychains you can use over and over again. When you are making your own keychains, there's no end to the ways you can create and grow your accessory list. You don't have to be stuck with the things they offer at the store, because you can make them yourself, and so much better.

I hope this book was able to give you the inspiration you need to create each and every one of these keychains, then to take what you have learned and create a whole bunch more. When you are able to create your own keychains, you open the door to being able to do whatever you want, when you want to.

Whether you are making them for yourself or you are making them for a friend, you can do anything with the world of accessories. Get creative with the colors and the size of the keychains, and make them be what you want them to be. There's no end to the ways you can create and modify these keychains to be what you want them to be, and when you do, you are going to get a whole new world of accessories like you have never seen before.

I hope this book opened the door to your creativity, and that you were able to take what you have learned here and apply it to any other project you wish to make. There's really no end to how you can make a collection of accessories, and this book is everything you need to do that very thing.

Dive into the world of crochet head first, and grab any and every pattern you see that will show you how to do this. You know you love these patterns, so why not take what you are doing and step further and make each of them, then make more for your friends and family?

When you are able to make your own accessories, you solve so many problems at once. No more stressing about what to do for holidays, no more feeling bored with your wardrobe and no more wondering if you are going to have something fresh to look forward to.

When you are making your own accessories, you are able to do anything you like, when you want to. This book is everything you need to make your keychain collection explode, and it's going to be exactly what you need to take your fashion statement up to the next level.

Happy crocheting!

Crochet:

18 Beautiful One-Night Crochet Projects To Try Right Now!

Introduction

It seems with your busy schedule, it's hard to find the time to sit back and relax, especially when you want to still work on your hobbies.

But it seems that no matter how hard you try to squeeze out a few minutes in your day, the things you want to do are always pushed until after dinner, when you are too tired to start anything big.

Of course, you know you can work on bigger projects a little at a time, but what's the fun in that? There are times when you just want to settle in with something that is low key and easy, and something you can start, and finish in a single afternoon.

"But aren't those small projects hard to make?"

"Don't they require that you pay more attention with all the fine details?"

"Don't they take just as much time as the bigger projects, since you aren't using a large hook?"

Of course when it comes to even small crochet, you can find patterns that are just as hard as the bigger ones, but with the patterns you find in this book, you are going to discover a world of easy, fast projects that you can make in an evening alone.

These patterns are designed to help you relax and let go of your day as you enjoy the hobby itself. Then, you are left with a cute little decoration or accessory before you head to bed.

With these one night projects, you can enjoy fast and easy crochet like never before. So grab your favorite hook and some of the yarn you are cleaning out of your stash, and let's get started.

You're going to fall in love with the little things.

Chapter 1 – Christmas Around the House

Pretty Party Napkin Ring

Photo made by: <u>Elin B</u>

You will need a ball of yarn in each color you wish to use and a size G crochet hook

Chain 15.

Single crochet across the row. Chain 1, turn, and single crochet across to the other side. Chain 1, turn, and single crochet across the row. Chain 1, turn, and single crochet back to the other side.

You are going to continue with this pattern until the napkin ring can wrap around your napkins when they are folded the way you wish.

Make sure they are able to reach around the napkin with enough overlap that you can fold one end over the other slightly.

Sew the ends in place, then attach the button at the top. The button is decorative, but if you like you can secure it with loops and a button hole.

Explore your own creativity and see what you can come up with. Make as many as you like in all the colors you like, and you are done!

Winter Chill Scarf

Photo made by: <u>Boupie</u>

You will need a ball of yarn in each color you wish to use and a size J crochet hook

Chain 20.

Single crochet across the row. Chain 1, turn, and single crochet back to the beginning. Chain 1, turn, and single crochet across the row.

For the next row, you are going to chain 10, and skip the next 4 stitches. Join with a slip stitch. Chain 10, skip the next 4 stitches, and join with a slip stitch. Repeat this across the row, and finish with a single crochet.

Chain 10, and join with a slip stitch to the center of the chain space. Chain 10, and join with a slip stitch to the center of the chain space.

Repeat across.

Continue with the last row until your scarf is as long as you want it to be.

Work 3 rows of single crochet to finish the piece, then tie off.

That's it! You're new scarf is done!

Snow Trinket Snowflakes

Photo made by: <u>Jam Project</u>

You will need a ball of yarn in each color you wish to use and a size G crochet hook

Chain 4 and join with a slip stitch to form a ring.

Chain 2, and double crochet in the center of the ring 2 times. Chain 4, then double crochet in the center of the ring 2 times. Chain 4, then double crochet in the center of the ring 2 times. Chain 4, then double crochet in the center of the ring 1 time. Join with a slip stitch.

Chain 2, skip the next 2 stitches, and double crochet in the chain space 2 times. Chain 2, skip the next 2 stitches, and double crochet in the chain space 2 times.

Repeat this around the row, and join with a slip stitch.

Chain 2, skip the next 2 stitches, and double crochet in the chain space 2 times. Chain 2, skip the next 2 stitches, and double crochet in the chain space 2 times.

Repeat this around the row, and join with a slip stitch.

You are going to repeat this pattern for as big as you want your snowflake to be, then you are ready for the final row:

Chain 1, and single crochet in the next stitch 3 times. Single crochet in the next stitch. Chain 1, and single crochet in the next stitch 3 times. Single crochet in the next stitch.

Winter Cranberry Phone Sock
You will need a ball of yarn in each color you wish to use and a size G crochet hook

Measure around your phone, and chain a length that is equal to this measurement.

Single crochet across the row. Chain 1, turn, and single crochet back to the beginning. Chain 1, turn, and single crochet across the row. Chain 1, turn, and single crochet back to the beginning. Chain 1, turn, and single crochet across the row.

Photo made by: vladimix

Continue until this is 2 rows taller than the top of your phone, and tie off.

Take your yarn needle and sew the bottom and open side, then turn your sock the right side out.

To assemble:

Start by making the flowers:

Chain 4 and join with a slip stitch to form a ring.

214

Single crochet in the center of this ring 9 times, and join with a slip stitch. Chain 1, turn, and single crochet around the row. Join with a slip stitch, chain 1, and turn.

Chain 1, and single crochet in the next stitch 3 times. Single crochet in the next stitch. Chain 1, and single crochet in the next stitch 3 times. Single crochet in the next stitch.

Repeat around, then tie off.

Repeat for as many flowers as you need, then join to the main piece with chains.

That's it! Your phone is ready to step out in style.

Chapter 2 – Last Minute Stocking Stuffers

Mini Doll Beanie

Photo made by: Iris

You will need a ball of yarn in each color you wish to use and a size G crochet hook

Chain 4 and join with a slip stitch to form a ring.

Single crochet in the center of this ring 9 times, and join with a slip stitch. Chain 1, turn, and single crochet around the row. Join with a slip stitch, chain 1, and turn.

Single crochet around, and join with a slip stitch. You are going to continue this until the beanie measures across the top of your doll's head.

For the next row, you are going to chain 1, and single crochet in the first 3 stitches, then skip the next stitch. Single crochet in the next 3 stitches, and skip the next stitch.

Repeat this around.

Join with a slip stitch, chain 1, and turn. Single crochet normally across the row.

Chain 1, turn, and single crochet in the first 3 stitches, then skip the next stitch.

Single crochet in the next 3 stitches, and skip the next stitch.

Decrease steadily so the beanie fits your doll as you go.

Continue until the beanie fits your doll, then tie off.

That's it!

Tiny Teddy

Photo made by: Guian Bolisay

You will need a ball of yarn in each color you wish to use and a size G crochet hook

For the head:

Chain 4 and join with a slip stitch to form a ring.

Single crochet in the center of this ring 9 times, and join with a slip stitch. Chain 1, turn, and single crochet around the row. Join with a slip stitch, chain 1, and turn.

Single crochet around, and join with a slip stitch. You are going to continue this for a total of 12 rows.

For the next row, you are going to chain 1, and single crochet in the first 3 stitches, then skip the next stitch. Single crochet in the next 3 stitches, and skip the next stitch.

Repeat this around.

Join with a slip stitch, chain 1, and turn. Single crochet normally across the row.

Chain 1, turn, and single crochet in the first 3 stitches, then skip the next stitch. Single crochet in the next 3 stitches, and skip the next stitch.

Repeat around, then join with a slip stitch.

You are going to continue with the steady decrease until you have nearly the perfect globe. Make sure you still have enough room to stuff this piece, but make the hole as small as you can.

Tie off and set aside.

For the body:

Chain 4 and join with a slip stitch to form a ring.

Single crochet in the center of this ring 9 times, and join with a slip stitch. Chain 1, turn, and single crochet around the row. Join with a slip stitch, chain 1, and turn.

Single crochet around, and join with a slip stitch. You are going to continue this for a total of 8 rows.

218

For the next row, you are going to chain 1, and single crochet in the first 3 stitches, then skip the next stitch. Single crochet in the next 3 stitches, and skip the next stitch.

Repeat this around.

Join with a slip stitch, chain 1, and turn. Single crochet normally across the row.

Chain 1, turn, and single crochet in the first 3 stitches, then skip the next stitch. Single crochet in the next 3 stitches, and skip the next stitch.

Repeat around, then join with a slip stitch.

You are going to continue with the steady decrease until you have nearly the perfect globe. Make sure you still have enough room to stuff this piece, but make the hole as small as you can.

Tie off and set aside.

For the ears:

Chain 4 and join with a slip stitch to form a ring.

Single crochet in the center of this ring 9 times, and join with a slip stitch. Chain 1, turn, and single crochet around the row. Tie off and repeat for the other side.

To assemble:

Stuff the head and body both with stuffing, then sew both to each other. Use your yarn needle, and make sure both are firm.

Use felt for the arms, legs, and bow.

Finish by attaching the ears, and you are done!

Smiling Snakes
You will need a ball of yarn in each color you wish to use and a size G crochet hook

For the head:

Chain 4 and join with a slip stitch to form a ring.

Photo made by: Arienne McCracken

Single crochet in the center of this ring 9 times, and join with a slip stitch. Chain 1, turn, and single crochet around the row. Join with a slip stitch, chain 1, and turn.

Single crochet around, and join with a slip stitch. You are going to continue this for a total of 8 rows.

For the next row, you are going to chain 1, and single crochet in the first 3 stitches, then skip the next stitch. Single crochet in the next 3 stitches, and skip the next stitch.

Repeat this around.

Join with a slip stitch, chain 1, and turn. Single crochet normally across the row.

Chain 1, turn, and single crochet in the first 3 stitches, then skip the next stitch. Single crochet in the next 3 stitches, and skip the next stitch.

Repeat around, then join with a slip stitch.

You are going to continue with the steady decrease until you have nearly the perfect globe. Make sure you still have enough room to stuff this piece, but make the hole as small as you can.

Tie off and set aside.

For the body:

Chain 10 and single crochet across the row. Chain 1, turn, and single crochet back to the other side. chain 1, turn, and single crochet across the row. You are going to continue with this until the body is as long as you want your snake to be, then tie off.

To assemble:

Stuff the head with stuffing, then sew firmly to the body. Make sure the head is nice and firm, and sew on the eyes with yarn and your needle. Use felt for the tongue, and you are done!

Photo made by: <u>Pat</u>

You will need a ball of yarn in each color you wish to use and a size G crochet hook

Chain 4 and join with a slip stitch to form a ring.

Single crochet in the center of this ring 9 times, and join with a slip stitch. Chain 1, turn, and single crochet around the row. Join with a slip stitch, chain 1, and turn.

Single crochet around, and join with a slip stitch. You are going to continue this for a total of 12 rows.

For the next row, you are going to chain 1, and single crochet in the first 3 stitches, then skip the next stitch. Single crochet in the next 3 stitches, and skip the next stitch.

Repeat this around.

Join with a slip stitch, chain 1, and turn. Single crochet normally across the row.

222

Chain 1, turn, and single crochet in the first 3 stitches, then skip the next stitch. Single crochet in the next 3 stitches, and skip the next stitch.

Repeat around, then join with a slip stitch.

You are going to continue with the steady decrease until you have nearly the perfect globe. Make sure you still have enough room to stuff this piece, but make the hole as small as you can.

Tie off and set aside.

For the ears:

Chain 4 and join with a slip stitch to form a ring.

Single crochet in the center of this ring 9 times, and join with a slip stitch. Switch to the main color of the body now, and join with a slip stitch. Chain 1, turn, and single crochet around the row. Tie off and repeat for the other side.

To assemble:

Stuff the body with stuffing, as firmly as you can get it without it being too tight, then sew the end closed. Add the details to the face with your yarn needle, too.

Finish by attaching the ears, and you are done!

Chapter 3 – Warm Crochet

One Night Neck Warmer

Photo made by: smittenkittenorig

You will need a ball of yarn in each color you wish to use and a size J crochet hook

Decide how long you want your cowl to be, then chain a length that is equal to this measurement. Typically, they are about 20 inches long, but you can adjust this to your own personal preference.

Single crochet across the row. Chain 1, turn, and single crochet across to the other side. Chain 1, turn, and single crochet across the row. Chain 1, turn, and single crochet back to the other side.

Continue with this pattern until your cowl is 20 inches long and 12 inches tall, then tie off.

Give the cowl a twist, and sew it together with a whip stitch. When you have sewn together the end, turn the cowl so the seam is on the inside of the cowl, then add the decorative buttons as you see in the photo.

That's it! Your new neck warmer is done and ready for action!

Winter Wind Beanie

Photo made by: Arienne McCracken

You will need a ball of yarn in each color you wish to use and a size J crochet hook

Chain 4 and join with a slip stitch to form a ring.

Single crochet in the center of this ring 9 times, and join with a slip stitch. Chain 1, turn, and single crochet around the row. Join with a slip stitch, chain 1, and turn.

Single crochet around, and join with a slip stitch. You are going to continue this until the beanie measures across the top of your head.

For the next row, you are going to chain 1, and single crochet in the first 3 stitches, then skip the next stitch. Single crochet in the next 3 stitches, and skip the next stitch.

Repeat this around.

Join with a slip stitch, chain 1, and turn. Single crochet normally across the row.

Chain 1, turn, and single crochet in the first 3 stitches, then skip the next stitch. Single crochet in the next 3 stitches, and skip the next stitch.

Continue until the beanie is as long as you want it to be.

For the next row, you are going to chain 10, and skip the next 4 stitches. Join with a slip stitch. Chain 10, skip the next 4 stitches, and join with a slip stitch. Repeat this across the row, and finish with a slip stitch.

Work 1 more row of single crochet now, joining with a slip stitch and tying off.

That's it! Your beanie is done!

For the Little One Mittens

Photo made by: Tare Panda

You will need a ball of yarn in each color you wish to use and a size G crochet hook

Measure around your baby's wrist. You want this to be snug enough to stay on while your baby is wearing it, but you don't want it to be too tight. A little on the loose side is better than tighter, keep that in mind as you measure.

Chain a length that matches this measurement.

Single crochet across the row and join with a slip stitch. Chain 1 turn, and single crochet back to the beginning, joining with a slip stitch. Chain 1, turn, and single crochet across the row, joining with a slip stitch.

When you get to your baby's thumb, you are going to single crochet around, then chain 2, and jump that space on the tube. Continue to work in the round on this smaller loop until the piece you make can reach up and over your baby's thumb.

Tie off, and return to where you left off on the main piece. Join with a slip stitch and work your way around the piece. Join with a slip stitch. Chain 1, turn, and repeat.

Continue until the piece reaches up and over the end of your baby's fingers.

Tie off and repeat for the other glove, then set aside.

For the cuff:

Chain a length that is 1 inch long.

Single crochet across the row, in the front loop only. Chain 1, turn, and single crochet across the row, in the front loop only. Chain 1, turn, and single crochet across the row, in the front loop only.

You are going to continue with this pattern until your strip will fit around your baby's wrist. Measure so it will run the same length as the base of the mitten you made. Tie off and repeat for the other side.

Take your yarn needle now and sew the cuff to the bottom of your mitten.

Sew both the main body of the mitten closed as well as the thumb, then turn the entire mitten the right side out.

Attach a little chain around the center for decoration, and you are done!

Sassy Headband

Photo made by: <u>becky bokern</u>

You will need a ball of yarn in each color you wish to use and a size G crochet hook

Chain 20.

Single crochet across the row. Chain 1, turn, and single crochet across to the other side. Chain 1, turn, and single crochet across the row. Chain 1, turn, and single crochet back to the other side.

Continue with this pattern until the piece can wrap around your head, and fit snugly, but not too tight.

When you are happy with how the headband fits, tie it off and take your yarn needle.

Whip stitch the seam together, making sure that the piece is lying flat against itself. You don't want any twist in this one.

Turn the headband to the right side out, and snip off the loose end.

That's it!

Chapter 4 – Winter Wonderland Crochet

Skater Ornament

Photo made by: regan76

You will need a ball of yarn in each color you wish to use and a size G crochet hook

Chain 12 and double crochet across the row.

Chain 2, turn, and double crochet in the first 6 stitches. Chain 2, turn, and double crochet back to the beginning.

Chain 1, and single crochet across the row. Tie off, and switch to white.

Join with a slip stitch, and single crochet across the row. Chain 1, turn, and single crochet back to the beginning. If you are at the back of the skate, chain 15, if not, then work 1 more single crochet row, then chain 15.

Tie off, and repeat the same steps for the other side. You want both of your skates to end with the length of chain at the back of them.

Take a paper clip and feed it through the bottom of the skates. Tie the end chains together with a knot in the center, and you are done!

Fast and Easy Lap Throw

Photo made by: Kristen Stubbs

You will need a ball of yarn in each color you wish to use and a size J crochet hook

Use the photo as a color reference. If you are going to follow the same color scheme as I did, make sure you change colors every three rows.

Chain 200.

Single crochet across the row. Chain 1, turn, and single crochet back to the other side. Chain 1, turn, and single crochet in the first 10, then skip the next stitch. Single crochet in the next 10 stitches, then skip the next stitch.

Single crochet in the next 10 stitches, then skip the next stitch. Continue to do this across the row.

231

When you get to the other side, you are going to chain 1, turn, and single crochet in each of the stitches across, skipping the same stitch that you skipped in the previous row.

Chain 1, turn, and single crochet across the row. By now, you shouldn't have to skip any stitches, just make sure that you are only putting 1 stitch in each stitch as you go across.

Change colors every 3 rows if you like, or use your own color scheme.

Tie off.

Take a DVD case, and wrap yarn around it several times. You are going to make the tassels all the same length, so continue to wrap until you have a nice, thick piece.

Divide this into even sections, and feed them through each of the points on your blanket. Secure them in place, tying a knot to hold them steady.

That's it! You're new lap throw is done!

Texting Gloves

Photo made by: becky bokern

You will need a ball of yarn in each color you wish to use and a size J crochet hook

Measure around your wrist, and chain a length that is equal to this measurement. You don't want it to be too tight, but you also need it to be snug enough to keep you warm during the winter weather.

Single crochet across the row. Chain 1 turn, and single crochet back to the beginning. Chain 1, turn, and single crochet across the row.

Continue with this pattern until you can wrap the piece around your hand, and it reaches from your wrist to the base of your fingers.

If you want more coverage, simply continue until you are happy with how high they ride on your fingers.

Tie off and repeat for the other glove, then set aside.

For the cuff:

Chain a length that is 2 inches long.

Single crochet across the row, in the front loop only. Chain 1, turn, and single crochet across the row, in the front loop only. Chain 1, turn, and single crochet across the row, in the front loop only.

You are going to continue with this pattern until your strip will fit around your entire wrist. Measure so it will run the same length as the base of your glove. Tie off and repeat for the other side.

Take your yarn needle now and sew the cuff to the bottom of your glove.

Next, you are going to run a single seam up the side of the glove, but measure as you go so you don't sew up the thumb hole. Once it is secure, turn the glove the other way so the seams are on the inside.

Repeat for the other side, and you are done!

Men's Smooth and Silky Scarf

You will need a ball of yarn in each color you wish to use and a size J crochet hook

Use the photo as a reference for colors, or make up your own as you go along.

Chain 159.

Single crochet across the row, in the front loop only. Chain 1, turn, and single crochet across to the other side. Chain 1, turn, and single crochet across the row, in the front loop only. Chain 1, turn, and single crochet back to the other side.

If you are going to change colors as I did, now is the time to do so. Tie off the first color, and join the next with a slip stitch.

Single crochet across the row, in the front loop only. Chain 1, turn, and single crochet across to the other side. Chain 1, turn, and single crochet across the row, in the front loop only. Chain 1, turn, and single crochet back to the other side.

If you are going to change colors as I did, now is the time to do so. Tie off the first color, and join the next with a slip stitch.

Continue for as many color blocks as you like. I used 4, then tied it off.

That's it! That special guy in your life is going to love it!

Chapter 5 – The Best of the Rest

Mantle Stockings

Photo made by: <u>Melissa Doroquez</u>

You will need a ball of yarn in each color you wish to use and a size G crochet hook

Chain 24 and single crochet across the row.

Chain 1, turn, and single crochet back to the beginning. Chain 1, turn, and single crochet across the row. Repeat for another 8 rows.

Chain 1, turn, and single crochet in the first 12 stitches. Chain 1, turn, and double crochet back to the beginning.

Chain 1, and single crochet across the row. Chain 1, turn, and single crochet back to the beginning. Chain 1, turn, and single crochet across the row. Repeat for another 14 rows.

Tie off and set aside, and repeat for the other side.

To assemble:

Take your yarn needle and sew up the border, leaving the top of your stocking open.

Once you have reached the other side, turn the piece the right side, out, and add a loop to the back for hanging.

That's it! Your stockings are ready for Santa!

Ho Ho Holidays

Photo made by: <u>Robin</u>

You will need a ball of yarn in each color you wish to use and a size G crochet hook

Use the photo for a color reference.

For the body:

Chain 4 and join with a slip stitch to form a ring.

Single crochet in the center of this ring 9 times, and join with a slip stitch. Chain 1, turn, and single crochet around the row. Join with a slip stitch, chain 1, and turn.

237

Single crochet around, and join with a slip stitch. You are going to continue this for a total of 10 rows.

For the next row, you are going to chain 1, and single crochet in the first 3 stitches, then skip the next stitch. Single crochet in the next 3 stitches, and skip the next stitch.

Repeat this around.

Join with a slip stitch, chain 1, and turn. Single crochet normally across the row.

Chain 1, turn, and single crochet in the first 3 stitches, then skip the next stitch. Single crochet in the next 3 stitches, and skip the next stitch.

Repeat around, then join with a slip stitch.

You are going to continue with the steady decrease until you have nearly the perfect globe. Make sure you still have enough room to stuff this piece, but make the hole as small as you can.

Tie off and set aside.

For the for the head:

Chain 4 and join with a slip stitch to form a ring.

Single crochet in the center of this ring 9 times, and join with a slip stitch. Chain 1, turn, and single crochet around the row. Join with a slip stitch, chain 1, and turn.

Single crochet around, and join with a slip stitch. You are going to continue this for a total of 8 rows.

For the next row, you are going to chain 1, and single crochet in the first 3 stitches, then skip the next stitch. Single crochet in the next 3 stitches, and skip the next stitch.

Repeat this around.

Join with a slip stitch, chain 1, and turn. Single crochet normally across the row.

Chain 1, turn, and single crochet in the first 3 stitches, then skip the next stitch. Single crochet in the next 3 stitches, and skip the next stitch.

Repeat around, then join with a slip stitch.

You are going to continue with the steady decrease until you have nearly the perfect globe. Make sure you still have enough room to stuff this piece, but make the hole as small as you can.

Tie off and set aside.

To assemble:

Stuff the head and body both with stuffing, then sew both to each other. Use your yarn needle, and make sure both are firm.

Now use white for the beard:

Chain 10 and single crochet across the row. Chain 1, turn, and skip the first stitch, then single crochet across the row and skip the last stitch. Chain 1, turn, and skip the first stitch, then single crochet across the row and skip the last stitch.

You are going to continue with this now until you come down to a nice point, then sew this on his face for the beard.

Repeat in red for the hat, making sure that the length will fit around the top of his head.

Sew in place, and your little Santa is done!

239

Conclusion

There you have it. Eighteen of the cutest crochet projects ever, and all small enough that you can create them in just a single evening.

I hope this book inspires you to take up some evening crochet, and that you are able to relax and unwind from your day as you create fun and cute little projects that make you happy.

The projects in this book are designed to help you relax, so heat up some tea and kick back with your favorite yarn. It's you time, and your projects are going to reflect just how happy you are.

Crochet Book Cover
15 Wonderful Crochet Patterns To Cover Your Books

Julianne Link

Crochet Book Covers

15 Wonderful Crochet Patterns To Cover Your Books

Introduction

Summer is drawing to a close, and with it our minds all turn back to books in one way or another. Perhaps you are a college student, and you are making ready to head off to school for the first time, the second time, or maybe it's even the last time.

Maybe you are entering high school, or maybe you are nearly finished. Maybe you are just happy to see all of the academic things come back into the picture, and you are getting your old books back off the shelves and enjoying them as you once did.

Perhaps you are ready to pick up book reading for the first time, and you are eager to start your very own personal library, getting only the books you want and the perfect personal touch added to each and every book you put onto your shelves.

No matter what you want to do, you have a good reason to get out your yarn, your crochet hook, and your favorite cup of coffee and get down to business. You are going to be able to add your own personal touch to each and every one of the titles.

Whether you are using soft cover, hard cover, repairing a cover that has long since seen better days, or simply redoing the cover to make it your own, you are going to find what you need in this book.

"I have never made a crochet cover before… is it hard?"

"I like to add my own touch to things, but I don't know how to make covers."

"I don't want it to look like I did it wrong, or like I didn't know what I was doing."

If you have ever felt any of these things, you aren't alone. Though making your own projects is exciting, it can be intimidating. But, you have everything you need right here to make your book a success, and it is going to give you the freedom you need to make your own covers any time you want, for any book you want.

And it just doesn't get any better than that.

Zig Zag Zipper

You will need one ball of each color. I also use buttons for a clasp and a size G crochet hook.

Measure the length you need around the base of the book. If you are going to fold in the ends for the flap, add 6 inches onto this measurement.

Chain a length that is equal to this measurement, turn, and single crochet across the row.

For the next row, single crochet in the first 4 stitches, then skip the next stitch. Single crochet in the next 4 stitches, then skip the next stitch.

Continue to do this across the row, forming that zig zag pattern. Switch to the different color on the third row, and continue this pattern.

You will keep going now, switching up colors every third row until the cover fits over the cover of your book.

Tie it off when you have the right size, and chain a length of 15 for the closing band.

You are now ready to assemble.

To assemble:

You have more than one option when you assemble this cover... either you can sew in panels to hold the book in place, or you can crochet an extra length and fold it over.

However you decide to do it, you are going to line up the ends, and sew the top and bottom of this row in place.

Attach the strap and the buttons, tie off and trim the loose threads, and your book is ready to slip inside!

Owl's Eyes Cover

You will need one ball of each color. I also use buttons for a clasp and a size G crochet hook.

Measure the length you need around the base of the book. If you are going to fold in the ends for the flap, add 6 inches onto this measurement.

247

Chain a length that is equal to this measurement, turn, and single crochet across the row.

For the next row, chain 1, and single crochet across the row. Chain 1, and single crochet back across the row.

Work until your cover is the size you need it to be. Measure as you go to ensure the proper fit, and tie off the end when you are finished.

For the eyes: Make 2

Start with black, and chain 5. Join with a slip stitch to form a ring.

Single crochet in the center of this 12 times. Change colors now to brown.

Work 1 row of brown before switching to white, and work 4 rows of white. Tie off and place on the cover as you see in the photo.

To assemble:

You have more than one option when you assemble this cover... either you can sew in panels to hold the book in place, or you can crochet an extra length and fold it over.

However you decide to do it, you are going to line up the ends, and sew the top and bottom of this row in place.

Attach the strap and the buttons, tie off and trim the loose threads, and your book is ready to slip inside!

You will need one ball of each color. I also use buttons for a clasp and a size G crochet hook.

Measure the length you need around the base of the book. If you are going to fold in the ends for the flap, add 6 inches onto this measurement.

Chain a length that is equal to this measurement, turn, and single crochet across the row.

For the next row, chain 2, and double crochet across the row. Chain 2, and double crochet back across the row.

Work until your cover is the size you need it to be. Measure as you go to ensure the proper fit, and tie off the end when you are finished with this section.

To assemble:

You have more than one option when you assemble this cover… either you can sew in panels to hold the book in place, or you can crochet an extra length and fold it over.

However you decide to do it, you are going to line up the ends, and sew the top and bottom of this row in place.

Attach the strap and the buttons, tie off and trim the loose threads, and your book is ready to slip inside!

Christmas Crashes

You will need one ball of each color. I also use buttons for a clasp and a size G crochet hook.

Measure the length you need around the base of the book. If you are going to fold in the ends for the flap, add 6 inches onto this measurement.

This is the total length you need your book cover to be, but you are going to start by chaining a length that is equal to the height of the book.

Single crochet across the row.

For the next row, chain 1, and single crochet back across the row. Chain 1, and single crochet across the row.

For the next row, you are going to work a single crochet row, working in the front row only.

251

Continue to single crochet back and forth across the row, every third row you are going to use the same single crochet, but you are going to only do it in the front loop only. Continue until it is the length you need.

To assemble:

You have more than one option when you assemble this cover... either you can sew in panels to hold the book in place, or you can crochet an extra length and fold it over.

However you decide to do it, you are going to line up the ends, and sew the top and bottom of this row in place.

Attach the strap and the buttons, tie off and trim the loose threads, and your book is ready to slip inside!

Green Striped Goodness

You will need one ball of each color. I also use buttons for a clasp and a size G crochet hook.

Measure the length you need around the base of the book. If you are going to fold in the ends for the flap, add 6 inches onto this measurement.

Chain a length that is equal to this measurement, turn, and single crochet across the row.

For the next row, chain 2, and double crochet across the row. Chain 2, and double crochet back across the row.

You are going to change colors every other row, so keep an eye on the photo to see when you change colors.

For the strap, you are going to chain 5, and single crochet across the row until it is long enough to close the book you want to cover.

For the flower:

Chain 5. Join with a slip stitch to form a ring.

Single crochet in the center of this 12 times. Join with a slip stitch, and chain 1. Single crochet in the next stitch 3 times, and single crochet in the next stitch. Single crochet in the next stitch 3 times, and single crochet in the next stitch.

Repeat around, and tie off.

To assemble:

You have more than one option when you assemble this cover... either you can sew in panels to hold the book in place, or you can crochet an extra length and fold it over.

However you decide to do it, you are going to line up the ends, and sew the top and bottom of this row in place.

Attach the strap and the buttons, tie off and trim the loose threads, and your book is ready to slip inside!

You will need one ball of each color. I also use buttons for a clasp and a size G crochet hook.

Measure the length you need around the base of the book. If you are going to fold in the ends for the flap, add 6 inches onto this measurement.

This is the total length you need your book cover to be, but you are going to start by chaining a length that is equal to the height of the book.

Single crochet across the row.

For the next row, chain 1, and single crochet back across the row. Chain 1, and single crochet across the row. Continue to single crochet back and forth across the row until it is the length you need.

Work 1 row of single crochet for the boarder.

For the strap, you are going to chain 5, and single crochet across the row until it is long enough to close the book you want to cover.

To assemble:

You have more than one option when you assemble this cover... either you can sew in panels to hold the book in place, or you can crochet an extra length and fold it over.

However you decide to do it, you are going to line up the ends, and sew the top and bottom of this row in place.

You are going to add in the details with a sewing needle, thread, and a yarn needle. Attach the decorations as you see in the photo.

Attach the strap and the buttons, tie off and trim the loose threads, and your book is ready to slip inside!

Chapter 3 – Just What You Wanted

Handy Handle

You will need one ball of each color. I also use buttons for a clasp and a size G crochet hook.

Measure the length you need around the base of the book. If you are going to fold in the ends for the flap, add 6 inches onto this measurement.

Chain a length that is equal to this measurement, turn, and single crochet across the row.

For the next row, single crochet across the row. Chain 1, turn, and single crochet back across the other way. Continue to do this until you have the right size, and tie off.

For the handle:

Measure the overall length you need for the book, and chain a length that is equal to this, plus 8 inches.

Work a single crochet pattern for the next 8 rows, and tie off.

Watch the photo for placement of the strap, and sew in place accordingly.

To assemble:

You have more than one option when you assemble this cover… either you can sew in panels to hold the book in place, or you can crochet an extra length and fold it over.

However you decide to do it, you are going to line up the ends, and sew the top and bottom of this row in place.

Attach the strap and the buttons, tie off and trim the loose threads, and your book is ready to slip inside!

The Lady of Lace

You will need one ball of each color. I also use buttons for a clasp and a size G crochet hook.

Measure the length you need around the base of the book. If you are going to fold in the ends for the flap, add 6 inches onto this measurement.

Chain a length that is equal to this measurement, turn, and single crochet across the row.

For the next row, single crochet across the row. Chain 1, turn, and single crochet back across the other way. Continue to do this until you have the right size, and tie off.

Now, repeat these steps once more, only this time with the other color. You are going to use your yarn needle to sew these two pieces in place, and tie off.

To assemble:

You have more than one option when you assemble this cover... either you can sew in panels to hold the book in place, or you can crochet an extra length and fold it over.

However you decide to do it, you are going to line up the ends, and sew the top and bottom of this row in place.

Attach the strap and the buttons, tie off and trim the loose threads, and your book is ready to slip inside!

You will need one ball of each color. I also use buttons for a clasp and a size G crochet hook.

Measure the length you need around the base of the book. If you are going to fold in the ends for the flap, add 6 inches onto this measurement.

This is the total length you need your book cover to be, but you are going to start by chaining a length that is equal to the height of the book.

Single crochet across the row.

For the next row, chain 1, and single crochet back across the row. Chain 1, and single crochet across the row. Continue to single crochet back and forth across the row until it is the length you need.

To assemble:

You have more than one option when you assemble this cover... either you can sew in panels to hold the book in place, or you can crochet an extra length and fold it over.

However you decide to do it, you are going to line up the ends, and sew the top and bottom of this row in place.

Attach the strap and the buttons, tie off and trim the loose threads, and your book is ready to slip inside!

Multi-Goodness Goddess

You will need one ball of each color. I also use buttons for a clasp and a size G crochet hook.

Measure the length you need around the base of the book. If you are going to fold in the ends for the flap, add 6 inches onto this measurement.

Chain a length that is equal to this measurement, turn, and single crochet across the row.

For the next row, chain 1, and single crochet back across the row. Chain 1, and single crochet across the row. Continue to single crochet back and forth across the row until it is the length you need.

To assemble:

You have more than one option when you assemble this cover… either you can sew in panels to hold the book in place, or you can crochet an extra length and fold it over.

However you decide to do it, you are going to line up the ends, and sew the top and bottom of this row in place.

Attach the strap and the buttons, tie off and trim the loose threads, and your book is ready to slip inside!

Pleased as a Plum

You will need one ball of each color. I also use buttons for a clasp and a size G crochet hook.

Measure the length you need around the base of the book. If you are going to fold in the ends for the flap, add 6 inches onto this measurement.

Chain a length that is equal to this measurement, turn, and single crochet across the row.

For the next row, chain 2, and double crochet back across the row. Chain 2, and double crochet across the row. Continue to single crochet back and forth across the row until it is the length you need.

Work 1 row of single crochet on the boarder, and repeat the main sequence for the strap.

For the flower:

Chain 5. Join with a slip stitch to form a ring.

Single crochet in the center of this 12 times. Join with a slip stitch, and chain 1. Single crochet in the next stitch 3 times, and single crochet in the next stitch. Single crochet in the next stitch 3 times, and single crochet in the next stitch.

Repeat around, and tie off.

To assemble:

You have more than one option when you assemble this cover... either you can sew in panels to hold the book in place, or you can crochet an extra length and fold it over.

However you decide to do it, you are going to line up the ends, and sew the top and bottom of this row in place.

Attach the strap and the buttons, tie off and trim the loose threads, and your book is ready to slip inside!

Green Machine

You will need one ball of each color. I also use buttons for a clasp and a size G crochet hook.

Measure the length you need around the base of the book. If you are going to fold in the ends for the flap, add 6 inches onto this measurement.

This is the total length you need your book cover to be, but you are going to start by chaining a length that is equal to the height of the book.

Single crochet across the row.

For the next row, chain 1, and single crochet back across the row. Chain 1, and single crochet across the row. Continue to single crochet back and forth across the row until it is the length you need.

You are now going to decrease with each row, skipping the first 2 stitches on each row, and stopping 2 stitches before the end of each row. When you are at a fine point, tie it off.

You are now ready to assemble.

To assemble:

You have more than one option when you assemble this cover... either you can sew in panels to hold the book in place, or you can crochet an extra length and fold it over.

However you decide to do it, you are going to line up the ends, and sew the top and bottom of this row in place.

Attach the strap and the buttons, tie off and trim the loose threads, and your book is ready to slip inside!

Chapter 5 – The Best of the Rest

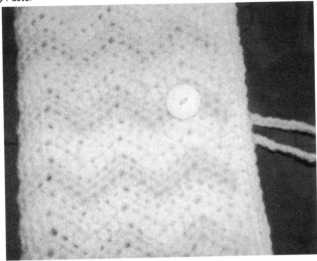

You will need one ball of each color. I also use buttons for a clasp and a size G crochet hook.

Measure the length you need around the base of the book. If you are going to fold in the ends for the flap, add 6 inches onto this measurement.

Chain a length that is equal to this measurement, turn, and single crochet across the row.

For the next row, single crochet in the first 4 stitches, then skip the next stitch. Single crochet in the next 4 stitches, then skip the next stitch.

Continue to do this across the row, forming that zig zag pattern. Switch to the different color on the third row, and continue this pattern.

You will keep going now, switching up colors every third row until the cover fits over the cover of your book.

Tie it off when you have the right size, and chain two lengths of 10 for the ties.

You are now ready to assemble.

To assemble:

You have more than one option when you assemble this cover... either you can sew in panels to hold the book in place, or you can crochet an extra length and fold it over.

However you decide to do it, you are going to line up the ends, and sew the top and bottom of this row in place.

Attach the strap and the buttons, tie off and trim the loose threads, and your book is ready to slip inside!

Rainbow Valley Beauty Book

266

You will need one ball of each color. I also use buttons for a clasp and a size G crochet hook.

Measure the length you need around the base of the book. If you are going to fold in the ends for the flap, add 6 inches onto this measurement.

This is the total length you need your book cover to be, but you are going to start by chaining a length that is equal to the height of the book.

Single crochet across the row.

For the next row, chain 1, and single crochet back across the row. Chain 1, and single crochet across the row. Continue to single crochet back and forth across the row until it is the length you need.

For the strap:

You are going to start with a chain 5 stitches long.

Continue to work until you are happy with the size of the length, and single crochet a boarder around the entire strap.

To assemble:

You have more than one option when you assemble this cover… either you can sew in panels to hold the book in place, or you can crochet an extra length and fold it over.

However you decide to do it, you are going to line up the ends, and sew the top and bottom of this row in place.

Attach the strap and the buttons, tie off and trim the loose threads, and your book is ready to slip inside!

You will need one ball of each color. I also use buttons for a clasp and a size G crochet hook.

Measure the length you need around the base of the book. If you are going to fold in the ends for the flap, add 6 inches onto this measurement.

Chain a length that is equal to this measurement, turn, and single crochet across the row.

For the next row, single crochet across the row. Chain 1, turn, and single crochet back across the other way. Continue to do this until you have the right size, and tie off.

To assemble:

You have more than one option when you assemble this cover... either you can sew in panels to hold the book in place, or you can crochet an extra length and fold it over.

However you decide to do it, you are going to line up the ends, and sew the top and bottom of this row in place.

268

Attach the strap and the buttons, tie off and trim the loose threads, and your book is ready to slip inside!

Chapter 6 – Making It Your Own

You will see that there are a lot of different ways you can make the covers for your books, you are going to find the same general pattern for each book. Since books are generally the same shape, you are going to use the same overall shape for each of your covers.

But, you don't have to stop there.

As you can see from the patterns in this book, you can add your own little touches here and there, but there is so much more you can do than just add a flower here or a strap there.

Every time you finish a cover, take a look at it and decide what you want to do with it.

You will find all kinds of patches, stamps, material, stickers, and tons of other options to use for each and every cover. Go to your local craft store and look over all of the various options you can choose from to customize your cover.

Add a different piece to each cover you make, and mix and match to create something entirely new each time. When you are being creative, there is no way you can go wrong. If you want to make a thicker strap, do it. If you want to have a thinner strap, or no strap at all, then you have the complete freedom to do that.

The main thing you want to keep in mind is that this should be fun. Add colors, add buttons, add anything you want. Make each and every book cover able to zip, or make them as open as the book itself.

In other words, treat each project as entirely unique and its own creation. You are going to be able to change and modify each and every one of these patterns to be just what you want them to be, or you can make each and every one as much the same as each other as you can.

The biggest benefit that comes from creating your own cover is that you have the freedom to make it your own.

So go ahead.

Make them your own.

Conclusion

There you have it, everything you need to know to completely make over your book collection, and to add your own personal taste to anything and everything you want in the book world.

You really don't need to have a reason to makeover your book collection, and the more you do it, the more you are going to find to do. I hope this book was able to inspire you to engage your other books, no matter how you want to do that.

I want you to have fun with the best collection you can ever have in life... your books. I want them to look like you want them to look, to give them your added touch of character. I want you to fall in love with your books for a whole new reason, and I want you to keep coming back to them over and over again.

This book is designed to help you make friends of your other books, and to fall in love with them, to give them your own little spin in any way you can think of. You don't have to be an author to make your mark on a book, and you don't need to be an artist to make your own book covers.

With this book, you are given everything you need to make your mark on any book, or even a tablet or computer if you want to. There's no way you can go wrong with your own creativity, and this book wants to give you everything you need to get started with your own personal library.

All you need is a few dollar's worth of supplies, a few minutes of your time, and a little bit of inspiration, and you have everything you need to get your project up and running. So if you are ready to say hello to the joys of making your own book covers, you have come to the right place.

Cover each and every book you own, buy more books to cover, and cover all your friends' books. No matter how you want to go about it, you are free to do as you please.

Let your creativity shine, and embrace your unique self. No matter how you want to do it, you are going to have it your way.

Crochet Mandala

Julianne Link

12 Most Gorgeous Patterns With Easy Instructions

Crochet Mandala:

12 Most Gorgeous Patterns With Easy Instructions

Introduction

Crochet craft is beneficial for everyone because it can improve your overall health and decrease your stress and tensions. You can learn the basic stitches of crochet to prepare these patterns easily. Crochet craft can fill your pocket with money because you can sell them in the market physically or via online stores. In this book, there are 12 beautiful mandala patterns with easy instructions. Follow them to design your own 12 mandalas.

These 12 patterns are easy to follow and perfect for you to decorate your house or send as gift to your friends:

Pattern 01: Blooming Mandala

Crochet Hook: 5mm or H/8

Weight of Yarn: (4) Aran and Worsted/Medium Weight (16 to 20 stitches to four inches)

Final Size: 12.5 to 13.5 inches

Notes:

- You will work in rounds with sl st (slip stitch) in the first stitch from the final stitch.
- You should learn to create slip knot on your hook.
- In some rows, the chain 1 will not be taken as a stitch.
- You will use nine colors in this pattern, and you are free to reduce them or use them all. You can repeat a few colors.

- Block the finish items and wet block can be a good choice for this.
- There is no need to fasten off any color until you are satisfied with the row.
- Monitor your stitches with any stitch counter.

Description:

Round 1: Color 1: Create a magic circle, ch 1, single crochet six times into the circle, slip stitch into the first st to secure – 6 single crochets

Round 2: Ch 7 (counts as treble + 3), *treble into the subsequent st, ch 3,* replicate from * to * 4 more times, slip stitch into the top of the ch 4 to secure – 6 trebles, six ch-3 spaces

Fasten off Color 1.

Round 3: Color 2: Create a slip knot on your hook, single crochet into a ch-3 space, single crochet 3 more times into the similar ch-3 space, ch 1, skip the subsequent treble, *single crochet 4 times into the following ch-3 space, ch 1, skip the subsequent treble,* replicate from * to * 4 more times, slip stitch into the first st to secure – 24 single crochets, 6 ch-1 spaces

Round 4: Ch 2 (counts as the first leg of the double-crochet4together), double-crochet3together the subsequent 3 sts, skip the subsequent ch 1 space, ch 8, *double-crochet4together the subsequent 4 sts, skip the subsequent ch 1 space, ch 8,* replicate from * to * 4 more times, slip stitch into the top of the double-crochet3together to secure – 6 double-crochet4togethers, 6 ch-8 spaces

Fasten off Color 2.

Round 5: 3rd color: Create a slip knot on your hook, single crochet 4 times into a ch-8 space, double-treble into the ch-1 space from round 2, single crochet 4 times into the similar ch-8 space, ch 3, skip the subsequent double-crochet4together, *[single crochet 4 times, double-treble (double-treble) into the ch-1 space from round 2, single crochet 4 times] into the subsequent ch-8 space, ch 3, skip the later double-crochet4together,* replicate from * to * 4 more times, slip stitch into the first st to secure – 48 single crochets, 6 double-treble, 6 ch-3 spaces

Fasten off 3rd color.

Round 6: 4th color: Ch 1, single crochet into the similar st as join, single crochet into the subsequent 8 sts (this includes both single crochet and double-treble), [2 single crochet, picot, 2 single crochet] into the following ch-3 space, *single crochet into the subsequent

278

9 sts, [2 single crochet, picot, 2 single crochet] into the subsequent ch-3 space,* replicate from * to * 4 more times, slip stitch into the first st to secure – 78 single crochets, 6 picots

Tie-up 4th color.

Round 7: 5th Color: Create a slip knot on your hook, spike single crochet around the first single crochet of the subsequent [2 single crochet, picot, 2 single crochet] in a ch-3 space, ch 10, spike single crochet around the last single crochet of the similar [2 single crochet, picot, 2 single crochet], ch 20, *spike single crochet spike single crochet around the first single crochet of the subsequent [2 single crochet, picot, 2 single crochet] in a ch-3 space, ch 10, spike single crochet around the last single crochet of the similar [2 single crochet, picot, 2 single crochet], ch 20,* replicate from * to * 4 more times, slip stitch into the first spike single crochet to secure – 12 spike single crochets, 6 ch-10 spaces, 6 ch-20 spaces

Tie up 5th color.

Round 8: 6th color: Create a slip knot on your hook, single crochet into a ch 20 space, single crochet 4 more times, ch 15, skip the subsequent [spike single crochet, ch-10, spike single crochet], *single crochet 5 times into the subsequent ch-20 space, ch 15, skip the subsequent [spike single crochet, ch-10, spike single crochet],*replicate from * to * 4 more times, slip stitch into the first st to secure – 30 single crochets, 6 ch-15 spaces

Round 9: Ch 1, single crochet into the similar st as join, single crochet into the subsequent st, picot, skip the subsequent st, single crochet into the subsequent 2 stitches, front post SeptTreble around the subsequent double-treble from round 5, [10 half-double-crochet, ch 5, 10 half-double-crochet] into the subsequent ch-20 space, *single crochet into the subsequent 2 sts, picot, skip the subsequent st, single crochet into the subsequent 2 sts, front post SeptTreble around the subsequent double-treble from round 5, [10 half-double-crochet, ch 5, 10 half-double-crochet] into the subsequent ch-20 space,* replicate from * to * 4 more times, slip stitch into the first st to secure – 24 single crochets, 6 picots, 6 ch-5 spaces, 6 SeptTrebles (septule-treble-crochet), 120 half-double-crochets

Tie up 6th color.

Round 10: 7th color: Pull up a loop in the first single crochet of a [2 single crochet, picot, 2 single crochet] section, ch 7 (counts as a treble and a ch 3 space), skip the subsequent [single crochet, picot, single crochet], treble into the subsequent st, ch 2, omit the subsequent 4 sts, half-double-crochet into the subsequent 5 sts, skip the subsequent 2 sts, half-double-crochet 6 times into the subsequent ch-5 space, skip the subsequent 2 sts, half-double-crochet into the subsequent 5 sts, ch 2, skip the subsequent 3 sts, *treble into the subsequent single crochet, ch 3, skip the subsequent [single crochet, picot, single crochet], treble into the subsequent st, ch 2, skip the subsequent 4 sts, half-double-crochet into the subsequent 5 sts, skip the subsequent 2 sts, half-double-crochet 6 times into the subsequent ch-5 space, skip the subsequent 2 sts, half-double-crochet into the subsequent 5 sts, ch 2, skip the subsequent 3 sts,* replicate from * to * 4 more times, slip stitch into the 4th st from the bottom of the original ch-7 to secure – 12 trebles, 96 half-double-crochets, 6 ch-3 spaces, 12 ch-2 spaces

Tie up the 7th color.

Round 11: 8th color: Create a slip knot on your hook, single crochet into a ch-3 space, ch 5, skip the subsequent [treble, ch-2 space, half-double-crochet], half-double-crochet into the subsequent 2 sts, SeptTreble into the ch-10 space from round 7 (skip the corresponding st on the round here and throughout this round), half-double-crochet into the subsequent st, ch 3, skip the subsequent 2 sts, single crochet into the subsequent st, ch 3, single crochet into the subsequent st, ch 3, skip the subsequent 2 sts, half-double-crochet into the subsequent St, SeptTreble into the ch-10 space from round 7, half-double-crochet into the subsequent 2 sts, ch 5, skip the subsequent [half-double-crochet, ch-2, treble], single crochet into the subsequent ch-3 space, ch 5, skip the subsequent [treble, ch-2 space, half-double-crochet], half-double-crochet into the subsequent 2 sts, SeptTreble into the ch-10 space from round 7 (skip the corresponding st on the round here and throughout this round), half-double-crochet into the subsequent st, ch 3, skip the subsequent 2 sts, single crochet into the subsequent st, ch 3, single crochet into the subsequent st, ch 3, skip the subsequent 2 sts, half-double-crochet into the subsequent st, SeptTreble into the ch-10 space from round 7, half-double-crochet into the subsequent 2 sts, ch 5, skip the subsequent [half-double-crochet, ch-2, treble],* replicate from * to * 4 more times, slip stitch into the first st to secure – 18 single crochets, 12 ch-5 spaces, 36 half-double-crochets, 12 SeptTrebles, 18 ch-3 spaces.

Tie up the 8th color.

Round 12: 9th color: Pull up a loop in the ch-5 space left of the first single crochet of the previous round, ch 4 (counts as a treble), [treble, Ch 3, 2 treble] into the similar ch 5 space, ch 2, skip the subsequent half-double-crochet, half-double-crochet into the subsequent 3 sts, double-crochet 3 times into the subsequent ch-3 space, ch 2, skip the subsequent single crochet, double-crochet 7 times into the subsequent ch-3 space, ch 2, skip the subsequent single crochet, double-crochet 3 times into the subsequent ch-3 space, half-double-crochet in the subsequent 3 sts, ch 2, skip the subsequent half-double-crochet, [2 treble, ch 3, 2 treble] into the subsequent ch-5 space, ch 2, skip the subsequent single crochet, *[2 treble, ch 3, 2 treble] into the subsequent ch-5 space, ch 2, skip the subsequent half-double-crochet, half-double-crochet into the subsequent 3 sts, double-crochet 3 times into the subsequent ch-3 space, ch 2, skip the subsequent single crochet, double-crochet 7 times into the subsequent ch-3 space, ch 2, skip the subsequent single crochet, double-crochet 3 times into the subsequent ch-3 space, half-double-crochet in the subsequent 3 sts, ch 2, skip the subsequent half-double-crochet, [2 treble, ch 3, 2 treble] into the subsequent ch-5 space, ch 2, skip the subsequent single crochet,* replicate from * to * 4 more times, slip stitch into the top of the original ch-4 to secure -48 trebles, 12 ch-3 spaces, 30 ch-2 spaces, 18 half-double-crochets, 78 double-crochets

Tie-up 9th color.

Carefully weave all ends.

Pattern 02: Flower Madala

Crochet Hook: 6.5mm or K/10.5

Weight of Yarn: Bulky Yarn (5) (12 to 15 stitches for four inches)

Round 1: With the first color, chain 2. Work 10 half-double-crochet in 2nd chain from hook. Join. (10 stitches)

Round 2: ch 1. Work 2 single crochet in each st around. Join. (20 stitches)

Round 3: chain 1. *Work 3 double crochet in subsequent st. Skip 1 st*. Replicate (*) around. Join. (30 stitches, or ten "clusters")

Round 4: ch 1. Working between the clusters for this round, *double crochet, three treble crochet, double crochet*. Replicate (*) around. Join. (50 stitches)

Round 5: Slip stitches over to the 2nd treble crochet. Chain 1. Single crochet in top of center treble crochet. Chain 5. *Skip subsequent four stitches. Single crochet in top of subsequent center treble crochet. Ch 5*. Replicate (*) around. Join. (10 stitches + 10 chain 5 spaces)

Round 6: ch 1. *Single crochet in single crochet st. Work {2 double crochet, treble crochet, ch 1. slip stitch in top of treble crochet just worked, treble crochet, two double crochet} in subsequent chain five space*. Replicate (*) around. Join. Tie-up and weave all ends.

Pattern 03: Mandala Beanie

- **Crochet Hook: 3.5mm or E/4 along with 4mm or G/6 hook**
- **Weight of Yarn: (0) Lace (33 to 40 stitches to four inches)**
- **Color A: Blue**
- **Color B: Cerise**
- **Color C: Purple**
- **Color D: Orange**
- **Weaving Needle**

Directions:

You will work top-down, and the brim is attached to the hat after finishing its body. This hat may look like different, and its fitting will be irregular than ordinary hats.

Guage:

- Four Rounds: 2.25 inches crossways

- Nine Rounds: 7.25 inches crossways

- Fifteen Rounds: 10.25 inches crossways

Special Stitches

Bltr (Beginning-linked-treble-crochet): Skip initial chain (insert crochet hook in the subsequent chain, yarn over, pull loop through) three times, (yarn over, pull through two loops o crochet hook) three times.

Ltr (Linked-Treble-Crochet): (insert crochet hook in the horizontal bar on one side of the previous stitch, yarn over and pull the loop through) two times, insert crochet hook in the subsequent chain, yarn over, pull loop through, [yarn over, pull through two loops on crochet hook] three times.

Directions:

Rnd 1: Start working with a larger crochet hook and use thread A, chain 4, link with slip stitch to the first ch to form a ring, ch 1, eight single crochet in ring, slip stitch to first single crochet. (Stitch count: 8 single crochet) Rnd 2: Chain 1, two single crochet in every single crochet all the way around, slip stitch to first single crochet. (Stitch count: 16 single crochet) Rnd 3: Chain 1, [single crochet in single crochet, two single crochet in subsequent single crochet] all the way around. (Stitch count: 24 single crochet) Tie up A.

Rnd 4: Use B color, working in bl (back loops) only for this rnd, join with slip stitch in any single crochet, chain 3 (it is considered as double crochet), double crochet in same single crochet as joining, *double crochet in subsequent single crochet, 2 double crochet in following single crochet, replicate from * to last single crochet, double crochet in last single crochet, slip stitch to top of beg ch-3. (Stitch count: 36 double crochet) Tie-upB.

Rnd 5: Use Color C, join with slip stitch in any double crochet, *ch 12, bltr, ltr in every remaining ch, skip 2 double crochet from rnd 4, slip stitch to subsequent double crochet with D (9 ltr-petal made), drop color C, now start with D, replicate from *, changing to C on slip stitch, carry on replicate from * until 12 petals are created, alternating colors, ending with slip stitch in first slip stitch. Carefully change color to avoid "cupping" of the project. If you want this strand on the back, you can cut off every petal to change colors. Or, alternatively, work this rnd in only one color. (Stitch count: 12 9-ltr petals created) Tie-upC and D.

Rnd 6: With A, join with slip stitch to the bottom of any petal on the base row side (where you did your initial chain 12), chain 1, *9 single crochet along side of petal, [2 single crochet in unused loop of chain at top of petal] 2 times, 9 single crochet along opposite side of petal, ch 3, slip stitch in unused corresponding front loop of single crochet of rnd 3, ch 3, replicate from * all the way around every of 12 petals, slip stitch to first single crochet.

Rnd 7: Slip stitch to 5th single crochet at side of the petal, ch 1, *single crochet in subsequent six single crochet, chain 1, single crochet in subsequent six single crochet, skip ten single crochet, replicate from * until all petals completed, slip stitch to first single crochet.

Rnd 8: Ch 1, *single crochet in subsequent five single crochet, three single crochet in ch-1 sp, single crochet in subsequent five single crochet, skip two single crochet, replicate from * until all petals are completed, slip stitch to first single crochet.

Rnd 9: Slip stitch to subsequent single crochet, ch 1, *single crochet in subsequent 4 single crochet, 3 single crochet in subsequent single crochet, single crochet in subsequent 4 single crochet, ch 3, skip 4 single crochet, replicate from * until all petals completed, slip stitch to first single crochet. Tie-upA.

Rnd 10: Join B with slip stitch in any ch-3 sp, ch 4 (counts as tr here and throughout), 8 tr in same ch 3 sp, *single crochet in 2nd single crochet of 3-single crochet group at top of petal, 9 treble in subsequent ch-3 sp, replicate from *, ending with single crochet in last petal, slip stitch to top of beginning ch-4. Tie-upB.

Rnd 11: Join A with slip stitch in any single crochet, ch 4, 6 tr in same single crochet, *skip tr, single crochet in subsequent 7 tr, skip tr, 7 tr in single crochet at top of subsequent petal, replicate from * to last 9-tr group, skip tr, single crochet in subsequent 7 tr, skip tr, slip stitch to top of beginning ch-4.

Rnd 12: Ch 1, single crochet in the same tr as joining and in subsequent six tr, *hdouble crochet in subsequent seven single crochet, single crochet in subsequent seven tr, replicate from * ending with hdouble crochet in last 7 single crochet, slip stitch to first single crochet. Tie-upA.

Rnd 13: Working in bl (back loops) only for this rnd, join D with slip stitch in top of same beginning st of previous rnd, ch 3, skip joining St, double crochet in every st all the way around, slip stitch to top of beginning ch-3. (Stitch count: 168 double crochet) Tie-upD.

Rnd 14: Join A with slip stitch in top of same beginning ch-3, ch 1, single crochet in same joining st, single crochet in subsequent 2 double crochet, *double crochet in corresponding unworked front loop of st from rnd below (in this rnd, you're looking at the stitches in rnd 12), skip double crochet behind double crochet just worked, single crochet in subsequent 3 double crochet, replicate from * to last st, double crochet in corresponding unworked front loop of single crochet from rnd below, skip double crochet behind double crochet just worked, slip stitch to first single crochet.

Rnd 15: Ch 1, single crochet in every stitch all the way around, slip stitch to first single crochet. (stitch count: 168 single crochet) Tie up A.

Rnd 16: Working in bl (back loops) only for this rnd, join C with slip stitch in top of same single crochet as joining, ch 3, skip joining st, double crochet in every st all the way around, slip stitch to top of beginning ch-3, (stitch count: 168 double crochet) Tie-up C.

Rnds 17-18: With A, replicate rnds 14-15. Tie-up A.

Rnd 19: Working in bl (back loops) only for this rnd, join B with slip stitch in top of same single crochet as joining, ch 3, skip joining st, double crochet in every st all the way around, slip stitch to top of beginning ch-3, (stitch count: 168 double crochet) Tie-upB.

Rnds 20-21: With A, replicate rnds 14to 15. Tie-up A.

Rnd 22: Working in bl (back loops) only for this rnd, join D with slip stitch in top of same single crochet as joining, ch 3, skip joining st, double crochet in every st all the way around, slip stitch to top of beginning ch-3, (stitch count: 168 double crochet) Tie-upD.

Rnds 23-24: Replicate rnds 14-15. Do not Tie-up A.

Brim

Row 1: (Still attached to hat, ribbing is worked vertically along stitches of hat.) With smaller hook and A, ch 9, single crochet in the second ch from hook and in subsequent seven ch, on hat body skip two single crochet from rnd 24, slip stitch in subsequent st, turn ribbing.

Row 2: Working in bl (back loops) only, single crochet in 8 single crochet, turn ribbing.

Row 3: Ch 1, working in bl (back loops) only, single crochet in 8 single crochet, on hat body skip 2 single crochet from rnd 24, slip stitch in subsequent st, turn ribbing.

Replicate rows 2-3 until all stitches used from rnd 24, carefully fasten off.

Finishing

It is time to use your yarn needle and stitch the brim, securely weave all ends.

Pattern 04: Crochet Doily

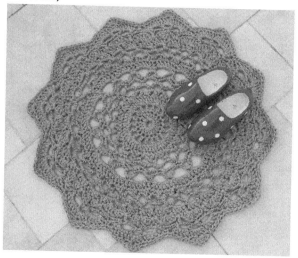

Start your work with 12mm crochet hook and two skeins yarn.

R1: Ch8, slip stitch in the first chain to link a ring. Ch3, 17double crochet in ring. Slip stitch in top of beginning ch3. (18double crochet)

R2: Ch4, do not flip. (Double crochet in subsequent st, ch1) around. Join with slip stitch in 3rd ch of beginning ch4.

R3: Slip stitch in subsequent ch sp. Ch3, 2double crochet in the same sp. 3double crochet in each remaining ch sp. Join with slip stitch to beginning ch3. (54double crochet)

R4: Ch1. Work the following crossways ea 3double crochet group: Single crochet in 1st double crochet, half-double-crochet in 2nd double crochet, double crochet in 3rd double crochet, chain 3.

R5: Slip stitch in beginning single crochet made. Slip stitch in double crochet. Single crochet in the three ch space. Ch5 (Single crochet in the space between the subsequent double crochet and three chains, ch5) around. Slip stitch in beginning single crochet made.

R6: Ch5. (Single crochet in subsequent ch5 space, ch5) around. Instead of finishing with ch5, end with ch2 and double crochet in first single crochet.

R7: Ch1. In the subsequent loop: (Single crochet, ch5, single crochet) chain 1 and subsequent loop (single crochet, ch5, single crochet). Continue around, and after last single crochet ch1 and slip stitch in beginning single crochet.

R8: Slip stitch in the initial 5ch loop, single crochet into a loop, ch6, single crochet in the subsequent loop, ch6 around. After the last ch6, slip stitch into initial single crochet.

R9: Ch3, five double crochet in the loop, one double crochet in subsequent single crochet, five double crochet in the loop, one double crochet in following single crochet. Continue around, finishing with 6double crochet in the last loop, and join with slip stitch to top of initial ch3.

R10: Ch1, single crochet in the same stitch, half-double-crochet in subsequent stitch, double crochet in following stitch, chain 3. Continue with single crochet,half-double-crochet,double crochet,ch3 sequence around and join with slip stitch to the first stitch.

R11: Slip stitches up to 3 ch loops. Single crochet in the loop, ch5, single crochet in a subsequent loop. After last ch5 join with slip stitch to initial single crochet.

R12: Single crochet in the loop, chain 5, single crochet in the subsequent loop, ch5. Continue around, and at finish ch2 and double crochet in first single crochet.

287

R13: Ch3, three double crochet in initial ch5 loop, 4double crochet in the subsequent loop, and four double crochet in every ch5 loop around. Join to initial chain with slip stitch.

R 14 chain 1 *Sk 1 st, six double crochet in subsequent st, sk 1 st, single crochet in subsequent st* continue around and slip stitch at first ch.

R15 chain 5 (counts as one double crochet + chain 2), *single crochet in 4th double crochet, chain 2, double crochet in single crochet between shells, chain 2* continue around and slip stitch at 3rd ch of the initial five ch.

R 16 *Chain 3, sc subsequent ch2 sp, (double crochet,ch2, double crochet) in subsequent single crochet (V-st made), ch3, sk following ch2 sp, slip stitch in subsequent six stitches, repeat from * continue around and slip stitch in initial st.

R 17 ch1, Sk subsequent ch2 sp of round 16, *5double crochet in each of following three ch3 spaces (fan made), sk subsequent three slip stitch single crochet in following slip stitch (above single crochet from round 15); repeat from * around, slip stitch in beginning ch to join.

R18: Optional. Single crochet around, for pointing, crochet 3double crochet in the middle double crochet in each of the fan. Tie up and weave in the end.

Pattern 05: Spring Rug

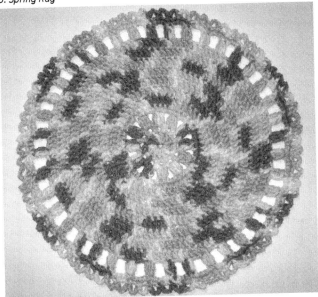

Materials: 2.5 oz. (4-ply worsted yarn)

Crochet Hook- J hook

Total Size: 13 1/2" crossways

Notes:

- Crochet tightly to adjust the size on the hook.
- Chain 2 at the start of rounds 5 to 10, it is not a stitch
- **Start cluster:** chain 2, yarn over, insert crochet hook in its space, yarn over, drag through yarn over, pull through two loops, yarn over, insert hook in the similar space, yarn over, pull through, yarn over, pull through two loops, yarn over, pull through last three loops.
- **Clusters:** yarn over, insert crochet hook in its space, pull through, yarn over, pull through two loops, yarn over, insert hook in the similar space, yarn over, pull through, yarn over, pull through two loops, yarn over, insert hook in the same place, yarn over, pull through, yarn over, pull through two loops, yarn over, pull through last four loops.

Directions:

Round 1: Ch 3 (make the 1st chain a little loose), 12 double crochet in 3rd ch from hook. Seam with a slip stitch to 1st double crochet.

Round 2: Ch 1, single crochet in the similar St as seaming, ch 2. (single crochet, ch 2) in subsequent double crochet around. Seam with a slip stitch to 1st single crochet.

Round 3: Slip stitch into the ch-2 space, beginning cluster in similar ch-2 space, ch 2. (cluster, ch 2) in subsequent ch-2 space around. Seam with a slip stitch to top of beginning cluster.

Round 4: Ch 1, two single crochet in similar st as seaming. 2 single crochet in each cluster and ch-2 space around. Seam with a slip stitch to 1st single crochet.

Round 5: Ch 2, double crochet in similar st as seaming. Double crochet in each single crochet around. Seam with a slip stitch to 1st double crochet.

Round 6: Ch 2, 2 double crochet in similar st as seaming, double crochet in subsequent 3 double crochet. *2 double crochet in subsequent double crochet, double crochet in subsequent 3 double crochet. Repeat from * around. Seam as before.

Round 7: Ch 2, 2 double crochet in similar st as seaming, double crochet in subsequent 4 double crochet. *2 double crochet in subsequent double crochet, double crochet in subsequent 4 double crochet. Repeat from * around. Seam as before.

Round 8: Ch 2, 2 double crochet in similar st as seaming, double crochet in subsequent 5 double crochet. *2 double crochet in subsequent double crochet, double crochet in subsequent 5 double crochet. Repeat from * around. Seam as before.

Round 9: Ch 2, 2 double crochet in similar st as seaming, double crochet in subsequent 6 double crochet. *2 double crochet in subsequent double crochet, double crochet in subsequent 6 double crochet. Repeat from * around. Seam as before.

Round 10: Ch 2, 2 double crochet in similar st as seaming, double crochet in subsequent 7 double crochet. *2 double crochet in subsequent double crochet, double crochet in subsequent 7 double crochet. Repeat from * around. Seam as before.

Round 11: Ch 2, 2 double crochet in similar st as seaming, double crochet in subsequent 8 double crochet. *2 double crochet in subsequent double crochet, double crochet in subsequent 8 double crochet. Repeat from * around. Seam as before.

Round 12: Beginning cluster in similar st as seaming, ch 3, skip subsequent two double crochet. *cluster in subsequent double crochet, ch 3, skip subsequent two double crochet. Repeat from * around. Seam with a slip stitch to top of beginning cluster.

Round 13: Ch 1, single crochet in similar st as seaming, three single crochet in ch-3 space. *single crochet in top of cluster, three single crochet in ch-3 space. Repeat from * around. Seam with a slip stitch to 1st single crochet.

Round 14: Ch 1, single crochet in similar st as seaming, ch 3, skip subsequent single crochet. *single crochet in subsequent single crochet, ch 3, skip subsequent single crochet. Replicate from * all the way around. Join as you do it before. Finish off.

Pattern 06: Colorful Mini Mandala

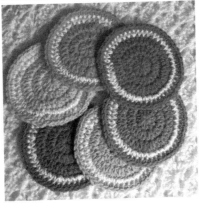

Finished Size: 4.5 inches diameter

Note: You can use different colors as per your choice.

Coaster: You can make more than one with different colors and in each coaster mandala, you will use White pulse.

291

Round 1: Start your choice. Using the "Magic Circle", Ch 1. Work 12 half-double-crochet in the circle. Join with sl st (slip stitch) to the top of first half-double-crochet. (12 half-double-crochet)

Round 2: Chain 1. Work 1 half-double-crochet in similar stitch as Ch 1. Work 2 half-double-crochet in each stitch around. Join to first half-double-crochet with sl st (slip stitch). (24 half-double-crochet)

Round 3: Chain 1. Work 1 half-double-crochet in similar stitch as Ch 1. *Work 1 half-double-crochet in subsequent stitch. Work 2 half-double-crochet in subsequent stitch.* Repeat from * to * around. Join to first half-double-crochet with sl st (slip stitch).

Round 4: Use White color. Chain 1. Work 1 single crochet in similar stitch as Ch 1. *Work 1 single crochet in subsequent two stitches. Work 2 single crochet in subsequent stitch. * Repeat from * to * around. Join to first single crochet with sl st (slip stitch).

Round 5: change to original color. Chain 1. Single crochet in every stitch around.

Tie up and weave all loose ends

Pattern 07: Flower Mandala

You have to make large hooks and use B color for chain 2, first round: 6 single crochet in the second chain from hook. Unite with slip stitch in first sc.

2nd round: Ch 1. You will start work in front rings, 1 single crochet in first single crochet. (1 half-double crochet. 2 double crochet. 1 half-double crochet) in subsequent single crochet. *1 single crochet in subsequent single crochet. (1 half-double crochet. 2 double crochet. 1 half-double crochet) in subsequent sc. Replicate from * once more. Do not join with slip stitch. 3 petals.

3rd round: Do not ch 1. Working in rem back rings of 1st round, 2 sc in every sc around. Join with slip stitch to first sc. 12 sc.

4th round: Ch 1. Working in front rings only, 1 sc in first sc. (1 half-double crochet. 2 double crochet. 1 half-double crochet) in subsequent sc. *1 sc in subsequent sc. (1 half-double crochet. 2 double crochet. 1 half-double crochet) in subsequent sc. Replicate from * 4 times more. Do not join with slip stitch. 6 petals.

5th round: Do not ch 1. Working in rem back rings of 3rd round, 2 sc in first sc. 1 sc in subsequent sc. (2 sc in subsequent sc. 1 sc in subsequent sc) 5 times. Join with slip stitch to first sc. 18 sc.

6th round: Ch 1. Working in front rings only, 1 sc in first sc. (1 half-double crochet. 2 double crochet. 1 half-double crochet) in subsequent sc. *1 sc in subsequent sc. (1 half-double crochet. 2 double crochet. 1 half-double crochet) in subsequent sc. Replicate from * 7 times more. Do not join with slip stitch. 9 petals.

7th round: Do not ch 1. Working in rem back rings of 5th round, 2 sc first sc. 1 sc in every of subsequent 2 sc. (2 sc in subsequent sc. 1 sc in every of subsequent 2 sc) 5 times. Join with slip stitch to first sc. 24 sc.

8th round: Ch 1. Working in front rings only, 1 sc in first sc. (1 half-double crochet. 2 double crochet. 1 half-double crochet) in subsequent sc. *1 sc in subsequent sc. (1 half-double crochet. 2 double crochet. 1 half-double crochet) in subsequent sc. Replicate from * 10 times more. Do not join with slip stitch. 12 petals.

9th round: Do not ch 1. It is time to handle rem back rings of seventh round , 2 single crochet first single crochet. 1 single crochet in every of subsequent 3 single crochet. (2 single crochet in subsequent single crochet. 1 single crochet in every of subsequent 3 single crochet) 5 times. Join with slip stitch to first single crochet. 30 single crochet.

10th round: Ch 1. Working in front rings only, 1 single crochet in first single crochet. (1 half-double crochet. 2 double crochet. 1 half-double crochet) in subsequent single crochet. *1 single crochet in subsequent single crochet. (1 half-double crochet. 2 double crochet. 1 half-double crochet) in subsequent single crochet. Replicate from * 13 times more. Join with slip stitch to first single crochet. Fasten off. It will be 15 petals.

- Worsted Weight yarn: 8ply black
- Crochet hook: 4mm
- Needles to weave ends

Directions:

Round 1 (Colour A): Make one slip-knot, chain four, and join with a slip-stitch to initiate the. Ch2, and work 11 double crochet (double crochet) into the middle of the ring. Join to the top of the initial ch2 with a slip-stitch, and fasten off Colour A.

Round 2 (Colour B): Use B color, chain 2, and work 1half-double-crochet (half-double crochet) into a similar place. Work 2half-double-crochet into each stitch of the previous round. Join to top of initial ch2 with a slip-stitch, and fasten off Colour B.

Round 3 (Black): Flip the side of the coaster, and join Black. Chain2, one half-double-crochet into a similar place. *1half-double-crochet in next stitch, then 2half-double-crochet in next stitch,* replicate from * to * until one stitch remains, 1half-double-crochet in final stitch. Join to top of initial ch2 with a slip-stitch.

Round 4: Ch2, 1half-double-crochet into a similar place. *1half-double-crochet, 1half-double-crochet, 2half-double-crochet,* replicate until one stitch remains, half-double-crochet in final stitch. Note: the 2half-double-crochet will fall between the 2half-double-crochet of the previous round. Seam to the top of initial ch2 with a slip-stitch.

Round 5: Ch2, 1half-double-crochet into a similar place. *1half-double-crochet, 1half-double-crochet, 1half-double-crochet, 2half-double-crochet,* replicate until 1 stitch remains, 1half-double-crochet. Join to top of initial ch2 with a slip-stitch.

Round 6: Ch1, 1single crochet into a similar place. Single crochet into each stitch of the previous round. Join to first single crochet with a slip-stitch.

Tie up yarn, weave all its ends.

Pattern 09: Mandala Blanket

- **Yarn: 104 yds or .95 m**
- **A Color: 4 balls**
- **B color: 2 balls**
- **C color: 2 balls**
- **D color: 2 Balls**
- **E Color: 2 balls**
- **F Color: 2 balls**
- **9mm or N/15 crochet hook**

Measurements: 185 cm or 73 inches in diameter

Directions:

Stripe Perfectly

Start with A color - 2 rounds. Use B color - 1 round. Use C color - 1 rnd. Use d color - 1 rnd. Use E color - 1 rnd. Use F color - 1 rnd.

These seven rounds to form Stripe perfectly.

Notes: You will use a new color for joining and work to last two loops on the hook. Yarn over the hook with a fresh color and drag through two loops on the crochet hook.

- Ch 3 at beg of round counts as a double crochet. Ch 4 at beg of round counts as treble.

- Link all rounds with sl st to first single crochet or top of ch 3 (4).

Start with A color, ch 2.

Proceed in Strebleipe Pat as follows:

1st round: 10 single crochet in 2nd ch from hook. Link with sl st to the top of ch 3. 10 single crochet.

2nd round: Ch 3. 1 double crochet in similar space as sl st. 2 double crochet in every double crochet around. Link B. 20 double crochet.

3rd round: Use B color, ch 1. *1 single crochet in subsequent double crochet. Two single crochet in subsequent double crochet. Replicate from * around. Link C. 30 single crochet.

4th round: Use C color, ch 4. 1 treble in every of subsequent two single crochet. *2 treble in subsequent single crochet. One treble in every of subsequent two single crochet. Replicate from * around. Link D. 40 treble.

296

5th round: Use d color, ch 1. *2 single crochet in the subsequent treble. One single crochet in every of subsequent three trebles. Replicate from * around. Link E. 50 single crochet.

6th round: Use E color, ch 3. one double crochet in subsequent single crochet. *2 double crochet in subsequent single crochet. One double crochet in every of subsequent four single crochet. Replicate from * to last two single crochet. One double crochet in every of last two single crochet. Link F. 60 double crochet.

7th round: Use F color, ch 1. *2 single crochet in subsequent double crochet. One single crochet in every of subsequent five double crochet. Replicate from * around. Link A. 70 single crochet.

8th round: Start with A color, ch 4. 1 treble in every of subsequent two single crochet. *2 treble in subsequent single crochet. One treble in every of subsequent six single crochet. Replicate from * to last four single crochet. Two treble in subsequent single crochet. One treble in every of last three single crochet. Link. 80 treble.

9th round: Ch 1. *2 single crochet in the subsequent treble. One single crochet in every of subsequent seven trebles. Replicate from * around. Link B. 90 single crochet.

10th round: Use B color, ch 3. one double crochet in every of subsequent two single crochet. *2 double crochet in subsequent single crochet. One double crochet in every of following eight single crochet. Replicate from * to last six single crochet. Two double crochet in subsequent single crochet. One double crochet in every of last five single crochet. Link C. 100 double crochet.

11th round: Use C color, ch 1. *2 single crochet in subsequent double crochet. One single crochet in every of subsequent nine double crochet. Replicate from * around. Link D. 110 single crochet.

12th round: Use d color, ch 4. 1 treble in every of subsequent three single crochet. *2 treble in subsequent single crochet. One treble in every of subsequent ten single crochet. Replicate from * to last seven single crochet. Two treble in subsequent single crochet. One treble in every of last six single crochet. Link E. 120 treble.

13th round: Use e color, ch 1. *2 single crochet in the subsequent treble. One single crochet in every of subsequent 11 trebles. Replicate from * around. Link F. 130 single crochet.

14th round: Use F color, ch 3. one double crochet in every of subsequent four single crochet. *2 double crochet in following single crochet. One double crochet in every of subsequent 12 single crochet. Replicate from * to last eight single crochet. Two double crochet in subsequent single crochet. One double crochet in every of last seven single crochet. Link A. 140 double crochet.

15th round: Start with A color, ch 1. *2 single crochet in subsequent double crochet. One single crochet in every of subsequent 13 double crochet. Replicate from * around. Link. 150 single crochet.

16th round: Ch 4. 1 treble in every of subsequent five single crochet. *2 treble in subsequent single crochet. One treble in every of subsequent 14 single crochet. Replicate from * to last nine single crochet. Two treble in subsequent single crochet. One treble in every of last eight single crochet. Link B. 160 treble.

Continue in a similar manner and include ten stitches in every round and work in the following sequence: single crochet round, double crochet round, single crochet round, treble round, until work measures almost 70" (178 cm) diameter. Tie-up.

Pattern 10: Mandala Pouch
- **Weight of Yarn:** Lace (33 to 40 stitches to four inches) (0)
- **Crochet Thread:** 8 Size Yarn
- **Hook:** Crochet hook of steel 2.20mm or 3 size hook
- **Lace ribbon:** 18 inches long to tie
- **Circumference:** 2 ¾ inches and Height: 3 ¾ inches

Special Stitches Instructions:

2dc-bobble: Yo (yarn over), insert crochet hook in stitch and pull yarn thread from side to side, yo and draw through two loops on crochet hook, Yo, put in in similar stitch and pull this thread through, yarn over and draw through two loops on hook, yarn over and draw through all three loops on crochet hook.)

dc2tog: Yarn over, put in crochet hook in stitch and draw thread through, yarn over and pull through two loops on hook, Yarn over, insert in subsequent stitch and drag thread through, yarn over and draw through two loops on crochet hook, yarn over and draw through all three loops on crochet hook.)

Directions:

Use cotton thread of size 8

chain 3 (consider as 1 double crochet).

Round 1: 11 double crochet in the initial chain (12 double crochet made). Slip stitch in top of initial double crochet to join.

Round 2: Chain 3, double crochet in same st, 2 double crochet in every double crochet, slip stitch in top of initial double crochet to join. (24 double crochet)

Round 3: Chain 3, *chain 1, double crochet in subsequent double crochet, replicate from * all around ending with chain 1, slip stitch in top of initial double crochet to join.

Round 4: Chain 3, double crochet in same double crochet, *chain 2, 2double crochet-bobble in subsequent double crochet, replicate from * all around ending with chain 2, slip stitch in top of initial double crochet to join.

Round 5: *Chain 7, skip 1 bobble, single crochet in a subsequent bobble, replicate from * all around. (12 chain-7 loops made)

Round 6: Slip stitch to the corner of chain-7 loop, chain 3 (consider as 1 double crochet), 6 double crochet in the loop, *chain 2, 7 double crochet in the subsequent loop, replicate from * all around, ending with chain 2, slip stitch in initial double crochet to join.

Round 7: Chain 3, double crochet in subsequent 6 double crochet, *chain 2, double crochet in subsequent 7 double crochet, skip 2-chain space, double crochet in subsequent 7 double crochet, replicate from * all around ending with slip stitch in initial double crochet to join.

Round 8: Slip stitch to top of 2nd double crochet, chain 3, double crochet in subsequent 5 double crochet, *chain 3, double crochet in subsequent 6 double crochet, skip 2 double crochet, double crochet in subsequent 6 double crochet, replicate from * all around ending with slip stitch in initial double crochet to join.

Round 9: Slip stitch to top of 2nd double crochet, chain 3, double crochet in subsequent 4 double crochet, *chain 3, 5 double crochet in chain-3 space, chain 3, double crochet in subsequent 5 double crochet, skip 2 double crochet, double crochet in subsequent 5 double crochet, replicate from * all around, ending with slip stitch in initial double crochet to join.

Round 10: Slip stitch to top of 2nd double crochet, chain 3, double crochet in subsequent 3 double crochet, *chain 3, [double crochet in subsequent double crochet, chain 1] 4 times, double crochet in subsequent double crochet, chain 3, double crochet in subsequent 4 double crochet, skip 2 double crochet, double crochet in subsequent 4 double crochet, replicate from * all around, ending with slip stitch in initial double crochet to join.

Round 11: Slip stitch to top of 2nd double crochet, chain 3, double crochet in subsequent 2 double crochet, *chain 3, skip chain-3 space[single crochet in chain-1 loop, chain 3] 3 times, single crochet in last chain-1 loop, chain 3, double crochet in subsequent 3 double crochet, skip 2 double crochet, double crochet in subsequent 3 double crochet, replicate from * all around, ending with slip stitch in initial double crochet to join.

Round 12: Slip stitch to top of 2nd double crochet, chain 3, double crochet in subsequent double crochet, *chain 3, skip chain-3 space, [single crochet in chain-3 loop, chain 3] 2 times, single crochet in last chain-3 loop, chain 3, double crochet in subsequent 2 double crochet, skip 2 double crochet, double crochet in subsequent 2 double crochet, replicate from * all around, ending with slip stitch in initial double crochet to join.

Round 13: Chain 3, double crochet in subsequent double crochet, *chain 3, skip chain-3 space, single crochet in chain-3 loop, chain 3, single crochet in subsequent chain-3 loop, chain 3, double crochet2tog in subsequent 2 double crochet, chain 5, double crochet2tog in subsequent 2 double crochet, replicate from * all around, ending with chain 5, slip stitch in top of initial double crochet to join.

Round 14: Chain 6 (make 1 double crochet, chain 3), *skip chain-3 space, single crochet in chain-3 loop, chain 3, 7 double crochet in the chain-5 loop, chain 3, replicate from * all around ending with 6 double crochet in last chain-5 loop. Slip stitch in top of double crochet (3rd chain of chain 6) to join.

300

Round 15: Chain 6 (make 1 double crochet, chain 3), *skip (3 chain, single crochet, 3 chain), double crochet in subsequent double crochet, [chain 1, double crochet in subsequent double crochet] 6 times, chain 3, replicate from * all around ending with chain 1, slip stitch in top of initial double crochet to join.

Round 16: Slip stitch to chain-1 space, *chain 3, double crochet in chain-3 space, [chain 3, single crochet in chain-1 space] 6 times, replicate from * all around.

Round 17: Slip stitch up chain 3 to tip of double crochet, chain 3, 2 double crochet in same double crochet, *[chain 3, single crochet in chain-3 loop] 5 times, chain 3, 3 double crochet in subsequent double crochet, replicate from * all around ending with chain 3, slip stitch in initial double crochet to join.

Round 18: Chain 4 (consider as 1 double crochet, chain 1), double crochet in subsequent double crochet, chain 1, double crochet in subsequent double crochet, *[chain 3, single crochet in chain-3 loop] 4 times, chain 3, [double crochet in subsequent double crochet, chain 1] 2 times, double crochet in subsequent double crochet, replicate from * all around ending with chain 3, slip stitch in initial double crochet in to join.

Round 19: Chain 3, double crochet in same double crochet, *[chain 1, 2 double crochet in subsequent double crochet] 2 times, [chain 3, single crochet in chain-3 loop] 3 times, chain 3, 2 double crochet in subsequent double crochet, replicate from * all around, ending with chain 3, slip stitch in initial double crochet to join.

Round 20: Chain 3, double crochet in same double crochet, *[chain 1, 2 double crochet in subsequent double crochet] 5 times, [chain 3, single crochet in chain-3 loop] 2 times, chain 3, 2 double crochet in subsequent double crochet, replicate from * all around, ending with chain 3, slip stitch in initial double crochet to join. (You should have 12 2-double crochet groups in every single each scallop)

Round 21: Chain 3, double crochet in subsequent double crochet, *[chain 3, slip stitch in 3rd chain from hook to make picot, double crochet2tog in subsequent 2 double crochet] 5 times, chain 3, single crochet in chain-3 loop, picot, chain 3, double crochet2tog in subsequent 2 double crochet, replicate from * all around, ending with chain 3, slip stitch in initial double crochet to join. Tie up.

Dry and block. Use lace ribbon to weave 14 rounds and keep ribbon behind 7 (dc) double crochet group. Tie all ends of lace ribbon and make a knot as per your desire.

Pattern 11: Mandala Bag for Market

- 2 balls of yarn
- Crochet hook: I hook or 5.5mm
- Yarn needle and scissors

Directions:

- Chain 2

- Rnd 1: Work 6 single crochet in the first chain

- Rnd 2: Work 2 single crochet in every single crochet around - 12 st

- Rnd 3: *2 single crochet in subsequent st, single crochet in subsequent st, replicate from * around - 18 st

- Rnd 4: *2 single crochet in subsequent st, single crochet in every of subsequent two stitches, replicate from * around - 24 stitches

- Rnd 5: *2 single crochet in subsequent st, single crochet in every of subsequent three stitches, replicate from * around - 30 stitches

- Rnd 6: *2 single crochet in subsequent st, single crochet in every of subsequent four stitches, replicate from * around - 36 stitches

- Rnd 7: *2 single crochet in subsequent st, single crochet in every of subsequent five stitches, replicate from * around - 42 stitches

- Rnd 8: *2 single crochet in subsequent st, single crochet in every of subsequent six stitches, replicate from * around - 48 stitches
- Rnd 9: *2 single crochet in subsequent st, single crochet in every of subsequent seven stitches, replicate from * around - 54 stitches

- Rnd 10: half-double-crochet -54 st

It is time to form a lattice, chain 5, skip two stitches, single crochet, replicate from * the last single crochet should be in the initial single crochet

*chain 6, single crochet to the middle of the subsequent loop, replicate from * till conclusion of row

*chain 7, single crochet to the middle of the subsequent loop, replicate from * until conclusion of your row

*chain 8, single crochet to the middle of the subsequent loop, replicate from * until the end of your row

*chain 9, single crochet to the midst of the subsequent loop, replicate from *work seven rows of chain 9

*Ch 5, single crochet to middle of the subsequent loop, replicate from *until the end

single crochet into chain 5 row and single crochet 2 to 3 extra rows

Finish the top row and mark the place of handles with single crochet. To make a handle, you can crochet 3 to 4 rows of single crochet, or you can get your desired length. Weave all ends, and the bag is ready.

Pattern 12: Mandala Shoulder Bag
- Crochet Hook: Size H
- Fabric for Cotton Lining: 1 yd
- Worsted Yarn: 1 ball or more
- Matching thread and needle

Notes:

Chain three at the finishing of every row will be counted as the first double crochet of the subsequent row.

Pattern:

Chain 4; join with a slip stitch to form a ring.

Round 1: Chain 3 to count as the first dc, work 7 more dc in the ring; chain 3, flip. (8 dc)

Round 2: Dc in the first dc, 2 dc in every remaining dc across; chain 3, flip. (16 dc)

Round 3: Replicate round 2. (32 dc)

Round 4: Dc in the first dc and in every dc across, 2 dc in the top of the flipping chain; chain 3, flip. (34 dc) (Increase at every finishing off the round.)

Round 5: Replicate round 4. (36 dc)

Round 6: Replicate round 2. (72 dc)

Round 7: Replicate round 4. (74 dc)

Round 8: Replicate round 4. (76 dc)

Round 9: Replicate round 4. (78 dc)

Round 10: Replicate round 4. (80 dc)

Round 11: Dc in the first dc (dc in the subsequent dc, 2 dc in the subsequent dc) across, dc in the flipping chain; chain 3, flip. (120 dc)

Round 12: Replicate round 4. (122 dc)

Round 13: Replicate round 4. (124 dc)

Round 14: Replicate round 4. (126 dc)

Round 15: Replicate round 4. (128 dc)

Round 16: Replicate round 4. (130 dc) Tie up. Weave in all ends.

Handle

Chain 220; being careful not to twist chain, join with a slip stitch to the first chain.

Round 1: Chain 3 to count as the first double crochet, double crochet in every chain around; join with a slip stitch to the top of the beginning chain 3. (220 double crochet)

Round 2: Replicate round 1.

Note: You will need additional yarn if you want to make 5 rows.

Rounds 3 to 5: Replicate round 1.

Assembly

Iron every crocheted part to block. If you want to line your bag, you can lay the crocheted parts of the fabric to trace the pattern of crocheted parts. Make sure to add seam allowance and cut along with traced line. Sew this lining to fit in the bag and flip its inside out. Slip stitch row 16 of one crocheted piece pieces to 130 stitches of row 5 of a handle, then carry on working slip stitch's in the leftover 90 handle stitches; seam with a slip stitch to the initial slip stitch; Tie up. Slip stitch row 16 of the other bag piece to 130 stitches of all free loops of the base chain of this handle, carry on working a slip stitch in the left over 90 handle stitches; seam with a slip stitch to the initial slip stitch; Tie up. Weave its ends.

Insert lining into your bag and whip stitch to the handle and opening of the bag. You can sew inside of the bag, after the initial ring.

Conclusion

Try these mandala patterns that are beautiful and easy to crochet. Step-by-step guidance is available with each pattern. You can use these patterns to design bags and gifts for your friends and family members.

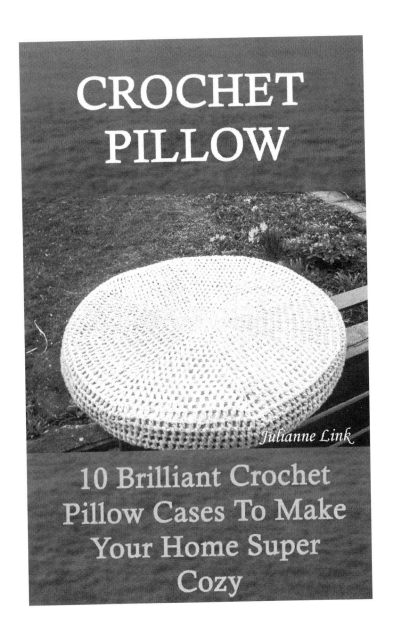

CROCHET PILLOW

Julianne Link

10 Brilliant Crochet Pillow Cases To Make Your Home Super Cozy

Crochet Pillow:

10 Brilliant Crochet Pillow Cases To Make Your Home Super Cozy

Introduction

Classic and stylish pillow covers with striking designs changes the look of place all together. They bring an ideal make over to interior and spruces up the décor of your room. These decorative crafts are adorable and have impact of lively and vibrant surroundings.

Crocheting has been practiced many years. They are being used to make hats, Beanies, jerseys, scarves and different other accessories plus frocks, dresses, blankets etc. It is basically a method of fabric creation. Crochet hook is used to inter lock the strands of thread, yarn or any other material. Different sort of stitches and patterns are used to create different crochet designs.

This book will get you through ten different crochet patterns or stitches for making cushion pillows. Everything you need to know about them is covered.

All you need to crochet is a crochet hook, some yarn and a pair of scissors, this eBook and that's set. Crochet hand books are also available to help you in making different patterns. Further crochet tutorials are available on internet, which will help you in learning different techniques and methods to be expert in it. These tutorials along with this book will be your ultimate solution to crochet pillows.

Remember don't lose heart on holding hook and if you are not able to dangle it. Practice again and again and that will not only make you capable of doing it but also to be an expert in it. Consider the following chart that will help you throughout the book to understand abbreviations. These abbreviations will be repeated throughout the book.

FREQUENTLY USED ABBREVIATIONS

beg	beginning
CC	contrast color
ch(s)	chain(s)
ch sp	chain space
cl(s)	cluster(s)
cont	continue
dc	double crochet
dec(ing)	decrease(ing)
ea	each
est	established
hdc	half double crochet
hk	hook
in(s)	inch(es)
inc(ing)	increase(ing)
MC	main color
pat st	pattern stitch
prev	previous
rem(ing)	remain(ing)
rep(s)	repeat(s)
rnd	round
RS	right side
sc	single crochet
sk	skip
sl	slip
sl st	slip stitch
sp(s)	space(s)
st(s)	stitch(es)
tog	together
tr	treble crochet
WS	wrong side
YO	yarn over

Here we will be discussing about ten different techniques and design to give you efficiency over versatile crochet designs.

Design no. 1 Checkerboard Pillow crochet Pattern

Requirements

- 9 oz weight yarn (one color)
- 8 oz weight yarn(second color)
- crochet hook
- needle
- 14" Pillow polyester for stuffing

(Here cornmeal and burgundy colors have been used as 1st and 2nd color respectively, but you may alter according to your choice.

instructions:

Strip A: (make 6)
Row 1: Take 1st selected color, start with ch and then single crochet in subsequent ch as of the hook and in every ch crossways, ch 1, twist

Rows 2-8: Single crochet in every sc crossways, ch 1, twist

Row 9: Single crochet in every sc crossways, shift to second color, ch 1, twist

Rows 10-17: Single crochet in every sc crossways, ch 1, twist

Row 18: Single crochet in every Sc crossways, change to first color, ch 1, twist

Row 19-26: Single crochet in every sc crossways, ch 1, twist

Row 27: Single crochet in every sc crossways, again shift to second color, ch 1, twist

Rows 28-35: Single crochet in every sc crossways, ch 1, twist

Row 36: Single crochet in every sc crossways, change to first color, ch 1, twist

Rows 37-44: Single crochet in every sc crossways, ch 1, twist

Row 45: Single crochet in every sc crossways, terminate off, and finally interlace in loose ends.

Strip B: (4)
Row 1: Take second color, ch 10, then single crochet in other ch as of hook and into every ch crossways, ch 1, and then twist

Rows 2-8: Single crochet in every sc crossways, ch 1, twist

Row 9: Single crochet in every sc crossways, change to first color, ch 1, twist

Rows 10-17: Single crochet in every sc crossways, ch 1, twist

Row 18: Single crochet in every Sc crossways, change to second color, ch 1, twist

Row 19-26: Single crochet in every sc crossways, ch 1, twist

Row 27: Single crochet in every sc crossways, change to first color, ch 1, twist

Rows 28-35: Single crochet in every sc crossways, ch 1, twist

Row 36: Single crochet in every sc crossways, change to second color, ch 1, twist

Rows 37-44: Single crochet in every sc crossways, ch 1, twist

Row 45: Single crochet in every sc crossways, finish off, again weave in wobbly ends.

Pillow Assembling and making Border:
Round 1: Put the two accomplished panels incorrect sides jointly. With second color yarn and operating through these two thicknesses and then sc two panels in concert all the length of three sides. Keep the checker squares creased up. Insert pillow form, sc fourth side closed, ch 1, and twist.

Round 2: Single crochet in every single crochet in the region of working 3 single crochet in corners, ch 1, twist

Rnd 3: RSingle crochet in every single crochet in the region of working 3 RSingle crochet in corners, stop it and interlace in slack ends.

Your adorable checker cushion is ready.

Design no. 2 Circular pillow at top

Requirements

- Yarn: four balls of first color and three balls of second color.
- Crochet Hook 2 / 0.
- A filling or polyester, Diameter: 15 inches
- GAUGE: 5 single crochet to make one inch; two double crochet and 1 single crochet Row to make 11 ¼ inches.

Method

Start with the first color at the middle, chain 5

1st round: 25 treble in 5th ch from hook, insert hook in top of starting chain, drop first color, attach second color and drag loop over chain and loop on crochet hook, now start joining round and keep on changing color in this way.

2nd round: 2 single crochet in similar place as slip stitch (1 st increased), * single crochet in subsequent treble, 2 single crochet in subsequent treble. Replicate from * around. Second color yarn, pick up first color.

3rd round: Ch 3, double crochet in similar place as slip stitch, double crochet in every single crochet, rising 12 double crochet equally in the similar order, drop second color, pick up first color and then Join.

4th round: Here Single crochet in similar position as slip stitch, single crochet in subsequent 2 double crochet, * thread over, insert hook into single crochet on previous single crochet round, draw loop throughout, twice; thread over and draw through all loops on hook, skip double crochet straight at the rear of puff st, single crochet in subsequent 3 double crochet. Replicate from * around, drop second color and pick up first color and finally join.

5th round: To be following in a way like 3rd round.

6th round: Single crochet in every single crochet around, escalating 19 single crochet uniformly around.

7th and 8th rounds: duplicate last 2 rounds.

9th round: Replicate 3rd round in similar way.

10th round: Then replicate 4th round similarly.

11th to 16th rounds including: Replicate 5th round to 10th round incl.

17th to 21st rounds including: Replicate 5th to 9th rounds incl.

At end of **last round,** join them and then break off the yarn.

Similarly make another piece. Keep both sides facing wrong and then work through both of the thicknesses to join them, attach second color to any double crochet, single crochet in equivalent position, single crochet in every double crochet about to within 10 inches from first single crochet, put in pillow and single crochet in every lasting double crochet. Join and again break off. And eye catching crochet cushion is ready.

318

Design no. 3 Second round pillow

Requirements:

- Yarn: 3 balls of one color and 2 balls of second.
- Crochet Hook
- 15" pillow foam
- GAUGE: 1" by 3 puff sts and approximately 4 rnds make 1½ inches.

Method:

In this method, initiate it with starting from the center with second color, ch 2.

1st rnd: 7 single crochet in 2nd ch as of hook and then connect.

2nd rnd: 2 single crochet in every sc around and again unite.

3rd rnd: Ch 3. Do it three times and thread above and sketch through all loops lying on hook. Build a puff st in every sc all around and then link to peak of first puff st.

4th rnd: Single crochet in rear loop of every puff st and in every ch around. Unite and break off.

320

5th rnd: Attach first color to similar place as slip stitch, ch 3, make a puff st in every sc and then unite.

6th rnd: Sc similar as slip stitch, * single crochet in next ch (1 single crochet increased), single crochet in next 2 puff sts. Repeat from * around. Combine and split off.

7th rnd: Unite second color to first sc and do again 5th rnd.

8th rnd: Single crochet in every sc around, mounting 14 sc consistently around. Unite and break off.

Do again last 2 rnds, change color on every added rnd until 18 rnds.

19th rnd: Single crochet in every sc around and increases it up to the demand and then unite.

Repeat l9th rnd until piece measures equal size as that of pillow.

After last rnd, unite and split off.

Other piece has to be made in the similar way. After completing, with incorrect sides opposite and working along both, attach Claret to any sc, sc directly in the region of within lo inches of first sc, pop in pillow and single crochet intimately around left over periphery. Fasten together and split off. And add the cushion to enhance your home's interior looks.

Design no. 4 Square Yellow Pillow

Requirements

- Yarn: 6 balls any color. I selected Yellow
- Crochet Hook
- 14 inches pillow foam of square shape.
- GAUGE: 1 shell and 2 sc make 1 ¾ inches

From the bottom, start making a chain 12 inches in length.

Method:

1st Row: Single crochet in 2nd ch as of hook, * skip 2 ch, 5 dc in subsequent ch, hop 2 ch, single crochet in after that ch,. Replicate from * crossways until there are 7 shells on Row, ending with an sc, hop 2 ch, 3 double crochet in preceding ch . Cut the left over chain. Ch 1, flip.

2nd Row: Single crochet in first dc, * shell in next sc, single crochet in center dc of subsequent shell. Do again from * transversely, till revery half shell in end sc. Ch 1. Flip. Do again 2nd Row until piece is finalized into a square.

For edging:

1st rnd: Sc closely around, making 3 single crochet in every corner.

2nd rnd: Single crochet in every sc around, making 3 single crochet in middle sc of every corner.

Do again 2nd rnd until the piece procedures 14 inch square. Unite it and then break off.

Other piece is to be made in the similar way. With incorrect sides in front of and functioning through both thicknesses, fasten the thread to some corner, single crochet in every sc around three sides, pop in pillow and sc crossways the left over side. Unite and smash off.

Decorate them in lounge and captivate your visitor's focus.

Design no. 5

This is another beautiful design for a crochet. All stitches in it are double crochet, chain or a skipped space, and it is named as filet crochet.

Level: Intermediate

Requirements:

- 2 oz cotton worsted yarn
- crochet hook of size E/4 (3.50 mm)

Instructions:

Chain 45

Row 1: sk first 3 ch , dc in second chain and across (42 sts)

Follow the chart for the rest of the directions.

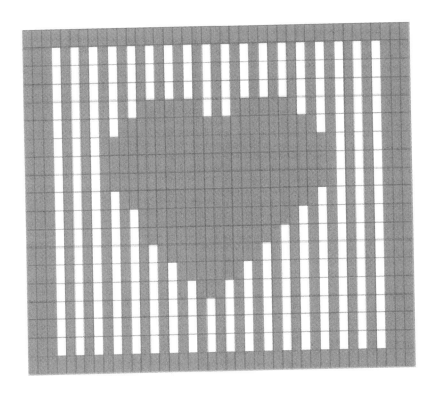

Design no. 6 Diagonal pillow

Pillow size: 14" x 14"

Requirements:

- Yarn: 3 balls of one color and 3 balls of second chosen color.
- Crochet Hook 3.5mm in size
- Yarn needle
- Pillow form of 14 inches.
- GAUGE: 2" in pattern which would be equal to 4 shells..

Method:

Pillow Front

Row 1 (work from Right Side): With A, ch 6, dc in 4th ch from hook, dc in next 2 ch; flip – 1 shell.

Row 2: Ch 6, dc in 4th ch initiating from hook, dc in next 2 ch – starting shell made; (slip st, ch 3, 3 dc) all over ch-3 of previous row shells made; flip – 2 shells.

Row 3: Starting shell, * shell; repeat from * across changing to B in last dc; flip – 3 shells.

Row 4: Starting shell, * shell; repeat from * across; flip.

Repeat Row 4 for pattern, increasing 1 shell every row, in the appropriate color chain:–
22 shells at finish of preceding row.

Row 23: With A, ch 1, slip st in first 3 dc, * shell; repeat from * to last shell; slide st in
last ch-3 changing to B; flip – 21 shells.

Row 24: Ch 1, slip st in first 3 dc, * shell; do it again from * to end shell; slip st in last
ch-3 space; go round – 20 shells.

Duplicate Row 24 for pattern, lessening 1 shell every row, in the appropriate color
sequence. Fasten off. Back Work similar as Front EXCEPT reverse the colors using first
color in place of second color and second color in place of first color.

Assemblage

Keeping wrong sides together and working through thicknesses, unite A and effort 1
round sc consistently in the region of 3 sides.

Slot in pillow foam; complete sc round.

Unite with a slip st in first sc. Fasten off. And finally it would be like this.

Get reminded of abbreviations again.

Design no. 7

Required materials

It will be a 14" **Pillow.**

- 3 balls of yarn of selected color
- **Hook of** U.S. Size H-8 [5mm].
- 14" or 16" sized pillow forms.
- **GAUGES: In sc rnds** - 14 sts = 4"; 18 rnds = 4".**Motif** – 3¾" square.

Check the gauge first. Utilize any size hook to get the gauges given.

FRONT-Motif (Make 9)-Rnd 1:

Ch 2; 8 single crochet in 2nd ch by hook and unite with a slip stitch to first sc.

Rnd 2: Ch 2; *holding at back last lp on hook, 2 dc in similar sc as joining, yo and through all 3 lps on hook* – **beg cl (cluster)** completed, *[ch 3; holding back last lp on hook, 3 double crochet in subsequent sc, yo and from side to side all 4 lps on hook* – **cl** made] 7 times; ch 1, dc in top of beg cl to connect and form last lp – 8 cl.

329

Rnd 3: Ch 1, 3 sc above dc, [5 single crochet in subsequent ch-3 sp] 7 times, 2 sc above ch-1; connect with a slip stitch to first sc.

Rnd 4: Ch 1, single crochet in similar sc as unification, * ch 4, skip subsequent 4 sc, single crochet in after that sc, ch 8, skip then 4 sc **, single crochet in subsequent sc; rep from * around, end at **; unite to first sc.

Rnd 5: Ch 1, * 4 single crochet in ch-4 lp, (5 sc, ch 2, 5 sc) all in ch-8 lp; rep from * around; connect and then tie up off. Interlace in ends.

Edging: Fasten together thread in last sc **ahead of** any corner.

Rnd 1: Ch 3, * 3 double crochet in corner sp, dc in every sc to subsequent corner, rep from * in the region of; join to top of ch-3 – 180 sts.

Rnd 2: Ch 3, dc in every dc around; unite and the Fasten off.

Back:

Create one motif similar as for front but do not tie up off at Rnd 5 ending .

Rnd 6: Ch 3, dc in subsequent sc and in all sc to corner sp, * all in corner sp, dc in every sc crossways; rep from * all around in that region, link to top of ch-3 – 18 sts between corner sps.

Rnd 7: Ch 3, dc in subsequent dc and all dc to corner, * (dc, ch 2, dc) everyone in corner sp, dc in every dc across; rep from * around; join – 20 sts between corner sps.

Rnd 8: Ch 3, dc in subsequent dc and every dc to corner, * (2 dc, ch 2, 2 dc) all in corner sp, dc in every dc crossways; rep from * all around and then join – 24 sts between corner sps.

Rnd 9: Rep Rnd 7 – 26 sts between corner sps.

Rnds 10, 11, 12, and 13: Follow similar as in Rnd 8 – 42 sts among corner sps at end of Rnd 13.

Rnd 14: Ch 3, dc in subsequent dc and every dc to corner, * 3 double crochet in corner sp, dc in every dc crossways; rep from * around; join – 180 sts around. Fasten off. Weave all ends.

WINDING UP:

Take wrong sides' jointly and match st for st, sc through both layers around front and back, popping in pillow form before closing last side and fasten together. Tie up.

And let your visitors remember you with the mesmerizing look of your living area.

Design no. 8 Simple Round pillow

Materials

- Yarn hook
- 7 oz of worsted weight of selected color of yarn

Procedure

If you have to make Round pillow form, you require making two pieces of them for front and back

Ch 4, slip stitch tog to form a ring.

Round 1: Ch 3, 13 double crochet in circle, slip stitch tog.

Rnd 2: Ch 3, dc in similar st, 2 dc in every st around, slip stitch tog.

Round 3: Ch 3, dc in similar st, *dc in subsequent 2 sts, 2dc. Replicate from * all around. Slip stitch tog.

Round 4: Ch 3, dc in similar st, *dc in subsequent 2 sts, 2dc. Replicate from * all around. Slip stitch tog.

Round 5: Ch 3, dc in similar st, *dc in subsequent 3 sts, 2dc. Repeat from * all around. Slip stitch tog.

Round 6: Ch 3, dc in similar st, *dc in subsequent 4 sts, 2dc. Repeat from * all around. Slip stitch tog.

Round 7: Ch 3, dc in similar st, *dc in subsequent 5 sts, 2dc. Repeat from * all around. Slip stitch tog.

Round 8: Ch 3, dc in similar st, *dc in subsequent 6 sts, 2dc. Repeat from * all around. Slip stitch tog.

Round 9: Ch 3, dc in similar st, *dc in subsequent 6 sts, 2dc. Repeat from * all around. Slip stitch tog.

Round 10: Ch 3, dc in similar st, *dc in subsequent 10 sts, 2dc. Repeat from * all around. Slip stitch tog.

Round 11: Ch 3, dc in similar st, dc in every st all around. Slip stitch tog.

Round 12: Replicate Round 11. tie off and then weave in end. On 2nd round, do not tie off.

Slip stitch tog opposite sides of pillow rounds. After halfway done, slip pillow foam between them. Then finish slip stitch all around. Fasten off and weave in end.

Design no. 9 Ribbon laced crochet cushion

Materials

- Yarn 1 skein of requires color
- Crochet Hook: H/8 [5.00mm]
- 12"-square pillow form
- fabric to match yarn of about size two 13" squares;
- thread for sewing
- needle
- Any colored ribbon 5⁄8"- I selected wide purple velvet ribbon, 27" length
- Again any colored ribbon I selected 5⁄8"-wide green velvet ribbon of lengths 14" and 46"
- 3"square piece of cardboard.
- GAUGE: Rounds 1–3 of pattern to make size 4¼" x 4¼".

Front = 12" square prior to amalgamation. Make sure to check the Gauge. Use any size needles to get the gauge.

Directions:

PATTERN STITCH Shell: Work 5 dc in specified st. FRONT Ch 4. Unite with slip stitch in first ch to form a ring.

Rnd 1 (right side): Ch 3 (counts as dc), work 15 dc in ring – 16 dc. Unite with slip stitch in 3rd chain of beginning ch-3.

Rnd 2: Ch 1, single crochet in similar ch as uniting, single crochet in subsequent 2 dc; *(sc, ch 2, sc) in subsequent dc, single crochet in subsequent 3 dc; replicate from * 2 times further (sc, ch 2, sc) in very last dc – 20 sc and 4 corner chain 2 spaces. Unite with slip stitch in beginning sc.

Rnd 3: Ch 4 (taken as double crochet and chain-1 sp), sk subsequent sc, dc in subsequent sc; *ch 1, sk subsequent sc, (dc, ch 1, dc, ch 2, dc, ch 1, dc) in corner ch-2 sp**; [ch 1, sk subsequent sc, dc in subsequent sc] twice*; replicate from * to * around, ending final replicate at **; ch 1, sk last sc – 24 dc, 20 ch-1 sps and 4 corner chain 2 spaces. Unite with slip stitch in 3rd chain of in start of ch-4.

Rnd 4: Chain 4 (taken as treble); *(2 treble, chain 2, 2 treble) in subsequent chain-1 sp, tr in subsequent dc, dc in subsequent chain-1 space and in subsequent dc, hdc in subsequent ch-1 sp, single crochet in subsequent dc, slip stitch in subsequent chain-2 sp, single crochet in subsequent dc, hdc in subsequent chain-1 sp, dc in subsequent dc and in subsequent chain-1sp**; tr in subsequent dc; replicate from * around, ending final replicate at ** - 24 tr, 16 dc, 8 hdc, 8 sc, 4 slip stitchs and 4 corner chain 2 spaces. Unite with slip stitch in 4th ch of beginning ch-4.

Rnd 5: Ch 1, single crochet in similar ch as uniteing and in every stitch around, working (sc, ch 2, sc) in every corner ch-2 sp – 68 sc and 4 corner chain 2 spaces. Unite with slip stitch in first sc. Ch 4 (it will be taken as double crochet and chain-1 sp on subsequent round), flip.

Rnd 6: (wrong side) Sk first sc, dc in subsequent sc; *ch 1, sk subsequent sc**, dc in subsequent sc; replicate from * all around, functioning (dc, ch 1, dc, ch 2, dc, ch 1, dc) in every corner ch-2 sp and ending final replicate at ** - 48 dc, 44 ch-1 sps and 4 corner chain 2 spaces. Unite with slip stitch in 3rd chain of flipping ch-4. Ch 1, flip.

Rnd 7: (right side) Single crochet in subsequent ch-1 sp, single crochet in every dc and in every ch-1 sp around, working (sc, ch 2, sc) in every corner ch-2 sp and ending with single crochet in similar ch as uniting – 100 sc and 4 corner chain 2 spaces. Unite with slip stitch in last sc. Do not flip.

Rnd 8: Ch 1, single crochet in subsequent sc; *sk subsequent 2 sc, shell in subsequent sc, sk subsequent 2 sc**, single crochet in subsequent sc; replicate from * around, working (shell in corner ch-2 sp, single crochet in subsequent sc) in every corner and ending final replicate at ** - 20 shells and 20 sc. Unite with slip stitch in beginning sc. Flip.

Rnd 9: (wrong side) Slip stitch in subsequent 2 dc, slip stitch in subsequent dc (center dc of shell), ch 1, single crochet in similar dc; *shell in subsequent sc, single crochet in center dc of subsequent shell; replicate from * around, working (shell in sc, sk subsequent dc, single crochet in subsequent dc, shell in subsequent dc (center dc of shell), single crochet in subsequent dc, skip subsequent dc, shell in sc) in every corner – 24 shells and 24 sc. Unite with slip stitch in beginning sc. Ch 5 (counts as double crochet and chain-2 sp on subsequent round), flip.

Rnd 10: (right side) Single crochet in center dc of subsequent shell, ch 2; *dc in subsequent sc, ch 2, single crochet in center dc of subsequent shell, ch 2; replicate

Working [dc in subsequent sc, chain 2, sk subsequent dc, dc in subsequent dc, ch 1, (dc, chain 2, dc) in subsequent dc, ch 1, dc in subsequent dc, chain 2, skip subsequent dc] in every corner – 40 dc, 20 sc, 52 ch- 2 sps and 8 ch-1 sps. Unite with slip stitch in 3rd chain of beginning ch-5. Do not flip.

Rnd 11: Ch 1, single crochet in similar ch as uniteing, single crochet in every st and in every ch-1 sp, operating 2 single crochet in every ch-2 sp and (sc, chain 2, sc) in every corner ch-2 sp – 172 sc. Unite with slip stitch in beginning sc. Ch 1, flip.

Rnd 12 (wrong side): Single crochet in subsequent sc; *ch 1, sk subsequent sc**; single crochet in subsequent sc; replicate from * around, working (sc, chain 2, sc) in every corner ch-2 sp and ending final replicate at ** - 92 sc, 88 ch-1 sps and 4 corner chain 2 spaces. Unite with slip stitch in beginning sc. Fasten off. Weave all ends.

Subsequent back work to be done similar as front.

WEAVE RIBBONS:

Weave ribbons on face of pillow as follows:

Weave shorter length of green ribbon inside and outside of ch sps on round 3. Weave purple ribbon inside and outside of ch sps on round 6.

Weave longer length of green ribbon inside and outside of ch sps on round 10. Trim ribbons as required. Sew ends of ribbons tog on wrong side of pillow front.

Fabric pillow cover

Taking right sides of fabric collectively, sew seam with ½" seam allowance on 3 sides of pillow using needle and thread. Trim corners and flip fabric right side outside. Pop in pillow form. Flip under left behind edges of fabric ½" to wrong side and sew closed.

JOINING:

With wrong sides of facing and rear tog and front facing, work throughout both thicknesses as follows:

Slot in hook in foremost ch-1 sp to left of corner ch-2 sp and draw up a lp, ch 1, single crochet in similar sp; *ch 1, sk next sc**; single crochet in subsequent ch-1 sp; replicate from * all around, operating (sc, chain 2, sc) in every corner ch-2 sp and ending final repeat at **.

Work around 3 sides of pillow; put in covered pillow form and complete last side – 96 sc, 92 ch-1 sps and 4 corner chain 2 spaces. Fasten together with slip stitch in beginning sc. tie off and Weave all ends.

Final Steps

Then prepare four yarn tassels in the following manner:

- Twist yarn all around cardboard for approximately fifteen times.
- Enclose 10" per 25.4cm piece of yarn all around wound yarn at one end of cardboard and tie a knot. Trim the other end of yarn and do away with from cardboard.
- Wind 10" piece of yarn several times around wound yarn, approximately ½"/1.3cm from tied end, fasten a granny knot and spruce ends.
- Fasten tassels to four corners of pillow by means of 10" tied end. Finally weave all ends.

Design no. 10

Essentials:

- Yarn: Balls of two different desired colors
- Crochet Hook of size 4mm [US G-6].
- Needle of yarn,
- Size of 12" pillow form.
- GAUGE: 15 sts = 4"

Method:

To alter Color in Sc:

Go through last st before changing color until 2 lps are left on hook, jump through color in use, gap up next color to be used and sketch through 2 lps on hook.

Continue with new color. Hold color which is not in use against wrong side of work, working above the strand for every 3 or 4 sts.

Rear:

With CA, ch 46.

Row 1 (work from Right Side): Single crochet in 2nd ch from hook and in every ch crossways and go round – 45 sc.

Row 2: Chain 1, single crochet in every sc crosswise; flip.

Replicate Row until 12" from beg. Fasten off.

FRONT:

With CA, ch 46.

Row 1 : Single crochet in 2nd ch as of hook and in every ch across; flip – 45 sc.

Row 2: Chain 1, single crochet in every sc across; flip.

Rows 3-10: Ch 1, single crochet in primary 2 sc with CA, * single crochet in subsequent 8 sc with CB, single crochet in subsequent 3 sc with CA; replicate from * across ending with 2 sc of CA as an alternative of 3; flip.

Rows 11-14: Replicate Row 2 with CA.

Rep Rows 3-14 two more times, then rep Rows 3-12 once more. Tie off and weave all ends.

Front Edging:

With right side in front of every other, connect CA in any sc; ch 1, work sc evenly around complete front, working 3 single crochet in every corner; fasten together with a slip stitch to first sc. Work 1 more round sc. tie off.

FINISHING:

With wrong sides together, sew pillow rear and front together leaving one side open. Place in pillow form and sew side closed.

ABBREVIATIONS:

beg = beginning; CA, CB = color A, B; ch = chain; rep = repeat; sc = single crochet; * = repeat whatever follows the * as indicated, mm = millimeters.

Conclusion

These were some of the mentioned designs. They would have definitely broadened your expertise. And now with application of some knowledge and tactics, you will be able to implement more and more designs in your cushion making.

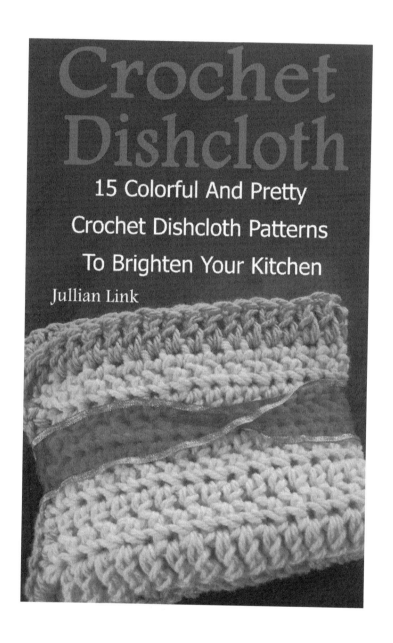

Crochet Dishcloth

15 Colorful And Pretty Crochet Dishcloth Patterns To Brighten Your Kitchen

Jullian Link

Crochet Dishcloth

15 Colorful And Pretty Crochet Dishcloth
Patterns To Brighten Your Kitchen

Introduction

There you are, browsing the aisles of the store once again, trying to find that one perfect set of cloths to put in your kitchen. You know what you want, but you just can't seem to find it on the shelves of the store, no matter how hard you look.

You could order online, but those are expensive, and you still aren't getting quite the look that you want. You want something that is new. Something that is fresh. Something that is unique to you and you alone, but all you can find are those same old patterns you see in your friend's houses.

You want something that represents you and your style. It's your kitchen, and you want to feel like you are expressing yourself while you are in it. You want to show off your flare to the world while you bake and cook, and to do that, you have to have the right tools for the job.

So, you simply are going to have to make it yourself.

"But I don't know if I can. These look hard."

"I have never made anything crocheted before... could I do it?"

"I want to make something by hand, but they look too difficult for what I have the time for... how can I make this work?"

If you have ever felt any of these things, you are not alone, but trust me, crochet is an easy hobby that you are going to fall in love with. The twisting and turning of the yarn is not only fun, but it's relaxing.

Unwind from your day with your favorite beverage and your favorite color yarn, and settle in to create and express yourself as often as you would like. You are going to end up with projects that show off your style, and you are going to amaze your friends and family with all of the pieces you are able to create.

So if you are done with browsing the stores, trying to find the unique items that you know you will only get if you make them yourself, you have come to the right place. Let me show you the wonderful world of crochet, and let me help you step into the land of arts and crafts.

You are going to open the door to complete creative freedom, and you are going to be free to make anything you like, whenever you like.

Are you ready to dive into a whole new world?

Good.

Let's get started.

Chapter 1 – Getting Started

Getting started with crochet can be both fun and intimidating if you have never done it before, but I am going to make it easy for you.

Here is a guide on how to create the stitches you are going to find in this book. They are all incredibly simply to create, you just have to practice them to perfect them.

Follow the directions, then dive into the patterns. You will be amazed at how easy they are!

Foundation chain – the foundation chain is the beginning of any crochet project. To create one, you are going to make a slip knot on the yarn, with a length hanging down. This length is going to be trimmed off when you are done.

Slip the knot over the hook and pull it firmly against the hook. To create a chain, grab the yarn with the hook, and pull it through the loop. You now have another loop on the hook, and a loop in the yarn beneath the hook. This is a chain.

When you see in a pattern that you must chain 10, you are going to continue this sequence until you have 10 of these loops on the yarn itself.

Single crochet – chain 10 for your foundation chain. To single crochet, you are going to wrap the yarn up and over the back, then push the hook through the center of the first chain next to the hook. Grab the yarn, and pull it through this loop.

Wrap the yarn up and over the hook, and pull it through the first loop you still have on your hook. Wrap it over once more, then pull it through the final loop.

This is your single crochet stitch. Repeat the sequence across the row.

Double crochet – chain 10 once more, only this time, you are going to wrap the yarn around 2 times. Push it through the center of the loop, and grab the yarn.

Pull it through, then wrap the yarn up and over the hook, and pull it through the first loop you still have on your hook. Wrap it over once more, then pull it through the next loop.

Bring the yarn up and over from the back one final time, and pull it through the last loop on the hook.

This is your double crochet. Repeat across the row.

Triple crochet – for triple crochet, chain 10.

Wrap the yarn around the hook 3 times. Push the hook through the center of the loop, and pull it through. Bring the yarn up and over, and pull it through the first loop on the hook.

Bring the yarn up and over again, and repeat. Do this again, then once more for the final loops on the hook.

This is your triple crochet. As you can see, the single, double, and triple are all referring to how many times you wrap the yarn around the hook, then how many times you need to pull it through to create your stitch. You can apply this to get any number of stitches you like.

Front loop only – as you have noticed, as you crochet, each stitch has 2 loops. When you are crocheting in the front loop only, you are pushing the hook through the center of these 2 loops instead of sliding it under them.

The front loop is the loop facing the front of the project. You are always going to use this loop with front loop only.

That's it! These are the only stitches you need to know for these projects. Practice them with the dishcloths, and you are going to be a master in no time.

Chapter 2 – Your First Dishcloths

It's finally time to get started! Take your time through each of these patterns, and keep an eye on your tension. Make sure you are pulling the yarn consistently the same throughout the cloth so you end up with a square.

You can follow the same colors that I chose, or you can use your own colors, just make sure you choose cotton yarn. Cotton comes in all kinds of colors, it's not expensive, and it's easy on the hands. Use this for all of your dishcloths and kitchen needs, and you will never want to use anything else again.

Easy Peasy Dishcloth

Photo made by: gillicious

You will need 1 ball of yarn in the color of your choice and a size G crochet hook

Chain a length that is 6 inches long.

Single crochet across the row. Chain 1, turn, and single crochet back to the beginning. Chain 1, turn, and single crochet across the row.

For row 3, chain 1, turn, and single crochet in the front loop only across the row. Chain 1, turn, and single crochet in the front loop only across the row once more.

For row 5, chain 1, turn, and single crochet normally across the row. Chain 1, turn, and single crochet normally back to the other side.

For row 7, chain 1, turn, and single crochet in the front loop only across the row. Chain 1, turn, and single crochet in the front loop only across the row once more.

Continue with this same pattern now, alternating between regular single crochet and front loop only single crochet every two rows. When you have a square, you are ready for the border.

For the border, you are going to single crochet across the row, then continue to single crochet down one side, across the bottom, and up the other side. Join with a slip stitch, and tie off.

That's it! You now have your first dishcloth.

White as Snow Dishcloth

Photo made by: Twanda Baker

You will need 1 ball of yarn in white of your choice and a size G crochet hook

Chain a length that is 6 inches long.

Chain 1, turn, and single crochet back to the beginning. Chain 1, turn, and single crochet back across the row.

Chain 1, turn, and single crochet back to the beginning. Chain 1, turn, and single crochet across the row.

You are going to repeat this same pattern now, always chaining 1 at the end of each row before you turn and begin again. Make sure your tension stays the same throughout, but make sure you keep the tension nice and snug. Continue to work until you have a square.

For the border, you are going to single crochet across the row, then continue to single crochet down one side, across the bottom, and up the other side. Join with a slip stitch, and tie off.

That's it! Your dishcloth is ready for work.

Photo made by: Stylva

You will need 1 ball of yarn in the color of your choice and a size G crochet hook

Chain a length that is 6 inches long.

Single crochet across the row. Chain 1, turn.

Single crochet in the first 4 stitches, then double crochet in the next 4 stitches. Single crochet in the next 4 stitches, then double crochet in the next 4 stitches.

Repeat this across the row, making sure you finish with a single crochet stitch. Chain 1, turn.

Single crochet in the first 4 stitches, then double crochet in the next 4 stitches. Single crochet in the next 4 stitches, then double crochet in the next 4 stitches.

351

Chain 1, turn, and repeat the pattern.

You are going to continue with this same pattern until you have a square.

Leave a raw edge on this border.

The Black and White Classics Dishcloth

You will need 1 ball of yarn in black and one in white and a size G crochet hook

Chain a length that is 6 inches long.

Chain 2, turn, and double crochet back to the beginning. Chain 2, turn, and double crochet back across the row.

Chain 2, turn, and double crochet back to the beginning. Chain 2, turn, and double crochet across the row.

You are going to repeat this same pattern now, always chaining 2 at the end of each row before you turn and begin again. Make sure your tension stays the same throughout, and continue to work until you have a square.

Tie off, then add the border.

For the border, join with the opposite color. Single crochet across the row, then continue to single crochet down one side, across the bottom, and up the other side. Join with a slip stitch, and tie off.

For variations in the look, try following the same pattern using either single crochet or triple crochet.

That's it!

Chapter 3 – Bringing In Your Style

Whether you want to celebrate your favorite time of year, you want to bring in your own favorite colors, or you are looking for something that is classy yet refined, you are sure to find the dishcloth you need here.

Use the same colors I used, or choose your own for your own original look. No matter how you do it, you are going to love the results.

Be My Valentine Dishcloths

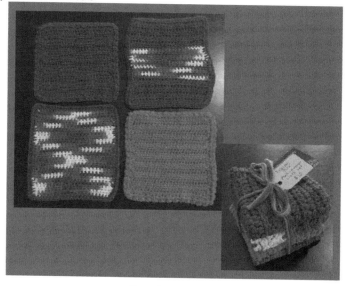

Photo made by: becky bokern

You will need 1 ball of yarn in the color of your choice and a size G crochet hook

Chain a length that is 6 inches long.

Chain 2, turn, and double crochet back to the beginning. Chain 2, turn, and double crochet back across the row.

Chain 2, turn, and double crochet back to the beginning. Chain 2, turn, and double crochet across the row.

You are going to repeat this same pattern now, always chaining 2 at the end of each row before you turn and begin again. Make sure your tension stays the same throughout, and continue to work until you have a square.

For the border, you are going to single crochet across the row, then continue to single crochet down one side, across the bottom, and up the other side. Join with a slip stitch, and tie off.

If you want to have the alternating stripe, work this pattern for 2 inches, then change colors to your stripe. Follow the pattern for another 2 inches, before you tie off and go back to your main color.

That's it!

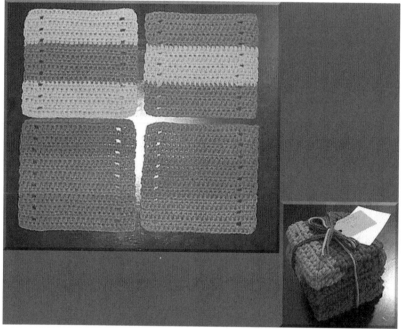

Photo made by: <u>becky bokern</u>

You will need 2 balls of yarn in the 2 colors of your choice and a size G crochet hook

Chain a length that is 6 inches long. Chain 2, and double crochet across the row.

Chain 2, turn, and double crochet in the first 3 stitches. Chain 4, skip the next 2 stitches, and double crochet in the next stitch. Continue to double crochet until you are 5 stitches away from the end of the row.

Chain 4, skip the next 2 stitches, and double crochet in the last 3 stitches.

For the next row, chain 2, turn, and double crochet in the first 3 stitches. Chain 4, skip the next 2 stitches, and double crochet in the next stitch. Continue to double crochet until you are 5 stitches away from the end of the row.

356

Chain 4, skip the next 2 stitches, and double crochet in the last 3 stitches.

Repeat this pattern until you are 2 inches up the side of the cloth.

Change colors now, and join with a slip stitch.

Chain 2, turn, and double crochet in the first 3 stitches. Chain 4, skip the next 2 stitches, and double crochet in the next stitch. Continue to double crochet until you are 5 stitches away from the end of the row.

Chain 4, skip the next 2 stitches, and double crochet in the last 3 stitches.

Repeat this pattern until you have a 2 inch stripe, then go back to your first color.

Chain 2, turn, and double crochet in the first 3 stitches. Chain 4, skip the next 2 stitches, and double crochet in the next stitch. Continue to double crochet until you are 5 stitches away from the end of the row.

Chain 4, skip the next 2 stitches, and double crochet in the last 3 stitches.

Leave a raw edge on this border.

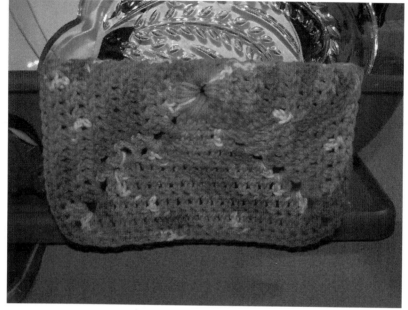

Photo made by: Lisa Plummer

You will need 1 ball of yarn in the color of your choice and a size G crochet hook

Chain 5, and join with a slip stitch to form a ring.

Single crochet in the center of this stitch 12 times. Chain 2, and turn.

Double crochet in the first 3 stitches, chain 5, and double crochet in the next 3 stitches. Chain 5, double crochet in the next 3 stitches, chain 5, and double crochet in the next 3 stitches.

Join with a slip stitch and chain 2. Double crochet in each of the stitches around, double crochet in the chain space 2 times, chain 2, and double crochet in the same space 2 times. Repeat this around.

Chain 2, turn, and double crochet in each of the stitches. When you reach the chain space, you are going to double crochet in it 1 time, chain 2, and double crochet in it once more. Repeat around.

358

Continue to follow this pattern until you have a square that is 6 inches tall by 6 inches wide. You are now ready to add the border.

For the border, you are going to single crochet across the row, then continue to single crochet down one side, across the bottom, and up the other side. Join with a slip stitch, and tie off.

That's it! You're done!

Fun and Flirty Dishcloths

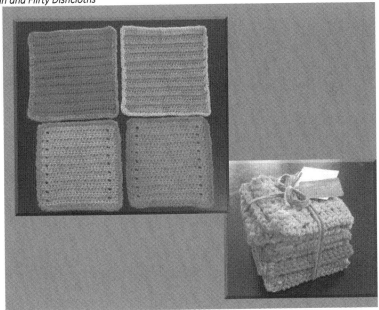

Photo made by: becky bokern

You will need 2 balls of yarn in the 2 colors of your choice and a size G crochet hook

Chain a length that is 6 inches long.

Chain 2, turn, and double crochet back to the beginning. Chain 2, turn, and double crochet back across the row.

359

Chain 2, turn, and double crochet back to the beginning. Chain 2, turn, and double crochet across the row.

You are going to repeat this same pattern now, always chaining 2 at the end of each row before you turn and begin again. Make sure your tension stays the same throughout, and continue to work until you have a square.

Tie off, then add the border.

You are going to use a different color, and join with a slip stitch. Single crochet across the top, then continue to single crochet down one side, across the bottom, and up the other side. Join with a slip stitch, and tie off.

Please note: If you want to have the open work ends, follow the directions for the spring mix crochet cloths, but use these colors.

Chapter 4 – The Jazzy Section

Whether you are feeling a little classic, a little funky, or a little jazzy, there is something in this chapter for you. Have fun with the patterns, have fun with the colors, and give your kitchen that pop it's been waiting for!

Triple Crochet Border Dishcloth

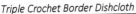

Photo made by: Lisa Plummer

You will need 1 ball of yarn in the color of your choice and a size G crochet hook

Chain a length that is 6 inches long.

Chain 1, turn, and single crochet back to the beginning. Chain 1, turn, and single crochet back across the row.

Chain 1, turn, and single crochet back to the beginning. Chain 1, turn, and single crochet across the row.

You are going to repeat this same pattern now, always chaining 1 at the end of each row before you turn and begin again. Make sure your tension stays the same throughout, and continue to work until you have a square.

Tie off, and change to another color for the border.

For the border, you are going to join with a slip stitch, and chain 3. Triple crochet across the top of the cloth, then continue to triple crochet down one side, across the bottom, and up the other side. Join with a slip stitch, and tie off.

Summer Patriot Dishcloths

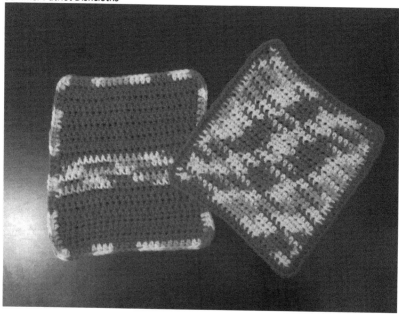

Photo made by: becky bokern

You will need 2 balls of yarn in the colors of your choice and a size G crochet hook

Chain a length that is 6 inches long.

Chain 2, turn, and double crochet back to the beginning. Chain 2, turn, and double crochet back across the row.

Chain 2, turn, and double crochet back to the beginning. Chain 2, turn, and double crochet across the row.

You are going to repeat this same pattern now, always chaining 2 at the end of each row before you turn and begin again. Make sure your tension stays the same throughout, and continue to work until you have a square.

Tie off, then add the border.

You are going to use a different color, and join with a slip stitch. Single crochet across the top, then continue to single crochet down one side, across the bottom, and up the other side. Join with a slip stitch, and tie off.

Please note: If you want to create a cloth with the stripe on one side, you are going to complete 5 rows, tie off, and join a different color with a slip stitch. Repeat the pattern for another 3 rows, before you tie off and go back to your main color.

Muted Moss Dishcloths

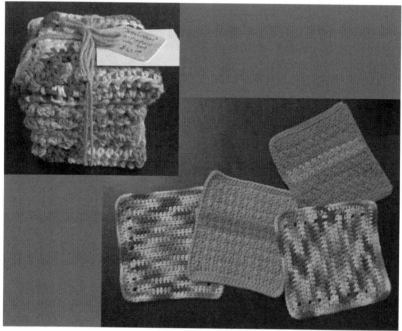

Photo made by: <u>becky bokern</u>

You will need 1 ball of yarn in the color of your choice and a size G crochet hook

Chain a length that is 6 inches long.

Chain 2, turn, and double crochet back to the beginning. Chain 2, turn, and double crochet back across the row.

Chain 2, turn, and double crochet back to the beginning. Chain 2, turn, and double crochet across the row.

You are going to repeat this same pattern now, always chaining 2 at the end of each row before you turn and begin again. Make sure your tension stays the same throughout, and continue to work until you have a square.

For the border, you are going to single crochet across the row, then continue to single crochet down one side, across the bottom, and up the other side. Join with a slip stitch, and tie off.

Please note: If you want to create a cloth with the stripe on one side, you are going to complete 5 rows, tie off, and join a different color with a slip stitch. Repeat the pattern for another 3 rows, before you tie off and go back to your main color.

That's it!

Chapter 5 – Variation Patterns

Here are a few patterns that show you how to use a single ball of yarn to get two entirely different looks for a washcloth.

First, you are going to use single crochet, then you are going to use triple, and the result is an entirely different outcome. Later on you will see the difference between a double crochet cloth from an open work cloth.

Make these patterns, then try mixing it up by throwing in variations with the stitches you are using. You can even change the border by using double crochet instead of single, or even alternating between single and double as you go along.

The point is to have fun, and let your imagination run wild!

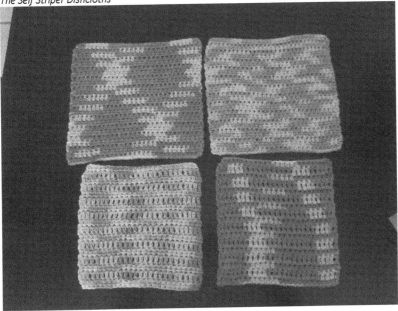

Photo made by: becky bokern

You will need 1 ball of yarn in the color of your choice and a size G crochet hook

Chain a length that is 6 inches long.

Chain 1, turn, and single crochet back to the beginning. Chain 1, turn, and single crochet back across the row.

Chain 1, turn, and single crochet back to the beginning. Chain 1, turn, and single crochet across the row.

You are going to repeat this same pattern now, always chaining 1 at the end of each row before you turn and begin again. Make sure your tension stays the same throughout, and continue to work until you have a square.

For the border, you are going to single crochet across the row, then continue to single crochet down one side, across the bottom, and up the other side. Join with a slip stitch, and tie off.

367

That's it! You're all set!

The Triple Crochet Self Striper Dishcloth (Photo Above)
You will need 1 ball of yarn in the color of your choice and a size G crochet hook

Chain a length that is 6 inches long.

Chain 3, turn, and triple crochet back to the beginning. Chain 3, turn, and triple crochet back across the row.

Chain 3, turn, and triple crochet back to the beginning. Chain 3, turn, and triple crochet across the row.

You are going to repeat this same pattern now, always chaining 3 at the end of each row before you turn and begin again. Make sure your tension stays the same throughout, and continue to work until you have a square.

For the border, you are going to single crochet across the row, then continue to single crochet down one side, across the bottom, and up the other side. Join with a slip stitch, and tie off.

That's it!

Storm Cloud Dishcloth

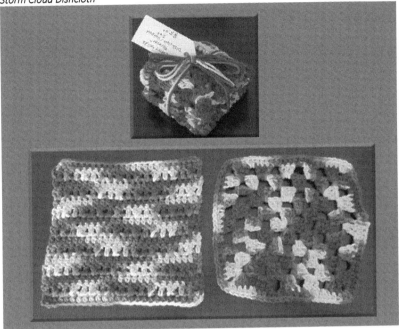

Photo made by: becky bokern

You will need 1 ball of yarn in the color of your choice and a size G crochet hook

Chain a length that is 6 inches long.

Chain 2, turn, and double crochet back to the beginning. Chain 2, turn, and double crochet back across the row.

Chain 2, turn, and double crochet back to the beginning. Chain 2, turn, and double crochet across the row.

You are going to repeat this same pattern now, always chaining 2 at the end of each row before you turn and begin again. Make sure your tension stays the same throughout, and continue to work until you have a square.

For the border, you are going to single crochet across the row, then continue to single crochet down one side, across the bottom, and up the other side. Join with a slip stitch, and tie off.

That's it! Your dishcloth is ready for action.

The Open Work Storm Cloud Dishcloth (Photo Above)
You will need 1 ball of yarn in the color of your choice and a size G crochet hook

Chain 5, and join with a slip stitch to form a ring.

Single crochet in the center of this stitch 12 times. Chain 2, and turn.

Double crochet in the first 3 stitches, chain 5, and double crochet in the next 3 stitches. Chain 5, double crochet in the next 3 stitches, chain 5, and double crochet in the next 3 stitches.

Chain 2, and double crochet in the chain space 4 times. Chain 3, and double crochet in the chain space 4 times. Chain 5, and skip the next 3, then double crochet in the chain space 4 times. Chain 5, and skip the next 3, and double crochet in the chain space 4 times.

Chain 2, and double crochet in the chain space 4 times. Chain 3, and double crochet in the chain space 4 times. Chain 5, and skip the next 3, then double crochet in the chain space 4 times. Chain 5, and skip the next 3, and double crochet in the chain space 4 times.

Continue this pattern around the other two corners.

Chain 2, and repeat the entire sequence once more. You are going to continue to group the double crochets in the chain spaces you create, and you are going to consistently chain 5, then skip the next 3 stitches to create more chain spaces.

Continue to work until you have a square that is 6 inches wide and 6 inches tall. You are now ready to add on the border.

For the border, you are going to single crochet across the row, then continue to single crochet down one side, across the bottom, and up the other side. Join with a slip stitch, and tie off.

That's it! Enjoy!

Conclusion

There you have it, everything you need to get started in crochet, and exactly what you need to create your very first dishcloths.

I hope this book was able to inspire you to create the items you want to put in your kitchen, and that you were able to ease into the world of crochet with the fun that this hobby provides. I know it can be frustrating at first, but I encourage you to stick with it.

The more you practice, the easier it's going to get, and the better you are going to be with each and every project.

I know you can do it, and I want you to get comfortable enough to branch out and try your own style. Throw in a bit of flare here, add in a touch of you there. You never know how many things you can modify and create until you try, and once you do, you will be hooked for life.

This book is designed for the beginner, so don't worry if you think you need to practice before you move on to more advanced projects. You can create these dishcloths at any level, and the more you practice, the easier they are going to get.

Have fun with it, and mix and match the stitches. See how many ways you can make the same dishcloth look different, and how many ways you can get the yarn to change based on the stitches you are using. Have fun with the entire process, and there won't be anything that is too hard for you.

I hope you enjoyed learning how to crochet, and I hope you take your skills to the next level. This is a hobby that is going to serve you well no matter how old you are, what you enjoy doing, or what kinds of projects you want to make.

Dive into the world of crochet, and enjoy the entire process. No project is going to be too hard.

Happy crocheting!

ALISA HATCHENSON

CROCHET OVALS
6 Afghan Patterns To Use For Cozy
Crochet Rugs

Crochet Ovals

6 Afghan Patterns To Use For Cozy Crochet Rugs

Introduction

You walk through your home, thinking about all the things you want to do. You want to have parties, you want to have fun for the holidays, and you want to show off what you are able to do to your friends and family. You want to create a new look that is going to be the envy of all who walk through your doors, and you want to be proud of the home you live in.

But, you also want to love the pieces you choose. You want to walk through your own home and know that you are going to love each and every piece that you choose, and you want to know without a doubt that it is going to go with the décor that you already have set in place. You don't want to settle for second best, you want to fall in love with your home and all the things you have inside.

Yet the stores don't offer the pieces that you want, and they don't give you everything you are looking for when it comes to the world of rugs. You know what you like and what you find in the stores are nice, but they aren't nearly the same thing.

So what are you going to do? Do you have to settle for second-best? Do you have to wish that you could have the rugs and décor that you dream of, but you have to go with the things that are on sale in the stores? Do you have to forget about everything you have wanted to do with your house and look like everyone else?

Thankfully, the answer is no. If you want your house to be exactly like you are dreaming, then you are going to have to decorate it yourself. You are going to have to be the one to create the pieces, and you are going to have to choose where you want them to be. It might sound intimidating, but it's not as hard as you think.

When it comes to the world of décor, all you need is a crochet hook and some imagination. You are going to find the inspiration with the patterns here, and you are going to see just how easy it is for you to create a variety of your own rugs. Each and every room in your house is going to look amazing, and you are going to be more than happy to show off what you can do to your friends and family.

Get ready to be the envy of all this holiday season, and fall in love with each of the pieces you create. Your rugs can be as large as you want, or you can keep them small and sweet.

Mix and match until you are happy with the perfect piece, and you are going to discover just how easy it is to find the rug of your dreams.

This book is going to change the way you decorate your home, and you are going to see for yourself just how easy it is to get what you want, when you want it. The world of home décor is far easier to get into than you think, and you'll love each and every piece you find. Grab your yarn and crochet hook and settle in!

The Patterns

Basic but Beautiful Rug

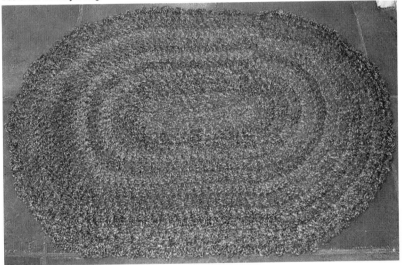

Photo made by: sharledskein

You will need 4 skeins of heavy weight yarn in the colors of your choice and a size N crochet hook. T-shirt yarn and plastic yarn both work as well, and you'll still be able to use the N hook for the project.

This project is worked until you are happy with the size of the piece, so you will need as much yarn as you like to achieve that size. For a minimum, you are going to need the equivalent of 2 skeins.

Chain 10 and single crochet across the row. instead of stopping at the end of the row, you are going to continue to single crochet down and around the bottom, working until you get back to the beginning. Join with a slip stitch, forming a rounded oval.

Chain 1, turn, and single crochet back to the beginning of the row, working 1 stitch in each of the stitches along the way, once again joining with a slip stitch when you get back to the beginning. Chain 1, turn, and once again single crochet back around the edge of the piece. You are going to join with a slip stitch when you get back to the beginning once more. Chain 1, turn, and repeat back to the beginning, remembering to join with a slip stitch.

You may find that you need to add an extra stitch to the end chain to ensure that you reach properly. This is normal, and you will continue to work with this new stitch that you add along the way. You can use scrap yarn to complete this project, or you can follow the photo as a reference guide of which kind of yarn to use.

If you are using multi-colored yarn, the piece is going to stripe itself, without you having to do anything. There is no wrong way to do it, as long as you are happy with the finished rug that you have created. Tie off the previous color, join the new color with a slip stitch, and continue along the edge of the project, following the same pattern as before.

Chain 1, turn, and single crochet back around the piece back to the beginning, joining with a slip stitch when you get there. Chain 1, turn, and single crochet back to the other side, joining with a slip stitch. Chain 1, turn, and single crochet back to the beginning, joining with a slip stitch when you get to the other side. Chain 1, turn, and single crochet back to the beginning, once again joining with a slip stitch.

Chain 1, turn, and single crochet back around the piece back to the beginning, joining with a slip stitch when you get there. Chain 1, turn, and single crochet back to the other side, joining with a slip stitch. Chain 1, turn, and single crochet back to the beginning, joining with a slip stitch when you get to the other side. Chain 1, turn, and single crochet back to the beginning, once again joining with a slip stitch.

Chain 1, turn, and single crochet back around the piece back to the beginning, joining with a slip stitch when you get there. Chain 1, turn, and single crochet back to the other side, joining with a slip stitch. Chain 1, turn, and single crochet back to the beginning, joining with a slip stitch when you get to the other side. Chain 1, turn, and single crochet back to the beginning, once again joining with a slip stitch.

Continue with this until you are happy with the size of the piece, once again remembering to change colors according to the photo or your own preference.

Tie off, and make sure all the ends are secure, and your rug is done!

If you are going to be using your rug on a hard surface, consider placing rug tabs at the bottom to ensure there is no sliding when you step on the rug. These can be purchased at most craft supply stores.

Rainbow Rug

Photo made by: punktoad

You will need heavy weight yarn in the colors of your choice and a size N crochet hook. T-shirt yarn and plastic yarn both work as well, and you'll still be able to use the N hook for the project.

This project is worked until you are happy with the size of the piece, so you will need as much yarn as you like to achieve that size. For a minimum, you are going to need the equivalent of 2 skeins.

Starting with the color of your choice, you are going to chain 5 and join with a slip stitch to form a ring. Single crochet in the center of this ring 12 times, and join with a slip stitch to the beginning.

Chain 1, turn, and single crochet back to the beginning of the row, working 1 stitch in each of the stitches along the way, once again joining with a slip stitch when you get back to the beginning. Chain 1, turn, and once again single crochet back around the edge of the piece. You are going to join with a slip stitch when you get back to the beginning once more. Chain 1, turn, and repeat back to the beginning, remembering to join with a slip stitch.

You may find that you need to add an extra stitch to the end chain to ensure that you reach properly. This is normal, and you will continue to work with this new stitch that you add along the way. You can use scrap yarn to complete this project, or you can follow the photo as a reference guide of which kind of yarn to use.

If you are going to be using the photo for reference, you are going to change colors every 10 to 15 rows, or as often as you prefer. There is no wrong way to do it, as long as you are happy with the finished rug that you have created. Tie off the previous color, join the new color with a slip stitch, and continue along the edge of the project, following the same pattern as before.

Chain 1, turn, and single crochet back around the piece back to the beginning, joining with a slip stitch when you get there. Chain 1, turn, and single crochet back to the other side, joining with a slip stitch. Chain 1, turn, and single crochet back to the beginning, joining with a slip stitch when you get to the other side. Chain 1, turn, and single crochet back to the beginning, once again joining with a slip stitch.

Chain 1, turn, and single crochet back around the piece back to the beginning, joining with a slip stitch when you get there. Chain 1, turn, and single crochet back to the other side, joining with a slip stitch. Chain 1, turn, and single crochet back to the beginning, joining with a slip stitch when you get to the other side. Chain 1, turn, and single crochet back to the beginning, once again joining with a slip stitch.

Chain 1, turn, and single crochet back around the piece back to the beginning, joining with a slip stitch when you get there. Chain 1, turn, and single crochet back to the other side, joining with a slip stitch. Chain 1, turn, and single crochet back to the beginning, joining with a slip stitch when you get to the other side. Chain 1, turn, and single crochet back to the beginning, once again joining with a slip stitch.

Continue with this until you are happy with the size of the piece, once again remembering to change colors according to the photo or your own preference.

Tie off, and make sure all the ends are secure, and your rug is done!

If you are going to be using your rug on a hard surface, consider placing rug tabs at the bottom to ensure there is no sliding when you step on the rug. These can be purchased at most craft supply stores.

Perfect for Fall Rug

Photo made by: storebukkebruse

You will need heavy weight yarn in the colors of your choice and a size N crochet hook. T-shirt yarn and plastic yarn both work as well, and you'll still be able to use the N hook for the project.

This project is worked until you are happy with the size of the piece, so you will need as much yarn as you like to achieve that size. For a minimum, you are going to need the equivalent of 2 skeins.

Starting with the color of your choice, you are going to chain 5 and join with a slip stitch to form a ring. Single crochet in the center of this ring 12 times, and join with a slip stitch to the beginning.

Chain 1, turn, and single crochet back to the beginning of the row, working 1 stitch in each of the stitches along the way, once again joining with a slip stitch when you get back to the beginning. Chain 1, turn, and once again single crochet back around the edge of the piece. You are going to join with a slip stitch when you get back to the beginning once more. Chain 1, turn, and repeat back to the beginning, remembering to join with a slip stitch.

You may find that you need to add an extra stitch to the end chain to ensure that you reach properly. This is normal, and you will continue to work with this new stitch that you add along the way. You can use scrap yarn to complete this project, or you can follow the photo as a reference guide of which kind of yarn to use.

If you are going to be using the photo for reference, you are going to change colors after the first 25 rows, then again after the 50th row, then again after the 75th, or as often as you prefer. There is no wrong way to do it, as long as you are happy with the finished rug that you have created. Tie off the previous color, join the new color with a slip stitch, and continue along the edge of the project, following the same pattern as before.

Chain 1, turn, and single crochet back around the piece back to the beginning, joining with a slip stitch when you get there. Chain 1, turn, and single crochet back to the other side, joining with a slip stitch. Chain 1, turn, and single crochet back to the beginning, joining with a slip stitch when you get to the other side. Chain 1, turn, and single crochet back to the beginning, once again joining with a slip stitch.

Chain 1, turn, and single crochet back around the piece back to the beginning, joining with a slip stitch when you get there. Chain 1, turn, and single crochet back to the other side, joining with a slip stitch. Chain 1, turn, and single crochet back to the beginning, joining with a slip stitch when you get to the other side. Chain 1, turn, and single crochet back to the beginning, once again joining with a slip stitch.

Chain 1, turn, and single crochet back around the piece back to the beginning, joining with a slip stitch when you get there. Chain 1, turn, and single crochet back to the other side, joining with a slip stitch. Chain 1, turn, and single crochet back to the beginning, joining with a slip stitch when you get to the other side. Chain 1, turn, and single crochet back to the beginning, once again joining with a slip stitch.

Continue with this until you are happy with the size of the piece, once again remembering to change colors according to the photo or your own preference.

Tie off, and make sure all the ends are secure, and your rug is done!

If you are going to be using your rug on a hard surface, consider placing rug tabs at the bottom to ensure there is no sliding when you step on the rug. These can be purchased at most craft supply stores.

Rags to Riches Rug

Photo made by: <u>Rick&Brenda Beerhorst</u>

You will need heavy weight yarn in the colors of your choice and a size N crochet hook. T-shirt yarn and plastic yarn both work as well, and you'll still be able to use the N hook for the project.

This project is worked until you are happy with the size of the piece, so you will need as much yarn as you like to achieve that size. For a minimum, you are going to need the equivalent of 2 skeins.

Starting with the color of your choice, you are going to chain 5 and join with a slip stitch to form a ring. Single crochet in the center of this ring 12 times, and join with a slip stitch to the beginning.

Chain 1, turn, and single crochet back to the beginning of the row, working 1 stitch in each of the stitches along the way, once again joining with a slip stitch when you get back to the beginning. Chain 1, turn, and once again single crochet back around the edge of the piece. You are going to join with a slip stitch when you get back to the beginning once more. Chain 1, turn, and repeat back to the beginning, remembering to join with a slip stitch.

You may find that you need to add an extra stitch to the end chain to ensure that you reach properly. This is normal, and you will continue to work with this new stitch that you add along the way. You can use scrap yarn to complete this project, or you can follow the photo as a reference guide of which kind of yarn to use.

If you are going to be using the photo for reference, you are going to change colors every 10 to 15 rows, or as often as you prefer. There is no wrong way to do it, as long as you are happy with the finished rug that you have created. Tie off the previous color, join the new color with a slip stitch, and continue along the edge of the project, following the same pattern as before.

Chain 1, turn, and single crochet back around the piece back to the beginning, joining with a slip stitch when you get there. Chain 1, turn, and single crochet back to the other side, joining with a slip stitch. Chain 1, turn, and single crochet back to the beginning, joining with a slip stitch when you get to the other side. Chain 1, turn, and single crochet back to the beginning, once again joining with a slip stitch.

Chain 1, turn, and single crochet back around the piece back to the beginning, joining with a slip stitch when you get there. Chain 1, turn, and single crochet back to the other side, joining with a slip stitch. Chain 1, turn, and single crochet back to the beginning, joining with a slip stitch when you get to the other side. Chain 1, turn, and single crochet back to the beginning, once again joining with a slip stitch.

Chain 1, turn, and single crochet back around the piece back to the beginning, joining with a slip stitch when you get there. Chain 1, turn, and single crochet back to the other side, joining with a slip stitch. Chain 1, turn, and single crochet back to the beginning, joining with a slip stitch when you get to the other side. Chain 1, turn, and single crochet back to the beginning, once again joining with a slip stitch.

Continue with this until you are happy with the size of the piece, once again remembering to change colors according to the photo or your own preference.

Tie off, and make sure all the ends are secure, and your rug is done!

If you are going to be using your rug on a hard surface, consider placing rug tabs at the bottom to ensure there is no sliding when you step on the rug. These can be purchased at most craft supply stores.

Seasonal Sensation Rug

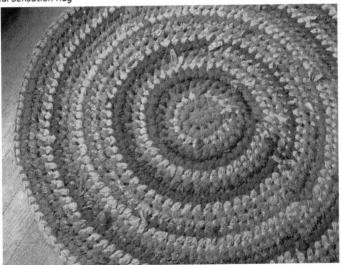

Photo made by: Rick&Brenda Beerhorst

You will need heavy weight yarn in the colors of your choice and a size N crochet hook. T-shirt yarn and plastic yarn both work as well, and you'll still be able to use the N hook for the project.

385

This project is worked until you are happy with the size of the piece, so you will need as much yarn as you like to achieve that size. For a minimum, you are going to need the equivalent of 2 skeins.

Starting with the color of your choice, you are going to chain 5 and join with a slip stitch to form a ring. Single crochet in the center of this ring 12 times, and join with a slip stitch to the beginning.

Chain 1, turn, and single crochet back to the beginning of the row, working 1 stitch in each of the stitches along the way, once again joining with a slip stitch when you get back to the beginning. Chain 1, turn, and once again single crochet back around the edge of the piece. You are going to join with a slip stitch when you get back to the beginning once more. Chain 1, turn, and repeat back to the beginning, remembering to join with a slip stitch.

You may find that you need to add an extra stitch to the end chain to ensure that you reach properly. This is normal, and you will continue to work with this new stitch that you add along the way. You can use scrap yarn to complete this project, or you can follow the photo as a reference guide of which kind of yarn to use.

If you are going to be using the photo for reference, you are going to change colors every other row, or as often as you prefer. There is no wrong way to do it, as long as you are happy with the finished rug that you have created. Tie off the previous color, join the new color with a slip stitch, and continue along the edge of the project, following the same pattern as before.

Chain 1, turn, and single crochet back around the piece back to the beginning, joining with a slip stitch when you get there. Chain 1, turn, and single crochet back to the other side, joining with a slip stitch. Chain 1, turn, and single crochet back to the beginning, joining with a slip stitch when you get to the other side. Chain 1, turn, and single crochet back to the beginning, once again joining with a slip stitch.

Chain 1, turn, and single crochet back around the piece back to the beginning, joining with a slip stitch when you get there. Chain 1, turn, and single crochet back to the other side, joining with a slip stitch. Chain 1, turn, and single crochet back to the beginning, joining with a slip stitch when you get to the other side. Chain 1, turn, and single crochet back to the beginning, once again joining with a slip stitch.

Chain 1, turn, and single crochet back around the piece back to the beginning, joining with a slip stitch when you get there. Chain 1, turn, and single crochet back to the other side, joining with a slip stitch. Chain 1, turn, and single crochet back to the beginning, joining with a slip stitch when you get to the other side. Chain 1, turn, and single crochet back to the beginning, once again joining with a slip stitch.

Continue with this until you are happy with the size of the piece, once again remembering to change colors according to the photo or your own preference.

Tie off, and make sure all the ends are secure, and your rug is done!

If you are going to be using your rug on a hard surface, consider placing rug tabs at the bottom to ensure there is no sliding when you step on the rug. These can be purchased at most craft supply stores.

Photo made by: <u>Max Barners</u>

You will need heavy weight yarn in the colors of your choice and a size N crochet hook. T-shirt yarn and plastic yarn both work as well, and you'll still be able to use the N hook for the project.

This project is worked until you are happy with the size of the piece, so you will need as much yarn as you like to achieve that size. For a minimum, you are going to need the equivalent of 2 skeins.

Starting with the color of your choice, you are going to chain 5 and join with a slip stitch to form a ring. Single crochet in the center of this ring 12 times, and join with a slip stitch to the beginning.

Chain 1, turn, and single crochet back to the beginning of the row, working 1 stitch in each of the stitches along the way, once again joining with a slip stitch when you get back to the beginning. Chain 1, turn, and once again single crochet back around the edge of the piece. You are going to join with a slip stitch when you get back to the beginning once more. Chain 1, turn, and repeat back to the beginning, remembering to join with a slip stitch.

You may find that you need to add an extra stitch to the end chain to ensure that you reach properly. This is normal, and you will continue to work with this new stitch that you add along the way. You can use scrap yarn to complete this project, or you can follow the photo as a reference guide of which kind of yarn to use.

If you are using multi-colored yarn, the piece is going to stripe itself, without you having to do anything. There is no wrong way to do it, as long as you are happy with the finished rug that you have created. Tie off the previous color, join the new color with a slip stitch, and continue along the edge of the project, following the same pattern as before.

Chain 1, turn, and single crochet back around the piece back to the beginning, joining with a slip stitch when you get there. Chain 1, turn, and single crochet back to the other side, joining with a slip stitch. Chain 1, turn, and single crochet back to the beginning, joining with a slip stitch when you get to the other side. Chain 1, turn, and single crochet back to the beginning, once again joining with a slip stitch.

Chain 1, turn, and single crochet back around the piece back to the beginning, joining with a slip stitch when you get there. Chain 1, turn, and single crochet back to the other side, joining with a slip stitch. Chain 1, turn, and single crochet back to the beginning, joining with a slip stitch when you get to the other side. Chain 1, turn, and single crochet back to the beginning, once again joining with a slip stitch.

Chain 1, turn, and single crochet back around the piece back to the beginning, joining with a slip stitch when you get there. Chain 1, turn, and single crochet back to the other side, joining with a slip stitch. Chain 1, turn, and single crochet back to the beginning, joining with a slip stitch when you get to the other side. Chain 1, turn, and single crochet back to the beginning, once again joining with a slip stitch.

Continue with this until you are happy with the size of the piece, once again remembering to change colors according to the photo or your own preference.

Tie off, and make sure all the ends are secure, and your rug is done!

If you are going to be using your rug on a hard surface, consider placing rug tabs at the bottom to ensure there is no sliding when you step on the rug. These can be purchased at most craft supply stores.

Conclusion

There you have it, everything you need to know to make your own afghan rugs, and the patterns to inspire you to create something wonderful with them to decorate every room in your house.

When it comes to home décor, the only way to get what you truly want is to make it yourself. Sure, you can find things in the store that you like. You can look at patterns and designs that you think are pretty, and you can find things that go with the rest of your house, but when you are looking for something that is created for your house – something that is going to make your house look wonderful and bring out just what you wanted in the room, you are going to have to do it yourself.

I hope this book was able to fill you with the inspiration you need to create a variety of beautiful rugs for your home, and that you are thrilled with each and every rug you have. There is no end to the ways you can fall in love with the rugs you wish to create, and you are going to find that each one is full of personality and charm.

Turn your home into the palace you have been dreaming of, and enjoy a variety of rugs that only you can create. Your friends and family will be amazed with the results, and you are going to find that there really is no end to the ways you can spice up the look of your home with just a simple piece.

So what are you waiting for? The holidays are on their way, and with them come all the family and friends. Hosting has never felt better than when you are able to take your home décor up to the next level, and the fun you are going to have as you show off each room to your friends and family is going to make all the hard work worth it.

Get out to the store, find your favorite yarn and crochet hook, and settle in. You are going to fall in love with the results, and you are going to be amazed at just how easy it is for you to create décor for your home that lasts a lifetime.

You'll be making memories as much as you are making the perfect decoration piece, and you'll see for yourself just how good it is to create what you want, when you want. There really is no end to the ways you can show off your style, all you have to do is imagine, take inspiration, and showcase your creativity. It all comes down to what you want to do with your look, and what you are able to make with your hook.

Getting that perfect room has never been so easy.

You've got the perfect look waiting for you – you just have to create it.

Good luck.

Crochet Dream Catcher

Alisa Hatchenson

10 Mystic Dream Catchers To Protect Your Sleep

393

Crochet Dream Catchers:

10 Mystic Dream Catchers To Protect Your Sleep

Introduction

You have dreams, hopes, and ambitions, and you want to follow all of them. You sleep well, you wake up, and you remember some of the dreams that you had, but other times, your dreams just feel like a distant memory.

There are times your dreams aren't so sweet, and you fear going back to sleep lest you somehow end up back inside one of them. You spend a night worried about this, and you wake up feeling tired and groggy the next day. It doesn't really matter what you do, when you fall asleep, it is little more than a gamble.

You want something that is going to help you sleep well. Something that is going to capture your imagination, fill you with motivation, and provide that sweet night you have been yearning for. No, you don't want medication and you certainly don't want to take any kind of pill – you want something that has been around longer than either of those.

You want a dreamcatcher.

But, how are you going to get one?

Sure, you can get online and order one. You can go to the store and buy one, but they aren't going to be personal. They aren't going to give you the end result you are looking for. To do that, you are going to have to do it yourself.

You are going to have to make one.

But, you ask – is that hard?

Is there a way you can do it without too much trouble?

How do you get them to fit inside those rings?

With all these questions in your head, it is easy to feel overwhelmed. But, this book is going to change all that, and it is going to provide you with the simple directions you need to create your very own dreamcatchers. This book is everything you have been searching for, and it is going to help you chase your dreams.

So what are you waiting for? All you need are a few tools to get the job done – and with this book, you've got them handed to you right here, and right now.

Let's get started – you have some dreaming to do.

The Dream Catchers

Mystic Mountain Dreamcatcher

You will need thread weight yarn in the colors of your choice and a size G crochet hook.

You will also need a needle and thread, a hoop in the size of your choice, and any decorations you wish to add to the finished catcher.

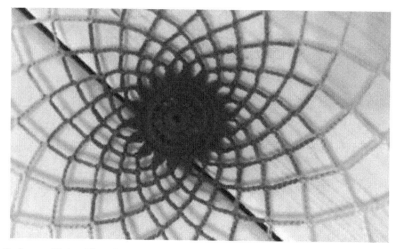

Chain 5 and join with a slip stitch to form a ring. Single crochet in the center of this ring 12 times, and join with a slip stitch. Chain 1, turn, and single crochet back to the other side, using 1 stitch in each stitch. Join with a slip stitch, chain 1, turn, and go back the other way, following the same pattern.

Continue to do this until the center measures 2 inches across.

For the next row, you are going to chain 5 and skip the next stitch and join with a slip stitch in the next stitch. Chain 5 and skip the next stitch then join with a slip stitch in the next stitch. Chain 5 and skip the next stitch then join with a slip stitch in the next stitch. Continue around.

Chain 5 and join with a slip stitch in the center of the chain space. Chain 5 once more and join with a slip stitch in the center of the next chain space. Continue around.

Repeat the last row until the piece is nearly as big as the hoop you are going to use. Tie off and set aside.

Repeat this sequence twice more for the two smaller hoops – set both aside.

To assemble:

398

Take your piece now and stretch it slightly to fit in the ring. Remember that you are going to make it slightly too small to fit the ring, so you have a nice, tight stretch when it is time to put it in.

Use your needle and thread to sew around the outside of the piece you have crocheted, wrapping it around the outside of the ring, and through the piece once more. Continue with even stitches all the way around the piece until you are happy with the center.

Tie off.

Add any additional ornaments you like to the centerpiece as well as the outside bottom of the ring. Attach a hook or a loop at the top to hang the piece, and you are done!

King of the Sea Dreamcatcher

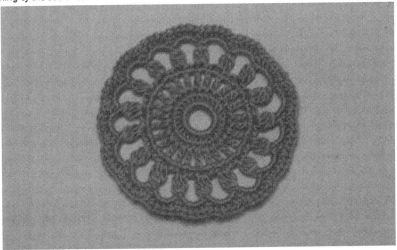

You will need thread weight yarn in the colors of your choice and a size G crochet hook.

You will also need a needle and thread, a hoop in the size of your choice, and any decorations you wish to add to the finished catcher.

Chain 10 and join with a slip stitch. Single crochet back around to the other side. Chain 1, turn, and single crochet back to the beginning. Join with a slip stitch. Chain 1, turn, and single crochet back to the other side. Continue for a total of 5 rows.

For the next row, you are going to chain 5 and skip the next stitch and join with a slip stitch in the next stitch. Chain 5 and skip the next stitch then join with a slip stitch in the next stitch. Chain 5 and skip the next stitch then join with a slip stitch in the next stitch. Continue around.

You are now going to go back to single crochet for the next 3 rows, joining the tops of the humps you have created from the previous row. You may have to chain a few extra stitches between the humps to ensure that you get the right shape to the piece, so work with the piece until you are happy with the shape.

For the next row, you are going to chain 8 and skip the next 4 stitches, then join with a slip stitch in the next stitch. For the next row, you are going to chain 8 and skip the next 4 stitches, then join with a slip stitch in the next stitch. For the next row, you are going to chain 8 and skip the next 4 stitches, then join with a slip stitch in the next stitch. For the next row, you are going to chain 8 and skip the next 4 stitches, then join with a slip stitch in the next stitch.

Repeat the last row until the piece is nearly as big as the hoop you are going to use.

For the next row, you are going to single crochet around the boarder of your piece 2 times. Again, you want this to still be smaller than the hoop of your choice, so don't make this border too thick.

When you are happy with the size, tie it off and set aside.

To assemble:

Take your piece now and stretch it slightly to fit in the ring. Remember that you are going to make it slightly too small to fit the ring, so you have a nice, tight stretch when it is time to put it in.

Use your needle and thread to sew around the outside of the piece you have crocheted, wrapping it around the outside of the ring, and through the piece once more. Continue with even stitches all the way around the piece until you are happy with the center.

Tie off.

Add any additional ornaments you like to the centerpiece as well as the outside bottom of the ring. Attach a hook or a loop at the top to hang the piece, and you are done!

Perfect for Fall Dreamcatcher

You will need thread weight yarn in the colors of your choice and a size G crochet hook.

You will also need a needle and thread, a hoop in the size of your choice, and any decorations you wish to add to the finished catcher.

Chain 5 and join with a slip stitch to form a ring. Single crochet in the center of this ring 12 times, and join with a slip stitch. Chain 1, turn, and single crochet back to the other side, using 1 stitch in each stitch. Join with a slip stitch, chain 1, turn, and go back the other way, following the same pattern.

Continue to do this until the center measures 2 inches across.

For the next row, you are going to chain 5 and skip the next stitch and join with a slip stitch in the next stitch. Chain 5 and skip the next stitch then join with a slip stitch in the next stitch. Chain 5 and skip the next stitch then join with a slip stitch in the next stitch. Continue around.

Chain 5 and join with a slip stitch in the center of the chain space. Chain 5 once more and join with a slip stitch in the center of the next chain space. Continue around.

Repeat the last row until the piece is nearly as big as the hoop you are going to use. Tie off and set aside.

Remember to attach beads to the ends as you stitch this to the hoop of your choice.

To assemble:

Take your piece now and stretch it slightly to fit in the ring. Remember that you are going to make it slightly too small to fit the ring, so you have a nice, tight stretch when it is time to put it in.

Use your needle and thread to sew around the outside of the piece you have crocheted, wrapping it around the outside of the ring, and through the piece once more. Continue with even stitches all the way around the piece until you are happy with the center.

Tie off.

Add any additional ornaments you like to the centerpiece as well as the outside bottom of the ring. Attach a hook or a loop at the top to hang the piece, and you are done!

Spring Center Dreamcatcher

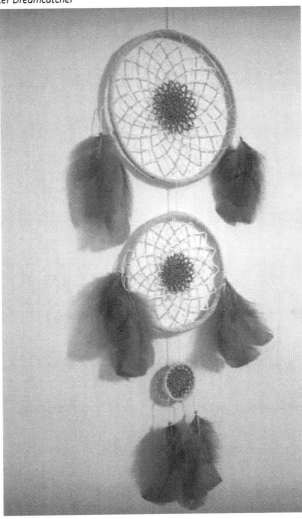

You will need thread weight yarn in the colors of your choice and a size G crochet hook.

You will also need a needle and thread, a hoop in the size of your choice, and any decorations you wish to add to the finished catcher.

Chain 5 and join with a slip stitch to form a ring. Single crochet in the center of this ring 12 times, and join with a slip stitch. Chain 1, turn, and single crochet back to the other side, using 1 stitch in each stitch. Join with a slip stitch, chain 1, turn, and go back the other way, following the same pattern.

Continue to do this until the center measures 2 inches across.

Tie off this color and join with the next color.

For the next row, you are going to chain 5 and skip the next stitch and join with a slip stitch in the next stitch. Chain 5 and skip the next stitch then join with a slip stitch in the next stitch. Chain 5 and skip the next stitch then join with a slip stitch in the next stitch. Continue around.

Chain 5 and join with a slip stitch in the center of the chain space. Chain 5 once more and join with a slip stitch in the center of the next chain space. Continue around.

Repeat the last row until the piece is nearly as big as the hoop you are going to use. Tie off and set aside.

Remember to repeat this two more times for the other hoops. You are going to follow the same sequence throughout, just alter the piece to fit the hoop you are currently making it for.

To assemble:

Take your piece now and stretch it slightly to fit in the ring. Remember that you are going to make it slightly too small to fit the ring, so you have a nice, tight stretch when it is time to put it in.

Use your needle and thread to sew around the outside of the piece you have crocheted, wrapping it around the outside of the ring, and through the piece once more. Continue with even stitches all the way around the piece until you are happy with the center.

Tie off.

Add any additional ornaments you like to the centerpiece as well as the outside bottom of the ring. Attach a hook or a loop at the top to hang the piece, and you are done!

You will need thread weight yarn in the colors of your choice and a size G crochet hook.

You will also need a needle and thread, a hoop in the size of your choice, and any decorations you wish to add to the finished catcher.

Chain 5 and join with a slip stitch to form a ring. Single crochet in the center of this ring 12 times, and join with a slip stitch. Chain 1, turn, and single crochet back to the other side, using 1 stitch in each stitch. Join with a slip stitch, chain 1, turn, and go back the other way, following the same pattern.

Continue to do this until the center measures 2 inches across.

Change colors and join with the next color (for the larger hoop only.)

For the next row, you are going to chain 5 and skip the next stitch and join with a slip stitch in the next stitch. Chain 5 and skip the next stitch then join with a slip stitch in the next stitch. Chain 5 and skip the next stitch then join with a slip stitch in the next stitch. Continue around.

Chain 5 and join with a slip stitch in the center of the chain space. Chain 5 once more and join with a slip stitch in the center of the next chain space. Continue around.

Repeat the last row until the piece is nearly as big as the hoop you are going to use. Tie off and set aside.

You are going to now go back and repeat this sequence for the smaller three hoops. Remember that you are not going to change colors for those pieces.

To assemble:

Take your piece now and stretch it slightly to fit in the ring. Remember that you are going to make it slightly too small to fit the ring, so you have a nice, tight stretch when it is time to put it in.

Use your needle and thread to sew around the outside of the piece you have crocheted, wrapping it around the outside of the ring, and through the piece once more. Continue with even stitches all the way around the piece until you are happy with the center.

Tie off.

Add any additional ornaments you like to the centerpiece as well as the outside bottom of the ring. Attach a hook or a loop at the top to hang the piece, and you are done!

Delicate Lace Dreamcatcher

You will need thread weight yarn in the colors of your choice and a size G crochet hook.

You will also need a needle and thread, a hoop in the size of your choice, and any decorations you wish to add to the finished catcher.

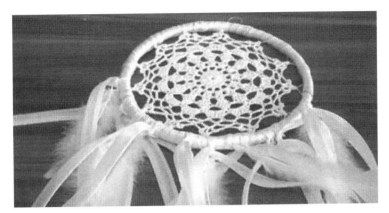

Chain 10 and join with a slip stitch. Single crochet back around to the other side. Chain 1, turn, and single crochet back to the beginning. Join with a slip stitch. Chain 1, turn, and single crochet back to the other side. Continue for a total of 5 rows.

For the next row, you are going to chain 5 and skip the next stitch and join with a slip stitch in the next stitch. Chain 5 and skip the next stitch then join with a slip stitch in the next stitch. Chain 5 and skip the next stitch then join with a slip stitch in the next stitch. Continue around.

You are now going to go back to single crochet for the next 7-8 rows, joining the tops of the humps you have created from the previous row. You may have to chain a few extra stitches between the humps to ensure that you get the right shape to the piece, so work with the piece until you are happy with the shape.

How thick you make this second piece is going to depend on the overall size of the hoop you are using, as well as the piece itself. Don't be afraid to adjust within the piece as you are working to ensure that you get the right shape and the right thickness – the good thing about these dreamcatchers is that you are able to adjust them to fit your needs as you work, instead of having to go with the black and white directions to get them the proper shape.

Make this thicker or even thinner if you are going to be using a smaller hoop, as long as you are happy with the end result, you are doing it the right way.

For the next row, you are going to chain 5 and skip the next stitch and join with a slip stitch in the next stitch. Chain 5 and skip the next stitch then join with a slip stitch in the next stitch. Chain 5 and skip the next stitch then join with a slip stitch in the next stitch. Continue around.

Chain 5 and join with a slip stitch in the center of the chain space. Chain 5 once more and join with a slip stitch in the center of the next chain space. Continue around.

Repeat the last row until the piece is nearly as big as the hoop you are going to use. Tie off and set aside.

To assemble:

Take your piece now and stretch it slightly to fit in the ring. Remember that you are going to make it slightly too small to fit the ring, so you have a nice, tight stretch when it is time to put it in.

Use your needle and thread to sew around the outside of the piece you have crocheted, wrapping it around the outside of the ring, and through the piece once more. Continue with even stitches all the way around the piece until you are happy with the center.

Tie off.

Add any additional ornaments you like to the centerpiece as well as the outside bottom of the ring. Attach a hook or a loop at the top to hang the piece, and you are done!

Photo made by: flyone1106

You will need thread weight yarn in the colors of your choice and a size G crochet hook.

You will also need a needle and thread, a hoop in the size of your choice, and any decorations you wish to add to the finished catcher.

Chain 5 and join with a slip stitch to form a ring. Single crochet in the center of this ring 12 times, and join with a slip stitch. Chain 1, turn, and single crochet back to the other side, using 1 stitch in each stitch. Join with a slip stitch, chain 1, turn, and go back the other way, following the same pattern.

Depending on the size of your piece, you can make the center as thick as you want, or leave it on the small side. Use the photo as a reference for the size of your piece.

For the next row, you are going to chain 5 and skip the next stitch and join with a slip stitch in the next stitch. Chain 5 and skip the next stitch then join with a slip stitch in the

411

next stitch. Chain 5 and skip the next stitch then join with a slip stitch in the next stitch. Continue around.

Chain 5 and join with a slip stitch in the center of the chain space. Chain 5 once more and join with a slip stitch in the center of the next chain space. Continue around.

Repeat the last row until the piece is nearly as big as the hoop you are going to use. Tie off and set aside.

To assemble:

Take your piece now and stretch it slightly to fit in the ring. Remember that you are going to make it slightly too small to fit the ring, so you have a nice, tight stretch when it is time to put it in.

Use your needle and thread to sew around the outside of the piece you have crocheted, wrapping it around the outside of the ring, and through the piece once more. Continue with even stitches all the way around the piece until you are happy with the center.

Tie off.

Add any additional ornaments you like to the centerpiece as well as the outside bottom of the ring. Attach a hook or a loop at the top to hang the piece, and you are done!

Mini Beaded Dreamcatcher

Photo made by: amylovesyah

You will need thread weight yarn in the colors of your choice and a size G crochet hook.

You will also need a needle and thread, a hoop in the size of your choice, and any decorations you wish to add to the finished catcher.

Chain 5 and join with a slip stitch to form a ring. Single crochet in the center of this ring 12 times, and join with a slip stitch. Chain 1, turn, and single crochet back to the other side, using 1 stitch in each stitch. Join with a slip stitch, chain 1, turn, and go back the other way, following the same pattern.

Depending on the size of your piece, you can make the center as thick as you want, or leave it on the small side. Use the photo as a reference for the size of your piece.

For the next row, you are going to chain 5 and skip the next stitch and join with a slip stitch in the next stitch. Chain 5 and skip the next stitch then join with a slip stitch in the next stitch. Chain 5 and skip the next stitch then join with a slip stitch in the next stitch. Continue around.

Chain 5 and join with a slip stitch in the center of the chain space. Chain 5 once more and join with a slip stitch in the center of the next chain space. Continue around.

413

Repeat the last row until the piece is nearly as big as the hoop you are going to use. Tie off and set aside.

Add the beads to the piece after you have it sewn in place.

To assemble:

Take your piece now and stretch it slightly to fit in the ring. Remember that you are going to make it slightly too small to fit the ring, so you have a nice, tight stretch when it is time to put it in.

Use your needle and thread to sew around the outside of the piece you have crocheted, wrapping it around the outside of the ring, and through the piece once more. Continue with even stitches all the way around the piece until you are happy with the center.

Tie off.

Add any additional ornaments you like to the centerpiece as well as the outside bottom of the ring. Attach a hook or a loop at the top to hang the piece, and you are done!

Triple Crown Dreamcatcher

Photo made by: mikeporterinmd

You will need thread weight yarn in the colors of your choice and a size G crochet hook.

You will also need a needle and thread, a hoop in the size of your choice, and any decorations you wish to add to the finished catcher.

Chain 5 and join with a slip stitch to form a ring. Single crochet in the center of this ring 12 times, and join with a slip stitch. Chain 1, turn, and single crochet back to the other side, using 1 stitch in each stitch. Join with a slip stitch, chain 1, turn, and go back the other way, following the same pattern.

Depending on the size of your piece, you can make the center as thick as you want, or leave it on the small side. Use the photo as a reference for the size of your piece.

For the next row, you are going to chain 5 and skip the next stitch and join with a slip stitch in the next stitch. Chain 5 and skip the next stitch then join with a slip stitch in the next stitch. Chain 5 and skip the next stitch then join with a slip stitch in the next stitch. Continue around.

Chain 5 and join with a slip stitch in the center of the chain space. Chain 5 once more and join with a slip stitch in the center of the next chain space. Continue around.

Repeat the last row until the piece is nearly as big as the hoop you are going to use. Tie off and set aside.

Add the beads to the main part of the piece after you have it sewn securely into place.

To assemble:

Take your piece now and stretch it slightly to fit in the ring. Remember that you are going to make it slightly too small to fit the ring, so you have a nice, tight stretch when it is time to put it in.

Use your needle and thread to sew around the outside of the piece you have crocheted, wrapping it around the outside of the ring, and through the piece once more. Continue with even stitches all the way around the piece until you are happy with the center.

Tie off.

Add any additional ornaments you like to the centerpiece as well as the outside bottom of the ring. Attach a hook or a loop at the top to hang the piece, and you are done!

Now that you have your dreamcatchers, it's time to decorate! Of course, you can follow each of the images and decorate them with real feathers, or you can crochet your own. For this final project, we are going to look at how you can crochet your own feathers.

Photo made by: <u>Regina Rioux</u>

You will need 1 ball of cotton yarn in the color of your choice and a size G crochet hook.

Decide how long you want your feather to be, and chain a length that is equal to this measurement. Single crochet back to the beginning. Next, take your hook and slip stitch to the base of where you want the feather to start fanning out.

Chain 10 and join with a slip stitch to the same stitch. Chain 10 and repeat on the other side. Now, move to the next stitch. Chain 10, and join with a slip stitch in the first stitch. Chain 10 and repeat on the other side. Chain 10 and join with a slip stitch to the same stitch. Chain 10 and repeat on the other side. Now, move to the next stitch. Chain 10, and join with a slip stitch in the first stitch. Chain 10 and repeat on the other side.

Chain 10 and join with a slip stitch to the same stitch. Chain 10 and repeat on the other side. Now, move to the next stitch. Chain 10, and join with a slip stitch in the first stitch. Chain 10 and repeat on the other side. Chain 10 and join with a slip stitch to the same stitch. Chain 10 and repeat on the other side. Now, move to the next stitch. Chain 10, and join with a slip stitch in the first stitch. Chain 10 and repeat on the other side.

Use the photo as reference, and as you get closer to the end, begin to chain fewer stitches to taper the end of the feather. Leave a point at the very end, and tie off the yarn.

That's it! Make as many of these as you like and your feathers are done!

Conclusion

There you have it, everything you need to know to make your own collection of dreamcatchers. It's no secret that these pieces are some of the most enchanting things you can use to decorate your home, and when you know how to make them yourself, you are giving yourself everything you need to decorate your house the right way.

I hope you make each and every one of the pieces you find in this book, and that you are able to take each of these and throw in your own creativity. There is no end to the ways you can show off your style, and with dreamcatchers, you're going to be sleeping well all night – every night.

Good luck, and sweet dreams.

Seasonal Crocheting

Winter Crochet

Wonderful Crochet Projects To Warm You And Your Loved Ones

Alisa Hatchenson

Winter Crochet:

Wonderful Crochet Projects To Warm You And
Your Loved Ones

Introduction

Sleigh bells are ringing, bells are jingling, and there are people singing in the streets. You don't know what it is, but it just seems as though people are nicer this time of the year. They are ready to hold the door open for you – they are ready to give a little more when they are standing in line, and they are ready to be a little nicer to those around them.

Suddenly, it doesn't matter so much that there are crowds in the streets or other people in line at the shopping mall. It doesn't matter that it is cold and snowy, or that you are going to have to wait a little longer to get things done. When it comes to the holidays, you are ready to set a lot aside for others.

This is the season of giving, and you want to enjoy every second of it – and you know one of the best ways to do that is by bundling up in your favorite style, and heading out to experience all the joys of the season.

When it comes to the holidays, you know that there are many different things you want to do and experience, and you want to do all of them feeling great. When you know you look good, you feel good, and you are going to do that by wearing your favorite – well – everything.

And what better way to know that you are going to get the custom fit than when you make it yourself? You'll get the perfect fit, you'll get the perfect color, and you'll get everything that you have been wanting in your winter wardrobe.

But where are you going to get these patterns? Where are you going to get these custom pieces that fit you just right in all the right places? Obviously, if you are going to get such a perfect thing, you are going to have to make it yourself.

And that's where this book comes in. In it, you are going to discover everything you need to create the perfect wardrobe no matter what you are looking for. This book is going to be your perfect inspiration, and with the dash of creativity you are going to add to the mix, you are going to end up with the perfect pieces no matter what.

Get ready to dive into a whole new world of fashion, and dive into this world with a whole new sense of style.

You know you want to, so what are you waiting for? You're brimming with creativity, so get ready to dive into a whole new world of fashion.

Let's get started.

Pretty Kitty Cuffs

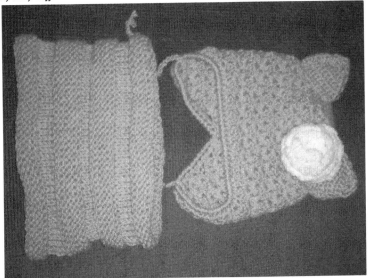

You will need 1 skein of yarn in the color of your choice and a size G crochet hook

You will also need a yarn needle and scissors.

For the hat:

Chain 4 and join with a slip stitch to form a ring. Single crochet in the center of this ring 8 times, and join with another slip stitch. Chain 1, turn, and single crochet across the row. Join with a slip stitch.

Chain 1, turn, and single crochet in the first stitch, then double crochet in the next stitch 2 times. Single crochet in the next stitch, then double crochet in the next stitch 2 times. Single crochet in the next stitch, then double crochet in the next stitch 2 times. Single crochet in the next stitch. Continue this around the row, and join with a slip stitch.

Chain 1, turn, and single crochet in the first stitch, then skip the next stitch. Single crochet in the next stitch, then skip the next stitch. Repeat this around, then join with a slip stitch at the end.

Chain 1, turn, and single crochet in the first stitch, then double crochet in the next stitch 2 times. Single crochet in the next stitch, then double crochet in the next stitch 2 times. Single crochet in the next stitch, then double crochet in the next stitch 2 times. Single crochet in the next stitch. Continue this around the row, and join with a slip stitch.

Chain 1, turn, and single crochet in the first stitch, then skip the next stitch. Single crochet in the next stitch, then skip the next stitch. Repeat this around, then join with a slip stitch at the end.

You are going to measure as you go with this, working until the top of the hat reaches across the top of your head. Usually you are going to increase for about 12 rows. Next, you are going to fit the hat to your head.

Chain 1, turn, and single crochet in the first stitch, then skip the next 2 stitches. Single crochet in the next stitch, then skip the next 2 stitches. Repeat this around, then join with a slip stitch at the end.

Chain 1, turn, and single crochet in the first stitch, then double crochet in the next stitch 2 times. Single crochet in the next stitch, then double crochet in the next stitch 2 times. Single crochet in the next stitch, then double crochet in the next stitch 2 times. Single crochet in the next stitch. Continue this around the row, and join with a slip stitch.

Repeat until the hat fits your head, then finish with a border around the base.

For each of the ears you are going to chain 10 and skip the first stitch, single crocheting across the row and skipping the last stitch. Single crochet across the row. Chain 1, skip the first stitch, and single crochet across the row, skipping the last stitch. Repeat until you have a triangle. Repeat for the other ear.

Sew the ears in place, and tie off.

For the scarf:

Chain a length that is 2 feet long. Single crochet across the row. Chain 1, turn, and single crochet back to the beginning. Chain 1, turn, and single crochet across the row. Chain 1, turn, and single crochet back to the beginning. Chain 1, turn, and single crochet across the row. Chain 1, turn, and single crochet back to the beginning. Chain 1, turn, and single crochet across the row.

Chain 1, turn, and single crochet across the row in the front loop only. Chain 1, turn, and single crochet back to the beginning in the front loop only. Chain 1, turn, and single crochet across the row in the front loop only. Chain 1, turn, and single crochet back to the beginning in the front loop only.

Chain a length that is 2 feet long. Single crochet across the row. Chain 1, turn, and single crochet back to the beginning. Chain 1, turn, and single crochet across the row. Chain 1, turn, and single crochet back to the beginning. Chain 1, turn, and single crochet across the row. Chain 1, turn, and single crochet back to the beginning. Chain 1, turn, and single crochet across the row.

Chain 1, turn, and single crochet across the row in the front loop only. Chain 1, turn, and single crochet back to the beginning in the front loop only. Chain 1, turn, and single crochet across the row in the front loop only. Chain 1, turn, and single crochet back to the beginning in the front loop only.

Repeat until the scarf measure six inches thick. Tie off.

Take your yarn needle and sew up the ends, creating an eternity scarf. Tie off, and you are done!

You will need 2 skeins of yarn in the color of your choice and a size J crochet hook

You will also need a yarn needle and scissors.

For the hat:

Chain 4 and join with a slip stitch to form a ring. Single crochet in the center of this ring 8 times, and join with another slip stitch. Chain 1, turn, and single crochet across the row. Join with a slip stitch.

Chain 1, turn, and single crochet in the first stitch, then double crochet in the next stitch 2 times. Single crochet in the next stitch, then double crochet in the next stitch 2 times. Single crochet in the next stitch, then double crochet in the next stitch 2 times. Single crochet in the next stitch. Continue this around the row, and join with a slip stitch.

Chain 1, turn, and single crochet in the first stitch, then skip the next stitch. Single crochet in the next stitch, then skip the next stitch. Repeat this around, then join with a slip stitch at the end.

Chain 1, turn, and single crochet in the first stitch, then double crochet in the next stitch 2 times. Single crochet in the next stitch, then double crochet in the next stitch 2 times. Single crochet in the next stitch, then double crochet in the next stitch 2 times. Single crochet in the next stitch. Continue this around the row, and join with a slip stitch.

Chain 1, turn, and single crochet in the first stitch, then skip the next stitch. Single crochet in the next stitch, then skip the next stitch. Repeat this around, then join with a slip stitch at the end.

You are going to measure as you go with this, working until the top of the hat reaches across the top of your head. Usually you are going to increase for about 12 rows. Next, you are going to fit the hat to your head.

Chain 1, turn, and single crochet in the first stitch, then skip the next 2 stitches. Single crochet in the next stitch, then skip the next 2 stitches. Repeat this around, then join with a slip stitch at the end.

Chain 1, turn, and single crochet in the first stitch, then double crochet in the next stitch 2 times. Single crochet in the next stitch, then double crochet in the next stitch 2 times. Single crochet in the next stitch, then double crochet in the next stitch 2 times. Single crochet in the next stitch. Continue this around the row, and join with a slip stitch.

Repeat until the hat fits your head, then finish with a border around the base.

Tie off.

For the scarf:

Chain a length that is 3 feet long.

Chain 2, turn, and double crochet back to the beginning. Chain 2, turn and double crochet across the row. Chain 2, turn, and double crochet back to the beginning. Chain 2, turn, and double crochet across the row. Chain 2, turn, and double crochet back to the beginning. Chain 2, turn, and double crochet across the row.

Chain 2, turn, and double crochet back to the beginning. Chain 2, turn and double crochet across the row. Chain 2, turn, and double crochet back to the beginning. Chain 2, turn, and double crochet across the row. Chain 2, turn, and double crochet back to the beginning. Chain 2, turn, and double crochet across the row.

Repeat until the scarf measure six inches thick. Tie off.

Take your yarn needle and sew up the ends, creating an eternity scarf. Tie off, and you are done!

Around the World Eternity Scarf

You will need 1 skein of yarn in the color of your choice and a size G crochet hook

You will also need a yarn needle and scissors.

Chain a length that is 4 feet long. Single crochet across the row. Chain 1, turn, and single crochet back to the beginning. Chain 1, turn, and single crochet across the row. Chain 1, turn, and single crochet back to the beginning. Chain 1, turn, and single crochet across the row. Chain 1, turn, and single crochet back to the beginning. Chain 1, turn, and single crochet across the row.

Chain 1, turn, and single crochet back to the beginning. Chain 1, turn, and single crochet across the row. Chain 1, turn, and single crochet back to the beginning. Chain 1, turn, and single crochet across the row. Chain 1, turn, and single crochet back to the beginning. Chain 1, turn, and single crochet across the row.

Repeat until the scarf measure six inches thick. Tie off.

Take your yarn needle and sew up the ends, creating an eternity scarf. Tie off, and you are done!

Magical Mermaid Cozy Blanket

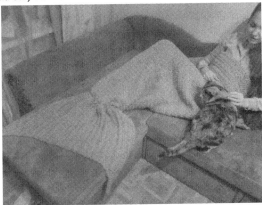

You will need 2 or 3 skeins of yarn in the color of your choice and a size J crochet hook

You will also need a yarn needle and scissors.

Chain a length that is 8 feet long – larger or smaller to adjust the size of the tale. When this is folded in half, it is going to fit around you, so make sure it is roomie enough.

Single crochet across the row. Chain 1, turn, and single crochet back to the beginning. Chain 1, turn, and single crochet across the row. Chain 1, turn, and single crochet back to the beginning. Chain 1, turn, and single crochet across the row. Chain 1, turn, and single crochet back to the beginning. Chain 1, turn, and single crochet across the row.

Single crochet across the row. Chain 1, turn, and single crochet back to the beginning. Chain 1, turn, and single crochet across the row. Chain 1, turn, and single crochet back to the beginning. Chain 1, turn, and single crochet across the row. Chain 1, turn, and single crochet back to the beginning. Chain 1, turn, and single crochet across the row. Keep going until this measures from your chest down past your feet.

Tie off.

Now, you are going to make the tail.

Chain a length that is 5 feet long. Single crochet across the row. Chain 1, turn, and single crochet back to the beginning. Chain 1, turn, and single crochet across the row. Chain 1, turn, and single crochet back to the beginning. Chain 1, turn, and single crochet across the row. Chain 1, turn, and single crochet back to the beginning. Chain 1, turn, and single crochet across the row.

This is the tail, continue until you are happy with the size, then tie off.

To finish:

Sew up the side of the larger piece you have made, creating the tube. Once this is sewn, you are going to gather the base by feeding a piece of yarn around the opening and pulling it closed. Insert the smaller square into this opening, pulling it closed into the shape of the tail.

Sew this securely into the blanket, and form the shape of the mermaid tale. Tie off, and you are done!

Snowball Fight Christmas Gloves

You will need scrap yarn or as many skeins of yarn in the colors of your choice and a size G crochet hook

You will also need a yarn needle and scissors.

Chain 1 length that is 4 inches long. Double crochet across the row, then down and across the bottom. Join with a slip stitch when you get back to the beginning. Chain 2, turn, and double crochet back up and around to the other side. Once again, you are going to join this with a slip stitch when you get back to the beginning.

You are going to follow this sequence until the size of your oval measures across your hand. Measure as you go to ensure you get the proper fit – and tie it off once you do.

Repeat this same sequence for the top of your hand, then once again for your thumbs.

Sew all the pieces together – the top and bottom of the hands, and the top and bottom of the thumbs – then you are going to sew the thumbs to the body of the mitten. Make sure there is enough room for your hands to slip in and out of the gloves easily, but not so easily that they fall off.

Next, you are going to make 3 strips for the cuff – make each one fit around your wrist, and follow the pattern for your glove.

Single crochet across the row. Chain 1, turn, and single crochet back to the beginning. Chain 1, turn, and single crochet across the row. Chain 1, turn, and single crochet back to the beginning. Tie off. Repeat for the next one. Do this 2 more times.

Sew each of these together and to the base of your glove – then repeat the process for the other hand. That's it! Your mittens are ready for anything!

The Diva Wrap

You will need 2 skeins of yarn in the color of your choice plus another skein in a different color for the trim and a size J crochet hook

You will also need a yarn needle and scissors.

For the body:

Measure from one shoulder to the other, then chain a length that is equal to this measurement. You are going to work the back of the piece first.

Chain 2, turn, and double crochet back to the beginning. Chain 2, turn and double crochet across the row. Chain 2, turn, and double crochet back to the beginning. Chain 2, turn, and double crochet across the row. Chain 2, turn, and double crochet back to the beginning. Chain 2, turn, and double crochet across the row.

Continue until it reaches from your shoulder to your hips.

Next, do the front of the piece. Starting at the bottom, chain a length that is equal to the first.

Chain 2, turn, and double crochet back to the beginning. Chain 2, turn and double crochet across the row. Chain 2, turn, and double crochet back to the beginning. Chain 2, turn, and double crochet across the row. Chain 2, turn, and double crochet back to the beginning. Chain 2, turn, and double crochet across the row.

When you reach your bust, start to move outward, creating the V.

Skip the first two stitches, then double crochet across the row. Double crochet back to the other side, once again skipping the last 2 stitches. Skip the first two stitches, then double crochet across the row. Double crochet back to the other side, once again skipping the last 2 stitches. Skip the first two stitches, then double crochet across the row. Double crochet back to the other side, once again skipping the last 2 stitches.

Continue until you reach the top of your shoulder.

For the other side, do the same thing, but using half the length.

Chain 2, turn, and double crochet back to the beginning. Chain 2, turn and double crochet across the row. Chain 2, turn, and double crochet back to the beginning. Chain 2, turn, and double crochet across the row. Chain 2, turn, and double crochet back to the beginning. Chain 2, turn, and double crochet across the row.

When you reach your bust, start to move outward, creating the V.

Skip the first two stitches, then double crochet across the row. Double crochet back to the other side, once again skipping the last 2 stitches. Skip the first two stitches, then double crochet across the row. Double crochet back to the other side, once again skipping the last 2 stitches. Skip the first two stitches, then double crochet across the row. Double crochet back to the other side, once again skipping the last 2 stitches.

Continue until you reach the top of your shoulder.

For the sleeves:

The sleeves are going to be made to fit your arm.

Chain 2, turn, and double crochet back to the beginning. Chain 2, turn and double crochet across the row. Chain 2, turn, and double crochet back to the beginning. Chain 2, turn, and double crochet across the row. Chain 2, turn, and double crochet back to the beginning. Chain 2, turn, and double crochet across the row.

Continue for the length you want your sleeves to be – this can be all the way down to your wrists, or stop at your elbows. When you are happy with the length, tie it off.

Repeat for the other side.

To finish:

Start by putting borders around all the open ends of your pieces. You want to have one end for both the cuffs, and a boarder around both the bottom and the neckline of your piece. You can do this with the same color or alternating colors – whichever you prefer.

Sew the front pieces to the back and up the sides, leaving a hole for the arms.

Next, you are going to sew the arms to the body, and snip off any of the loose ends. Add any ties you would like to have on the body of the piece, and tie the ends to keep them from unraveling. Make sure all is secure, and you are done!

Fireside Warmth Cardigan

You will need scrap yarn or as many skeins in as many colors as you would like to use – the equivalent of 3 skeins of yarn total. You will also need a size J crochet hook

You will also need a yarn needle and scissors.

For the body:

Measure from one shoulder to the other, then chain a length that is equal to this measurement. You are going to work the back of the piece first.

Chain 2, turn, and double crochet back to the beginning. Chain 2, turn and double crochet across the row. Chain 2, turn, and double crochet back to the beginning. Chain 2, turn, and double crochet across the row. Chain 2, turn, and double crochet back to the beginning. Chain 2, turn, and double crochet across the row.

You are going to make this as long as you want – but try to go down below your knees. You can use the photo as a reference guide for changing colors, or you can change according to your own preference. Do this for the front as well.

Next, do the front of the piece. Starting at the bottom, chain a length that is half the length of the first. Remember you are going to change colors according to the photo, or as you prefer.

When you reach your bust, start to move outward, creating the V.

Skip the first two stitches, then double crochet across the row. Double crochet back to the other side, once again skipping the last 2 stitches. Skip the first two stitches, then double crochet across the row. Double crochet back to the other side, once again skipping the last 2 stitches. Skip the first two stitches, then double crochet across the row. Double crochet back to the other side, once again skipping the last 2 stitches.

Continue until you reach the top of your shoulder.

For the other side, do the same thing, once again using half the length.

When you reach your bust, start to move outward, creating the V.

Skip the first two stitches, then double crochet across the row. Double crochet back to the other side, once again skipping the last 2 stitches. Skip the first two stitches, then double crochet across the row. Double crochet back to the other side, once again skipping the last 2 stitches. Skip the first two stitches, then double crochet across the row. Double crochet back to the other side, once again skipping the last 2 stitches.

Once again, continue until you reach the top of your shoulder.

For the sleeves:

The sleeves are going to be made to fit your arm.

Single crochet across the row. Chain 1, turn, and single crochet back to the beginning. Chain 1, turn, and single crochet across the row. Chain 1, turn, and single crochet back to the beginning. Chain 1, turn, and single crochet across the row. Chain 1, turn, and single crochet back to the beginning. Chain 1, turn, and single crochet across the row.

Sew the front pieces to the back and up the sides, leaving a hole for the arms.

Continue for the length you want your sleeves to be – this can be all the way down to your wrists, or stop at your elbows. When you are happy with the length, tie it off.

Repeat for the other side.

To finish:

Start by putting borders around all the open ends of your pieces. You want to have one end for both the cuffs, and a boarder around both the bottom and the neckline of your piece. You can do this with the same color or alternating colors – whichever you prefer.

Next, you are going to sew the arms to the body, and snip off any of the loose ends. Add any ties you would like to have on the body of the piece, and tie the ends to keep them from unraveling. Make sure all is secure, and you are done!

Holiday Happiness Winter Cardigan

You will need 2 skeins of yarn in the color of your choice and a size J crochet hook

You will also need a yarn needle and scissors.

For the body:

Measure from one shoulder to the other, then chain a length that is equal to this measurement. You are going to work the back of the piece first.

Single crochet across the row. Chain 1, turn, and single crochet back to the beginning. Chain 1, turn, and single crochet across the row. Chain 1, turn, and single crochet back to the beginning. Chain 1, turn, and single crochet across the row. Chain 1, turn, and single crochet back to the beginning. Chain 1, turn, and single crochet across the row. Continue until it reaches from your shoulder to your hem.

Next, do the front of the piece. Starting at the bottom, chain a length that is equal to the first.

Single crochet across the row. Chain 1, turn, and single crochet back to the beginning. Chain 1, turn, and single crochet across the row. Chain 1, turn, and single crochet back to the beginning. Chain 1, turn, and single crochet across the row. Chain 1, turn, and single crochet back to the beginning. Chain 1, turn, and single crochet across the row.

When you reach your bust, start to move outward, creating the V.

Skip the first two stitches, then double crochet across the row. Double crochet back to the other side, once again skipping the last 2 stitches. Skip the first two stitches, then double crochet across the row. Double crochet back to the other side, once again skipping the last 2 stitches. Skip the first two stitches, then double crochet across the row. Double crochet back to the other side, once again skipping the last 2 stitches.

Continue until you reach the top of your shoulder.

For the other side, do the same thing, but using half the length.

Single crochet across the row. Chain 1, turn, and single crochet back to the beginning. Chain 1, turn, and single crochet across the row. Chain 1, turn, and single crochet back to the beginning. Chain 1, turn, and single crochet across the row. Chain 1, turn, and single crochet back to the beginning. Chain 1, turn, and single crochet across the row.

When you reach your bust, start to move outward, creating the other half of the V.

Skip the first two stitches, then double crochet across the row. Double crochet back to the other side, once again skipping the last 2 stitches. Skip the first two stitches, then double crochet across the row. Double crochet back to the other side, once again skipping the last 2 stitches. Skip the first two stitches, then double crochet across the row. Double crochet back to the other side, once again skipping the last 2 stitches.

Continue until you reach the top of your shoulder.

For the sleeves:

The sleeves are going to be made to fit your arm.

Single crochet across the row. Chain 1, turn, and single crochet back to the beginning. Chain 1, turn, and single crochet across the row. Chain 1, turn, and single crochet back to the beginning. Chain 1, turn, and single crochet across the row. Chain 1, turn, and single crochet back to the beginning. Chain 1, turn, and single crochet across the row.

Sew the front pieces to the back and up the sides, leaving a hole for the arms.

Continue for the length you want your sleeves to be – this can be all the way down to your wrists, or stop at your elbows. When you are happy with the length, tie it off.

Repeat for the other side.

To finish:

Start by putting borders around all the open ends of your pieces. You want to have one end for both the cuffs, and a boarder around both the bottom and the neckline of your piece. You can do this with the same color or alternating colors – whichever you prefer.

Next, you are going to sew the arms to the body, and snip off any of the loose ends. Add any ties you would like to have on the body of the piece, and tie the ends to keep them from unraveling. Make sure all is secure, and you are done!

Conclusion

There you have it, everything you need to make a collection of warm and cozy winter wear for yourself, your friends, and all the loved ones in your life. You know this is one of the most joyful times in the year, and you want nothing more than to enjoy each and every part of it from being inside to going out and doing new things.

You know there is nothing better than when you dress up and head out into the chilly afternoon to have fun with your friends, and it's even better when you know that you look good doing it. I hope you were able to find the inspiration you need to create all kinds of warm and cozy items for your wardrobe – and as gifts for your friends and family.

There is nothing better than homemade Christmas presents, and you know you have a list of people you want to surprise with the things you can create for them. This book is going to give you the tools you need to do that, now all you need is the inspiration to make it happen.

Christmas is on the way, and you want to dive into all the festivities with a passion. You are going to find there are nothing but smiles and good times rolling when you spread the Christmas cheer with these wonderful gifts.

The meadow is full of glistening snow, and the stores are filled with all the decorations and joy of the season. You know you want to dive into all the fun of this wonderful time of year, and you can do that with nothing more than a crochet hook, your favorite yarn, and a bit of creativity and inspiration.

This book is everything you need to get started, so embrace the joy of the season with all the passion and fun you have in you, and dive into a whole new way to celebrate what this time of year has to offer. You are about to create a Christmas you are never going to forget, and you're going to love every second of it.

What are you waiting for? It's the most wonderful time of the year, and it's just waiting for you to dive in and take part in the joy of the season.

Good luck, and have a very happy holidays.

6 CROCHET MITTENS:
CROCHET MITTENS PATTERNS FOR THE WHOLE FAMILY
JULIANNE LINK

Crochet Mittens:

6 Crochet Mittens Patterns For The Whole Family

Introduction

Everyone loves to stay warm during the winters and the best thing to stay warm is having mittens. Some people actually search for the mittens because naturally they your hands warmer than other things. The fabric of the mitten is so strong which does not leave a space in your hand to get colder. When you are outside and dealing with the snow, then obviously you would need the gloves but if you are just stepping out for shopping, then mittens would be the best thing.

A mother always cares for everyone in the home which is why here is the guide for you to make the mittens for the family. You can protect your entire family especially the babies of the family from the cold weather. Babies already look adorable and the mittens add up to their cuteness. You can make different patterns and styles out of mittens of your favorite colors. There are flapped mittens, designed, pockets, fingerless and many other types of mittens.

They are not hard to make instead once you understand its pattern, you will be happy to be creative and make more out of them. Instead of buying the mittens, you can check out this eBook which will guide you step by step to get done with patterning the mittens. The materials and the directions are listen for you accordingly for the family so you can look into it. There are some mittens which cover your entire hand without even the space for thumb whereas others have the separation of thumb. All kinds of mittens patterns would be found here with different colors of your own choice. The colors depends on the yarn you choose. You need to make a design in your brain first and then consider starting the work. You can take some examples from below and get started now!

Chapter 1 – Mittens for Male Members

Mostly males think it is childish to wear the mittens but the main reason is the protection. You can check out the amazing patterns of male mittens which will not make you feel awkward at all. The coloring and the patterns are defined specifically by keeping the male aspect in mind. People do not really differentiate between the gloves and mittens but mittens are made of yarn rather than the gloves could be made of different materials. Mittens are used for long term as well and you need to keep in mind while stitching that it does not leave a loop of any opening in future as well. Here is a perfect pattern for the male mitten which you can start at home during these winters.

Crochet hook: G/6/4mm, H/8/5mm

Weight of Yarn: 5 ounces Camouflage 971, 6 pattern stitches, 5 pattern rows.

Required Yarn: 300 Yards

Size: 2 inches

Stitches Used: ch (chain), sl st (slip stitch), sc (single crochet), dc (double crochet), dec sc (decrease single crochet), dec dc (decrease double crochet).

Making for Male Mittens

Round 1: Take the Hook G, chain 13 into the single crochet in the 2nd chain inside the hook. And cross it over each chain. Keep turning it until you get the 12 single crochet.

Round 2: Getting to the back loops now, single crochet should cross each of the single crochet which you yarned before starting from chain 1. Continuous for 12 chains.

Round 3- 30: Repeat the same round 2 on the 12 single crochets by yarning inside.

Round 31: The top of rubbing should be worked within the 21 single crochet with turning into chain 1.

Round 32: Use the H hook, cross the single crochet into each of the crochet for the 21 single crochet.

Round 33: Repeat round 32.

Round 34: In the first single crochet, double crochet the second single crochet. Keep on doing this for 5 times. Next, start with the double crochet and repeat that for about 7 times. Reach to chain 1 and do it again till the 32 round stitch.

Round 35: Repeat the same procedure as 34 for 7 times to complete it till round 34.

Round 36: Single crochet the double crochet again and repeat it for 5 times. Reach till the 36 slip stitch and do it for about 7 times.

Round 37: Now you have to move forward with the 37 round to 38 by doing the same procedure of single crochet to first double crochet then second crochet to second double crochet. Do it for 5 times to reach to 38th round.

Round 38: Repeat the same procedure as round 37 to reach to round 39 and 40.

Round 40: Now move backward by doing the same procedure to reach round 30 single stitches. This is to strengthen the mittens.

Round 41: Single crochet in the double crochet and do it for about 13 times returning to chain 1 and coming back to 30 stitches.

Round 42: Repeat the same procedure of round 41 until 50 rounds.

Round 51: Close the work by leaving a tail open for the thumb space to be worked. Decrease the double crochet for 1 stitch and close it there.

Working for the Thumb:

Round 1: Get the yarn from the piece near the thumb tail and stitch it by single crochet from round 40. Repeat it for about 4 times by turning till chain 1. It needs total of 12 stitches.

Round 2: Single crochet the double crochet and repeat that in the same area for about 5 times. 12 stitches in total.

Round 3: Repeat the same procedures until 5 rounds. Single crochets for the 12 stitches which you have done in round 2.

Round 6: Decrease the double chain stitches and take it to chain 1 by totaling of 6 stitches.

Round 7: Decrease the double chain again by 6 stitches and leave the space open from the front for the thumb. Fix your thumb inside and then stitch it over by adjusting by closing the mitten.

Now, at the end, switch it to the other side and cut off the weaves which may be visible. If there are any ends remaining then attach the yarn and by single stitching, do it for 6-7 stitches.

Here are the sizes for men's hand and the inches which may be suitable:

Small: 64 inches

Medium: 66 inches

Large: 68 inches

X-large 70 inches.

Chapter 02: Crochet Mitten for Adult Girls

Girls tend to love mittens because it makes them look cute. It also serves the purpose of staying warm as well as some prefer to match the mittens with their clothes color. It looks adorable and keeps your hands warm whether you are traveling for work or school. As you can see the image below, this type of mittens helps you pick anything by separating the thumb on the other side. Mostly these are preferable for the outdoors such as if you are having a coffee, you can still wear these. They are simple to make with just following the directions accordingly. You can weave them in different colors with the pattern of three colors or more than that but the more colors you choose, the more complicated it will be for you so it is better to stick to one color if you are a beginner. Once you get an idea about the pattern then you can weave it with different combinations.

When you are knitting, not only your brain is working actively but you are actually making a difference to your body physically as well. Such as you are using your fingers to weave the yarn which helps your cartilages relax and be flexible even more. You won't get tired of weaving at all but it will make your finger stronger than before. If you get tired somehow, then you can soak your hand in warm water and see the effect. It will leave you relaxed and you will be able to weave longer. There are a lot of hidden benefits of knitting which you will get to now once you are in it doing it physically. If you feel like it, grab a needle and a yarn and get started. It is not a lot of expense but rather than buying the mittens, you can have your own made with your favorite colors right at your home.

Once you understand the in and out of the knitting, you would not want to leave the habit of knitting. It is exciting and you can teach your siblings or kids too. It is easy but you just need to understand some of its aspects clearly. Whether you are designing it for male, female, babies or adults, you need to have a clear picture in your mind first in order to get started and ending up with good results.

Crochet hook: 5.5mm, needle (yarn)

Weight of Yarn: 16 single chains, 4 inches; 17 rows of 4 inches

Required Yarn: 300 Yards

Size: 7 ½ x 11 ½ inches

Making of Adult Girls Mitten:

The adult girl's mittens would be worked through the row of 7 rounds ending at the fingertips. It will follow only 1 row. Will be working with the back loops in single chain and the hook from one chain to another turn by turn.

For Hand:

Round 1: Coming from the cuffs, stitch around for 18 stitches with keeping it consistent.

Round 2: Chain 1 should be placed into the second chain for the next 8 times. Join them together by single stitching.

Round 3: Chain 1 in single chain and repeat that two times. Slip the single stitch in round of 20 and 30.

Round 4: Getting back to chain 1, in the other 10-14 stitches, move forward for 24-32 single triple stitches.

Continue the stitches until it reaches a shape of solid chain1 and single chain of each round together with the single triple chain. Repeat the entire process, one more time.

Preparing the thumb:

For the thumb opening, continue it with the chain 1 and skip the other single triple stitches. Slip the single stitch for the upper side of the hand.

Round 1: Single chain in the rounds of 24, 31 and 38. Decrease it for the last round which comes in further.

Round 2: Single chain two times for 22, 28 and 36 single triple stitches

Round 3: Repeat round 2 for 3 more times.

Round 4: Fasten it and move to the thumb side by ending at its last round of the hand stitching.

Round 5: Single chain for 7 and 8 rounds. Continue it for the working of single chain in size 4 and 5 and weave at the end to finish it off.

Chapter 03: Crochet Mitten for Baby Girl

It is essential to keep the babies warm during winters which is why mother prefer mittens. Little mittens are so cute that they would even fit a kitten. Mittens are safe for the babies because they are unable to take them off but you need to be careful that they do not get that warm. Do not make them wear during the night time as it is the time when you as a mother would be sleeping deep as well and won't be able to keep a check on the baby as you do during the day time. You can weave the baby mittens faster than doing it for the adults because they take less yarn and are easy to make. You do not have to measure any size for their hands because they are so small. Mostly people prefer the color pink for the baby girl mittens but you can make combinations.

When you are knitting, it is actually the focus and it keeps you away from the stress and depression of your life. You can turn on your favorite music and starting weaving. It also normalizes your blood pressure as you sit at one place and knit without any tension in your head. It is actually a whole brain procedure and once your brain is aware of that process, it does not function actively but relaxes and your cognitive abilities help you to repeat the processes. It keeps your brain health normal and you can stay active for longer time which means you would not feel sleepy in the day time even if you have good hours of sleep. You can learn more crafts if you get efficient at this. Mostly people are not creative which this why they find it hard to improvise knitting but the ones who get it, can be really good at crafting other things.

Crochet hook: H crochet hook, needle (yarn)

Weight of Yarn: 5 ounces, chains 4.

Required Yarn: 200 Yards

Size: 2 inches

Making of Mitten for Baby Girl

By creating a chain 4 start with the Rounds.

Round 1: Single crochet in the chain 2 by the hook by taking it across chain 3. Bring it from the other side and make it total of 6 single crochets joining it with chain 1.

Round 2: By working on the double crochet join it with single crochet and align it with chain 1. It should have total of 12 double crochets.

Round 3: Join the single crochet with chain 1 and continue it 3 more times.

Round 4: Double crochet for the first single stitch and repeat it 2 more times. Join it with single line and crochet with compiling it to 18 double crochets.

Round 5: Make it all even on the palm side from single stitch to chain 1.

Round 6: Take the double crochet and work with the first double crochet in round 1. Do it accordingly to all the double crochets from here.

Round 7: From this round, take it till round 12 and continuous do it accordingly like round 6.

Working with the Wrist:

Round 13: Single crochet it with all the single stitches.

Round 14: Double crochet all the ones by totaling 21 stitches.

Round 15: Hold the double crochets and continue 10 more times.

Round 16-20: Work from the back by fixing it and weaving the ends. Finish it off by cutting off the yarn from the end neatly.

Chapter 04: Crochet Mitten for Baby Boy

As we see blue little mittens, we can tell that these are for the baby boys. It is somehow allocated that the color blue is for the boys. Babies are always sensitive whether it is a baby girl or baby boy. You need to care for them the same way because they are newly born and are sensitive to everything including the weather. Consider making your baby wear mittens if it is his first winters in this world. You need to make sure that he is protected fully especially when you step out. His needs to be inside and be covered so that he does not catch any cold.

The instructions of the baby mittens are quite clear which you will be able to understand once you have the yarn and its needle in your hand. Make sure to weave it around when your baby is not near you because of the needle. You need to keep it all away because it might hurt them intentionally.

You will be surprised to know during the process of learning that knitting actually helps you relax in your daily life routine. We do not get to know and we get stressed for no reason. By setting up the knitting project, you can simply reduce your stress once you are aware of the pattern and without any thought in mind, your hands would be knitting the yarn as however you thought it to be in your head. There are repetitive rounds which will help you relax by body and mind which would definitely work as a meditation for you.

Photo made by: Tare Panda

Crochet hook: G crochet hook, needle (yarn)

Weight of Yarn: 5 ounces, chain 9.

Required Yarn: 200 Yards

Size: 2 inches of G hook, loop on each side

Making of Mitten for Baby Boy

For the Cuff:

Round 1: This is the first row with chain 9 starting from the hook and each crossing it down to 8 and further.

Round 2: This is the second row continuing from chain 1 and back looping across the single crochet 8 chains.

Now, we have to repeat both of the rows for about 24 times in order to make the cuff.

For the Hand:

It will be total of 26 stitches all together making rows in between. It will be better to keep the numbers even.

Round 1: Starting from row 1 and single crochet at the same time by the last 2 single crochets tied.

Round 2: The chain 1 needs to go with row 1 by taking the single stitches over the row and behind it. Make sure to take the stitches to the thumbs side as well to complete the row of 26 stitches of total. We will be increasing the rows further with the stitches. There will be 14 single stitches more.

Round 3: Single crochet in each row with the single stitch with totaling 13 stitches and repeating it for the hand completely.

Round 4: Start the row 2 with the chain 1 being tied in the single crochet and the second crochet in the next step and continue for 3 more times.

Round 5: Chain 1 with row 4 for the next single stitch following the first single crochet and with singles stitches.

Round 6: Chain 1 being turned into the single stitch for the next stitch. Continue it for the next 6 chains.

For the thumb:

Depends on the size of the thumb, but since this is for the baby boy, we will not be needing bigger size.

Round 7: Continuing to the next row with the chain 1 and in the single crochet with the single stitching. It should continue for the 12 counts total. Depends on the inches you are continuing the thumb for. If it is smaller then you will need to do the 4 single stitches and a little bigger will keep on getting with the even number.

Round 8: Repeat the rows for the 4 single crochets. Do the single crochets and turn it back by weaving it completely.

There are two ways through which you are able to sew the thumbs perfectly:

1. Make sure to cut the yarn accordingly and then get the needle by the single stitches by pulling them tightly. Leave one side of the yarn completely out so you can sew it easily. Make a base row and then start the single crochet by pulling the single stitches together. Hold it tightly.

2. Now, put the needle through another side and weave the other side by holding it tightly. Make sure you have the crochet hook pulled with the single stitches as well. If you see a loop on the top, fix it right away because it needs to get tightened right away. When the base is ready, end it with the single crochet and take it all the way across to complete the weaving.

Chapter 05: Crochet Mitten with Flaps

Flappy mittens are popular with the teenage girls because they find it adorable to wear. they like to have any kind of animal shaped on it which would be flapped and mostly the sea animals are make on the mittens such as fishes, whales, dolphins and many others. They look cute while you wear it and you can play around with it also. Mittens are warmer than gloves and you will experience that once you start wearing them in winters.

Winters season is beautiful but always hard because you have to keep yourself covered otherwise you can get sick. People wear mittens to stay warm so that they do not end up on bed falling ill.

A lot of people cannot knit so when you know how to do it, it is something to be proud of. You can show it to your loved ones how to manage the yarn and it is like a trick to them that how could you even do that when it seems so complicated. This easy guide helps you in weaving the mittens. This is like a new skill learned which will get you a lot of compliments which you cannot even think of. It will also give you a sense of accomplishment that you have done something different and new in your life.

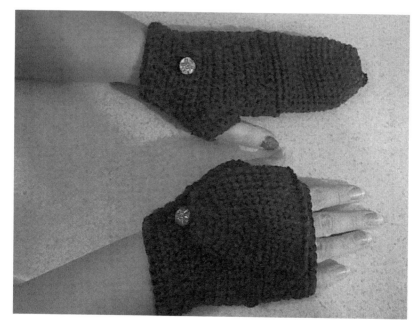

Picture made by: becky bokern

Crochet hook: F crochet hook, needle (tapestry)

Weight of Yarn: 6 single crochet for 1 inches; 6 rows with 1 inches.

Required Yarn: 300 Yards

Size: 2 inches

Making for Mitten with Flaps

For Wrists:

Round 1: Create the chain with the base which should be for total 30 chains.

Round 2: create row 1 with the 15 single crochets with the main color which you have chosen and then 15 single crochets after that totaling to 30 single crochets.

Round 3: Now take the other color rather than the main color and add 15 more single crochet with the 15 single crochet at the bottom of it.

Round 4: With the other color, increase 1 stitch in the 15 single crochets and in the other 15 crochets as well making it 32 single crochets.

Round 5: Again repeat the same as round 4 till 10 rounds.

For Fingers:

Round 11: Now comes the third color in between. You have to make 2 single crochets with 6 chains here. With attaching the row before and creating the other 6 rows. There will be total of 36 single crochets here.

Round 12: The third color should be there with the second color of 18 single crochets.

Round 13: Third color following decrease in one stitch with 16 single crochets and on the back other 16 single crochets.

Round 14: Keep on decrease the stitches for each single crochets until round 20.

Round 21: Decrease 5 single stitches in the end and weave it off by finishing it completely.

For the Thumb (creating the flap)

Round 22: With the third color carry on with the 6 single crochets at the side. With bringing in the loops of thumbhole.

Round 23: Decrease 1 stitch from the single crochet and finish it off here.

Round 24: Create the flap over it by the second color and weave the single crochet of 16 stitches here. Finish it off by repeating round 23 here.

Flaps on the other side of the Mitten

Round 25: With the second color get the 8 single crochets.

Round 26: Decrease 1 stitch and add the 6 single crochets.

Round 27: Keep on decreasing each stitch by keeping the single crochets similar.

Round 28: At the end, keep the single crochets up to 10 and then finish it off.

Upper Flap and Lower Flap

You would need to create the flap on the top as well to make it look cute. Well, take the yarn and tie a knot to it with the hook. Keep the edges open and make the upper opening with stitching it row by row now. You have to make 3 rows with the loops which can be fixed in the next stitching which would be under it. When you have made the 3 rows with the single stitching then repeat the same procedure for the lower flap.

Chapter 06: Fingerless Crochet Mitten

Most people who smoke consider the fingerless crochet mittens because it is easier for them not to take them off again and again. Well, making the patterns for the fingerless mittens is easier than anything because it covers half of your hand. It does not cover your fingers due to which you can pick or hold anything easily. The fingerless crochets have the simplest pattern to be followed which you can check below. Choose the color according to your choose and try them now. They look stylish and you won't even feel cold on your hands.

As people are fond of cellphones nowadays, it gets easier for you to handle your smartphone and work with it. The touch screens can only detect your finger touch so you won't need to take them off back and forth. If you are unable to find the fingerless mittens then buy a yarn and a needle. That is all you need and proper direction to make it. This is where you will find the best clear directions which will get you through some rounds and you will be done with the weaving of the mittens.

Photo made by: Kim Piper Werker

Crochet hook: 3.5 mm, E/4 hook

Weight of Yarn: 20-32 stitches of 4 inches each. Super fine quality (1)

Required Yarn: 213 yards

Size: 5 inches (tapestry needle)

Making for Fingerless Crochet Mittens

The Palms:

Round 1: Make sure not to twist the pieces by join it to the first chain. Leave a loop in the beginning before starting the body of the mitten.

Round 2: Start from the chain 5 and continue it for the same single stitching. Now move to third stitching and then continue it for about 5 times.

Round 3: Turn the body of the mitten and repeat the process from chain 3. In the chain 2, add the single crochet and slip to the side of the mitten. Do not end it here since this is going towards the thumb knitting.

The Thumbs:

Round 4: Since the thumbs are going to be open, you will start with the same chain 3 and turn it around with the next chain on the other side. Join it with the clusters to make it compact. Taking it from the 2nd to 8th cluster, keep joining it by single crochet.

Round 5: Chain 3 needs to be turned by moving to next step of chain 3 single stitching. Do not decrease the stitching. Unless you need to weave the bottom of the mitten. But that step has not come yet.

Round 6: Slip in the chain 4 to the 5th and repeat the same pattern as round 5. Repeat from the rounds and with joining it to single stitching.

Round 7: At the end of this thumb, turn it around with keeping it attached with the cluster and repeat chain 5. Do the same single stitching on it and finish it off.

For the Cuff

Round 1: Keep the mitten to the right side and work towards the chain at the base of it. Attach the yarn with chain 3 and join them by the hook. Pull up the loop which you left at the beginning and stitch it until it reaches the chain 32 by 4 inches each.

Round 2: Chain 2 needs to start here by joining it back to chain 3 with the back and front. Slip it through and weave it by ending the pattern here neatly.

Conclusion

We have winters right across the corner and mittens become a need in the areas where we get to see snow especially. They keep your hands warm in the cold winter's nights. You can wear them outdoor and indoor as well to keep your hand away from the cold stormy nights. It is said that if your hands and feet are warm, then your body temperature stays normal too. Well, learning how to make the perfect pattern for the mittens for family is a fun thing to do. You can sit, turn on the music and enjoy the weaving time with this amazing guide. It will not only help you with the rounds but you can also see the images which you will be seeing by the end.

The yarn is too warm to keep your hands normal all day long. Choose your own colors to make the mittens for your family whether you have babies or adult girls. Mostly mothers prefer to do this for their family because they are the care takers and love to weave especially at the time when they are expecting a new child. Well, this is the best place to get started. Check out the amazing tips on the patterns with the exact size to fit your hand accordingly.

People believe that mittens are worn more by women than the men. Well, it is true but you can weave one for your spouse and you will see that he will love it. Start from making it for him and then weave it for your entire family. This will take time at first but once you have your hands frequent on it, you won't even see the needle and the yarn and make it like anything within some hours. Get started now!

CROCHET NECK WARMER

Julianne Link

15 Beautiful Neck Warmers To Keep You Nice And Cozy

Crochet Neck Warmer

15 Beautiful Neck Warmers To Keep You Nice
And Cozy

Introduction

Winter is coming, and with it comes cold weather, chilly nights, and snow. You know you love the fun and coziness of the holidays, but no one wants to be chilly during this time. With all the time you have to spend outdoors, running errands, getting a tree, making sure the lights are on the house and the snow is shoveled out of the driveway... you need something that will keep you warm and cozy.

But when you look at the scarves at the store, you know that's not what you want. They are long and cumbersome, and they get in the way. You can wrap it around your neck, but you still have a lot of fabric hanging down and getting in the way of what you are trying to accomplish.

No, you need something that will keep the chill out and the warmth in, but something that's going to stay close to your body and not get in the way of your day. You need a neck warmer.

But where do you get those? Again, when you look in the stores, you see there are a few to choose from, but nothing that makes you want to spend your hard earned money on it. You want something that's cute, fashionable, and comfortable, as well as effective.

You want something that you can feel good about wearing, and feel good while you wear it. You want something that's going to get the job done and look good doing it... basically, you need something that is custom made, and to do that, you need to make it yourself.

But how? Aren't cowls hard to make? Aren't neck warmers difficult to get the right fit? How am I going to make something that looks good and gets the job done?

Don't worry, you aren't alone. Many people who have never made these before wonder if they are going to be able to do it, and the answer is, yes... you can. Neck warmers are really easy to make, and they are great ways to express yourself with what you can do.

In this book, I am going to give you 15 different patterns to choose from, giving you the ability to make your own neck warmers, and to make them your own. With this book, you have it all... comfort and coziness with fashion and fun. Dive into the world of crocheted neck warmers, and never go back to the store purchased items again.

Winter might be on its way, but when you have these warm wraps sitting on your shoulders, you know the winter winds can do their worst. You are safe and sound, and snug as a bug. Now let's get started.

Chapter 1 – Beautiful Holiday Warmers

Snowflake Slate Neck Warmer

Photo made by: smittenkittenorig

You will need 1 ball of yarn and a size G crochet hook

Chain a length that is 18 inches long.

Single crochet across the row. Chain 2, turn, and double crochet in the first stitch. Double crochet in the next stitch 3 times, then double crochet in the next stitch. Double crochet in the next stitch 3 times, then double crochet in the next stitch. Double crochet in the next stitch 3 times, then double crochet in the next stitch.

Repeat this across the row, ending with 1 double crochet in the last stitch. Chain 2, turn, and double crochet in the first stitch. Double crochet in the next stitch 3 times, then double crochet in the next stitch. Double crochet in the next stitch 3 times, then double crochet in the next stitch. Double crochet in the next stitch 3 times, then double crochet in the next stitch.

Continue with this pattern until the neck warmer measures 12 inches tall. Tie off.

To assemble:

Take your yarn needle now and sew up the open end. Use a whip stitch and keep your stitches both close together and even. Run the full length of the side, then tie off.

Turn the neck warmer the right side out, so the seam is on the inside.

Rose Garden Warmer

You will need 1 ball of yarn and a size G crochet hook

Chain 20.

Single crochet across the row. Chain 1, turn, and single crochet across the row. Chain 1, turn, then single crochet across the row once more. Chain 1, turn, then single crochet back to the other side.

Continue with this pattern, keeping an eye on your tension. Make sure you don't pull it in, or that you hold the yarn too loose. Keep a steady, even tension on the piece the entire time, and continue to work until the piece is 16 inches long.

Photo made by: <u>Kim Piper Werker</u>

To assemble:

There are two different ways you can assemble this piece. I prefer to secure the ends together and use it as a pullover, but if you like, you can make the buttons functional instead.

For the pullover style:

Fold the piece as you see in the photo, and sew one end of the warmer to the other end. I prefer to sew a seam on both ends directly, securing the scarf in place as you see in the photo.

Attach the buttons as accent pieces, and your warmer is ready to go!

For the button style:

Attach the buttons where you want them on the neck warmer, and place loops on the other end. If you would rather, place snaps on both ends instead. Make sure everything is secure, and tie off the loose ends.

That's it! Your neck warmer is ready for the chill of the coldest winter night.

Hippy Holiday Neck Warmer

You will need 1 ball of yarn and a size G crochet hook

Chain 120.

Double crochet across the row. Chain 2, and double crochet back to the beginning. Chain 2, turn, and double crochet across the row. Chain 2, turn, and double crochet back to the beginning.

Chain 2, turn, and double crochet across the row. Chain 2, turn, and double crochet bac to the beginning. Continue with this pattern, keeping an eye on your tension. Make sure you don't pull it in, or that you hold the yarn too loose. Keep a steady, even tension on the piece the entire time, and continue to work until the piece is 12 inches tall.

Tie off.

To assemble:

Take your yarn needle now and sew up the open end. Use a whip stitch and keep your stitches both close together and even. Run the full length of the side, then tie off.

Turn the neck warmer the right side out, so the seam is on the inside. I like to wear this warmer open, but you can also twist the piece as you put it on for an added fashion statement.

That's it! Wrap around your neck once, or multiple times for a closer fitting neck warmer. No matter how you decide to wear it, get out there and enjoy the cold winter air.

Flower Power Neck Warmer

Photo made by: <u>becky bokern</u>

You will need 1 ball of yarn and a size G crochet hook

Chain 34.

Single crochet across the row. Chain 1, turn, and single crochet across the row. Chain 1, turn, then single crochet across the row once more. Chain 1, turn, then single crochet back to the other side.

Continue with this pattern, keeping an eye on your tension. Make sure you don't pull it in, or that you hold the yarn too loose. Keep a steady, even tension on the piece the entire time, and continue to work until the piece is 12 inches long.

Tie off, then grab your crochet hook and attach it with a slip stitch to the side of the piece.

Single crochet in the first stitch, then double crochet in the next 3 stitches. Single crochet in the next stitch, then double crochet in the next 3 stitches. Single crochet in the first stitch, then double crochet in the next 3 stitches. Single crochet in the next stitch, then double crochet in the next 3 stitches.

Repeat until you get back to the beginning, and join with a slip stitch.

To assemble:

Take your yarn needle now and sew up the open end. Use a whip stitch and keep your stitches both close together and even. Run the full length of the side, then tie off.

Turn the neck warmer the right side out, so the seam is on the inside.

That's it!

Either wear this warmer folded down for a subtle bit of warmth, or feel free to pull it up when you need that extra sense of cozy!

Camo Colored Neck Warmer

You will need 1 ball of yarn and a size G crochet hook

Chain 14.

Single crochet across the row. Chain 1, turn, and single crochet across the row. Chain 1, turn, then single crochet across the row once more. Chain 1, turn, then single crochet back to the other side.

Continue with this pattern, keeping an eye on your tension. Make sure you don't pull it in, or that you hold the yarn too loose. Keep a steady, even tension on the piece the entire time, and continue to work until the piece is 12 inches long.

To assemble:

Attach the button or snap to the ends of both pieces of the warmer, and wrap securely around your neck when you are ready to wear.

Another way you can assemble this is to sew up the open end of both, then use the buttons as accent pieces.

Royally Wise Neck Warmer

You will need 1 ball of yarn and a size G crochet hook

Chain a length that is 22 inches long.

Single crochet across the row. Chain 2, turn, and double crochet in the first stitch. Double crochet in the next stitch 3 times, then double crochet in the next stitch. Double crochet in the next stitch 3 times, then double crochet in the next stitch. Double crochet in the next stitch 3 times, then double crochet in the next stitch.

Photo made by: smittenkittenorig

Repeat this across the row, ending with 1 double crochet in the last stitch. Chain 2, turn, and double crochet in the first stitch. Double crochet in the next stitch 3 times, then double crochet in the next stitch. Double crochet in the next stitch 3 times, then double crochet in the next stitch. Double crochet in the next stitch 3 times, then double crochet in the next stitch.

Continue with this pattern until the neck warmer measures 18 inches tall.

To assemble:

Take your yarn needle now and sew up the open end. Use a whip stitch and keep your stitches both close together and even. Run the full length of the side, then tie off.

Turn the neck warmer the right side out, so the seam is on the inside.

That's it! Wear this up or folded down for multiple wearing options.

Insider's tip:

Making the neck warmer a bit bigger allows you to wear it up without having to bend it.

Buttoned Burgundy Wrap

Photo made by: smittenkittenorig

You will need 1 ball of yarn and a size G crochet hook

Chain 120.

Single crochet across the row. Chain 1, and single crochet back to the beginning. Chain 1, turn, and single crochet across the row. Chain 1, turn, and single crochet back to the beginning.

Chain 1, turn, and single crochet across the row. Chain 1, turn, and single crochet bac to the beginning.

482

Continue with this pattern, keeping an eye on your tension. Make sure you don't pull it in, or that you hold the yarn too loose. Keep a steady, even tension on the piece the entire time, and continue to work until the piece is 12 inches tall.

Tie off.

To assemble:

Take your yarn needle now and sew up the open end. Use a whip stitch and keep your stitches both close together and even. Run the full length of the side, then tie off.

Turn the neck warmer the right side out, so the seam is on the inside. Attach the buttons as accents to the side.

That's it! Wrap around your neck once, or multiple times for a closer fitting neck warmer. No matter how you wear your warmer, give it a twist to show the buttons on the inside.

Photo made by: <u>becky bokern</u>

You will need 1 ball of yarn in each of the colors of your choice and a size G crochet hook

This neck warmer is created using the Catherine Wheel stitch. If you are unfamiliar with this stitch, look it up. It's incredibly easy to do though it's not as common as many of the other stitches that are seen around today, and you will be able to create wonderful things once you know how to do it.

With this pattern, you will use 2 different kinds of yarn, changing colors every 4 rows. Again, follow the pattern for the Catherine Wheel, and this is all going to make sense and come together beautifully.

Start by chaining 116. Follow the Catherine Wheel stitch pattern to work your way across the row, then follow the other half of the pattern on your way back. When you finish the first half of the sequence, tie off the work and change colors.

Join with a slip stitch, then begin again, following the same pattern back across the row.

You are going to continue with this now until you have a neck warmer as thick as you want it to be. Tie off, and you are ready to assemble.

To assemble:

Take your yarn needle now and sew up the open end. Use a whip stitch and keep your stitches both close together and even. Run the full length of the side, then tie off.

Turn the neck warmer the right side out, so the seam is on the inside.

That's it! Wrap around your neck once, or multiple times for a closer fitting neck warmer.

Highland Hooded Cowl

Photo made by: smittenkittenorig

You will need 1 ball of yarn and a size G crochet hook

Chain 180.

Single crochet across the row. Chain 1, and single crochet back to the beginning. Chain 1, turn, and single crochet across the row. Chain 1, turn, and single crochet back to the beginning.

Chain 1, turn, and single crochet across the row. Chain 1, turn, and single crochet bac to the beginning.

Continue with this pattern, keeping an eye on your tension. Make sure you don't pull it in, or that you hold the yarn too loose. Keep a steady, even tension on the piece the entire time, and continue to work until the piece is 12 inches tall.

Tie off.

To assemble:

Take your yarn needle now and sew up the open end. Use a whip stitch and keep your stitches both close together and even. Run the full length of the side, then tie off.

Turn the neck warmer the right side out, so the seam is on the inside.

That's it! Wrap around your neck once, or multiple times for a closer fitting neck warmer.

Wear up and over your head for a hooded effect whenever you want added warmth.

Spectacular Striped Neck Warmer

Photo made by: <u>becky bokern</u>

You will need 1 ball of yarn in each of the colors of your choice and a size G crochet hook

Use the photo as a reference for colors, or make your own. To do what I did, you will work 5 rows of navy blue, then 3 rows of green, followed by 5 rows of navy, then 3 rows of pink.

Work your way around the neck warmer, making it as large as you want.

Start with the navy blue.

Chain 25.

Double crochet in the front loop only on the first stitch, then the back loop only on the next stitch. Double crochet in the front loop only on the next stitch, then the back loop only on the next stitch. Double crochet on the front loop only in the next stitch, then the back loop only in the next stitch.

Repeat this across the row.

When you get to the end of the row, chain 2, and turn.

Double crochet in the front loop only on the first stitch, then the back loop only on the next stitch. Double crochet in the front loop only on the next stitch, then the back loop only on the next stitch. Double crochet on the front loop only in the next stitch, then the back loop only in the next stitch.

Again, work as many rows per color as you want, and create the stripes you want. Have fun with it, and once the scarf has reached the length you prefer, tie off.

You are now ready to assemble.

To assemble:

Take your yarn needle now and sew up the open end. Use a whip stitch and keep your stitches both close together and even. Run the full length of the side, then tie off.

Turn the neck warmer the right side out, so the seam is on the inside.

That's it! Wrap around your neck once, or multiple times for a closer fitting neck warmer.

Photo made by: <u>smittenkittenorig</u>

You will need 1 ball of yarn and a size G crochet hook

Chain a length that is 17 inches.

Single crochet across the row. Chain 1, and single crochet back to the beginning. Chain 1, turn, and single crochet across the row. Chain 1, turn, and single crochet back to the beginning.

Chain 1, turn, and single crochet across the row. Chain 1, turn, and single crochet bac to the beginning.

Continue with this pattern, keeping an eye on your tension. Make sure you don't pull it in, or that you hold the yarn too loose. Keep a steady, even tension on the piece the entire time, and continue to work until the piece is 12 inches tall.

Tie off.

To assemble:

Take your yarn needle now and sew up the open end. Use a whip stitch and keep your stitches both close together and even. Run the full length of the side, then tie off.

Turn the neck warmer the right side out, so the seam is on the inside. Attach the buttons on as accent pieces, spaced where you want them to be.

That's it! Wear the warmer up around your face, or fold it down on warmer days.

Buttoned Back Around Neck Warmer

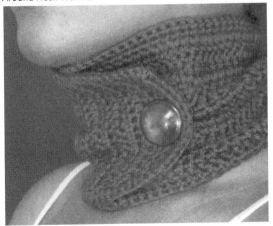

Photo made by: Sedie Meruska

You will need 1 ball of yarn and a size G crochet hook

Chain 25.

Single crochet across the row. Chain 2, turn, and double crochet back to the beginning. Chain 1, turn, and single crochet across the row. Chain 2, turn, and single crochet back to the beginning.

Single crochet across the row. Chain 2, turn, and double crochet back to the beginning. Chain 1, turn, and single crochet across the row. Chain 2, turn, and single crochet back to the beginning.

Notice the pattern you are creating goes like this:

Row of single, row of double, row of single, row of double, row of single, row of single, row of double, row of single, row of double, row of single, row of single, row of double.

Pay attention as you work your way along this neck warmer, and stick with the same pattern throughout. When you reach the desired length, tie off and assemble.

To assemble:

Attach the button or snap to the ends of both pieces of the warmer, and wrap securely around your neck when you are ready to wear. This piece can also be folded down when you put it on for an entirely different look.

Two Toned Warmer

Photo made by: smittenkittenorig

You will need 1 ball of yarn in each of the colors of your choice and a size G crochet hook

This neck warmer is worked with 2 different color sequences. I work 15 rows in one color, tie it off, and finish with 15 rows in the other color.

Start with black:

Chain a length that is 19 inches.

Single crochet across the row. Chain 1, and single crochet back to the beginning. Chain 1, turn, and single crochet across the row. Chain 1, turn, and single crochet back to the beginning.

Chain 1, turn, and single crochet across the row. Chain 1, turn, and single crochet bac to the beginning.

Continue with this pattern, keeping an eye on your tension. Make sure you don't pull it in, or that you hold the yarn too loose. Keep a steady, even tension on the piece the entire time, and continue to work with black until you have a total of 15 rows.

Tie off, and change to the variegated yarn. Join with a slip stitch, and work 1 row of single crochet. Chain 1, and turn.

Single crochet across the row. Chain 1, and single crochet back to the beginning. Chain 1, turn, and single crochet across the row. Chain 1, turn, and single crochet back to the beginning.

Chain 1, turn, and single crochet across the row. Chain 1, turn, and single crochet bac to the beginning.

Continue with this pattern, once again keeping an eye on your tension. Make sure you don't pull it in, or that you hold the yarn too loose. Keep a steady, even tension on the piece the entire time, and continue to work with variegated until you have a total of 15 more rows, or 30 rows for the entire scarf.

To assemble:

Take your yarn needle now and sew up the open end. Use a whip stitch and keep your stitches both close together and even. Run the full length of the side, then tie off.

Turn the neck warmer the right side out, so the seam is on the inside.

That's it! To wear, give your warmer a twist to show both sides of the piece at once.

Lovely Lady's Scalloped Neck Warmer
You will need 1 ball of yarn and a size G crochet hook

Chain 88.

Single crochet across the row.

For the next row, double crochet in the next stitch 3 times, chain 1, skip the next stitch, then double crochet in the next stitch 3 times. Chain 1, skip the next stitch, and double crochet in the next stitch 3 times. Chain 1, skip the next stitch, and double crochet in the next stitch 3 times.

Photo made by: Ny

Repeat this across the row. When you reach the end of the row, make sure you end with a double crochet in the last stitch. Chain 2, and turn.

Double crochet in the first stitch, chain 1, and double crochet in the chain space 3 times. Chain 1, skip the next stitch, and double crochet in the chain space 3 times. Repeat this across the row. When you get to the end of the row, chain 2 and turn.

Double crochet in the first stitch, chain 1, and double crochet in the chain space 3 times. Chain 1, skip the next stitch, and double crochet in the chain space 3 times. Repeat this across the row. When you get to the end of the row, chain 2 and turn.

Work this sequence once or twice more, until you are happy with the thickness of the neck warmer. Finish with 1 more row of single crochet.

To assemble:

Take your yarn needle now and sew up the open end. Use a whip stitch and keep your stitches both close together and even. Run the full length of the side, then tie off.

Turn the neck warmer the right side out, so the seam is on the inside.

That's it! Your warmer is done!

Wavy Wonder Neck Warmer

Photo made by: <u>becky bokern</u>

You will need 1 ball of yarn and a size G crochet hook

Chain 29.

Single crochet across the row. Chain 1, turn, and single crochet across the row. Chain 1, turn, then single crochet across the row once more. Chain 1, turn, then single crochet back to the other side.

Continue with this pattern, keeping an eye on your tension. Make sure you don't pull it in, or that you hold the yarn too loose. Keep a steady, even tension on the piece the entire time, and continue to work until the piece is 12 inches long.

Tie off, then grab your crochet hook and attach it with a slip stitch to the side of the piece.

Single crochet in the first stitch, then double crochet in the next 3 stitches. Single crochet in the next stitch, then double crochet in the next 3 stitches. Single crochet in the first stitch, then double crochet in the next 3 stitches. Single crochet in the next stitch, then double crochet in the next 3 stitches.

Repeat until you get back to the beginning, and join with a slip stitch.

For an extra wave added to this pattern, I prefer to go around the border once more, only using single crochet this time. Still follow the waves you have created, and don't fill in the gaps.

When you get back to the beginning, tie it off.

To assemble:

Take your yarn needle now and sew up the open end. Use a whip stitch and keep your stitches both close together and even. Run the full length of the side, then tie off.

Turn the neck warmer the right side out, so the seam is on the inside.

That's it! Wrap around your neck once, or multiple times for a closer fitting neck warmer.

Conclusion

There you have it, everything you need to know to make your own crocheted neck warmers, and the inspiration you need to make it your own. I hope this book was able to inspire you to create a variety of neck warmers, both with the patterns found within this book, and to use your creativity to make your own.

There's no way you can go wrong when you let your imagination run wild, and I hope this book inspires you to do that very thing. Have fun with the creations you make, give them to your friends and family, and never run out of a new look whenever you want.

With this book, you have what you need to completely redo your accessory wardrobe whenever you want to. Whether there's an event coming up, you are in the mood for a little more color, or you simply want to spend some time making something that you can then wear, you have what you need right here.

Mix and match the sizes for children, or throw in a variety of different colors to make custom pieces for everyone on your gift list. Christmas is right around the corner, and you know you want to get a start on your shopping. What better way to spread the cheer than with handmade gifts from you with love?

This book is the inspiration you need to make it happen, and I know you will get the results you are after, without having to stress about it. Get your crochet hook, grab your favorite yarn, and get ready to get busy with fun patterns you will love to make.

With the weather turning cold and the days getting shorter, you know you want to wear something cozy and warm, and with these patterns, you not only get that, but you will also get the latest and greatest in the fashion world.

Jump on board with any and every look you want, and dive into a new way of doing things. With this book, you have everything you need to redo your accessories, and spice up the season faster than a pumpkin spice latte.

You know you want to, so go ahead and dive in. with this book in hand, nothing is going to hold you back.

Now get out there and make some neck warmers!

Happy crocheting.

Crochet Angels

15 Wonderful Crochet Angel Patterns To Prepare Your Home For Christmas Miracle

Julianne Link

Crochet Angel

15 Wonderful Crochet Angel Patterns To
Prepare Your Home For Christmas Miracle

Introduction

It's Christmastime again, and you are ready to decorate your house. You know you love all the Christmas decorations, but you don't want to have to pick from the same old selection that you find in stores.

You want to be unique, you want to have your own style, and you want to have your own look everywhere in your home.

But how are you going to do this unless you make it yourself?

If you stick to the stores, you have to stick with the same old selection that you have always had, but when you make it yourself, you can throw in any custom look you want.

Bring in the glitter, bring in the glue, and bring in anything you want to give the look that perfect touch.

In this book, I am going to show you exactly what you need to do to make angels of your own. Have fun with the various patterns, mix and match to bring in your own flare, and express yourself in this Christmas season like never before. Are you ready to enjoy this Christmas season? Get your yarn and hook, and let's get started.

Chapter 1 – Angels From On High

The Angel Choir

Photo made by: Tobias Vemmenby

You will need 1 ball of yarn and a size G crochet hook

For the head:

Chain 5 and join with a slip stitch to form a ring. Single crochet in the center of this ring 10 times, and join with a slip stitch. Chain 1, turn, and single crochet back around to the other side. Chain 1, turn, and single crochet back to the beginning.

Chain 1, turn, and single crochet back to the other side. Continue with this now for a total of 10 rows.

For the next row, chain 1, turn, and single crochet in the next 3 stitches, then skip the next stitch. Single crochet in the next 3 stitches, and skip the next stitch. Continue to the beginning, and join with a slip stitch.

Work the next row as you normally would, then work another decrease row.

You are going to steadily decrease until you have nearly a perfect globe. Set aside.

For the body:

Chain 5 and join with a slip stitch to form a ring. Single crochet in the center of this ring 10 times, and join with a slip stitch. Chain 1, turn, and single crochet back around to the other side. Chain 1, turn, and single crochet back to the beginning.

Chain 1, turn, and single crochet back to the other side. Continue with this now for a total of 10 rows.

For the next row, chain 1, turn, and single crochet in the next 3 stitches, then skip the next stitch. Single crochet in the next 3 stitches, and skip the next stitch. Continue to the beginning, and join with a slip stitch.

Chain 5, skip the next 3 and join with a slip stitch. Chain 5, skip the next 3 and join with a slip stitch. Chain 5, and skip the next 3, then join with a slip stitch. Repeat this around.

For the next row, you are going to chain 5, and join with a slip stitch to the top of the chain space. Chain 5, and join with a slip stitch to the chain space. Repeat this sequence for as long as you want your angel's gown to be.

For the wings:

Chain 15. Single crochet across the row. Chain 1, skip the first stitch, and single crochet across the row, chain 1, turn, and single crochet across the row, skipping the last stitch. Chain 1, turn, and skip the first stitch. Single crochet across the row.

Chain 1, skip the first stitch, and single crochet across the row, skipping the last stitch. Chain 1, and skip the first stitch and continue across the row. You are going to be decreasing on both sides of the piece, but you are going to decrease faster on the one side than the other.

When you only have a length of 4 stitches, tie off and repeat for the other side.

To assemble:

Stuff the head firmly with stuffing, then take your yarn needle and sew the bottom closed. Make sure it's packed tightly before sewing shut. Sew the base of the head directly to the body, and cut any loose ends. Attach the wings next, making sure there are no loose ends. Attach another loop for a hanger, or hooks in the back, and you are set!

Highlight Angel

Photo made by: Jennifer Snyder

You will need 1 ball of yarn in white, black, and grey, and a size G crochet hook

For the head:

Chain 5 and join with a slip stitch to form a ring. Single crochet in the center of this ring 10 times, and join with a slip stitch. Chain 1, turn, and single crochet back around to the other side. Chain 1, turn, and single crochet back to the beginning.

Chain 1, turn, and single crochet back to the other side. Continue with this now for a total of 20 rows.

For the next row, chain 1, turn, and single crochet in the next 3 stitches, then skip the next stitch. Single crochet in the next 3 stitches, and skip the next stitch. Continue to the beginning, and join with a slip stitch.

Work the next row as you normally would, then work another decrease row.

You are going to steadily decrease until you have nearly a perfect globe. Tie off.

Take lengths of yarn now, and feed them through the top of the head. Follow the photo as a reference for colors and placement, and feed through as many lengths of yarn as you can get to fit. Once you are happy with the hair, set aside.

For the body:

Chain 5 and join with a slip stitch to form a ring. Single crochet in the center of this ring 10 times, and join with a slip stitch. Chain 1, turn, and single crochet back around to the other side. Chain 1, turn, and single crochet back to the beginning.

Continue until you have a total of 12 rows.

For the next row, chain 1, turn, and single crochet in the next 3 stitches, then skip the next stitch.

Chain 1, turn, and single crochet around the row. Join with a slip stitch, chain 1, turn, and single crochet around the row. Continue with this pattern, creating a cylinder shape until the tube measures about 5 inches tall.

Next, decrease sharply to a narrow opening, tie off, and set aside.

507

For the legs:

Chain 5 and join with a slip stitch to form a ring. Single crochet in the center of this ring 10 times, and join with a slip stitch. Chain 1, turn, and single crochet back around to the other side. Chain 1, turn, and single crochet back to the beginning.

Continue until you have a total of 5 rows.

For the next row, chain 1, turn, and single crochet in the next 3 stitches, then skip the next stitch.

Chain 1, turn, and single crochet around the row. Join with a slip stitch, chain 1, turn, and single crochet around the row. Continue with this pattern, creating a cylinder shape until the tube measures about 3 inches tall.

Next, decrease sharply to a narrow opening, tie off, and repeat for the other leg.

For the wings:

Chain 25. Single crochet across the row. Chain 1, skip the first stitch, and single crochet across the row, chain 1, turn, and single crochet across the row, skipping the last stitch. Chain 1, turn, and skip the first stitch. Single crochet across the row.

Chain 1, skip the first stitch, and single crochet across the row, skipping the last stitch. Chain 1, and skip the first stitch and continue across the row. You are going to be decreasing on both sides of the piece, but you are going to decrease faster on the one side than the other.

When you only have a length of 7 stitches, tie off and repeat for the other side.

To assemble:

Stuff the head firmly with stuffing, then take your yarn needle and sew the bottom closed. Make sure it's packed tightly before sewing shut.

Stuff the body firmly, but not as plump as you did the head. Also stuff the arms separately from the rest of the pieces and sew each piece closed. Start by sewing the arms in place. Sew the wings on next, then the legs after that. Sew the base of the head directly to the body, and cut any loose ends. Make sure the head, wings, legs, and arms are sewn in place securely, and you are done!

Glorious Day Angel

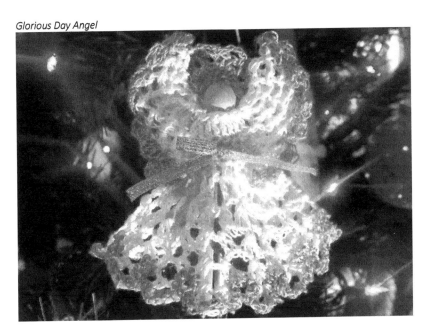

Photo made by: Irish American Mom

You will need 1 ball of yarn in white and 1 ball of yarn in gold and a size G crochet hook

Use the photo as a color reference.

Chain 5, and join with a slip stitch to form a ring. Chain 1, and single crochet in the center of this ring 10 times. Chain 4, turn, and skip the next 2 stitches, then join with a slip stitch. Chain 4, skip the next 2 stitches, and join with a slip stitch on the next stitch.

Repeat for 5 rows. Tie off.

Bend this in half, and fold up and around the head as you see in the photo.

For the body:

Chain 5 and join with a slip stitch to form a ring. Single crochet in the center of this ring 10 times, and join with a slip stitch. Chain 1, turn, and single crochet back around to the other side. Chain 1, turn, and single crochet back to the beginning.

Chain 1, turn, and single crochet back to the other side. Continue with this now for a total of 10 rows.

For the next row, chain 1, turn, and single crochet in the next 3 stitches, then skip the next stitch. Single crochet in the next 3 stitches, and skip the next stitch. Continue to the beginning, and join with a slip stitch.

Chain 5, skip the next 3 and join with a slip stitch. Chain 5, skip the next 3 and join with a slip stitch. Chain 5, and skip the next 3, then join with a slip stitch. Repeat this around.

For the next row, you are going to chain 5, and join with a slip stitch to the top of the chain space. Chain 5, and join with a slip stitch to the chain space. Repeat this sequence for as long as you want your angel's gown to be.

To assemble:

Attach the wings to the top of the skirt, then glue the head to the body. Add features if you like, or leave it as is.

Either way, your new angel is done!

Chapter 2 – Small Packages

Elegant Wraps

Photo made by: Jo Naylor

You will need 1 ball of yarn and a size G crochet hook

Take your yarn and wrap it around a DVD case. When you have a small handful of yarn, cut the bottom of the wrap off the DVD case.

Use the bundle to tie a knot in the middle, then take 2 small lengths of yarn to form the body, and the arms.

For the wings:

Bend crafting wire in the shape of a set of wings, then take your yarn. Wrap the yarn around this wire, forming extra loops on the ends. When you have completely covered the wire, tie off. Attach the wings to the back of the angel, and you are done!

Mini Little Singer

Photo made by: <u>Robin</u>

You will need 1 ball of yarn in white, tan, and yellow and a size G crochet hook

For the head:

Chain 5 and join with a slip stitch to form a ring. Single crochet in the center of this ring 10 times, and join with a slip stitch. Chain 1, turn, and single crochet back around to the other side. Chain 1, turn, and single crochet back to the beginning.

Chain 1, turn, and single crochet back to the other side. Continue with this now for a total of 10 rows.

For the next row, chain 1, turn, and single crochet in the next 3 stitches, then skip the next stitch. Single crochet in the next 3 stitches, and skip the next stitch. Continue to the beginning, and join with a slip stitch.

Work the next row as you normally would, then work another decrease row.

You are going to steadily decrease until you have nearly a perfect globe. Set aside.

For the body:

Chain 5 and join with a slip stitch to form a ring. Single crochet in the center of this ring 10 times, and join with a slip stitch. Chain 1, turn, and single crochet back around to the other side. Chain 1, turn, and single crochet back to the beginning.

Chain 1, turn, and single crochet back to the other side. Continue with this now for a total of 10 rows.

For the next row, chain 1, turn, and single crochet in the next 3 stitches, then skip the next stitch. Single crochet in the next 3 stitches, and skip the next stitch. Continue to the beginning, and join with a slip stitch.

Work the next row as you normally would, then work another decrease row.

Continue with this pattern, adding a yellow strip around the center of the ball. When you have a small opening, tie off.

For the wings:

Chain 10.

Single crochet across the row, chain 1, turn, and skip the first stitch. Single crochet across the row and skip the last stitch. Chain 1, turn, and skip the first stitch, single crochet across the row, and skip the last stitch.

Chain 1, and single crochet across the row. Chain 1, turn, and single crochet in the first stitch 2 times. Single crochet across the row, and single crochet in the last stitch 2 times.

Chain 1, and single crochet across the row. Chain 1, turn, and single crochet in the first stitch 2 times. Single crochet across the row, and single crochet in the last stitch 2 times.

Finish with a single crochet around the entire border, and tie off.

To assemble:

Stuff the head firmly with stuffing, then take your yarn needle and sew the bottom closed. Make sure it's packed tightly before sewing shut. Sew the wings in place next. Stuff the body firmly, make sure you go as firmly as you did for the head. Sew the base of the head directly to the body, and cut any loose ends.

That's it, your little cherub is done!

Chubby Little Cherub
You will need 1 ball of yarn in white, tan, yellow, and a size G crochet hook

For the head:

Chain 5 and join with a slip stitch to form a ring. Single crochet in the center of this ring 10 times, and join with a slip stitch. Chain 1, turn, and single crochet back around to the other side. Chain 1, turn, and single crochet back to the beginning.

Chain 1, turn, and single crochet back to the other side. Continue with this now for a total of 20 rows.

Photo made by: <u>Robin</u>

For the next row, chain 1, turn, and single crochet in the next 3 stitches, then skip the next stitch. Single crochet in the next 3 stitches, and skip the next stitch. Continue to the beginning, and join with a slip stitch.

Work the next row as you normally would, then work another decrease row.

You are going to steadily decrease until you have nearly a perfect globe. Set aside.

For the body:

515

Chain 5 and join with a slip stitch to form a ring. Single crochet in the center of this ring 10 times, and join with a slip stitch. Chain 1, turn, and single crochet back around to the other side. Chain 1, turn, and single crochet back to the beginning.

Chain 1, turn, and single crochet back to the other side. Continue with this now for a total of 30 rows.

For the next row, chain 1, turn, and single crochet in the next 3 stitches, then skip the next stitch. Single crochet in the next 3 stitches, and skip the next stitch. Continue to the beginning, and join with a slip stitch.

Work the next row as you normally would, then work another decrease row.

You are going to steadily decrease until you have nearly a perfect globe. Set aside.

For the arms:

Chain 5 and join with a slip stitch to form a ring. Single crochet in the center of this ring 10 times, and join with a slip stitch. Chain 1, turn, and single crochet back around to the other side. Chain 1, turn, and single crochet back to the beginning.

Continue until you have a total of 5 rows.

For the next row, chain 1, turn, and single crochet in the next 3 stitches, then skip the next stitch.

Chain 1, turn, and single crochet around the row. Join with a slip stitch, chain 1, turn, and single crochet around the row. Continue with this pattern, creating a cylinder shape until the tube measures about 3 inches tall.

Next, decrease sharply to a narrow opening, tie off, and repeat for the other arm.

For the wings:

Chain 25. Single crochet across the row. Chain 1, skip the first stitch, and single crochet across the row, chain 1, turn, and single crochet across the row, skipping the last stitch. Chain 1, turn, and skip the first stitch. Single crochet across the row.

516

Chain 1, skip the first stitch, and single crochet across the row, skipping the last stitch. Chain 1, and skip the first stitch and continue across the row. You are going to be decreasing on both sides of the piece, but you are going to decrease faster on the one side than the other.

When you only have a length of 7 stitches, tie off and repeat for the other side.

To assemble:

Stuff the head firmly with stuffing, then take your yarn needle and sew the bottom closed. Make sure it's packed tightly before sewing shut.

Stuff the body firmly, but not as plump as you did the head. Also stuff the arms separately from the rest of the pieces and sew each piece closed. Start by sewing the arms in place.

Sew the wings in place next. Sew the base of the head directly to the body, and cut any loose ends. Make sure the head and arms are sewn in place securely, and you are done!

Greetings from the Lamp Post

Photo made by: JAM Project

You will need 1 ball of yarn and a size G crochet hook

Chain 5 and join with a slip stitch to form a ring. Single crochet in the center of this ring 10 times, and join with a slip stitch. Chain 1, turn, and single crochet back around to the other side. Chain 1, turn, and single crochet back to the beginning.

Chain 1, turn, and single crochet back to the other side. Continue with this now for a total of 10 rows. Tie off.

For the body:

Chain 6.

Double crochet across the row. Chain 2, and double crochet in the first stitch 2 times. Double crochet across the row, then double crochet in the last stitch 2 times.

Repeat this 4 more times.

For the last row, chain 1, and single crochet in the next stitch 3 times. Chain 1, and single crochet in the next stitch 3 times. Repeat across the row.

For the wings, simply work a chain 2 rows thick of single crochet, and attach to the back.

That's it! Assemble the angel, and you are done!

Photo made by: <u>Matt Brown</u>

You will need 1 ball of yarn in white, tan, yellow, and a size G crochet hook

For the head:

Chain 5 and join with a slip stitch to form a ring. Single crochet in the center of this ring 10 times, and join with a slip stitch. Chain 1, turn, and single crochet back around to the other side. Chain 1, turn, and single crochet back to the beginning.

Chain 1, turn, and single crochet back to the other side. Continue with this now for a total of 10 rows.

For the next row, chain 1, turn, and single crochet in the next 3 stitches, then skip the next stitch. Single crochet in the next 3 stitches, and skip the next stitch. Continue to the beginning, and join with a slip stitch.

Work the next row as you normally would, then work another decrease row.

You are going to steadily decrease until you have nearly a perfect globe. Feed the golden cord through the top of the head for hair, adding as much and as long as you want.

Set aside.

For the body:

Chain 5 and join with a slip stitch to form a ring. Single crochet in the center of this ring 10 times, and join with a slip stitch. Chain 1, turn, and single crochet back around to the other side. Chain 1, turn, and single crochet back to the beginning.

Chain 1, turn, and single crochet back to the other side. Continue with this now for a total of 10 rows.

For the next row, chain 1, turn, and single crochet in the next 3 stitches, then skip the next stitch. Single crochet in the next 3 stitches, and skip the next stitch. Continue to the beginning, and join with a slip stitch.

Work the next row as you normally would, then work another decrease row.

Continue with this pattern, adding a yellow strip around the center of the ball. When you have a small opening, tie off.

Attach the arms directly to the side of the body.

To assemble:

Stuff the head firmly with stuffing, then take your yarn needle and sew the bottom closed. Make sure it's packed tightly before sewing shut.

Stuff the body firmly as well, then sew the bottom closed. Attach the arms to the sides of the body as you can see in the photo.

Sew the base of the head directly to the body, and cut any loose ends.

Attach another loop for a hanger, or hooks in the back, and you are set!

Candy Corny Angel

Photo made by: <u>Dina Wirawan</u>

You will need 1 ball of yarn in orange, white, yellow, light yellow, and a size G crochet hook

Use the photo as a color chart.

Chain 5 and join with a slip stitch to form a ring. Single crochet in the center of this ring 10 times, and join with a slip stitch. Chain 1, turn, and single crochet back around to the other side. Chain 1, turn, and single crochet back to the beginning.

Chain 1, turn, and single crochet back to the other side. Continue with this now for a total of 40 rows.

For the next row, chain 1, turn, and single crochet in the next 3 stitches, then skip the next stitch. Single crochet in the next 3 stitches, and skip the next stitch. Continue to the beginning, and join with a slip stitch.

Continue to decrease all the way to the top, following the photo as a color chart.

For the wings:

Chain 25. Single crochet across the row. Chain 1, skip the first stitch, and single crochet across the row, chain 1, turn, and single crochet across the row, skipping the last stitch. Chain 1, turn, and skip the first stitch. Single crochet across the row.

Chain 1, skip the first stitch, and single crochet across the row, skipping the last stitch. Chain 1, and skip the first stitch and continue across the row. You are going to be decreasing on both sides of the piece, but you are going to decrease faster on the one side than the other.

When you only have a length of 7 stitches, tie off and repeat for the other side.

Sew to each side of the candy corn angel, and you are done!

Chapter 4 – Unique Little Cherubs

Mini Wing Angel's Sing

Photo made by: Picture Institute- Bristol Margate Nida London

You will need 1 ball of yarn in blue, orange, white, yellow, and a size G crochet hook

For the body:

Chain 5 and join with a slip stitch to form a ring. Single crochet in the center of this ring 10 times, and join with a slip stitch. Chain 1, turn, and single crochet back around to the other side. Chain 1, turn, and single crochet back to the beginning.

Chain 1, turn, and single crochet back to the other side. Continue with this now for a total of 10 rows.

For the next row, chain 1, turn, and single crochet in the next 3 stitches, then skip the next stitch. Single crochet in the next 3 stitches, and skip the next stitch. Continue to the beginning, and join with a slip stitch.

Chain 5, skip the next 3 and join with a slip stitch. Chain 5, skip the next 3 and join with a slip stitch. Chain 5, and skip the next 3, then join with a slip stitch. Repeat this around.

Single crochet in each of the stitches 2 times. Chain 1, turn, and single crochet in each of the stitches 2 times. Repeat this sequence for as long as you want your skirt to be.

Stuff the body generously, then close the base.

Glue the wooden ball to the top, and add your features. Add small wings to the back, tie off, and you are done!

Golden Glory Angel

Photo made by: <u>Alyson Hurt</u>

You will need 1 ball of yarn in white and 1 ball of yarn in gold and a size G crochet hook

You are going to glue the wooden ball to the top of the wings, or you can use a clothespin for the body.

For the wings:

Chain 5. Single crochet across the row. Chain 1, and single crochet in each of the stitches across the row 2 times. Chain 1, turn, and repeat.

For the next row, chain 4, and skip the next stitch, and join with a slip stitch. Chain 4, and skip the next stitch, and join with a slip stitch. Repeat across the row.

For the next row, chain 4, and join with a slip stitch in the chain space. Chain 4, and join with a slip stitch in the chain space. Repeat across. Continue until you are happy with the size of the wings, then tie off. Repeat for the other side.

For the body:

Chain 5 and join with a slip stitch to form a ring. Single crochet in the center of this ring 10 times, and join with a slip stitch. Chain 1, turn, and single crochet back around to the other side. Chain 1, turn, and single crochet back to the beginning.

Chain 1, turn, and single crochet back to the other side. Continue with this now for a total of 10 rows.

For the next row, chain 1, turn, and single crochet in the next 3 stitches, then skip the next stitch. Single crochet in the next 3 stitches, and skip the next stitch. Continue to the beginning, and join with a slip stitch.

Chain 5, skip the next 3 and join with a slip stitch. Chain 5, skip the next 3 and join with a slip stitch. Chain 5, and skip the next 3, then join with a slip stitch. Repeat this around.

For the next row, you are going to chain 5, and join with a slip stitch to the top of the chain space. Chain 5, and join with a slip stitch to the chain space. Repeat this sequence for as long as you want your angel's gown to be.

To assemble:

Sew the wings to the body and fit around the clothespin, or simply sew them together and attach the ball for the head.

527

That's it! Attach a loop to hang your piece, and you are done!

Twist and Turned Angel

Photo made by: Jo Naylor

You will need 1 ball of yarn and a size G crochet hook

Take your yarn and wrap it around a DVD case. When you have a small handful of yarn, cut the bottom of the wrap off the DVD case.

Use the bundle to tie a knot in the middle, then take 2 small lengths of yarn to form the body, and the arms.

For the wings:

Use another bundle of yarn for the wings, following the same steps as you did for the rest of the body. Wrap securely.

You can also crochet a small belt for the center of the angel, but this is up to you.

Attach the wings to the back of the angel, and you are done!

Open Work Joy

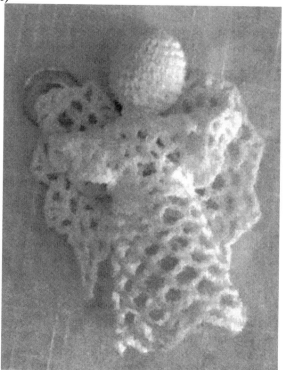

Photo made by: <u>chrtphre campbell</u>

You will need 1 ball of yarn and a size G crochet hook

For the head:

Chain 5 and join with a slip stitch to form a ring. Single crochet in the center of this ring 10 times, and join with a slip stitch. Chain 1, turn, and single crochet back around to the other side. Chain 1, turn, and single crochet back to the beginning.

Chain 1, turn, and single crochet back to the other side. Continue with this now for a total of 10 rows.

For the next row, chain 1, turn, and single crochet in the next 3 stitches, then skip the next stitch. Single crochet in the next 3 stitches, and skip the next stitch. Continue to the beginning, and join with a slip stitch.

Work the next row as you normally would, then work another decrease row.

You are going to steadily decrease until you have nearly a perfect globe. Set aside.

For the body:

Chain 5 and join with a slip stitch to form a ring. Single crochet in the center of this ring 10 times, and join with a slip stitch. Chain 1, turn, and single crochet back around to the other side. Chain 1, turn, and single crochet back to the beginning.

Chain 1, turn, and single crochet back to the other side. Continue with this now for a total of 10 rows.

For the next row, chain 1, turn, and single crochet in the next 3 stitches, then skip the next stitch. Single crochet in the next 3 stitches, and skip the next stitch. Continue to the beginning, and join with a slip stitch.

Chain 5, skip the next 3 and join with a slip stitch. Chain 5, skip the next 3 and join with a slip stitch. Chain 5, and skip the next 3, then join with a slip stitch. Repeat this around.

For the next row, you are going to chain 5, and join with a slip stitch to the top of the chain space. Chain 5, and join with a slip stitch to the chain space. Repeat this sequence for as long as you want your angel's gown to be.

For the wings:

Chain 5. Single crochet across the row. Chain 1, and single crochet in each of the stitches across the row 2 times. Chain 1, turn, and repeat.

For the next row, chain 4, and skip the next stitch, and join with a slip stitch. Chain 4, and skip the next stitch, and join with a slip stitch. Repeat across the row.

For the next row, chain 4, and join with a slip stitch in the chain space. Chain 4, and join with a slip stitch in the chain space. Repeat across. Continue until you are happy with the size of the wings, then tie off. Repeat for the other side.

To assemble:

Stuff the head firmly with stuffing, then take your yarn needle and sew the bottom closed. Make sure it's packed tightly before sewing shut.

Sew the base of the head directly to the body, and cut any loose ends. Pinch the side of the body on both ends, creating the arm folds. Sew in place.

Attach the wings next, and snip the loose string off the end. Attach another loop for a hanger, or hooks in the back, and you are set!

Little Miss Silent Night

Photo made by: <u>Son of Groucho</u>

You will need 1 ball of yarn and a size G crochet hook, some gold string, a ball, and some glue

Chain 5 and join with a slip stitch to form a ring. Single crochet in the center of this ring 10 times, and join with a slip stitch. Chain 1, turn, and single crochet back around to the other side. Chain 1, turn, and single crochet back to the beginning.

Chain 1, turn, and single crochet back to the other side. Continue with this now for a total of 10 rows.

For the next row, chain 1, turn, and single crochet in the next 3 stitches, then skip the next stitch. Single crochet in the next 3 stitches, and skip the next stitch. Continue to the beginning, and join with a slip stitch.

Chain 5, skip the next 3 and join with a slip stitch. Chain 5, skip the next 3 and join with a slip stitch. Chain 5, and skip the next 3, then join with a slip stitch. Repeat this around.

For the next row, you are going to chain 5, and join with a slip stitch to the top of the chain space. Chain 5, and join with a slip stitch to the chain space. Repeat this sequence for as long as you want your angel's gown to be.

To assemble:

Use a bulb or a wooden ball for the head, and use mesh for the wings. Add in finer details for each of the features and add in your own little touch.

That's it! She's done!

Photo made by: Chris RubberDragon

You will need 1 ball of yarn and a size G crochet hook

For the head:

Chain 5 and join with a slip stitch to form a ring. Single crochet in the center of this ring 10 times, and join with a slip stitch. Chain 1, turn, and single crochet back around to the other side. Chain 1, turn, and single crochet back to the beginning.

Chain 1, turn, and single crochet back to the other side. Continue with this now for a total of 10 rows.

For the next row, chain 1, turn, and single crochet in the next 3 stitches, then skip the next stitch. Single crochet in the next 3 stitches, and skip the next stitch. Continue to the beginning, and join with a slip stitch.

Work the next row as you normally would, then work another decrease row.

534

You are going to steadily decrease until you have nearly a perfect globe. Set aside.

For the body:

Chain 5 and join with a slip stitch to form a ring. Single crochet in the center of this ring 10 times, and join with a slip stitch. Chain 1, turn, and single crochet back around to the other side. Chain 1, turn, and single crochet back to the beginning.

Chain 1, turn, and single crochet back to the other side. Continue with this now for a total of 10 rows.

For the next row, chain 1, turn, and single crochet in the next 3 stitches, then skip the next stitch. Single crochet in the next 3 stitches, and skip the next stitch. Continue to the beginning, and join with a slip stitch.

Chain 5, skip the next 3 and join with a slip stitch. Chain 5, skip the next 3 and join with a slip stitch. Chain 5, and skip the next 3, then join with a slip stitch. Repeat this around.

For the next row, you are going to chain 5, and join with a slip stitch to the top of the chain space. Chain 5, and join with a slip stitch to the chain space. Repeat this sequence for as long as you want your angel's gown to be.

For the wings:

Chain 5. Single crochet across the row. Chain 1, and single crochet in each of the stitches across the row 2 times. Chain 1, turn, and repeat.

For the next row, chain 4, and skip the next stitch, and join with a slip stitch. Chain 4, and skip the next stitch, and join with a slip stitch. Repeat across the row.

For the next row, chain 4, and join with a slip stitch in the chain space. Chain 4, and join with a slip stitch in the chain space. Repeat across. Continue until you are happy with the size of the wings, then tie off. Repeat for the other side.

To assemble:

Stuff the head firmly with stuffing, then take your yarn needle and sew the bottom closed. Make sure it's packed tightly before sewing shut.

Sew the base of the head directly to the body, and cut any loose ends. Sew the wings on next, and again snip any loose ends. Attach another loop for a hanger, or hooks in the back, and you are set!

Conclusion

There you have it, everything you need to make your own little angels to decorate your home for the holidays. Whether you are putting up a tree, want to have them on various knobs, or just want them on the shelf, you have what you need here.

Let this book inspire you to make the most of crafting this holiday season, and spread the Christmas cheer!

Christmas Crochet

15 Beautiful Christmas Crochet Patterns To Give Your Home A Christmas Look

Julianne Link

Christmas Crochet

15 Beautiful Christmas Crochet Patterns To Give
Your Home A Christmas Look

Introduction

Christmas time is here, and your house is in need of a makeover. Of course, you know you are picky about what you put into your house, even if it is only for a few months out of the year. You have to use decorations that are cute, that are simple, and that go with the overall tone of your house.

There's nothing worse than a house that has decorations splattered through it, but nothing seems to go with anything. You know it's only for a few weeks of the year, but you simply must have everything be perfect, or it's going to be an awfully long three weeks.

What better way to get exactly what you want then making things yourself? If you are making your own decorations, you are in control of the outcome, and you are guaranteed to get just what you want, when you want it. And this book is going to show you how.

Let me give you the patterns to fifteen different projects that you can fall in love with over and over again. This book is full of patterns that aren't going to go out of style, and no matter how old you are, what kind of style you have, or what you want to put in your house, you will get what you want.

Throw in your own style with each of these little pieces, and you will get what you want no matter what. This book is full of patterns and decorations you can use all over the house, and if you change various little things with color or embellishment, you can make them suitable for your kid's room, for fancy dinners, or for anything that comes to mine.

The patterns in this book are easy, and you will soon discover that no matter what skill level you have, you will enjoy making them and throwing in your own personal touch.

Christmas is just around the corner, but you still have time to make any or all of these projects before it gets here. Let your imagination run wild, and show off your style in any of these little patterns. It's the most wonderful time of the year, so why not celebrate it in as many ways possible?

Grab your crochet hook, grab your yarn, and get to work. You know you love crochet, and this is an excellent time to embrace the best of both worlds. Finish your gift shopping, have fun in the process, and most of all, get down to crocheting!

Now let's get started.

Chapter 1 – Simplicity Crochet

Simple little patterns to get you started… make any or all of these in a single afternoon, and decorate every corner of your house!

Simple Little Snowflake

Photo made by: Miia Sample

You will need 1 ball of yarn and a size G crochet hook

Chain 10 and join with a slip stitch to form a ring. Single crochet in the center of this ring 20 times, and join with a slip stitch. Chain 5, and skip the next 2 stitches, and join with a slip stitch.

Chain 5, and skip the next 2 stitches, and join with a slip stitch. Repeat this around. Join with a slip stitch, chain 1, and turn.

Work 1 row of single crochet, then join with a slip stitch, and turn once more. Chain 5, and skip the next 2 stitches, and join with a slip stitch.

Chain 5, and skip the next 2 stitches, and join with a slip stitch. Repeat this around. Join with a slip stitch, chain 1, and turn.

Single crochet in the first stitch 3 times. Chain 1, and double crochet in the next stitch 2 times. Chain 1, and single crochet in the next stitch 3 times. Single crochet in the next stitch.

Single crochet in the next stitch 3 times. Chain 1, and double crochet in the next stitch 2 times. Chain 1, and single crochet in the next stitch 3 times. Single crochet in the next stitch.

Repeat this sequence around the edge of the snowflake, and join with a slip stitch when you get back to the beginning.

Secure a hook or a string to the top of the piece for hanging, and you are done!

Photo made by: <u>Robin</u>

You will need 1 ball of yarn for each of the colors you use and a size G crochet hook

For the head, select color for the piece you are making, then:

Chain 5, and join with a slip stitch to form a ring. Single crochet in the center of this ring 10 times, and join with another slip stitch.

Chain 1, turn, and single crochet around the other way. Chain 1, turn, and single crochet back to the beginning. You are going to continue this pattern for a total of 5 rows.

For the next row, chain 1, and single crochet in the first 2 stitches, then skip the next stitch. Single crochet in the next 2 stitches, and skip the next stitch. Repeat around.

Join with a slip stitch and chain 1 before turning.

single crochet in the first 2 stitches, then skip the next stitch. Single crochet in the next 2 stitches, and skip the next stitch. Repeat around.

Continue with a steady decrease until you have a small ball. Set aside.

For the body:

Chain 5, and join with a slip stitch to form a ring. Single crochet in the center of this ring 10 times, and join with another slip stitch.

Chain 1, turn, and single crochet around the other way. Chain 1, turn, and single crochet back to the beginning. You are going to continue this pattern for a total of 10 rows.

For the next row, chain 1, and single crochet in the first 3 stitches, then skip the next stitch. Single crochet in the next 3 stitches, and skip the next stitch. Repeat around.

Join with a slip stitch and chain 1 before turning.

single crochet in the first 3 stitches, then skip the next stitch. Single crochet in the next 3 stitches, and skip the next stitch. Repeat around.

If you are creating the elf, remember to change colors about halfway through the body, then go back to the main color after you work the belt.

Continue with a steady decrease until you have a small ball. Set aside.

To assemble:

Stuff both head and body, then sew them together.

Add eyes with beads or embroidery, then add on any other details:

Crochet a small hat for the elf by making a small triangle using a base of 5 stitches, and decreasing. For the hat for the snowman, do the same, only make a rectangle and draw it in when you get to the center.

Do a simple chain 5 and work 1 single crochet row 2 times for the antlers for the reindeer.

Attach details, and you are done!

Noel, the Mini Angel

Photo made by: <u>Robin</u>

You will need 1 ball of yarn for each of the colors you use and a size G crochet hook

Use the photo as a reference guide for colors

For the head, select color for the piece you are making, then:

Chain 5, and join with a slip stitch to form a ring. Single crochet in the center of this ring 10 times, and join with another slip stitch.

Chain 1, turn, and single crochet around the other way. Chain 1, turn, and single crochet back to the beginning. You are going to continue this pattern for a total of 5 rows.

546

For the next row, chain 1, and single crochet in the first 2 stitches, then skip the next stitch. Single crochet in the next 2 stitches, and skip the next stitch. Repeat around.

Join with a slip stitch and chain 1 before turning.

single crochet in the first 2 stitches, then skip the next stitch. Single crochet in the next 2 stitches, and skip the next stitch. Repeat around.

Continue with a steady decrease until you have a small ball. Set aside.

For the body:

Chain 5, and join with a slip stitch to form a ring. Single crochet in the center of this ring 10 times, and join with another slip stitch.

Chain 1, turn, and single crochet around the other way. Chain 1, turn, and single crochet back to the beginning. You are going to continue this pattern for a total of 10 rows.

For the next row, chain 1, and single crochet in the first 3 stitches, then skip the next stitch. Single crochet in the next 3 stitches, and skip the next stitch. Repeat around.

Join with a slip stitch and chain 1 before turning.

single crochet in the first 3 stitches, then skip the next stitch. Single crochet in the next 3 stitches, and skip the next stitch. Repeat around.

Remember to add the yellow belt in the center of the body.

Continue with a steady decrease until you have a small ball. Set aside.

To assemble:

Stuff both head and body, then sew them together.

Add eyes with beads or embroidery, then add on any other details:

I use a section of glittery pipe cleaner for the halo, and the wings are simple as well.

Chain 15 and single crochet across the row. Chain 1, turn, and single crochet back to the beginning. Chain 2, and skip the first stitch, then single crochet across the row, and skip the last stitch.

Chain 1, turn, and single crochet across the row.

Chain 2, and skip the first stitch, then single crochet across the row, and skip the last stitch.

Chain 1, turn, and single crochet across the row.

Continue with this decrease until you have the size of wings you prefer, and embellish them with gold around the end. Sew them in place, and your mini angel is done!

Chapter 2 – Christmas Everywhere

Christmas ornaments or coasters… there are tons of ways you can bring in little crochet patterns throughout the house!

Christmas Bulb Cover

Photo made by: Catherine

You will need 1 ball of yarn and a size G crochet hook

Chain 5, and join with a slip stitch to form a ring. Single crochet in the center of this ring 10 times, and join with another slip stitch.

Chain 1, turn, and single crochet around the other way. Chain 1, turn, and single crochet back to the beginning. You are going to continue this pattern until it covers the top of the bulb you are using. Join with a slip stitch.

Chain 5, and skip the next 2 stitches, and join with a slip stitch. Repeat this around. Join with a slip stitch, chain 1, and turn.

Chain 5, and skip the next 2 stitches, and join with a slip stitch. Repeat this around. Join with a slip stitch, chain 1, and turn.

Work 1 row of single crochet, join with a slip stitch, chain 1, and turn.

For the next row, chain 1, and single crochet in the first 3 stitches, then skip the next stitch. Single crochet in the next 3 stitches, and skip the next stitch. Repeat around.

Join with a slip stitch and chain 1 before turning.

single crochet in the first 3 stitches, then skip the next stitch. Single crochet in the next 3 stitches, and skip the next stitch. Repeat around.

Slide your bulb into the center of this covering now, and continue to work your way around the bulb, using a steady decrease.

Stop when you are at the base of the bulb, and tie off.

Photo made by: <u>Styla</u>

You will need 1 ball of yarn and a size G crochet hook

Chain 5 and join with a slip stitch to form a ring. Chain 2, and double crochet in the center of the ring 2 times. Chain 5, then double crochet in the center of the ring 3 times. Chain 5 and double crochet in the center of the ring 5 times. Chain 5, then join with a slip stitch.

For the next row, chain 5, and skip the next 3 stitches, then double crochet in the chain space 3 times. Chain 8, and double crochet in the same chain space 3 times. Chain 5, skip the next 3 stitches, and single crochet in the chain space 3 times. Repeat this for the third edge of the tree.

551

Join with a slip stitch. Chain 2, and double crochet in the chain space 8 times. Chain 1, skip the next stitch, and double crochet in the chain space 8 times. Chain 5 and double crochet in the same space 8 times, this is forming the top of the tree.

Continue with the pattern of double crochet in the chain space 8 times, chaining 1, and skipping the next stitch until you have reached the point where you began. Join with a slip stitch and tie off.

Join the yarn to the center of the base with a slip stitch, and single crochet in the next 5 stitches, chain 1, turn, and single crochet back across the row. Chain 1, turn, and single crochet in the next 5 stitches. Repeat this for a total of 6 rows. Tie off, and you are done.

Christmas Skate Ornaments

Photo made by: Regan76

You will need 1 ball of yarn and a size G crochet hook

552

Chain 10 and double crochet across the row, skipping the last 4 stitches. Chain 2, turn, and double crochet in the 6 stitches going to the back of the skate. Chain 2, turn, and work toward the front of the boot once more.

Tie off, and go to white. Join this with a slip stitch, chain 2, and work 1 row of double crochet across the top in white.

Chain a length of 15 stitches, and tie off.

Repeat for the other side.

Tie a knot in the center, bringing the two skates together. Use a paper clip to slide under the base of the boots, and your skates are done!

Chapter 3 – That Little Touch

Prepare for any family dinner with these napkin rings, and be the star of the show!

Elegant Napkin Holders

Photo made by: Elin B

You will need 1 ball of yarn and a size G crochet hook

Chain 12 and double crochet across the row. Chain 2, turn, and double crochet back to the beginning. Chain 2, turn, and double crochet across the row. Continue with this pattern until you are happy with the length of your strip, and tie off.

Secure a button to one end and a loop to the other, and repeat in an alternating red and green pattern for all your napkins!

Christmas Pine Throw

Photo made by: Amy Truter

You will need 1 ball of yarn for each of the colors you use and a size G crochet hook

Create 24 of each of the 3 colors.

Chain 30 and single crochet across the row. Chain 5, and skip the next 2 stitches, then chain 5, and skip the next 2 stitches. Chain 5, and skip the next 2 stitches. Repeat this across the row.

Chain 6, skip the chain space, and double crochet in the chain space 2 times. Chain 5, skip the chain space, and double crochet in the chain space 2 times. Repeat across the row.

Chain 6, skip the chain space, and double crochet in the chain space 2 times. Chain 5, skip the chain space, and double crochet in the chain space 2 times. Repeat across the row.

Repeat until you have a square, tie off, and set aside.

Repeat for as many squares as you need, then lay them out in the pattern you see in the photo, and sew them together with your yarn needle.

Perfect Ornaments for Every Tree

Photo made by: <u>Becky Bokern</u>

You will need 1 ball of yarn for each of the colors you use and a size G crochet hook

For the snowmen:

Chain 5, and join with a slip stitch to form a ring. Single crochet in the center of this ring 10 times, and join with another slip stitch.

Chain 1, turn, and single crochet around the other way. Chain 1, turn, and single crochet back to the beginning. Continue for 4 rows for the first round, 6 rows for the next round, and 8 rows for the final round. Sew them end to end, and tie a red chain around the neck.

Secure a hook or length of thread at the top, and your snowmen are done!

For the stars:

Chain 5, and join with a slip stitch to form a ring. Single crochet in the center of this ring 10 times, and join with another slip stitch.

Chain 1, turn, and single crochet around the other way. Chain 1, turn, and single crochet back to the beginning. Continue for 5 rows. Tie off.

For the spikes on the stars, join with a slip stitch, and single crochet in the next 8 stitches. Chain 1, turn, and go back across this row. Chain 1, turn, and skip the first stitch, working a single crochet across the row and skipping the last stitch. Chain 1, turn, and skip the first stitch, and single crochet across the row, skipping the last stitch.

Repeat this until you are at a fine point, and tie off. Go back to the beginning, and join once again with a slip stitch, 8 stitches away from the base of this first spike.

Single crochet in the next 8 stitches. Chain 1, turn, and go back across this row. Chain 1, turn, and skip the first stitch, working a single crochet across the row and skipping the last stitch. Chain 1, turn, and skip the first stitch, and single crochet across the row, skipping the last stitch.

Repeat this until you are at a fine point, and tie off. Repeat for as many spikes as your star is going to have. Secure a hook or length of thread at the top, and your stars are done!

Chapter 4 – Christmas Cheer

Small decorations for any room in the house, you can make any of these in just an hour!

Starry Night Christmas Garland

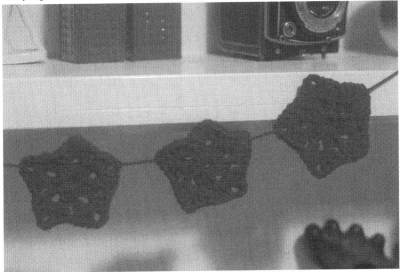

Photo made by: Helen

You will need 1 ball of yarn for each of the colors you use and a size G crochet hook

Chain 10 and join with a slip stitch to form a ring. Single crochet in the center of this ring 20 times, and join with a slip stitch. Chain 5, and skip the next 2 stitches, and join with a slip stitch.

Chain 5, and skip the next 2 stitches, and join with a slip stitch. Repeat this around. Join with a slip stitch, chain 1, and turn.

Work 1 row of single crochet, then join with a slip stitch, and turn once more. Chain 5, and skip the next 2 stitches, and join with a slip stitch.

Chain 5, and skip the next 2 stitches, and join with a slip stitch. Repeat this around. Join with a slip stitch, chain 1, and turn.

Chain 2, and double crochet in the next 8 stitches, then double crochet in the next stitch 3 times. Double crochet in the next 8 stitches, then double crochet in the next stitch 8 times. Continue this around the edge of the star, creating the points for each one.

Repeat for as many stars as you want, until you are ready to assemble:

To assemble:

String your stars on lengths of yarn, and secure them in place with knots. That's it! Your garland is ready for anything.

Christmas Stocking Mini Decoration

Photo made by: JAM Project

You will need 1 ball of yarn for each of the colors you use and a size G crochet hook

Chain 20 and double crochet across the row, chain 2, turn, and double crochet across to the other side. Chain 2, turn, and double crochet across the row. Repeat for 10 rows.

For the next row, continue to double crochet, skipping the last 10 stitches. Chain 2, turn, and double crochet in the 10 stitches going to the back of the stocking. Chain 2, turn, and work toward the front of the stocking once more.

Continue for another 5 rows.

Tie off, and go to white. Join this with a slip stitch, chain 2, and work 3 rows of double crochet across the top in white.

Chain a length of 15 stitches, and tie off.

Repeat this entire sequence for the other side, then take your yarn needle and sew up the two halves of the boot.

For the second half, you aren't going to chain the final 15 stitches at the end, just leave it as it is.

Join this final chain to both sides, and you are done!

Photo made by: JAM Project

You will need 1 ball of yarn and a size G crochet hook

Chain 5, and join with a slip stitch to form a ring. Single crochet in the center of this ring 10 times, and join with another slip stitch.

Chain 1, turn, and single crochet around the other way. Chain 1, turn, and single crochet back to the beginning.

For the next row, chain 5, then single crochet across the row, across the bottom of the circle, and chain 5 out on the other side. chain 1, and single crochet across this row back to the base of the circle once more.

563

Chain 2 and double crochet in the next 5 stitches.

Chain 2, turn, and double crochet in the first stitch 2 times, then double crochet across the row and double crochet in the last stitch 2 times. Chain 2, turn, and double crochet in the first stitch 2 times, then double crochet across the row and double crochet in the last stitch 2 times.

Work 1 more double crochet row, and chain 1 at the end.

Single crochet in the first stitch, then double crochet in the next 2 stitches. Single crochet in the first stitch, then double crochet in the next 2 stitches. Repeat across the row. Tie off when you get to the end, and you are done!

Chapter 5 – The Best of Christmas Decorations

Have fun with bigger projects, and show off your style all over the house!

Basket Bundle

Photo made by: <u>Garett</u>

You will need 1 ball of yarn for each of the colors you use and a size G crochet hook

Chain 5, and join with a slip stitch to form a ring. Single crochet in the center of this ring 10 times, and join with another slip stitch.

Chain 1, turn, and single crochet around the other way. Chain 1, turn, and single crochet back to the beginning. You are going to continue this pattern for a total of 30 rows.

For the next row, chain 1, and single crochet in the first 3 stitches, then skip the next stitch. Single crochet in the next 3 stitches, and skip the next stitch. Repeat around.

Join with a slip stitch and chain 1 before turning.

single crochet in the first 3 stitches, then skip the next stitch. Single crochet in the next 3 stitches, and skip the next stitch. Repeat around.

Join with a slip stitch, chain 1, and turn. You are going to begin a single crochet pattern now, without any more decreases. Follow the color scheme in the photo, and continue to work until you are happy with the size of your basket, then tie off.

Finish with chains for the handles of the baskets, or weave an embellishment through the side, however you want to finish your Christmas basket and embrace all the festivities to come!

Photo made by: <u>Robin</u>

You will need 1 ball of yarn for each of the colors you use and a size G crochet hook

For the wreath:

Measure how much you need to wrap around the ring you have chosen, and chain a length that is equal to this measurement. Chain 1, turn, and single crochet back to the beginning. Chain 1, turn, and single crochet across the row. Chain 1, turn, and single crochet back to the beginning.

Repeat until you can fit this around the ring, then tie off and set aside.

For the ribbon:

Chain 10 and single crochet across the row. Chain 1, turn, and single crochet back to the beginning. Chain 1, turn, and single crochet across the row. Chain 1, turn, and single crochet back to the beginning. Repeat 2 more times, and tie off.

567

Take a length of red and tie securely around the center of the piece, and your bow is done!

For the bell:

Chain 1, turn, and single crochet across the row.

Chain 2, and skip the first stitch, then single crochet across the row, and skip the last stitch.

Chain 1, turn, and single crochet across the row.

Continue with this decrease until you have the size of bell you want, and tie off.

To assemble:

Wrap the green strip around the ring you have, and sew in place. Twist this so the seam is on the inside, then whip stitch the ribbon on next.

Finish with the bell as you see in the photo, and you are done!

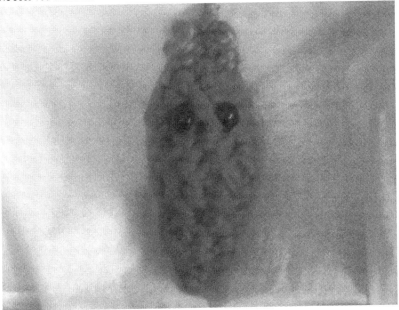

Photo made by: <u>Robin</u>

You will need 1 ball of yarn for each of the colors you use and a size G crochet hook

Chain 10 and single crochet across the row. Chain 1, turn, and single crochet back to the beginning. Chain 1, turn, and single crochet across the row. Continue for a total of 15 rows, and tie off.

Take your yarn needle and sew the side of the piece, along with one of the ends. Stuff as well as you can with stuffing (using a pencil helps), then sew the end into a point.

Add the eyes, and embellish with some lengths of yarn from your scrap bag, and you are done!

Conclusion

There you have it, everything you need to make your own little variety of crochet Christmas ornaments for this holiday season. There are so many things you can make with crochet, and once you have learned how to use this skill for Christmas, the options are endless.

This book is full of patterns that you can use for ornaments, stand-alone decorations for your mantle, or for a cute little stocking stuffer for someone you love.

When you crochet, there's no limit to the possibilities, and I hope this book was able to inspire you to create as many Christmas items as you can. There is so much joy in this season, and the more you celebrate with the things you make, the more fun you have.

I designed this book to suit everyone, no matter what their particular style is. You can choose these patterns if you are a seasoned hobbyist, or if this is your first time. Either way, you are going to see just how much fun it is to create each and every piece, and to fall in love with the results time and time again.

Don't stop at just one, decorate your entire tree in bulbs and other decorations you have made, or make your own little nativity scene with what you have on hand. There's no limit to how you can express your love for the season, and with crochet, you are going to find that your results are as unique as you.

So, if you want to show off your love for all things crochet, you have come to the right place. This book is your key to all things holiday crochet, and as soon as you get started, you won't be able to stop.

Try making some of these patterns larger than the pattern calls, try making some of them smaller. There's no end to the possibilities, and the more you work at it, the more expressive you can become. Have fun with the patterns, and have fun with the designs, and you will have everything you need to enjoy this holiday season.

Get into the true spirit Christmas with your crochet projects, and express your love for the season.

Merry Christmas!

CROCHET BIKINI

5 Masterpiece Crochet Bikinis To Rock On The Beach

Crochet Bikini For Everyone

5 Masterpiece Crochet Bikinis To Rock On The Beach

Introduction

The sun is out, school is out, and you are due for your summer vacation. Right now, nothing sounds better than sipping on your favorite drink next to a pool or on the beach, or even next to the ocean. Perhaps you have a vacation destination in mind, perhaps you are going to staycation in your own back yard.

No matter what you are going to do, you know you want to look good doing it, and to do that, you are going to need the right swimsuit.

But, bikinis haven't always been your friend. There are times when you felt that you looked good, until you looked in the mirror. There were times when you scoured the shelves of the store to find something that would work for you, but you find that the sets simply don't fit, or the tops or bottoms just don't seem to fit the right way.

So what does that mean? Does that mean that you are stuck with swimsuits that you don' t want to wear? Does that mean that you have to suffer through with pieces that you don' t think make you look good, or that don't help you to feel good about yourself?

Of course not!

When it comes to swimsuits, you can turn to the world of crochet for your answer.

But, you wonder, isn't it difficult to crochet a bikini? What kind of yarn do you use? How do you know it's going to fit you?

If you have wondered about these things yourself, you have come to the right place. In this book, you are going to discover everything that you need to know to make your own bikinis. You are going to learn the tips and tricks that you need to make swimsuits to fit your body, and you are going to learn how to put in the details that you want.

You are going to get exactly what you want with each and every one of these pieces, and you are going to rock your style on the beach like never before. So what are you waiting for? Grab your favorite cotton yarn, grab your favorite crochet hook, and settle in with a cold glass of iced tea.

You are going to fall in love with the results, and you are going to love each and every piece that you make. There's no end to the wonderful pieces you can make, or how good you can feel when you wear them.

You deserve the best of the best, so let's get started.

Chapter 1 – The Bikini Patterns

Ruby Red Bikini Set

You will need 2 skeins of cotton yarn in ruby red (or the color of your choice) and a size G crochet hook.

For the Top:

Using an unlined bra or a bikini that you already own, chain a length from the top of the cup to the bottom.

Single crochet across the row, and continue to single crochet up and around the top, down to the same point on the other side. Join with a slip stitch, chain 1, turn, and single crochet back around the row. Do not join with a slip stitch this time. Instead, chain 1, turn, and single crochet back to the other side of the row. Again, do not join with a slip stitch. Chain 1, turn, and single crochet back to the beginning.

You are going to see a triangle forming.

Continue to work with this pattern, until you have a cup that is equal to the cup of your bra top or bikini. Tie off the first cup and set aside.

Repeat this for the other cup, then tie off and set aside.

Next, you are going to take your crochet hook and join with a slip stitch to the bottom of one of the cups. Single crochet across this bottom, then continue across the bottom of the other cup. Chain 1, turn, and single crochet back to the beginning. Chain 1, turn, and single crochet back to the other side. Chain 1, turn, and single crochet across the row. Chain 1, turn, and single crochet back to the beginning.

Continue now with this pattern, until you are happy with how far down the piece reaches. Tie off.

Chain 4 chains now, 2 for the neck ties and 2 for the side ties. Single crochet across the row. Chain 1, turn, and single crochet back to the beginning. Tie off each one and set aside.

Attach the chains to the top of the cups, then attach the other two to the sides of the piece. Make sure it is all secure, then you are done! Create 2 tassels using a DVD case, then secure these tassels to the sides of the piece alone

For the Bottoms:

Use either a bikini bottom or a pair of underwear that you already have to get the right size.

Chain a length that is equal to the top of the front of the piece. Chain 1, turn, and single crochet across the row. Chain 1, turn, and single crochet back to the other side. Chain 1, turn, and single crochet across the row. Chain 1, turn, and single crochet back to the other side. Chain 1, turn, and single crochet across the row. Chain 1, turn, and single crochet back to the beginning.

You are going to be using your bikini bottoms or underwear as the template for the piece, and you are going to follow this as a guide for the size of the bottoms.

Following the template, begin to decrease.

Chain 1, skip the first stitch on the row, and single crochet across the row, skipping the last stitch. Chain 1, skip the first stitch on the row, and single crochet across the row, skipping the last stitch. Chain 1, skip the first stitch on the row, and single crochet across the row, skipping the last stitch. Chain 1, skip the first stitch on the row, and single crochet across the row, skipping the last stitch. Chain 1, skip the first stitch on the row, and single crochet across the row, skipping the last stitch.

When you reach the center of the bottoms, you are going to go back to normal crochet, without any decreases:

Chain 1, turn, and single crochet across the row. Chain 1, turn, and single crochet back to the other side. Chain 1, turn, and single crochet across the row. Chain 1, turn, and single crochet back to the other side. Chain 1, turn, and single crochet across the row. Chain 1, turn, and single crochet back to the beginning.

When you get through between your legs, you are going to continue to follow the pattern as you increase once more:

Chain 1 and single crochet in the first stitch 2 times, then single crochet across the row, and single crochet in the last stitch 2 times. Chain 1 and single crochet in the first stitch 2 times, then single crochet across the row, and single crochet in the last stitch 2 times. Chain 1 and single crochet in the first stitch 2 times, then single crochet across the row, and single crochet in the last stitch 2 times.

Continue until you have reached the proper size on the other side. Tie off.

Chain 2 lengths of chain now, 6 inches each. Feed these through the sides of the bottoms, and use as a drawstring when you wear. Create 2 tassels using a DVD case, then secure these tassels to the sides of the bottom of the piece only. Make sure it is all secure, and that there are no loose ends anywhere on the piece. Tie off.

That's it! You're done!

Mesmerizing Pearl Top

You will need 2 skeins of cotton yarn in ivory or off white (or the color of your choice) and a size G crochet hook.

Using an unlined bra or a bikini that you already own, chain a length from the top of the cup to the bottom.

Single crochet across the row, and continue to single crochet up and around the top, down to the same point on the other side. Join with a slip stitch, chain 1, turn, and single crochet back around the row. Do not join with a slip stitch this time. Instead, chain 1, turn, and single crochet back to the other side of the row. Again, do not join with a slip stitch. Chain 1, turn, and single crochet back to the beginning.

You are going to see a triangle forming.

Continue to work with this pattern, until you have a cup that is equal to the cup of your bra top or bikini. Tie off the first cup and set aside.

Repeat this for the other cup, then tie off and set aside.

Next, you are going to take your crochet hook and join with a slip stitch to the bottom of one of the cups. Single crochet across this bottom, then continue across the bottom of the other cup. Chain 1, turn, and single crochet back to the beginning.

For the next row, you are going to chain 5, skip the first 3 stitches, then join with a slip stitch into the next stitch. Chain 5, skip the next 3 stitches, then join with a slip stitch in the next stitch. Chain 5, skip the next 3 stitches, then join with a slip stitch in the next stitch. Chain 5, skip the next 3 stitches, then join with a slip stitch in the next stitch. Chain 5, skip the next 3 stitches, then join with a slip stitch in the next stitch. Repeat this across the row.

For the next row, you are going to chain 5 and join with slip stitch in the middle of the chain space. Chain 5, then join with a slip stitch into the center of the chain space. Chain 5, then join with a slip stitch into the center of the chain space. Chain 5, then join with a slip stitch into the center of the chain space. Chain 5, then join with a slip stitch into the center of the chain space.

Continue now with this pattern, until you are happy with how far down the piece reaches. Tie off.

Chain 4 chains now, 2 for the neck ties and 2 for the side ties. Single crochet across the row. Chain 1, turn, and single crochet back to the beginning. Tie off each one and set aside.

Sew each of these lengths to the cups on the bikini and to the sides, then make sure all is secure. Finish with adding fringe across the front of the piece, using the photo as a reference for placement.

Tie off, and you are done!

580

Flirty Ruffle Bottoms

You will need 2 skeins of cotton yarn in tan (or the color of your choice) and a size G crochet hook.

Use either a bikini bottom or a pair of underwear that you already have to get the right size.

Chain a length that is equal to the top of the front of the piece. Chain 1, turn, and single crochet across the row. Chain 1, turn, and single crochet back to the other side. Chain 1, turn, and single crochet across the row. Chain 1, turn, and single crochet back to the other side. Chain 1, turn, and single crochet across the row. Chain 1, turn, and single crochet back to the beginning.

You are going to be using your bikini bottoms or underwear as the template for the piece, and you are going to follow this as a guide for the size of the bottoms.

Following the template, begin to decrease.

Chain 1, skip the first stitch on the row, and single crochet across the row, skipping the last stitch. Chain 1, skip the first stitch on the row, and single crochet across the row, skipping the last stitch. Chain 1, skip the first stitch on the row, and single crochet across the row, skipping the last stitch. Chain 1, skip the first stitch on the row, and single crochet across the row, skipping the last stitch. Chain 1, skip the first stitch on the row, and single crochet across the row, skipping the last stitch.

When you reach the center of the bottoms, you are going to go back to normal crochet, without any decreases:

Chain 1, turn, and single crochet across the row. Chain 1, turn, and single crochet back to the other side. Chain 1, turn, and single crochet across the row. Chain 1, turn, and single crochet back to the other side. Chain 1, turn, and single crochet across the row. Chain 1, turn, and single crochet back to the beginning.

When you get through between your legs, you are going to continue to follow the pattern as you increase once more:

Chain 1 and single crochet in the first stitch 2 times, then single crochet across the row, and single crochet in the last stitch 2 times. Chain 1 and single crochet in the first stitch 2 times, then single crochet across the row, and single crochet in the last stitch 2 times. Chain 1 and single crochet in the first stitch 2 times, then single crochet across the row, and single crochet in the last stitch 2 times.

Continue until you have reached the proper size on the other side. Tie off.

Go back to the top now with a contrasting color, and join with a slip stitch. Chain 1, and single crochet in the first stitch. Double crochet in the next 3 stitches, and single crochet in the next stitch. Double crochet in the next 3 stitches, then single crochet in the next stitch. Double crochet in the next 3 stitches, then single crochet in the next stitch. Join both the front and the back this way, working your way around the entire top so the bikini will pull on without strings.

If you would like more security, add a drawstring. Tie off and you are done!

High Wasted Bikini Set

You will need 2 skeins of cotton yarn in grey (or the color of your choice) and a size G crochet hook.

For the Top:

Using an unlined bra or a bikini that you already own, chain a length from the top of the cup to the bottom.

Single crochet across the row, and continue to single crochet up and around the top, down to the same point on the other side. Join with a slip stitch, chain 1, turn, and single crochet back around the row. Do not join with a slip stitch this time. Instead, chain 1, turn, and single crochet back to the other side of the row. Again, do not join with a slip stitch. Chain 1, turn, and single crochet back to the beginning.

You are going to see a triangle forming.

Continue to work with this pattern, until you have a cup that is equal to the cup of your bra top or bikini. Tie off the first cup and set aside.

Repeat this for the other cup, then tie off and set aside.

Next, you are going to take your crochet hook and join with a slip stitch to the bottom of one of the cups. Single crochet across this bottom, then continue across the bottom of the other cup. Chain 1, turn, and single crochet back to the beginning. Chain 1, turn, and single crochet back to the other side. Chain 1, turn, and single crochet across the row. Chain 1, turn, and single crochet back to the beginning.

Continue now with this pattern, until you are happy with how far down the piece reaches. As this is a two piece that is designed to have more coverage than most, you are going to work your way further down the piece than you would with the other pieces. Tie off.

Chain 4 chains now, 2 for the neck ties and 2 for the side ties. Single crochet across the row. Chain 1, turn, and single crochet back to the beginning. Tie off each one and set aside.

Secure these 4 ties to the bikini, making sure they are all sewn securely and will not break off when the bikini is wet. Using a contrasting color, feed this through the bottom part of the piece, adding an accent to the bikini. Tie a bow or allow to hang loose, however you prefer.

That's it! Tie it off and you are done!

For the Bottoms:

Use either a bikini bottom or a pair of underwear that you already have to get the right size.

Chain a length that is equal to the top of the front of the piece. Chain 1, turn, and single crochet across the row. Chain 1, turn, and single crochet back to the other side. Chain 1, turn, and single crochet across the row. Chain 1, turn, and single crochet back to the other side. Chain 1, turn, and single crochet across the row. Chain 1, turn, and single crochet back to the beginning.

Remember you are going to make these high rise, so continue with this pattern until you are happy with the rise of the bottoms.

Just as with other pieces, you are going to be using your bikini bottoms or underwear as the template for the piece, and you are going to follow this as a guide for the size of the bottoms.

When you are happy with the rise, you are going to use the template to begin to decrease.

Chain 1, skip the first stitch on the row, and single crochet across the row, skipping the last stitch. Chain 1, skip the first stitch on the row, and single crochet across the row, skipping the last stitch. Chain 1, skip the first stitch on the row, and single crochet across the row, skipping the last stitch. Chain 1, skip the first stitch on the row, and single crochet across the row, skipping the last stitch. Chain 1, skip the first stitch on the row, and single crochet across the row, skipping the last stitch.

When you reach the center of the bottoms, you are going to go back to normal crochet, without any decreases:

Chain 1, turn, and single crochet across the row. Chain 1, turn, and single crochet back to the other side. Chain 1, turn, and single crochet across the row. Chain 1, turn, and single crochet back to the other side. Chain 1, turn, and single crochet across the row. Chain 1, turn, and single crochet back to the beginning.

When you get through between your legs, you are going to continue to follow the pattern as you increase once more:

Chain 1 and single crochet in the first stitch 2 times, then single crochet across the row, and single crochet in the last stitch 2 times. Chain 1 and single crochet in the first stitch 2 times, then single crochet across the row, and single crochet in the last stitch 2 times. Chain 1 and single crochet in the first stitch 2 times, then single crochet across the row, and single crochet in the last stitch 2 times.

Continue until you have reached the proper size and rise on the other side of the piece. Tie off.

Chain 2 lengths of chain now 1 foot long each. Using the photo as reference, feed these through the sides of the bottoms, and use as a drawstring when you wear.

You will need 2 skeins of cotton yarn in each of the colors that you choose to use and a size G crochet hook.

If you are going to follow the same color scheme as the photo, you are going to be changing the color of yarn every 2 rows. Pay attention and use the photo as a reference, or simply create your own color scheme.

For the Top:

Using an unlined bra or a bikini that you already own, chain a length from the top of the cup to the bottom.

Single crochet across the row, and continue to single crochet up and around the top, down to the same point on the other side. Join with a slip stitch, chain 1, turn, and single crochet back around the row. Do not join with a slip stitch this time. Instead, chain 1, turn, and single crochet back to the other side of the row. Again, do not join with a slip stitch. Chain 1, turn, and single crochet back to the beginning.

You are going to see a triangle forming. Remember if you are going to be changing colors with this that you need to do so every couple of rows. It's simple to do – all you need to do is tie off the row after 2 rows, then join with the next color. Work 2 rows then tie off, and join with the next color.

Continue to work with this pattern, until you have a cup that is equal to the cup of your bra top or bikini. Tie off the first cup and set aside.

Repeat this for the other cup, then tie off and set aside, once again following the same alternating color pattern as you did in the previous cup, if you chose to stripe your piece.

Now, take your crochet hook and join with a slip stitch on the bottom of one of the cups. Single crochet across the bottom of the row, continuing across the bottom of the second cup, joining the two cups together. Chain 1, turn, and single crochet back to the beginning of the row. Now, you are going to add the ruffle to the bottom of the piece:

Chain 1, and single crochet in the first stitch. Double crochet in the next 3 stitches, and single crochet in the next stitch. Double crochet in the next 3 stitches, then single crochet in the next stitch. Double crochet in the next 3 stitches, then single crochet in the next stitch. Join both the front and the back this way, working your way across the bottom of the piece. Tie off when you reach the beginning.

Chain 4 chains now, 2 for the neck ties and 2 for the side ties. Single crochet across the row. Chain 1, turn, and single crochet back to the beginning. Tie off each one and set aside.

Attach the chains to the top of the cups, then attach the other two to the sides of the piece. Make sure it is all secure, then you are done and ready to head out to rock those waves!

For the Bottoms:

For the ruffle bottoms you are going to follow the same method as before, only if you are going to make them match the top, feel free to stripe them as you did with the top of the piece. Remember to change colors after every couple of rows.

Use either a bikini bottom or a pair of underwear that you already have to get the right size.

Chain a length that is equal to the top of the front of the piece. Chain 1, turn, and single crochet across the row. Chain 1, turn, and single crochet back to the other side. Chain 1, turn, and single crochet across the row. Chain 1, turn, and single crochet back to the other side. Chain 1, turn, and single crochet across the row. Chain 1, turn, and single crochet back to the beginning.

You are going to be using your bikini bottoms or underwear as the template for the piece, and you are going to follow this as a guide for the size of the bottoms.

Following the template, begin to decrease.

Chain 1, skip the first stitch on the row, and single crochet across the row, skipping the last stitch. Chain 1, skip the first stitch on the row, and single crochet across the row, skipping the last stitch. Chain 1, skip the first stitch on the row, and single crochet across the row, skipping the last stitch. Chain 1, skip the first stitch on the row, and single crochet across the row, skipping the last stitch. Chain 1, skip the first stitch on the row, and single crochet across the row, skipping the last stitch.

When you reach the center of the bottoms, you are going to go back to normal crochet, without any decreases:

Chain 1, turn, and single crochet across the row. Chain 1, turn, and single crochet back to the other side. Chain 1, turn, and single crochet across the row. Chain 1, turn, and single crochet back to the other side. Chain 1, turn, and single crochet across the row. Chain 1, turn, and single crochet back to the beginning.

When you get through between your legs, you are going to continue to follow the pattern as you increase once more:

Chain 1 and single crochet in the first stitch 2 times, then single crochet across the row, and single crochet in the last stitch 2 times. Chain 1 and single crochet in the first stitch 2 times, then single crochet across the row, and single crochet in the last stitch 2 times. Chain 1 and single crochet in the first stitch 2 times, then single crochet across the row, and single crochet in the last stitch 2 times.

Continue until you have reached the proper size on the other side. Tie off.

Go back to the top now with a contrasting color, and join with a slip stitch. Chain 1, and single crochet in the first stitch. Double crochet in the next 3 stitches, and single crochet in the next stitch. Double crochet in the next 3 stitches, then single crochet in the next stitch. Double crochet in the next 3 stitches, then single crochet in the next stitch. Join both the front and the back this way, working your way around the entire top so the bikini will pull on without strings. Make sure all is secure, and you are done!

Conclusion

There you have it, everything you need to know to make your own crochet bikinis. You know as soon as summer arrives you are ready to hit the beach, but that can be difficult finding your style in the stores. You don't want to follow what everyone else is doing, you want to show off your own style, and the only way you can do that for sure is to make your own.

I hope you feel inspired by this book, and that you are able to make your own bikini collection to rock this summer. You know you deserve the best of the best, and when you make your own, you are going to ensure you get that very thing. Dive into the world of crochet head first, then dive into the pool head first in your sizzling bikini.

The heat of summer is here already, and you know you are more than ready to hit the beach. So, grab your crochet hook, your favorite kind of yarn (just make sure it's cotton!) and your favorite crochet hook, and you are going to be set for all the heat waves of summer.

Flaunt your bikini body, and show the world what hard work can do. You are one of a kind, you are beautiful, and you have what it takes to turn heads everywhere you go. Whip up a collection of your own bikinis now, and embrace summer for all that you can.

Don't waste these summer months – there's no limit to the number of bikinis you can make, so go wild. Make them in every color of the rainbow, make them in multiple colors themselves. Whatever you do, just make them.

The sky is the limit with your swimsuit collection, and you deserve to have each and every one of these pieces. You work hard for your body, now you need something that fits you in a custom way and shows off each and every one of your curves.

Make the suits to fit you, and forget about trying to fit inside the suits. You can have custom, you can have everything you want, and you can show off your skills to your friends and to the world. Now settle in with your favorite summer beverage, grab your favorite crochet hook, and get ready to show off everything you have worked so hard for.

Happy crocheting.

CROCHET BAG DIY

10 PRETTY AND TRENDY CROCHET BAG PATTERNS

Crochet Bag DIY:

10 Pretty and Trendy Crochet Bag Patterns

Introduction

Each successful project will help you to increase your self-esteem and self-expression. With constant practice, you will be able to build new crocheting skills. This new skill will help you to deal with the fear of unemployment because you can earn money by selling crocheted projects. Several studies show that crafting can postpone or reduce dementia. Dementia is related to memory loss with age.

This book has 10 interesting crochet bag patterns for you to try.

Chapter 1 – Beach Crochet Bags

If you want beautiful beach crochet bags, there are two patterns for you. These are extremely easy and beautiful:

Pattern 01: Cutest Beach Bag

Photo made by: Audrey B.

- **Crochet Hook:** 5mm or H/8
- **Weight of Yarn:** (5) Chunky/Bulky (12 to 15 stitches for four inches)
- Red Ribbon: 4 to 5 skeins (7/8" width)
- Safety pin or stitch marker
- Red thread and needle

Pattern:

Start with base

Chain 36.

Row 1 to 13: Single crochet into every of the 36 chain, chain 1, and flip.

Row 14: Single crochet in the subsequent 35 single crochet, 3 single crochet in the subsequent single crochet at the closing of the row (i.e. 36 single crochet stitch) (this will be the first corner, single crochet in the stitches to make the width of your bag (about 12 single crochet), 3 in the previous stitch that makes up the width (2nd corner) and you are on the opposite side of the length of foundation where you have chained 36. Single crochet in every of the subsequent 35 stitch, 3 single crochet in the subsequent single crochet at the closing of the row (i.e. 36 chain stitch) (This will again make the 3rd corner), single crochet in the stitches to make width of bag (about 12 single crochet), 3 in the preceding stitch for width and slip stitch to seam the beginning row.

Get Ready to Construct Body of Bag:

Row 15: Chain 1, single crochet in the Back Loop only in every single crochet in the round. Slip stitch to seam round.

Row 16: Chain 1, single crochet in both loops in every single crochet in the round. Slip stitch to seam round.

Row 17,21,25,29,33,37: Chain 3 (counts 1 double crochet), double crochet in both loops in every single crochet in the round. Slip stitch to seam round.

Row 18,22,26,30,34,38: Chain 1, single crochet in both loops in every double crochet in the round. Slip stitch to seam round.

Row 19,23,27,31,35: Chain 4 (consider as 1 double crochet and chain 1), skip single crochet, *double crochet in the subsequent single crochet, chain 1, skip the subsequent single crochet, ** replicate * to ** 54 x, slip stitch to seam round.

Row 20,24,28,32,36: chain 1, single crochet in every space in the round. Slip stitch to seam round.

Design Shoulder Straps:

Put the bag flat and measure 5" on your right & left closing of this bag and mark with one stitch marker or use a safety pin. You can replicate this on the other side of the bag. The 5" marker is the center of every strap. There will be 4 stitch markers (2 on every side of your bag) Crochet the straps with the help of given pattern:

*Row 1: Slip stitch into the single crochet that 2.5" from the closing of the bag and the stitch marker. Chain 1, single crochet in the subsequent 7 single crochet. (you will need stitch marker to do this).

Row 2: 1 chain, single crochet in the subsequent 3 single crochet, chain 1, skip subsequent single crochet, single crochet in the subsequent 3 single crochet.

The pattern for (Odd numbered) Rows: Single crochet in the subsequent single crochet.

The pattern for (Even number) Rows: Chain, single crochet in the subsequent 3 single crochet, chain 1, skip subsequent single crochet, single crochet in the subsequent 3 single crochet.

You have to replicate both odd and even rows until you get total 77 rows. Single crochet the strap to 2nd closing of your bag on the similar side of the bag. Make sure to keep the middle strap to its place with another stitch marker. Take off your stitch marker to complete your work. ** Replicate from * to ** for the second side of this bag.

Adding the Ribbon Embellishment

You will create gaps in the body for 19, 23, 27, 31 and 35. You will add ribbons in this gap.

Step 1: Safety pin your ribbon to its place where you started to create tension. You need to weave horizontally from outside to inside in the gaps. If the ribbon fills gap on 1 row, you can move ribbon without cutting. There is no need to cut because cutting can mess up everything and you will have to stitch it later. Fill al gaps in the body of the bag and if your run out of your skein, close with a safety pin to close one skein and start a new skein of your ribbon.

Step 2: Once you are satisfied with placement, cut off the leftover ribbon and secure hand stitch at all closings.

Step 3: Use a needle to hand-stitch and thread ribbon to the inner side of your bag. There is no need to stitch the long ribbons outside the bags. Embellishment of ribbon for the straps is made in a similar way. You can buy an extra skein of ribbon for both straps and sew ribbons inside of straps at the closing point.

Pattern 02: Triple Pattern Beach Bag

Photo made by: Lindy Zubairy

MATERIALS:

- Color A: 3 skeins
- Colors B: 2 skeins
- Color C: 2 skeins
- Color D: 2 skeins
- Size J crochet hook

First Pattern: With Color D, chain 96. Seam with a slip stitch into the ring, careful not to twist chain.

Row 1: Chain 1, work 1 single crochet in same st as seam, * chain 1, skip 1 chain, 1 single crochet in subsequent chain, replicate from * around, chain 1, skip the last chain, drop D; with A, slip stitch to top of first single crochet, chain 1: 48 mesh.

Row 2: With A, work 1 single crochet in the seam, *chain 1, 1 single crochet in subsequent space, replicate from * around, end chain 1; with color D, slip stitch to first single crochet, chain 1.

Row 3: With color D, replicate Row 2.

Replicate Rows 2 and 3 until there are 5 rows of A. Increasing 1 pattern in every 6th pattern, work 1 more row of D, seam and tie up: 56 patterns.

2ND Pattern: Row 1: With loop of B on hook, work 1 single crochet in first st, * 4-double crochet shell in subsequent space, skip subsequent chain-1 space, 1 single crochet in subsequent space, skip subsequent space, replicate from * around, end last 4-double crochet shell in last space, drop B; with C, seam with slip stitch to first single crochet: 14 shells.

Row 2: Chain 3 for first double crochet, work 1 double crochet in the same place as seam, * 1 single crochet in space between 2nd and 3rd double crochet of subsequent shell, 4 double crochet in subsequent single crochet, replicate from * around, end 1 single crochet in middle of the last shell, 2 double crochet in the same place as first 2 double crochet, drop color C; with B, seam.

Row 3: 1 single crochet in the seam, 1 shell in every single crochet and 1 single crochet in the middle of every shell, drop B; with A, seam to first single crochet.

Rows 4 through 7: Continue in shell pattern, working 1 row every of A, B, C and B, seam. Tie up all colors.

3RD PATTERN: Row 1: On the wrong side of one loop of A on hook, work * 2 single crochet in single crochet, 1 single crochet in every of 4 double crochet, replicate from * around, drop A, with C, seam with slip stitch to first single crochet, chain 3, turn: 84 stitches.

Row 2: 2 double crochet in the base of chain-3. * skip 2, work 3 double crochet in subsequent st, replicate from * around, drop C, with A, seam with slip stitch to top of chain-3, turn. 28 shells.

Row 3: * Chain 2, 1 single crochet in the middle of the subsequent shell, replicate from * around, drop A, with C - chain 3, turn.

Rows 4, 5, 6 and 7: Replicate Rows 2 and 3. Tie up C.

Row 8: With A, * work 1 single crochet in subsequent single crochet, 2 single crochet in space, replicate from * around, drop A, with B, slip stitch to first single crochet, chain 2, turn.

4TH Pattern: Row 1: With chain 2 as first half-double-crochet, work 1 more half-double-crochet at the base of chain-2 for the first group, * 2 half-double-crochet in subsequent st, skip 1 st, replicate from * around; 42 half-double-crochet groups; with A, seam, chain 2, turn.

Row 2: With chain-2 as first half-double-crochet work 1 more half-double-crochet in first space for the first group, 2 half-double-crochet in space between every 2-half-double-crochet groups, end 2 half-double-crochet in space before turning-chain, tie up.

Row 3: Seam B in space after 12th group, chain 2, turn, 1 half-double-crochet in same space, 2 half-double-crochet in every of 19 spaces, change to A, chain 2, turn.

Row 4: 2 half-double-crochet in subsequent space and in every space, end 2 half-double-crochet in last space, 1 half-double-crochet in turning chain; change to B, chain 2, turn.

Row 5: 2 half-double-crochet in space between first and 2nd groups, 2 half-double-crochet in every space, end 1 half-double-crochet in turning chain, change to A, chain 2, turn.

Alternating 1 row every of A and B, replicate Row 5 until 4 groups rem.

Subsequent row works two groups, one group in turning chain, chain two, turn.

Still alternating colors, work in the three groups for 9", tie up. With a loop of B on the hook, skip 3 groups on last long row, work two half-double-crochet in subsequent space and work another side the same.

Finishing: Sew ends of handle tog. Seam edges of foundation chain. With C, work 1 row of single crochet around the opening and handle then with D, work 1 row of slip stitches through back loops only. If desired, you can line with felt.

601

Chapter 2 – Summer Crochet Bags

There are some beautiful summer crochet bags that are easy to crochet with the help of given pattern:

Pattern 03: Sling Pattern for Summer

Photo made by: <u>Samm</u>

- Worsted Yarn: 1 ball or more
- Crochet Hook: Size H
- Fabric for Cotton Lining: 1 yd
- Matching thread and needle

Notes:

Chain 3 at the finishing of every row will be counted as the first double crochet of the subsequent row.

Pattern:

Chain 4; join with a slip stitch to form a ring.

Row 1: Chain 3 to count as the first double crochet, work 7 more double crochet in the ring; chain 3, flip. (8 double crochet)

Row 2: Double crochet in the first double crochet, 2 double crochet in every remaining double crochet across; chain 3, flip. (16 double crochet)

Row 3: Replicate row 2. (32 double crochet)

Row 4: Double crochet in the first double crochet and in every double crochet across, 2 double crochet in the top of the flipping chain; chain 3, flip. (34 double crochet) (Increase at every finishing off the row.)

Row 5: Replicate row 4. (36 double crochet)

Row 6: Replicate row 2. (72 double crochet)

Row 7: Replicate row 4. (74 double crochet)

Row 8: Replicate row 4. (76 double crochet)

Row 9: Replicate row 4. (78 double crochet)

Row 10: Replicate row 4. (80 double crochet)

Row 11: Double crochet in the first double crochet (double crochet in the subsequent double crochet, 2 double crochet in the subsequent double crochet) across, double crochet in the flipping chain; chain 3, flip. (120 double crochet)

Row 12: Replicate row 4. (122 double crochet)

Row 13: Replicate row 4. (124 double crochet)

Row 14: Replicate row 4. (126 double crochet)

Row 15: Replicate row 4. (128 double crochet)

Row 16: Replicate row 4. (130 double crochet) Tie up. Weave in all ends.

Handle

Chain 220; being careful not to twist chain, join with a slip stitch to the first chain.

Round 1: Chain 3 to count as the first double crochet, double crochet in every chain around; join with a slip stitch to the top of the beginning chain 3. (220 double crochet)

Round 2: Replicate round 1.

Note: You will need additional yarn if you want to make 5 rows.

Rounds 3 to 5: Replicate round 1.

Assembly

Iron every crocheted part to block. If you want to line your bag, you can lay the crocheted parts of the fabric to trace the pattern of crocheted parts. Make sure to add seam allowance and cut along with traced line. Sew this lining to fit in the bag and flip its inside out. Slip stitch row 16 of one crocheted piece pieces to 130 stitches of row 5 of a handle, then carry on working slip stitch's in the leftover 90 handle stitches; seam with a slip stitch to the initial slip stitch; Tie up. Slip stitch row 16 of the other bag piece to 130 stitches of all free loops of the base chain of this handle, carry on working a slip stitch in the left over 90 handle stitches; seam with a slip stitch to the initial slip stitch; Tie up. Weave its ends.

Insert lining into your bag and whip stitch to the handle and opening of the bag. You can sew inside of the bag, after the initial ring.

Pattern 04: Flower Crochet Bag

Photo made by: Lindy Zubairy

- Crochet Hook: 5 mm or H/8
- Weight of Yarn: (4) Aran, Worsted Weight/ Medium Weight (16 to 20 stitches to four inches)

MATERIALS

- Main color (MC): 4 balls
- Color A: 2 balls
- Color B: 2 balls
- Color C: 2 balls
- Color D: 2 balls

Measurements:

Almost 18½" or 47 cm wide X 12½" or 32 cm high.

GAUGE: 14 single crochet and almost 16 rows = 4 inches or 10 cm

Directions:

Motif

605

With color 1, chain 2.

1st round: 6 single crochet in 2nd chain from hook. Now join withslip stitch to initial single crochet.

2nd round: Chain 3 (counts as double crochet). 2 double crochet in same space

as last slip stitch. 3 double crochet in every single crochet around. Now join with

slip stitch to top of chain 3. 18 double crochet. Tie up.

Flower: Initial Petal: 1st row: Now join color 2 with slip stitch to front loop only of any double crochet. *Chain 3 (counts as double crochet). 1 double crochet in same space as last slip stitch. 1 double crochet in front loop only of subsequent double crochet. 2 double crochet in front loop only of subsequent double crochet. 5 double crochet for the petal. Flip.

2nd row: Chain 3 (counts as double crochet). 1 double crochet in every double crochet of petal. Flip.

3rd row: Chain 3 (counts as double crochet). (Yarn over hook and draw up a loop in subsequent st. Yarn over hook and draw through 2 loops on hook) 3 times. Yarn over hook and draw through all loops on hook – double crochet3tog made. 1 double crochet in last double crochet. Tie up leaving a long end. *

Second Petal: **Join color 2 again with slip stitch to front loop of subsequent unworked single crochet of 2nd round. Replicate from * to * once. **

Third to Sixth Petals: Replicate from ** to ** 4 times more. 6 petals.

3rd round: Now join color 3 with slip stitch to remaining back loop of any double crochet of 2nd round. Chain 3. 1 double crochet in same space. 2 double crochet in every remaining back loop around. Now join with slip stitch to top of chain 3. 36 double crochet.

4th round: Chain 3. 1 double crochet in same space as last slip stitch. *1 double crochet in subsequent double crochet. 2 double crochet in subsequent double crochet. Replicate

606

from * to last 5 double crochet. 2 double crochet in every of subsequent 4 double crochet. 1 double crochet in last double crochet. Now join with slip stitch to top of chain 3. 56 double crochet.

5th round: Chain 1. 1 single crochet in same space as last slip stitch. 1 single crochet in every of subsequent 4 double crochet. *1 half-double crochet in every of subsequent 2 double crochet. 1 double crochet in every of subsequent 2 double crochet. 5 treble in subsequent double crochet for a corner. 1 double crochet in every of subsequent 2 double crochet. 1 half-double crochet in every of subsequent 2 double crochet. ** 1 single crochet in every of subsequent 5 double crochet. Replicate from * twice more, then from * to ** once.

Now join with slip stitch to initial single crochet.

6th round: Chain 1. 1 single crochet in every stitch around, working 3 single crochet in corners. Now join with slip stitch to initial single crochet. Tie up.

Using yarn ends from every petal, sew around outer edges of petals.

Motif I (make 2)

Using Main Color for color 1, and A for color two and C for 3rd color.

Motif II (make 2)

Use D for 1st color, C for 2nd color and B for 3rd color.

Motif III (make 2)

Use A for 1st color, D for 2nd color and Main Color for 3rd color.

Motif IV (make 2)

Use C for color 1, D for 2nd color and Main Color for 3rd color.

Motif V (make 2)

Use B for color 1, Main Color for 2nd color and A for 3rd color.

Motif VI (make 2)

Use Main Color for color 1, B for 2nd color and C for 3rd color.

Stitch Motifs together as shown in the image for back and front.

Side and Bottom Section

Note: While changing color, make sure to work to previous 2 loops on crochet hook of the last stitch, then pull new color via remaining two loops and continue.

With Main Color, chain 11.

1st row: (Right Side). 1 double crochet in 4th chain from hook (counts as 2 double crochet). 1 double crochet in every chain across. 9 stitches. Now join A. Flip.

2nd row: With A, chain 1. 1 single crochet in every double crochet across. Now join MAIN COLOR. Flip.

3rd row: With MAIN COLOR, chain 3 (consider as double crochet). 1 double crochet in every single crochet across. Now join A. Flip.

4th row: As 2nd row. Now join B. Flip.

5th row: With B, as 3rd row. Now join C. Flip.

6th row: With C, as 2nd row. Now join B. Flip.

7th row: Similar to 5th row.

8th row: With C, as 2nd row. Now join A. Flip.

9th row: With A, as 3rd row. Now join MAIN COLOR. Flip.

10th row: With MAIN COLOR, as 2nd row. Now join A. Flip.

11th row: With A, as 3rd row. Now join Main Color. Flip.

12th row: With MAIN COLOR, as 2nd row. Now join C. Flip.

13th row: With C, as 3rd row. Now join B. Flip.

14th row: With B, as 2nd row. Now join C. Flip.

15th row: With C, as 3rd row. Now join B. Flip.

16th row: With B, as 2nd row. Now join MAIN COLOR. Flip.

17th row: With MAIN COLOR, as 3rd row. Now join A. Flip.

Replicate 2nd to 17th rows until work from beg measures length to fit down one side of Back or Front, across the bottom, then up remaining side. Tie up.

Pin one Side and base Section to the Front and the Back along three sides.

Edging: 1st round: Now join MAIN COLOR with slip stitch in top left corner of Front or Back of Bag. Chain 1. 3 single crochet in same space as slip stitch. Work single crochet equally around, working three single crochet in corners and through both widths where Front and Side sections meet. Now join with slip stitch to initial single crochet.

2nd round: Chain 1. You will work from left side to right, instead of right side to left, as usual, work one reverse single crochet in every single crochet around. Now join with slip stitch to initial single crochet. Tie up.

Replicate border to design back.

Handles (you will make 2)

Start with MAIN COLOR, chain 50.

1st row: (Right Side). 1 double crochet in 4th chain from hook (consider as 2 double crochet). 1 double crochet in every chain across. 48 stitches. Flip.

2nd and 3rd rows: Chain 3 (consider as double crochet). 1 double crochet in every double crochet across. Flip.

Fold Handle in half lengthwise and work 1 row of single crochet through 3rd row and remaining loops of foundation chain. Tie up.

Sew handles as you can see in the picture.

Chapter 3 – Crochet Clutch Bags

There are some stylish clutch bags made of crochet and you can have them in your collection. Try these pattern:

Pattern 05: Cash and Card Case

Photo made by: Krystyn Wukitsch Foran

Crochet Hook: 4mm or G/6 hook
Weight of Yarn: Aran and Worsted/Medium Weight Yarn (4) (16 to 20 stitches to four inches)
Matching Thread
Large Eye Needle

Gauge: 8 single crochet = 2", 7 single crochet = 2"
Chain 15. Read note 1.

ROUND 1: Make 2 single crochet in 2nd chain from hook, single crochet in every chain (12) to last chain, you need to work over the yarn tail for rest of this round, three single crochet in the last chain, work in opposite side of starting chain and single crochet in every of 13 chain stitches; [30 single crochet]

ROUND 2: Slip stitch in BACK loop of first single crochet of round 1 (counts as first single crochet), single crochet in BACK loop of every single crochet around. [30 single crochet] There is no need to join rounds. Read second note.

ROUNDS 3 to 8: Single crochet in BACK loop of subsequent single crochet and in BACK loop of every single crochet around. [30 single crochet]

ROUND 9: Single crochet in BACK loop of subsequent single crochet and in BACK loop of every single crochet around to the last 2 stitches before the side edge fold. Slip stitch in last 2 single crochet ending at the fold. Chain 1, flip.

Now work back and forth in rows.

Row 1: Single crochet in 2 slip stitches, single crochet in 12 single crochet. Chain 1, flip. (14 single crochet)

Row 2: Single crochet in 14 single crochet. (14 single crochet)

Tie up.

Replicate for the second pocket. But do not fasten off after row 2.

Row 3: Keep pockets together with the small side of your pockets on the inner side. Chain 1, single crochet through both pocket upper edges crossways.

Notes!

If you are using multicolor yarn, you will need chain 17 and work almost 10 rows before starting flap. Some multicolor yarns can be thinner than the single color. You need to work 2 rows over 16 stitches.

It looks easy to work the inside case out while working in back loop, flipping the right side out for almost 9 rounds.

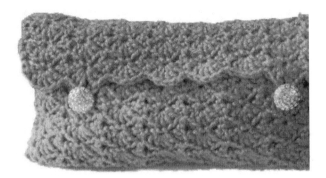

Crochet Hook: 4mm or G/6

Weight of Yarn: Aran and Worsted/Medium Weight (16 to 20 stitches to four inches)

Yarn: Two Skeins in any color almost 75 yards or 50g

Size of Finished Product (when the bag is closed):

Width: 10 inches or 25cm

Height: 5 inches or 14 cm

Buttons: 2

Fabric: Silk Fabric or cotton fabric almost 20 inches. You should select thin fabric; otherwise, the clutch becomes bulky.

Pattern:

Foundation   Chain (ch) 49

Row 1   Ch 1, 1 sc in last ch of the foundation row. Replicate 8 times: [Skip 2, 5 dc in ch st, skip 2, 1 sc in ch st]. Flip.

Row 2   Ch 5, 1 sc in the third dc of the 5 dc cluster in the previous row, ch 2, 1 dc in previous row's sc. Replicate 7 times: [Ch 2, 1 sc in the third dc of the 5 dc cluster in the previous row, ch 2, 1 dc in previous row's sc.] Flip

Row 3   Ch 1, 1 sc in last row's dc. Replicate 8 times: [Skip 2, 5 dc in sc, skip 2, 1 sc into last row's dc st]. Flip

Replicate row 2 & 3 until it measures 30 cm or 12 inches. You will end with one row 2.

Last Row: You can make eyelets to close this clutch.

Ch 1, 1 sc in last row's dc. Skip 2, 5 dc in last row's sc st, skip 2, 1 sc in last row's dc st. Skip 2, 2 dc in last row's sc st, ch 5, 3 dc in same sc st, skip 2, 1 sc in last row's dc st. Replicate 4 times: [Skip 2, 5 dc in previous row's sc st , skip 2, 1 sc in previous row's dc st.] Then you crochet the second eyelet: Skip 2, 3 dc in sc st, ch 5, 2 dc in same sc st, skip 2, 1 sc in last row's dc st. Skip 2, 5 dc in last row's sc st , skip 2, 1 sc in last row's dc st.

Finally, you will cut yarn and weave all ends. See the image:

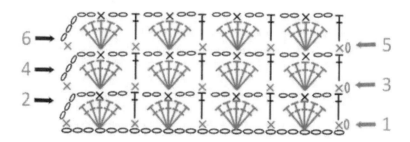

614

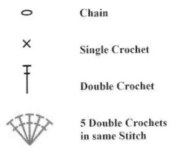

o	Chain
×	Single Crochet
⊤	Double Crochet
	5 Double Crochets in same Stitch

Finished Product:

Sew Button on Fabric:

Sew buttons on the top side of fabric and attach fabric of lining and then stitch it from inside.

Chapter 4 – Flowery Crochet Patterns

There are a few patterns that are designed with beautiful flowers. You should try these patterns:

Pattern 07: Flower Crochet Bag

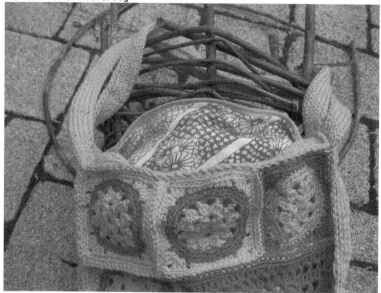

Photo made by: petuniad

Crochet Hook: 3.75 mm or F/5

Weight of Yarn: Fine (2) (23 to 26 stitches to four inches)

1 package yarn

Gauge: 7 inches wide and 7 inches tall without handle

Directions:

Single Layer Flower: (Make 5)

Round 1: With Color A, chain 2. Work 6 single crochet in 2nd chain from hook. Now join. (6 stitches)

Round 2: chain 1. Work 2 single crochet in every stitch around. Now join. Tie up. (12 stitches)

Round 3: Now join Color B. *Chain 3. Work 3 treble or triple crochet in subsequent stitch. Chain 3, slip stitch in subsequent stitch*. Replicate (*) around, for a total of 6 petals. Now join. Tie up.

Round 4: Now join Color C in the top of 1st treble or triple crochet stitch. Chain 1. Single crochet in similar stitch. Single crochet in every of the subsequent 2 treble or triple crochet stitches. Chain 1. *Treble or triple crochet in subsequent slip stitch, between petals. Chain 1. Single crochet in every of the subsequent 3 treble or triple crochet stitches. Chain 1*. Replicate (*) around. Now join.

Round 5: chain 1. Half-double-crochet in similar stitch as Now joining. Half-double-crochet in every of the subsequent 2 single crochet stitches. *Half-double-crochet in chain 1 space. Work {half-double-crochet, chain 2, half-double-crochet} all in subsequent treble or triple crochet stitch. Half-double-crochet in subsequent chain 1 space. Half-double-crochet in every of the subsequent 3 single crochet stitches*. Replicate (*) around, working 1 half-double-crochet in last chain 1 space. Now join. Tie up. Weave in all ends.

Double Layer Flower: (Make 2)

Round 1: With Color A, chain 2. Work 6 single crochet in 2nd chain from hook. Now join. (6 stitches)

Round 2: chain 1. Work 2 single crochet in every stitch around. Now join. Tie up. (12 stitches)

Round 3: Now join Color B. Working in FLO for this round, *Chain 2. Work 2 double crochet in subsequent stitch. Chain 2, slip stitch in subsequent stitch*. Replicate (*) around, for a total of 6 petals. Now join. Slip stitch into an unused back loop of the 1st stitch.

Round 4: Now work in BLO of the similar round~ *Chain 3. Work 3 treble or triple crochet in subsequent stitch. Chain 3, slip stitch in subsequent stitch*. Replicate (*) around, for a total of 6 petals. Now join. Tie up.

Round 5: Now join Color C in the top of 1st treble or triple crochet stitch, of back petals. This entire round is worked in the back petals only, leaving the front petals free. Chain 1. Single crochet in similar stitch. Single crochet in every of the subsequent 2 treble or triple crochet stitches. Chain 1. *Treble or triple crochet in subsequent slip stitch, between petals. Chain 1. Single crochet in every of the subsequent 3 treble or triple crochet stitches. Chain 1*. Replicate (*) around. Now join.

Round 6: chain 1. Half-double-crochet in similar stitch as Now joining. Half-double-crochet in every of the subsequent 2 single crochet stitches. *Half-double-crochet in chain 1 space. Work {half-double-crochet, chain 2, half-double-crochet} all in subsequent treble or triple crochet stitch. Half-double-crochet in subsequent chain 1 space. Half-double-crochet in every of the subsequent 3 single crochet stitches*. Replicate (*) around, working 1 half-double-crochet in last chain 1 space. Now join. Tie up. Weave in all ends.

Handle:

Chain 51. Slip stitch in 2nd chain from hook, and every remaining chain. Tie up, leaving a long tail for sewing.

Now join a contrasting color to either end, and slip stitch in every stitch across. Tie up, leaving a long tail for sewing. (You should have one long tail at every end)

You have to set your motifs as given in the pattern and sew them.

Assembly:

After creating all motifs, you can set them as shown in the picture and stitch them by putting one motif at one time and keep right sides together. You can use any method to stitch. For model, you can slip stitch via BLO for every motif to join them. Put one double layer of motifs in the middle and stitch one single layer motif on each side. One side of motif should touch another motif.

Fold every side half motif, and stitch together.

After stitching front pieces, you can put a second dual layer of motif and stitch right sides to each other. Fold solo motifs in the half to meet the dual layer motif and deal with one at one time and stitch all sides together.

Once it is done, you can weave all ends and flip the side of the bag. Stitch handle by sewing its one end in the chain 2 space at the top part of every side. Weave all ends and the bag is done.

Pattern 08: Roses Tote

Photo made by: Cacauli

Crochet Hook: 4 mm or G/6

Weight of Yarn: Chunky or Super Bulky (6) (4 to 11 stitches for four inches)

MATERIALS:

Premier Yarns

- A: (1 skein)
- B: (1 skein)
- C: (1 skein)
- Thread
- Sewing Needle
- Sixty wooden beads (1 cm)
- Woven tote handles (24 inches wide x 16 inches high)

GAUGE:

8 chains = 4 inches

BAG

Rose (you will make 20 with each color yarn A and B, & C)

Open your yarn and work down to the middle of yarn, insert hook through the center almost 1 1/2" from its end and there will be 1 loop on hook. * insert crochet hook once again through middle of yarn 1" apart (there will be 2 loops on crochet hook), pull 2nd loop on crochet hook through 1st loop on hook – 1 chain form; replicate from * 7 times again. Cut your yarn 1½" from the last chain form, pull a final bit of yarn through the last stitch.

Finishing

* Attach your thread to tie-up end of "A" Rose. Use fingers, coil every Rose into one Rose shape, and pulling out the yarn as you try to make a complete flower. Nail down the middle of the Rose with the help of small stitches and use sewing needle as well as a thread for this purpose. Sew one bead to the middle of each Rose. Sew the "A" Rose to its place on the base of one side of woven tote with numerous stitches. Replicate from * for every Rose, change colors. You have to adjust 12 roses in one row and there are five rows on 24" by 16" tote.

After sewing all roses to your Tote, open sides of all roses with our fingers and fill out their empty spaces one by one. You need needle and thread to manage the edges of roses.

Chapter 5 – Crochet Pouch Bags

You can crochet some pretty pouch bags and there are a few patterns for your assistance:

Pattern 09: Crochet Pouch

Photo made by: <u>alexxis</u>

- **Weight of Yarn:** Lace (33 to 40 stitches to four inches) (0)
- **Crochet Thread:** 8 Size Yarn
- **Hook:** Crochet hook of steel 2.20mm or 3 size hook
- **Lace ribbon:** 18 inches long to tie
- **Circumference:** 2 ¾ inches and Height: 3 ¾ inches

Directions:

Special Stitches Instructions:

2dc-bobble: Yo (yarn over), insert crochet hook in stitch and pull yarn thread from side to side, yo and draw through two loops on crochet hook, Yo, put in in similar stitch and pull this thread through, yarn over and draw through two loops on hook, yarn over and draw through all three loops on crochet hook.)

dc2tog: Yarn over, put in crochet hook in stitch and draw thread through, yarn over and pull through two loops on hook, Yarn over, insert in subsequent stitch and drag thread through, yarn over and draw through two loops on crochet hook, yarn over and draw through all three loops on crochet hook.)

Directions:

Use cotton thread of size 8

chain 3 (consider as 1 double crochet).

Round 1: 11 double crochet in the initial chain (12 double crochet made). Slip stitch in top of initial double crochet to join.

Round 2: Chain 3, double crochet in same st, 2 double crochet in every double crochet, slip stitch in top of initial double crochet to join. (24 double crochet)

Round 3: Chain 3, *chain 1, double crochet in subsequent double crochet, replicate from * all around ending with chain 1, slip stitch in top of initial double crochet to join.

Round 4: Chain 3, double crochet in same double crochet, *chain 2, 2double crochet-bobble in subsequent double crochet, replicate from * all around ending with chain 2, slip stitch in top of initial double crochet to join.

Round 5: *Chain 7, skip 1 bobble, single crochet in a subsequent bobble, replicate from * all around. (12 chain-7 loops made)

Round 6: Slip stitch to the corner of chain-7 loop, chain 3 (consider as 1 double crochet), 6 double crochet in the loop, *chain 2, 7 double crochet in the subsequent loop, replicate from * all around, ending with chain 2, slip stitch in initial double crochet to join.

Round 7: Chain 3, double crochet in subsequent 6 double crochet, *chain 2, double crochet in subsequent 7 double crochet, skip 2-chain space, double crochet in subsequent

7 double crochet, replicate from * all around ending with slip stitch in initial double crochet to join.

Round 8: Slip stitch to top of 2nd double crochet, chain 3, double crochet in subsequent 5 double crochet, *chain 3, double crochet in subsequent 6 double crochet, skip 2 double crochet, double crochet in subsequent 6 double crochet, replicate from * all around ending with slip stitch in initial double crochet to join.

Round 9: Slip stitch to top of 2nd double crochet, chain 3, double crochet in subsequent 4 double crochet, *chain 3, 5 double crochet in chain-3 space, chain 3, double crochet in subsequent 5 double crochet, skip 2 double crochet, double crochet in subsequent 5 double crochet, replicate from * all around, ending with slip stitch in initial double crochet to join.

Round 10: Slip stitch to top of 2nd double crochet, chain 3, double crochet in subsequent 3 double crochet, *chain 3, [double crochet in subsequent double crochet, chain 1] 4 times, double crochet in subsequent double crochet, chain 3, double crochet in subsequent 4 double crochet, skip 2 double crochet, double crochet in subsequent 4 double crochet, replicate from * all around, ending with slip stitch in initial double crochet to join.

Round 11: Slip stitch to top of 2nd double crochet, chain 3, double crochet in subsequent 2 double crochet, *chain 3, skip chain-3 space[single crochet in chain-1 loop, chain 3] 3 times, single crochet in last chain-1 loop, chain 3, double crochet in subsequent 3 double crochet, skip 2 double crochet, double crochet in subsequent 3 double crochet, replicate from * all around, ending with slip stitch in initial double crochet to join.

Round 12: Slip stitch to top of 2nd double crochet, chain 3, double crochet in subsequent double crochet, *chain 3, skip chain-3 space, [single crochet in chain-3 loop, chain 3] 2 times, single crochet in last chain-3 loop, chain 3, double crochet in subsequent 2 double crochet, skip 2 double crochet, double crochet in subsequent 2 double crochet, replicate from * all around, ending with slip stitch in initial double crochet to join.

Round 13: Chain 3, double crochet in subsequent double crochet, *chain 3, skip chain-3 space, single crochet in chain-3 loop, chain 3, single crochet in subsequent chain-3 loop, chain 3, double crochet2tog in subsequent 2 double crochet, chain 5, double crochet2tog in subsequent 2 double crochet, replicate from * all around, ending with chain 5, slip stitch in top of initial double crochet to join.

623

Round 14: Chain 6 (make 1 double crochet, chain 3), *skip chain-3 space, single crochet in chain-3 loop, chain 3, 7 double crochet in the chain-5 loop, chain 3, replicate from * all around ending with 6 double crochet in last chain-5 loop. Slip stitch in top of double crochet (3rd chain of chain 6) to join.

Round 15: Chain 6 (make 1 double crochet, chain 3), *skip (3 chain, single crochet, 3 chain), double crochet in subsequent double crochet, [chain 1, double crochet in subsequent double crochet] 6 times, chain 3, replicate from * all around ending with chain 1, slip stitch in top of initial double crochet to join.

Round 16: Slip stitch to chain-1 space, *chain 3, double crochet in chain-3 space, [chain 3, single crochet in chain-1 space] 6 times, replicate from * all around.

Round 17: Slip stitch up chain 3 to tip of double crochet, chain 3, 2 double crochet in same double crochet, *[chain 3, single crochet in chain-3 loop] 5 times, chain 3, 3 double crochet in subsequent double crochet, replicate from * all around ending with chain 3, slip stitch in initial double crochet to join.

Round 18: Chain 4 (consider as 1 double crochet, chain 1), double crochet in subsequent double crochet, chain 1, double crochet in subsequent double crochet, *[chain 3, single crochet in chain-3 loop] 4 times, chain 3, [double crochet in subsequent double crochet, chain 1] 2 times, double crochet in subsequent double crochet, replicate from * all around ending with chain 3, slip stitch in initial double crochet in to join.

Round 19: Chain 3, double crochet in same double crochet, *[chain 1, 2 double crochet in subsequent double crochet] 2 times, [chain 3, single crochet in chain-3 loop] 3 times, chain 3, 2 double crochet in subsequent double crochet, replicate from * all around, ending with chain 3, slip stitch in initial double crochet to join.

Round 20: Chain 3, double crochet in same double crochet, *[chain 1, 2 double crochet in subsequent double crochet] 5 times, [chain 3, single crochet in chain-3 loop] 2 times, chain 3, 2 double crochet in subsequent double crochet, replicate from * all around, ending with chain 3, slip stitch in initial double crochet to join. (You should have 12 2-double crochet groups in every single each scallop)

Round 21: Chain 3, double crochet in subsequent double crochet, *[chain 3, slip stitch in 3rd chain from hook to make picot, double crochet2tog in subsequent 2 double crochet] 5 times, chain 3, single crochet in chain-3 loop, picot, chain 3, double crochet2tog in subsequent 2 double crochet, replicate from * all around, ending with chain 3, slip stitch in initial double crochet to join. Tie up.

Dry and block. Use lace ribbon to weave 14 round and keep ribbon behind 7 (dc) double crochet group. Tie all ends of lace ribbon and make a knot as per your desire.

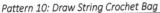

Pattern 10: Draw String Crochet Bag

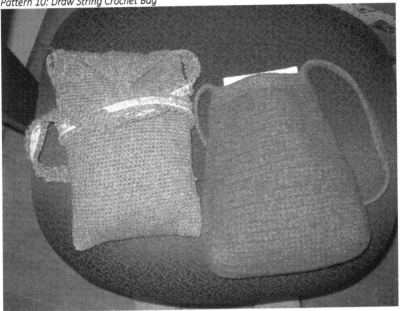

Photo made by: <u>noricum</u>

Crochet Hook: 5mm or H/8

Weight of Yarn: Aran and Wrosted/Medium Yarn (16 to 20 stitches to four inches)

Final Size: 12" long and 18" Around

Cotton Yarn: 129 yds or 3 oz.

Directions:

R: 1 - chain 34, 1 double crochet in the 4th chain from the hook, 1double crochet in the same chain as 1st double crochet,

1 double crochet in the following 29 chains, 2 double crochet in the last chain (33double crochet)

Turn working down the opposite side of the chain, 2 double crochet in the 1st chain,

1double crochet in the following 29 chains, 2 double crochet in the last chain, join to top of the 1st double crochet with a slip stitch,

(33double crochet + 33double crochet = 66double crochet)

R: 2 - chain3, (considers as a double crochet) 1 double crochet in every double crochet around, join, (66double crochet)

R: 3 -chain4, (considers as double crochet, chain1) *skip the following double crochet, 1 double crochet in the following double crochet, chain1*

Replicate from * to * around, join to top of chain 3 with a slip stitch, (33double crochet= 33chain1=66sts)

R: 4 - chain4, (considers as double crochet, chain1) *skip the following chain1 space, 1 double crochet in the following double crochet, chain1*

Replicate from * to * around, join to top of chain 3 with a slip stitch, (33double crochet= 33chain1=66sts)

R: 5 - R: 21 - Replicate R: 4

R: 6 - chain2, *1 half-double-crochet in the following double crochet, 1half-doublt-crochet in the following chain1 space*

626

Replicate from * to * around, join to 1st half-double-crochet with a slip stitch.

tie off and weave in your ends. (66half-doublt-crochet)

Drawstring:

using two strands of your cotton yarn, chain 100, tie up.

Weave ends of chain through Row 21

You can draw the drawstring to 1 side, for 1 side handle.

Or you can draw both ends, for two side handles.

Conclusion

Crafting can be really soothing for those people who are suffering from Dementia. Insomnia is a horrible feeling, but with the help of crocheting, you can get rid of this problem. Focus on soft and easy crochet and your mind and body will be relaxed to get to your bed. You can improve the quality of your sleep and reduce the need for sleep medications. This book is designed for you with 10 pretty crochet bag patterns. You can practice these patterns and improve your overall health. By selling these patterns, you can strengthen your financial position.

Alisa Hatchenson

Crochet Jewelry

20 Crochet Bracelets, Earrings, and Rings You Can Make Yourself!

Crochet Jewelry

20 Crochet Bracelets, Earrings, and Rings You Can Make Yourself!

Introduction

Every day is a good day to set a new trend, and you are always ready to strut your stuff. But, this isn't always easy when you have a limited selection of items to choose from.

Sure, you can mix and match, but how many times can you do that without being bored? You want something new and exciting. You want something that makes you feel amazing as you walk down the street, and you want something that is going to show the world that you know how to set trends, and you aren't afraid to do it.

But, you feel overwhelmed.

Where do you start?

How do you know you are going to get the pieces that you want?

How to you express your style when you feel like you've hit a creative roadblock?

If you have been feeling this way, you have come to the right place. In this book, you are going to learn everything you need to know to create your own jewelry pieces, and to show off to the world your own unique style. Whether you choose to make these each as they are exactly, or you take what you see here and turn them into something that is your own, you are going to find that making your own jewelry line is easier than ever.

This book is going to give you everything you need to crochet your own jewelry pieces, and you are going to find the inspiration to be endless. So go ahead, put on your own creative thinking cap, and get ready to dive into a new world of jewelry and trends like you have never imagined before.

There's no way you can do it wrong when you are happy with the results, and this book is the little push you need to get there. Settle in with your favorite crochet hook, your favorite color yarn, and a glass of your favorite ice cold beverage, and you are going to get everything you have ever wanted for your accessory collection.

Get ready to dive into the world of fashion design, and learn for yourself what it feels like to create pieces that you are happy to show off to the world. You know you want to, so don't let anything hold you back.

Let's get started.

Chapter 1 – Crochet Earrings

Red as a Ruby Dangle Earrings

Photo made by: kaylkels

You will need:

Earring hooks

Size E crochet hook

Needle and thread

Jewelry wire

Thread yarn

Directions:

Chain 14 and join with a slip stitch to form a ring.

Single crochet in the center of this ring 16 times, and join with a slip stitch. Chain 1, turn, and single crochet back to the other side. Join with a slip stitch. Chain 1, turn, and single crochet back to the beginning. Join with a slip stitch.

Continue until you are happy with the size of the earring, then finish with a border.

To shape the petals, you are going to:

Chain 3 and skip the first 2 stitches, then join with a slip stitch in the next stitch. Chain 3 and skip the next 2 stitches, then join with a slip stitch in the next stitch. Chain 3 and skip the next 2 stitches, and join with a slip stitch in the next stitch. Repeat around.

Repeat for the other earring.

To assemble:

Using the photo as a reference, assemble your earrings as you see here. Use tight, even stitches as you work, ensuring that none of the wire shows through the piece.

Tie off, and cut off all the loose threads. That's it!

Key Lime Earring Set

Photo made by: <u>moiracrochetsplarn</u>

You will need:

Earring hooks

Size E crochet hook

Needle and thread

Cross Beads

Thin lengths of plastic in the color of your choice (cut up plastic bags work well)

Directions:

Chain 4 and join with a slip stitch to form a ring.

Single crochet in the center of this ring 8 times, and join with a slip stitch. Chain 1, turn, and single crochet back to the other side. Join with a slip stitch. Chain 1, turn, and single crochet back to the beginning. Join with a slip stitch. Chain 1, turn, and single crochet back to the other side.

Continue until you are happy with the size of the earring, then finish with a border.

Repeat for the other earring.

To assemble:

Using the photo as a reference, assemble your earrings as you see here. Use tight, even stitches as you work, ensuring that none of the wire shows through the piece. Attach the beads as you see in the photo as well.

Tie off, and cut off all the loose threads. That's it!

All the Gum Drops Earrings

Photo made by: <u>moiracrochetsplarn</u>

You will need:

Earring hooks

Size E crochet hook

Needle and thread

Thin lengths of plastic in the color of your choice (cut up plastic bags work well)

Directions:

Chain 4 and join with a slip stitch to form a ring.

Single crochet in the center of this ring 8 times, and join with a slip stitch. Chain 1, turn, and single crochet back to the other side. Join with a slip stitch. Chain 1, turn, and single crochet back to the beginning. Join with a slip stitch. Chain 1, turn, and single crochet back to the other side.

Continue until you are happy with the size of the earring, then tie off.

Repeat for the other earring.

To assemble:

Using the photo as a reference, assemble your earrings as you see here. Use tight, even stitches as you work, ensuring that none of the wire shows through the piece.

Tie off, and cut off all the loose threads. That's it!

Bleeding Heart Earrings

Photo made by: moiracrochetsplarn

You will need:

637

Earring hooks

Size E crochet hook

Needle and thread

Thin lengths of plastic in the color of your choice (cut up plastic bags work well)

Directions:

Chain 4 and join with a slip stitch to form a ring.

Single crochet in the center of this ring 8 times, and join with a slip stitch. Chain 1, turn, and single crochet back to the other side. Join with a slip stitch. Chain 1, turn, and single crochet back to the beginning. Join with a slip stitch. Chain 1, turn, and single crochet back to the other side.

Continue until you are happy with the size of the earring, then finish with a border.

To shape the petals, you are going to:

Chain 5 and skip the first 2 stitches, then join with a slip stitch in the next stitch. Chain 5 and skip the next 2 stitches, then join with a slip stitch in the next stitch. Chain 5 and skip the next 2 stitches, and join with a slip stitch in the next stitch. Repeat around.

Repeat for the other earrings, adjusting the size according to the photo.

To assemble:

Using the photo as a reference, assemble your earrings as you see here. Use tight, even stitches as you work, ensuring that none of the wire shows through the piece.

Tie off, and cut off all the loose threads. That's it!

Photo made by: <u>Maria Panayiotou</u>

You will need:

Earring hooks

Size E crochet hook

Needle and thread

Jewelry wire

Thread weight yarn in the color of your choice

Directions:

Decide how large you want the finished piece to be, then chain a length that is equal to this measurement. Single crochet across the row. Chain 1, turn, and single crochet back to the other side. Chain 1, turn, and single crochet back to the beginning. Chain 1, turn, and single crochet back to the other side. Chain 1, turn, and single crochet back to the beginning.

You are going to continue with this until the strip that you create is large enough to wrap entirely around the wire you have chosen. When you are happy with the size, tie off.

Repeat for the other earring.

To assemble:

Using the photo as a reference, assemble your earrings as you see here. Use tight, even stitches as you work, ensuring that none of the wire shows through the piece.

Tie off, and cut off all the loose threads. That's it!

Mottled Magic Earrings

Photo made by: moiracrochetsplarn

You will need:

Earring hooks

Size E crochet hook

Needle and thread

Thin lengths of plastic in the color of your choice (cut up plastic bags work well)

Directions:

Chain 4 and join with a slip stitch to form a ring.

Single crochet in the center of this ring 8 times, and join with a slip stitch. Chain 1, turn, and single crochet back to the other side. Join with a slip stitch. Chain 1, turn, and single crochet back to the beginning. Join with a slip stitch. Chain 1, turn, and single crochet back to the other side.

Continue until you are happy with the size of the earring, then finish with a border.

To shape the petals, you are going to:

Chain 5 and skip the first 2 stitches, then join with a slip stitch in the next stitch. Chain 5 and skip the next 2 stitches, then join with a slip stitch in the next stitch. Chain 5 and skip the next 2 stitches, and join with a slip stitch in the next stitch. Repeat around.

Repeat for the other earring.

To assemble:

Using the photo as a reference, assemble your earrings as you see here. Use tight, even stitches as you work, ensuring that none of the wire shows through the piece.

Tie off, and cut off all the loose threads. That's it!

Star of the Show Earring Set

Photo made by: mccordworks

You will need:

Earring hooks

Size E crochet hook

Needle and thread

Jewelry wire

Thin lengths of plastic in the color of your choice (cut up plastic bags work well)

Directions:

Chain 4 and join with a slip stitch to form a ring.

Single crochet in the center of this ring 8 times, and join with a slip stitch. Chain 1, turn, and single crochet back to the other side. Join with a slip stitch. Chain 1, turn, and single crochet back to the beginning.

Continue until you are happy with the size of the earring, then finish with a border.

To shape the petals, you are going to:

Chain 5 and skip the first 2 stitches, then join with a slip stitch in the next stitch. Slip stitch down the side of the circle until you are ready to form another point. Chain 5 and skip the next 2 stitches, then join with a slip stitch in the next stitch.

Slip stitch down the side of the piece until you are ready to make another point. Chain 5 and skip the next 2 stitches, and join with a slip stitch in the next stitch.

Repeat around. When you are finished, tie off.

Repeat for the other earring.

To assemble:

Using the photo as a reference, assemble your earrings as you see here. Use tight, even stitches as you work, ensuring that none of the wire shows through the piece.

Tie off, and cut off all the loose threads. That's it!

Chapter 2 – Crochet Bracelets

Sea Bracelet

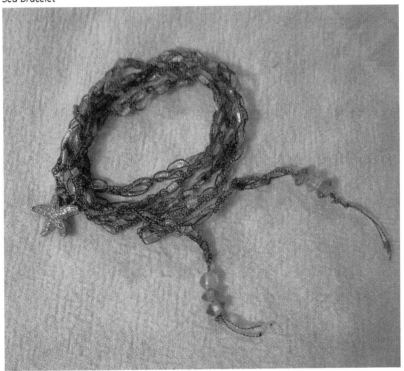

Photo made by: wisewellwoman

What you will need:

Size E crochet hook

Beads

Charms

Needle and thread

Thread weight yarn of your choice

Directions:

Decide how large you want the finished piece to be, then chain a length that is equal to this measurement. Single crochet across the row. Chain 1, turn, and single crochet back to the other side.

This is going to remain a thin length of chain, as you are going to then wrap it around the beads you have selected. After you are happy with how long and thick the first piece is, and you know it's going to fit the beads, you are going to tie off and set it aside.

Chain another length that is equal to the first. Single crochet across the row. Chain 1, turn, and single crochet back to the other side.

Once again, this is going to remain a thin length of chain, as you are going to then wrap it around the beads you have selected. After you are happy with how long and thick the first piece is, and you know it's going to fit the beads, you are going to tie off and set it aside.

Once more, chain another length that is equal to the first. Single crochet across the row. Chain 1, turn, and single crochet back to the other side.

When you have finished the three chains, you are ready to assemble.

To assemble:

Use the photo as a reference for assembly, and don't be afraid to throw in some of your own creativity. Intertwine the pieces together, make sure they are all secure, and attach any and all charms that you wish to be on your piece.

When you are happy with how it looks, snip off any loose ends, and attach a clasp, if desired.

That's it!

Photo made by: tafkabecky

What you will need:

Size E crochet hook

Needle and thread

Thread weight yarn of your choice

Directions:

Decide how large you want the finished piece to be, then chain a length that is equal to this measurement. Single crochet across the row. Chain 1, turn, and single crochet back to the other side.

This is going to remain a thin length of chain, as you are going to braid them together when you are done. After you are happy with how long and thick the first piece is, you are going to tie off and set it aside.

Chain another length that is equal to the first. Single crochet across the row. Chain 1, turn, and single crochet back to the other side.

Once again, this is going to remain a thin length of chain, as you are going to braid them together when you are done. After you are happy with how long and thick the first piece is, you are going to tie off and set it aside.

Once more, chain another length that is equal to the first. Single crochet across the row. Chain 1, turn, and single crochet back to the other side.

When you have finished the three chains, you are ready to assemble.

To assemble:

Use the photo as a reference for assembly, and don't be afraid to throw in some of your own creativity. Intertwine the pieces together, make sure they are all secure, and attach any and all charms that you wish to be on your piece.

When you are happy with how it looks, snip off any loose ends, and attach a clasp, if desired.

And you are done!

The Cage of Glory Bracelet

Photo made by: moiracrochetsplarn

What you will need:

Size E crochet hook

Thin plastic strips – cutting up a plastic bag works well.

Needle and thread

Directions:

Chain 12.

Single crochet across the row. Chain 16 now, and join with a slip stitch to the opposite side of the bracelet. Single crochet in the first stitch. Chain 16 once more, and join with a slip stitch to the other side of the bracelet. Single crochet in the first stitch.

Continue until the bracelet can fit around your wrist, then assemble.

To assemble:

Use the photo as a reference for assembly, and don't be afraid to throw in some of your own creativity. Intertwine the pieces together, make sure they are all secure, and attach any and all charms that you wish to be on your piece.

When you are happy with how it looks, snip off any loose ends, and attach a clasp, if desired.

That's it! You're done!

It's Hip to be a Square

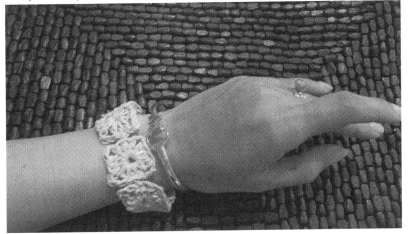

Photo made by: <u>tracey leigh</u>

What you will need:

Size E crochet hook

Thread weight yarn in the color of your choice

Needle and thread

Directions:

Chain 4 and join with a slip stitch to form a ring.

Single crochet in the center of this ring 8 times, and join with a slip stitch. Chain 1, turn, and single crochet back to the other side. Join with a slip stitch. Chain 1, turn, and single crochet back to the beginning. Join with a slip stitch. Chain 1, turn, and single crochet back to the other side.

Continue until you are happy with the size of the center.

To form the square shape, you are going to single crochet across the top, then chain 3 before continuing to single crochet in the very next stitch. This will form the angle. Single crochet across the side and chain 3 to form the next angle. Repeat for the other two sides.

Work 1 more row of single crochet, following your new pattern. Tie off and repeat until you have enough squares to fit around your wrist.

To assemble:

Use the photo as a reference for assembly, and don't be afraid to throw in some of your own creativity. Intertwine the pieces together, make sure they are all secure, and attach any and all charms that you wish to be on your piece.

When you are happy with how it looks, snip off any loose ends, and attach a clasp, if desired.

That's it, your new bracelet is ready for anything!

The Simple Solution

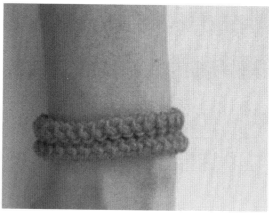

Photo made by: mariatenorio

What you will need:

Size E crochet hook

Thread weight yarn in the color of your choice

Needle and thread

Directions:

Decide how large you want the finished piece to be, then chain a length that is equal to this measurement. Single crochet across the row. Chain 1, turn, and single crochet back to the other side.

This is going to remain a thin length of chain, as you are going to sew them together when you are done. After you are happy with how long and thick the first piece is, you are going to tie off and set it aside.

Chain another length that is equal to the first. Single crochet across the row. Chain 1, turn, and single crochet back to the other side.

Once again, this is going to remain a thin length of chain, as you are going to sewing it to the other strip. After you are happy with how long and thick the first piece is, you are going to tie off.

To assemble:

Use the photo as a reference for assembly, and don't be afraid to throw in some of your own creativity. Intertwine the pieces together, make sure they are all secure, and attach any and all charms that you wish to be on your piece.

When you are happy with how it looks, snip off any loose ends, and attach a clasp, if desired.

That's it!

Sunny Day Bracelet

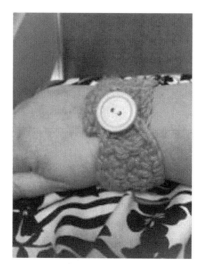

Photo made by: <u>nikijulian</u>

What you will need:

Size G crochet hook

Large button

Cotton yarn in the color of your choice

Needle and thread

Directions:

Decide how large you want the finished piece to be, then chain a length that is equal to this measurement. Single crochet across the row. Chain 1, turn, and single crochet back to the other side. Chain 1, turn, and single crochet back to the beginning. Chain 1, turn, and single crochet back to the other side. Chain 1, turn, and single crochet back to the beginning.

When you are happy with how thick the strip is, you are going to tie it off. You are now ready to assemble.

To assemble:

Use the photo as a reference for assembly, and don't be afraid to throw in some of your own creativity. Intertwine the pieces together, make sure they are all secure, and attach any and all charms that you wish to be on your piece.

When you are happy with how it looks, snip off any loose ends, and attach a clasp, if desired.

That's it! You can leave it as it is, or add more buttons to it if you like, get creative!

Fall Fantasy Bracelet

Photo made by: reginarioux

What you will need:

Size E crochet hook

Needle and thread

Thread weight yarn in the color of your choice

Bangle wire or jewelry wire you can bend to fit your wrist

Directions:

Start with chaining a length that is as long as you want the feather to be – about 2 inches is standard. Tie off and set aside.

Next, begin chaining shorter lengths, tying each one off and setting it aside when you are happy with the size. Make the lengths that are closer to the top of the feather longer than the lengths that are at the tip, forming the feather shape.

Use the photo as reference.

To assemble:

Use the photo as a reference for assembly, and don't be afraid to throw in some of your own creativity. Intertwine the pieces together, make sure they are all secure, and attach any and all charms that you wish to be on your piece.

When you are happy with how it looks, snip off any loose ends, and attach a clasp, if desired.

That's it! Try making the bracelet over again in as many colors as you can think of!

Chapter 3 – Crochet Rings

The Simple Things Ring

Photo made by: poptoplady

What you will need:

Size E crochet hook

Thread weight yarn in the color of your choice

Soda caps

Needle and thread

Directions:

Chain 4 and join with a slip stitch to form a ring.

Single crochet in the center of this ring 8 times, and join with a slip stitch. Chain 1, turn, and single crochet back to the other side. Join with a slip stitch. Chain 1, turn, and single crochet back to the beginning. Join with a slip stitch. Chain 1, turn, and single crochet back to the other side.

When you are happy with the size of the center, take your soda caps and lay them as you see in the photo. You are ready to assemble.

To assemble:

Use the photo as a reference for assembly, and don't be afraid to throw in some of your own creativity. Intertwine the pieces together, make sure they are all secure, and attach any and all charms that you wish to be on your piece.

When you are happy with how it looks, take a length of thread, a crocheted chain, wire, or metal chain and cut it to the proper length to fit around your finger. Sew the main pendant of the piece to this length, and make sure you have all pieces entirely secure.

When you are happy with how it looks, you are ready to rock your new style!

The Fairy Garden Ring

Photo made by: kaylkels

What you will need:

Size E crochet hook

Thread weight yarn in the color of your choice

Needle and thread

Directions:

Chain 4 and join with a slip stitch to form a ring.

Single crochet in the center of this ring 8 times, and join with a slip stitch. Chain 1, turn, and single crochet back to the other side. Join with a slip stitch. Chain 1, turn, and single crochet back to the beginning. Join with a slip stitch. Chain 1, turn, and single crochet back to the other side.

Continue until you are happy with the size of the earring, then finish with a border.

To shape the petals, you are going to:

Chain 4 and skip the first 2 stitches, then join with a slip stitch in the next stitch. Chain 4 and skip the next 2 stitches, then join with a slip stitch in the next stitch. Chain 4 and skip the next 2 stitches, and join with a slip stitch in the next stitch. Repeat around.

To assemble:

Use the photo as a reference for assembly, and don't be afraid to throw in some of your own creativity. Intertwine the pieces together, make sure they are all secure, and attach any and all charms that you wish to be on your piece.

When you are happy with how it looks, crochet a length that will fit around your finger. Single crochet across the row. Chain 1, turn, and single crochet back to the beginning. Chain 1, turn, and single crochet back to the other side. Chain 1, turn, and single crochet back to the beginning.

Continue until you are happy with how the wrap looks around your finger, then tie off. You can make this as thin or as thick as you like.

When you are happy with how it looks, you are ready to rock your new style!

Barely There White Ring

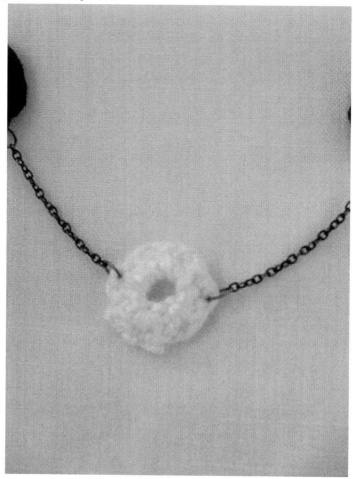

What you will need:

Size E crochet hook

Thread weight yarn in the color of your choice

Needle and thread

Directions:

Chain 4 and join with a slip stitch to form a ring.

Single crochet in the center of this ring 8 times, and join with a slip stitch. Chain 1, turn, and single crochet back to the other side. Join with a slip stitch. Chain 1, turn, and single crochet back to the beginning. Join with a slip stitch. Chain 1, turn, and single crochet back to the other side.

Continue until you are happy with the size of the earring, tie off.

To assemble:

Use the photo as a reference for assembly, and don't be afraid to throw in some of your own creativity. Intertwine the pieces together, make sure they are all secure, and attach any and all charms that you wish to be on your piece.

When you are happy with how it looks, take a length of thread, a crocheted chain, wire, or metal chain and cut it to the proper length to fit around your finger. Sew the main pendant of the piece to this length, and make sure you have all pieces entirely secure.

When you are happy with how it looks, you are ready to rock your new style!

The Oversized Statement Ring

Photo made by: <u>sionakaren</u>

What you will need:

Size E crochet hook

Thread weight yarn in the color of your choice

Needle and thread

Directions:

Chain 4 and join with a slip stitch to form a ring.

Single crochet in the center of this ring 8 times, and join with a slip stitch. Chain 1, turn, and single crochet back to the other side. Join with a slip stitch. Chain 1, turn, and single crochet back to the beginning. Join with a slip stitch. Chain 1, turn, and single crochet back to the other side.

Continue until you are happy with the size of the earring, then finish with a border.

To shape the petals, you are going to:

658

Chain 10 and skip the first 2 stitches, then join with a slip stitch in the next stitch. Chain 10 and skip the next 2 stitches, then join with a slip stitch in the next stitch. Chain 10 and skip the next 2 stitches, and join with a slip stitch in the next stitch. Repeat around.

To assemble:

Use the photo as a reference for assembly, and don't be afraid to throw in some of your own creativity. Intertwine the pieces together, make sure they are all secure, and attach any and all charms that you wish to be on your piece.

When you are happy with how it looks, take a length of thread, a crocheted chain, wire, or metal chain and cut it to the proper length to fit around your finger. Sew the main pendant of the piece to this length, and make sure you have all pieces entirely secure.

When you are happy with how it looks, you are ready to rock your new style!

The Plum Summer Ring

Photo made by: sammy4586

What you will need:

Size E crochet hook

Thread weight yarn in the color of your choice

Needle and thread

Directions:

Chain 4 and join with a slip stitch to form a ring.

Single crochet in the center of this ring 8 times, and join with a slip stitch. Chain 1, turn, and single crochet back to the other side. Join with a slip stitch. Chain 1, turn, and single crochet back to the beginning. Join with a slip stitch. Chain 1, turn, and single crochet back to the other side.

Continue until you are happy with the size of the earring, then finish with a border.

To shape the petals, you are going to:

Chain 4 and skip the first 2 stitches, then join with a slip stitch in the next stitch. Chain 4 and skip the next 2 stitches, then join with a slip stitch in the next stitch. Chain 4 and skip the next 2 stitches, and join with a slip stitch in the next stitch. Repeat around.

To assemble:

Use the photo as a reference for assembly, and don't be afraid to throw in some of your own creativity. Intertwine the pieces together, make sure they are all secure, and attach any and all charms that you wish to be on your piece.

When you are happy with how it looks, take a length of thread, a crocheted chain, wire, or metal chain and cut it to the proper length to fit around your finger. Sew the main pendant of the piece to this length, and make sure you have all pieces entirely secure.

When you are happy with how it looks, you are ready to rock your new style!

Oh So Tiny Ring

Photo made by: nicasaurusrex

What you will need:

Size E crochet hook

Thread weight yarn in the color of your choice

Needle and thread

Directions:

Chain 4 and join with a slip stitch to form a ring.

Single crochet in the center of this ring 4 times, and join with a slip stitch. Chain 1, turn, and single crochet back to the other side. Join with a slip stitch. Chain 1, turn, and single crochet back to the beginning.

Continue until you are happy with the size of the earring, then finish with a border.

To shape the petals, you are going to:

Chain 3 and skip the first stitch, then join with a slip stitch in the next stitch. Chain 3 and skip the next stitch, then join with a slip stitch in the next stitch. Chain 3 and skip the next stitch, and join with a slip stitch in the next stitch. Repeat around.

661

To assemble:

Use the photo as a reference for assembly, and don't be afraid to throw in some of your own creativity. Intertwine the pieces together, make sure they are all secure, and attach any and all charms that you wish to be on your piece.

When you are happy with how it looks, take a length of thread, a crocheted chain, wire, or metal chain and cut it to the proper length to fit around your finger. Sew the main pendant of the piece to this length, and make sure you have all pieces entirely secure.

When you are happy with how it looks, you are ready to rock your new style!

Conclusion

There you have it, everything you need to know about making your own crochet jewelry, and a variety of patterns you can choose from to rock your style today. I hope this book is able to inspire you to create your very own jewelry collection, and that you take what you have learned here and create all kinds of pieces for your accessory needs.

There is no end to the ways you can create your own jewelry, or to how you can express your creativity while you do it. Have fun, show off your skills, and wow your friends and family with your new accessories every time you see them.

You know you want to, and now it's never been easier to do that very thing. You can be a fashion designer, you can get exactly what you want, when you want it, and you can do it all on your own.

Good luck!

Alisa Hatchenson

Fall Crochet Patterns

20 Cozy Fall Crochet Projects For You And Your Home

Fall Crochet Patterns

20 Cozy Fall Crochet Projects For You And Your Home

Introduction

It's getting on to be that time of the year, and you are ready to celebrate. From holidays and getting together with friends and family to enjoying all kinds of good times with those you love, you are ready for the days to come.

You know amid all the festivities you want to decorate. You want to embrace your style, and you want to enjoy all this season has to offer. Of course, in order to do that, you are going to have to express your creative side in a whole new way – and this book is going to show you how.

Discover all kinds of new ways to create a style that is uniquely yours. From all the things you can make to decorate your house to the things you can create to show off your style, you are going to find it here.

This book is going to show you how to create anything and everything you like, and you are going to discover that there really is no way you can go wrong. This book is everything you have been looking for and then some, and you are going to get just what you are looking for.

Unleash your inner creativity, and you are going to get the projects you have been dreaming of. You know you want to, and now you can. Let's get started.

Pumpkin Patch

Photo made by: oCassandraoClevengero

You will need 1 skein of yarn in each of the colors you wish to use and a size G crochet hook

Chain 4 and join with a slip stitch to form a ring. Single crochet in the center of this ring 10 times, and join with another slip stitch.

Chain 1, turn, and single crochet around the row. Chain 1, turn, and single crochet back around, joining with a slip stitch when you get back to the beginning. Chain 1, turn, and single crochet back to the beginning. Chain 1, turn, and single crochet back to the beginning, joining with a slip stitch.

Continue with this until you have a disc that is 8 inches across, then begin your decrease.

Chain 1, turn, and single crochet in the first 5 stitches, then skip the next stitch. Single crochet in the next 5 stitches, then skip the next stitch. Single crochet in the next 5 stitches, then skip the next stitch. Single crochet in the next 5 stitches, then skip the next stitch. Single crochet in the next 5 stitches, then skip the next stitch.

Once the pumpkin begins to form, you are going to work a few rows without decreasing, before returning to the decrease to finish the ball shape.

Stuff the pumpkins with stuffing, and when you are done, sew the bottom. Take a yarn needle and lengths of yarn, then form the shapes of the pumpkins. Tie off, and make sure all is secure.

That's it! Your pumpkins are done!

Photo made by: smittenkittenoriginals

You will need 1 skein of yarn in each of the colors you wish to use and a size J crochet hook

Chain a length that is 6 feet long.

Single crochet across the row. Chain 1, turn, and single crochet back to the beginning, in the front loop only. Chain 2, turn, and double crochet across the row. Chain 2, turn, and double crochet back to the beginning, in the front loop only. Chain 2, turn, and double crochet across the row in the front loop only. Chain 2, turn, and double crochet back to the beginning, in the front loop only.

Chain 2, turn, and double crochet across the row, in the front loop only. Chain 2, turn, and double crochet back to the beginning in the front loop only. Chain 2, turn, and double crochet back to the beginning in the front loop only. Chain 2, turn, and double crochet back to the beginning in the front loop only. Chain 2, turn, and double crochet back to the beginning in the front loop only.

Continue until you are happy with the size of the scarf, and tie off. Add fringe to the end and you are done!

Carrie the Cranberry

Photo made by: snarledskein

You will need 1 skein of yarn in each of the colors you wish to use and a size G crochet hook

Chain 4 and join with a slip stitch to form a ring. Single crochet in the center of this ring 10 times, and join with another slip stitch.

Chain 1, turn, and single crochet around the row. Chain 1, turn, and single crochet back around, joining with a slip stitch when you get back to the beginning. Chain 1, turn, and single crochet back to the beginning. Chain 1, turn, and single crochet back to the beginning, joining with a slip stitch.

Continue with this until you have a disc that is 4 inches across, then begin your decrease.

Chain 1, turn, and single crochet in the first 2 stitches, then skip the next stitch. Single crochet in the next 2 stitches, then skip the next stitch. Single crochet in the next 2 stitches, then skip the next stitch. Single crochet in the next 2 stitches, then skip the next stitch. Single crochet in the next 2 stitches, then skip the next stitch.

Once the cranberry begins to form, you are going to work a few rows without decreasing, before returning to the decrease to finish the ball shape.

Stuff the cranberry with stuffing, and when you are done, sew the bottom. Use green and smaller discs to form the leaves, then attach these with chains.

Sew on the buttons for the eyes and stitch on the remaining details, and your cranberry is done!

The Fall Bangle

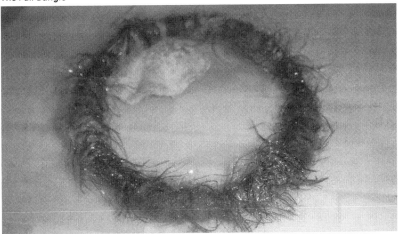

Photo made by: Maria Panayiotou

You will need 1 skein of yarn in each of the colors you wish to use and a size G crochet hook

Using fun fur yarn, wrap around your bangle. Make sure that there are no spaces in between the strands. Continue to wrap until you reach the other side, then take your crochet hook and feed it through the bottom of the piece.

Make sure everything is secure, then tie off.

Not Your Mother's Scarf

Photo made by: macrak

You will need 1 skein of yarn in each of the colors you wish to use and a size J crochet hook

Choose 5 or 6 colors and take your crochet hook. Chain a length that is 4 feet long, then tie it off and set it aside. Repeat this for the other colors, making each one the same length.

672

Once you have all the colors, hold them together and tie knots in the chain. Tie one final knot, securing the scarf together, and you are done!

Fall Bash Beanie

Photo made by: paeonia1

You will need 1 skein of yarn in each of the colors you wish to use and a size G crochet hook

Chain 4 and join with a slip stitch to form a ring. Single crochet in the center of this ring 10 times, and join with another slip stitch.

Chain 1, turn, and single crochet around the row. Chain 1, turn, and single crochet back around, joining with a slip stitch when you get back to the beginning. Chain 1, turn, and single crochet back to the beginning. Chain 1, turn, and single crochet back to the beginning, joining with a slip stitch.

Continue with this until you have a disc fits across the top of your head, then begin your decrease.

Chain 1, turn, and single crochet in the first 5 stitches, then skip the next stitch. Single crochet in the next 5 stitches, then skip the next stitch. Single crochet in the next 5 stitches, then skip the next stitch. Single crochet in the next 5 stitches, then skip the next stitch. Single crochet in the next 5 stitches, then skip the next stitch.

Once the hat fits the shape of your head, you are going to work a few rows without decreasing, continuing until the hat is the length that you prefer.

Once the hat as reached your desired length, tie off and you are done!

The Fall Collection Washcloths

Photo made by: smittenkittenoriginals

You will need 1 skein of yarn in each of the colors you wish to use and a size G crochet hook

Chain a length that is 8 inches long.

Single crochet across the row. Chain 1, turn, and single crochet back to the beginning. Chain 1, turn, and single crochet across the row. Chain 1, turn, and single crochet back to the beginning. Chain 1, turn, and single crochet back to the beginning. Chain 1, turn, and single crochet across the row. Chain 1, turn, and single crochet back to the beginning. Chain 1, turn, and single crochet back to the beginning. Chain 1, turn, and single crochet across the row. Chain 1, turn, and single crochet back to the beginning.

Chain 1, turn, and single crochet across the row. Chain 1, turn, and single crochet back to the beginning. Chain 1, turn, and single crochet back to the beginning. Chain 1, turn, and single crochet across the row. Chain 1, turn, and single crochet back to the beginning. Chain 1, turn, and single crochet back to the beginning. Chain 1, turn, and single crochet across the row. Chain 1, turn, and single crochet back to the beginning.

Continue until you have a square, then tie off. Single crochet around the border, and you are done!

Repeat for the other washcloths, and you are done!

Maroon Madness

You will need 1 skein of yarn in each of the colors you wish to use and a size J crochet hook

Chain a length that is 5 feet long.

Single crochet across the row. Chain 1, turn, and single crochet back to the beginning, in the front loop only. Chain 2, turn, and double crochet across the row. Chain 2, turn, and double crochet back to the beginning, in the front loop only. Chain 2, turn, and double crochet across the row in the front loop only. Chain 2, turn, and double crochet back to the beginning, in the front loop only.

Chain 2, turn, and double crochet across the row, in the front loop only. Chain 2, turn, and double crochet back to the beginning in the front loop only. Chain 2, turn, and double crochet back to the beginning in the front loop only. Chain 2, turn, and double crochet back to the beginning in the front loop only. Chain 2, turn, and double crochet back to the beginning in the front loop only.

When you are happy with how thick your scarf is, tie it off and add tassels to the ends.

Around the Globe Cowl

You will need 1 skein of yarn in each of the colors you wish to use and a size J crochet hook

Chain a length that is 4 feet long.

Single crochet across the row. Chain 1, turn, and single crochet back to the beginning. Chain 1, turn, and single crochet across the row. Chain 1, turn, and single crochet back to the beginning. Chain 1, turn, and single crochet back to the beginning. Chain 1, turn, and single crochet across the row. Chain 1, turn, and single crochet back to the beginning. Chain 1, turn, and single crochet back to the beginning. Chain 1, turn, and single crochet across the row. Chain 1, turn, and single crochet back to the beginning.

Chain 1, turn, and single crochet across the row. Chain 1, turn, and single crochet back to the beginning. Chain 1, turn, and single crochet back to the beginning. Chain 1, turn, and single crochet across the row. Chain 1, turn, and single crochet back to the beginning. Chain 1, turn, and single crochet back to the beginning. Chain 1, turn, and single crochet across the row. Chain 1, turn, and single crochet back to the beginning.

Continue until the cowl is nice and thick – use the photo for reference. When you are happy with the size of the piece, tie it off.

Sew up the ends of the cowl, and turn the right side out. That's it! You are done!

Super Stripes Autumn Throw

You will need 1 skein of yarn in each of the colors you wish to use and a size J crochet hook

Chain a length that is 5 feet long.

Single crochet across the row. Chain 1, turn, and single crochet back to the beginning. Chain 1, turn, and single crochet across the row. Chain 1, turn, and single crochet back to the beginning. Chain 1, turn, and single crochet back to the beginning. Chain 1, turn, and single crochet across the row. Chain 1, turn, and single crochet back to the beginning. Chain 1, turn, and single crochet back to the beginning. Chain 1, turn, and single crochet across the row. Chain 1, turn, and single crochet back to the beginning.

Use the photo as a reference for color, changing colors as often as you like.

Chain 1, turn, and single crochet across the row. Chain 1, turn, and single crochet back to the beginning. Chain 1, turn, and single crochet back to the beginning. Chain 1, turn, and single crochet across the row. Chain 1, turn, and single crochet back to the beginning.

Chain 1, turn, and single crochet back to the beginning. Chain 1, turn, and single crochet across the row. Chain 1, turn, and single crochet back to the beginning.

When you are happy with the size of the blanket, you are going to add a single crochet row around the entire border. Tie off, and you are done!

Every Season Throw

Photo made by: kpwerker

You will need 1 skein of yarn in each of the colors you wish to use and a size J crochet hook

Chain a length that is 8 feet long.

Single crochet across the row. Chain 1, turn, and single crochet back to the beginning. Chain 1, and single crochet in the first 10 stitches, then skip the next stitch. Single crochet in the next 10 stitches, and skip the next stitch. Single crochet in the next 10 stitches, and skip the next stitch. Continue to the end.

Chain 1, and single crochet in the first 10 stitches, then skip the next stitch. Single crochet in the next 10 stitches, and skip the next stitch. Single crochet in the next 10 stitches, and skip the next stitch. Continue to the end.

Chain 1, turn, and single crochet across the row. Chain 1, turn, and single crochet back to the beginning. Chain 1, turn, and single crochet back to the beginning. Chain 1, turn, and single crochet across the row. Chain 1, turn, and single crochet back to the beginning. Chain 1, turn, and single crochet back to the beginning. Chain 1, turn, and single crochet across the row. Chain 1, turn, and single crochet back to the beginning.

Chain 1, turn, and single crochet across the row. Chain 1, turn, and single crochet back to the beginning. Chain 1, turn, and single crochet back to the beginning. Chain 1, turn, and single crochet across the row. Chain 1, turn, and single crochet back to the beginning. Chain 1, turn, and single crochet back to the beginning. Chain 1, turn, and single crochet across the row. Chain 1, turn, and single crochet back to the beginning.

Use the photo as reference, and change colors as much as you like. When you are done, add a border, and enjoy!

Fall Harvest Coasters

Photo made by: hellomomo

You will need 1 skein of yarn in each of the colors you wish to use and a size G crochet hook

Chain 4 and join with a slip stitch to form a ring. Single crochet in the center of this ring 10 times, and join with another slip stitch.

Chain 1, turn, and single crochet around the row. Chain 1, turn, and single crochet back around, joining with a slip stitch when you get back to the beginning. Chain 1, turn, and single crochet back to the beginning. Chain 1, turn, and single crochet back to the beginning, joining with a slip stitch.

Chain 1, turn, and single crochet around the row. Chain 1, turn, and single crochet back around, joining with a slip stitch when you get back to the beginning. Chain 1, turn, and single crochet back to the beginning. Chain 1, turn, and single crochet back to the beginning, joining with a slip stitch.

Chain 1, turn, and single crochet around the row. Chain 1, turn, and single crochet back around, joining with a slip stitch when you get back to the beginning. Chain 1, turn, and single crochet back to the beginning. Chain 1, turn, and single crochet back to the beginning, joining with a slip stitch.

Use short chains of green for the leaves of the fruit, and sew in place.

Continue until you are happy with the size of your coaster, then tie off. Repeat for the other coasters, and you are done!

Droopy Back Beanie

Photo made by: <u>smittenkittenoriginals</u>

You will need 1 skein of yarn in each of the colors you wish to use and a size G crochet hook

Chain 4 and join with a slip stitch to form a ring. Single crochet in the center of this ring 10 times, and join with another slip stitch.

Chain 1, turn, and single crochet around the row. Chain 1, turn, and single crochet back around, joining with a slip stitch when you get back to the beginning. Chain 1, turn, and single crochet back to the beginning. Chain 1, turn, and single crochet back to the beginning, joining with a slip stitch.

Continue with this until you have a disc fits across the top of your head, then begin your decrease.

Chain 1, turn, and single crochet in the first 5 stitches, then skip the next stitch. Single crochet in the next 5 stitches, then skip the next stitch. Single crochet in the next 5 stitches, then skip the next stitch. Single crochet in the next 5 stitches, then skip the next stitch. Single crochet in the next 5 stitches, then skip the next stitch.

Once the hat fits the shape of your head, you are going to work a few rows without decreasing, continuing until the hat is the length that you prefer. Remember that this is a slouchy beanie, so continue until the beanie is long – longer than what you would normally use for a beanie.

Once the hat as reached your desired length, tie off and you are done!

Fall's Fun Fur Scarf

Photo made by: madaise

You will need 1 skein of yarn in each of the colors you wish to use and a size G crochet hook

Chain a length that is 5 inches.

Single crochet across the row. Chain 1, turn, and single crochet back to the beginning. Chain 1, turn, and single crochet across the row. Chain 1, turn, and single crochet back to the beginning. Chain 1, turn, and single crochet back to the beginning. Chain 1, turn, and single crochet across the row. Chain 1, turn, and single crochet back to the beginning. Chain 1, turn, and single crochet back to the beginning. Chain 1, turn, and single crochet across the row. Chain 1, turn, and single crochet back to the beginning.

Chain 1, turn, and single crochet across the row. Chain 1, turn, and single crochet back to the beginning. Chain 1, turn, and single crochet back to the beginning. Chain 1, turn, and single crochet across the row. Chain 1, turn, and single crochet back to the beginning. Chain 1, turn, and single crochet back to the beginning. Chain 1, turn, and single crochet across the row. Chain 1, turn, and single crochet back to the beginning.

When you are happy with the length of the scarf, tie off and you are done!

Pumpkin Spice Scarf

Photo made by: smittenkittenoriginals

You will need 1 skein of yarn in each of the colors you wish to use and a size G crochet hook

Chain a length that is as long as you want your scarf to be.

Single crochet across the row. Chain 1, turn, and single crochet back to the beginning, in the front loop only. Chain 2, turn, and double crochet across the row. Chain 2, turn, and double crochet back to the beginning, in the front loop only. Chain 2, turn, and double crochet across the row in the front loop only. Chain 2, turn, and double crochet back to the beginning, in the front loop only.

Chain 2, turn, and double crochet across the row, in the front loop only. Chain 2, turn, and double crochet back to the beginning in the front loop only. Chain 2, turn, and double crochet back to the beginning in the front loop only. Chain 2, turn, and double crochet back to the beginning in the front loop only. Chain 2, turn, and double crochet back to the beginning in the front loop only.

Change colors as you prefer, using the photo as a reference guide. When you are happy with the size of your scarf, you are done!

Tabletop Owl

You will need 1 skein of yarn in each of the colors you wish to use and a size G crochet hook

Chain 4 and join with a slip stitch to form a ring. Single crochet in the center of this ring 10 times, and join with another slip stitch.

Chain 1, turn, and single crochet around the row. Chain 1, turn, and single crochet back around, joining with a slip stitch when you get back to the beginning. Chain 1, turn, and single crochet back to the beginning. Chain 1, turn, and single crochet back to the beginning, joining with a slip stitch.

Continue with this until you have a disc that is 8 inches across, then begin your decrease.

Chain 1, turn, and single crochet in the first 5 stitches, then skip the next stitch. Single crochet in the next 5 stitches, then skip the next stitch. Single crochet in the next 5 stitches, then skip the next stitch. Single crochet in the next 5 stitches, then skip the next stitch. Single crochet in the next 5 stitches, then skip the next stitch.

Once the owls body is forming, continue with the single crochet rows without any kinds of decreases. When you are happy with the size of the body, you are going to tie off the end and stuff the owl. Sew across the top, forming the shape of your decoration.

Repeat the steps to make 2 discs for eyes, then sew onto the body – following the details that you see in the photo. When you are happy with the final look of the bird, tie off and you are done!

Bright and Bold Pumpkin Scarf

You will need 1 skein of yarn in each of the colors you wish to use and a size J crochet hook

Chain a length that is 6 feet long.

Single crochet across the row. Chain 1, turn, and single crochet back to the beginning. Chain 1, turn, and single crochet across the row. Chain 1, turn, and single crochet back to the beginning. Chain 1, turn, and single crochet back to the beginning. Chain 1, turn, and single crochet across the row. Chain 1, turn, and single crochet back to the beginning. Chain 1, turn, and single crochet back to the beginning. Chain 1, turn, and single crochet across the row. Chain 1, turn, and single crochet back to the beginning.

Chain 1, turn, and single crochet across the row. Chain 1, turn, and single crochet back to the beginning. Chain 1, turn, and single crochet back to the beginning. Chain 1, turn, and single crochet across the row. Chain 1, turn, and single crochet back to the beginning. Chain 1, turn, and single crochet back to the beginning. Chain 1, turn, and single crochet across the row. Chain 1, turn, and single crochet back to the beginning.

When you are happy with the thickness of the scarf, tie off and you are done!

Basic Fall Nights Pillow

Photo made by: <u>dainec</u>

You will need 1 skein of yarn in each of the colors you wish to use and a size J crochet hook

Measure a pillow and chain a length that will fit over the side.

Single crochet across the row. Chain 1, turn, and single crochet back to the beginning. Chain 1, turn, and single crochet across the row. Chain 1, turn, and single crochet back to the beginning. Chain 1, turn, and single crochet back to the beginning. Chain 1, turn, and single crochet across the row. Chain 1, turn, and single crochet back to the beginning. Chain 1, turn, and single crochet back to the beginning. Chain 1, turn, and single crochet across the row. Chain 1, turn, and single crochet back to the beginning.

Chain 1, turn, and single crochet across the row. Chain 1, turn, and single crochet back to the beginning. Chain 1, turn, and single crochet back to the beginning. Chain 1, turn, and single crochet across the row. Chain 1, turn, and single crochet back to the beginning. Chain 1, turn, and single crochet back to the beginning. Chain 1, turn, and single crochet across the row. Chain 1, turn, and single crochet back to the beginning.

688

When you can fit this over your pillow, tie off.

Take your yarn needle now, and sew this around your pillow. Secure an oversized button to the front, and you are done!

Fall Toaster Coasters

Photo made by: Rebecca Kahn

You will need 1 skein of yarn in each of the colors you wish to use and a size G crochet hook

Chain 4 and join with a slip stitch to form a ring. Single crochet in the center of this ring 10 times, and join with another slip stitch.

Chain 1, turn, and single crochet around the row. Chain 1, turn, and single crochet back around, joining with a slip stitch when you get back to the beginning. Chain 1, turn, and single crochet back to the beginning. Chain 1, turn, and single crochet back to the beginning, joining with a slip stitch.

Chain 1, turn, and single crochet around the row. Chain 1, turn, and single crochet back around, joining with a slip stitch when you get back to the beginning. Chain 1, turn, and single crochet back to the beginning. Chain 1, turn, and single crochet back to the beginning, joining with a slip stitch.

Chain 1, turn, and single crochet around the row. Chain 1, turn, and single crochet back around, joining with a slip stitch when you get back to the beginning. Chain 1, turn, and single crochet back to the beginning. Chain 1, turn, and single crochet back to the beginning, joining with a slip stitch.

Continue until you are happy with the size of your coaster, then tie off. Repeat for the other coasters, and you are done!

Fireside Warmth

Photo made by: <u>tonyandshayna</u>

You will need 1 skein of yarn in each of the colors you wish to use and a size J crochet hook

Chain a length that is 6 feet long.

Single crochet across the row. Chain 1, turn, and single crochet back to the beginning, in the front loop only. Chain 2, turn, and double crochet across the row. Chain 2, turn, and double crochet back to the beginning, in the front loop only. Chain 2, turn, and double crochet across the row in the front loop only. Chain 2, turn, and double crochet back to the beginning, in the front loop only.

Chain 2, turn, and double crochet across the row, in the front loop only. Chain 2, turn, and double crochet back to the beginning in the front loop only. Chain 2, turn, and double crochet back to the beginning in the front loop only. Chain 2, turn, and double crochet back to the beginning in the front loop only. Chain 2, turn, and double crochet back to the beginning in the front loop only.

Use the photo as a reference for color, changing color as much as you like. Continue to work until your blanket is a square, or until it is the size that you wish it to be. When you are happy with the size, tie off and put a single crochet border around the entire thing.

Tie off the blanket and make sure there are no loose threads, and you are done!

Conclusion

There you have it, everything you need to create a variety of autumn designs, and to make your house cozy and sweet this season! You are going to fall in love with each and every one of these patterns, and you are going to find that each one brings in the joy of the season.

The nights are getting longer, the days are getting colder, and you are ready for the upcoming holidays.

Don't wait – you know this is one of the greatest times of year, and you are going to enjoy each and every second of it. Have fun with your creations, and you are going to embrace all this fall has to offer!

46447835R00384